THE

LAKE REGIONS OF CENTRAL AFRICA

VOL. II.

NAVIGATION OF THE TANGANYIKA LAKE.

THE

LAKE REGIONS OF CENTRAL AFRICA

A PICTURE OF EXPLORATION

BY

SIR RICHARD F. BURTON

Capt. H. M. I. Army : Fellow and Gold Medallist of the Royal Geographical Society

INTRODUCTION BY
ALAN MOOREHEAD

—————

" Some to discover islands far away" — Shakespeare

—————

IN TWO VOLUMES
VOLUME II.

HORIZON PRESS   NEW YORK

CONTENTS

OF

THE SECOND VOLUME.

Page

CHAPTER XII.

The Geography and Ethnology of Unyamwezi. — The Fourth
Region 1

CHAP. XIII.

At length we sight the Lake Tanganyika, the " Sea of Ujiji."   34

CHAP. XIV.

We explore the Tanganyika Lake 80

CHAP. XV

The Tanganyika Lake and its Periplus 134

CHAP. XVI.

We return to Unyanyembe 155

CHAP. XVII.

The Down-march to the Coast 223

Page

CHAP. XVIII.

Village Life in East Africa 278

CHAP. XIX.

The Character and Religion of the East Africans; their
Government, and Slavery. 324

Conclusion 379

APPENDICES.

APPENDIX I.: Commerce, Imports, and Exports . . . 387
APPENDIX II.: Official Correspondence 420

LIST OF ILLUSTRATIONS

IN

THE SECOND VOLUME.

FULL-PAGE ILLUSTRATIONS

Navigation of the Tanganyika Lake . . . . . *Frontispiece.*
View in Usagara . . . . . . *to face page* 1
Snay bin Amir's House . . . . . „ 155
Saydumi, a native of Uganda . . . . . „ 223
The Basin of Maroro . . . . . . „ 255
The Basin of Kisanga . . . . . . „ 278

TEXT ILLUSTRATIONS

Iwanza, or public-houses ; with Looms to the left . . . 1
My Tembe near the Tangangika 34
Head Dresses of Wanyamwezi 80
African heads, and Ferry-boat 134
Portraits of Muinyi Kidogo, the Kirangozi, the Mganga, &c. . 155
Mgongo Thembo, or the Elephant's Back 223
Jiwe la Mkoa, the Round Rock 242
Rufita Pass in Usagara 259
The Ivory Porter, the Cloth Porter, and Woman in Usagara . 278
Gourd, Stool, Bellows, Guitar, and Drum 292
Gourds 313
A Mnyamwezi and a Mheha 324
The Bull-headed Mabruki, and the African standing position . 378
The Elephant Rock 384

VIEW IN USAGARA.

THE

LAKE REGIONS OF CENTRAL AFRICA.

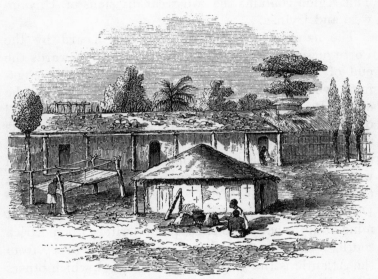

A village interior in the Land of the Moon.

Utanta or loom.   Iwanza, or public houses.

CHAPTER XII.

THE GEOGRAPHY AND ETHNOLOGY OF UNYAMWEZI.—THE FOURTH REGION.

The fourth division is a hilly table-land, extending from the western skirts of the desert Mgunda Mk'hali, in E. long. 33° 57′, to the eastern banks of the Malagarazi River, in E. long. 31° 10′: it thus stretches diagonally over 155 rectilinear geographical miles. Bounded on the north by Usui and the Nyanza Lake, to the south-eastwards by Ugala, southwards by Ukimbu, and south-westwards by Uwende, it has a depth of from twenty-five to thirty marches. Native caravans, if lightly laden, can accomplish it in twenty-five days, including four halts. The maximum altitude observed by B. P. therm. was 4050 feet, the minimum 2850. This region contains the two great divisions of Unyamwezi and Uvinza.

The name of Unyamwezi was first heard by the Portuguese, according to Giovanni Botero, towards the end of the sixteenth century, or about 1589. Pigafetta, who, in 1591, systematised the discoveries of the earlier Portuguese, placed the empire of " Monemugi " or Munimigi in a vast triangular area, whose limits were Monomotapa, Congo, and Abyssinia : from his pages it appears that the people of this central kingdom were closely connected by commerce with the towns on the eastern coast of Africa. According to Dapper, the Dutch historian, (1671,) whose work has been the great mine of information to subsequent writers upon Africa south of the equator, about sixty days' journey from the Atlantic is the kingdom of Monemugi, which others call " Nimeamaye," a name still retained under the corrupted form " Nimeaye " in our atlases. M. Malte-Brun, senior, mentioning Mounemugi, adds, " ou, selon une autographe plus authentique, *Mou-nimougi*." All the Portuguese authors call the people Monemugi or Mono-emugi ; Mr. Cooley prefers Monomoezi, which he derives from "Munha Munge," or "lord of the world," the title of a great African king in the interior, commemorated by the historian De Barros. Mr. Macqueen ('Geography of Central Africa'), who also gives Manmoise, declares that " Mueno-muge, Mueno-muize, Monomoise, and Uniamese," relate to the same place and people, comprehending a large extent of country in the interior of Africa : he explains the word erroneously to mean the "great Moises or Movisas." The Rev. Mr. Erhardt asserts that for facility of pronunciation the coast merchants have turned the name "Wanamesi" into "Waniamesi," which also leads his readers into error. The Rev. Mr. Livingstone thus endorses the mistake of Messrs. Macqueen and Erhardt : "The names Monomoizes, spelt also Monemuigis and Monomuizes, and Monomotapistas, when applied to the tribes, are exactly the same as if we should call the Scotch the Lord Douglases . . . Monomoizes was formed from Moiza or Muiza, the singular of the word Babisa or Aiza, the proper name of a large tribe to the north." In these sentences there is a confusion between the lands of the Wanyamwezi, lying under the parallel of the Tanganyika Lake, and the Wabisa (in the singular Mbísá, the Wavisa of the Rev. Mr. Rebmann), a well-known commercial tribe dwelling about the Maravi or Nyassa Lake, S.W. of Kilwa, whose name in times of old was corrupted by the Portuguese to Movizas or Movisas. Finally M. Guillain, in a work already alluded to, states correctly the name of the people to be Oua-nyamouczi, but in designating the country "payš de Ņyamouezi," he shows little knowledge of the Zangian dialects. M. V. A. Malte-Brun, junior ('Bulletin de Géographie,' Paris, 1856, Part II. p. 295) correctly writes Wanyamwezi.

A name so discrepantly corrupted deserves some notice. Unyamwezi is translated by Dr. Krapf and the Rev. Mr. Rebmann, "Possessions of the Moon." The initial U, the causal and locative prefix, denotes the land, nya, of, and mwezi, articulated m'ezí with

semi-elision of the w, means the moon. The people
sometimes pronounce their country name Unyamiezi,
which would be a plural form, miezi signifying moons
or months. The Arabs and the people of Zanzibar, for
facility and rapidity of pronunciation, dispense with
the initial dissyllable, and call the country and its race
Mwezi. The correct designation of the inhabitants of
Unyamwezi is, therefore, Mnyamwezi in the singular,
and Wanyamwezi in the plural: Kinyamwezi is the
adjectival form. It is not a little curious that the Greeks
should have placed their τὴς σελήνης ὄρος—the mountain
of the moon—and the Hindus their Soma Giri (an expression probably translated from the former), in the
vicinity of the African "Land of the Moon." It is
impossible to investigate the antiquity of the vernacular
term; all that can be discovered is, that nearly 350
years ago the Portuguese explorers of Western Africa
heard the country designated by its present name.

There is the evidence of barbarous tradition for a
belief in the existence of Unyamwezi as a great empire,
united under a single despot. The elders declare that
their patriarchal ancestor became after death the first
tree, and afforded shade to his children and descendants. According to the Arabs the people still perform
pilgrimage to a holy tree, and believe that the penalty
of sacrilege in cutting off a twig would be visited by
sudden and mysterious death. All agree in relating
that during the olden time Unyamwezi was united
under a single sovereign, whose tribe was the Wakalaganza, still inhabiting the western district, Usagozi. According to the people, whose greatest chronical measure
is a Masika, or rainy season, in the days of the grandfathers of their grandfathers the last of the Wanyamwezi emperors died. His children and nobles divided
and dismembered his dominions, further partitions en-

sued, and finally the old empire fell into the hands of a rabble of petty chiefs. Their wild computation would point to an epoch of 150 years ago—a date by no means improbable.

These glimmerings of light thrown by African tradition illustrate the accounts given by the early Portuguese concerning the extent and the civilisation of the Unyamwezi empire. Moreover, African travellers in the seventeenth century concur in asserting that, between 250 and 300 years ago, there was an outpouring of the barbarians from the heart of Æthiopia and from the shores of the Central Lake towards the eastern and southern coasts of the peninsula, a general waving and wandering of tribes which caused great ethnological and geographical confusion, public demoralisation, dismemberment of races, and change, confusion, and corruption of tongues. About this period it is supposed the kingdom of Mtándá, the first Kazembe, was established. The Kafirs of the Cape also date their migration from the northern regions to the banks of the Kei about a century and a half ago.

In these days Unyamwezi has returned to the political status of Eastern Africa in the time of the Periplus. It is broken up into petty divisions, each ruled by its own tyrant; his authority never extends beyond five marches; moreover, the minor chiefs of the different districts are virtually independent of their suzerains. One language is spoken throughout the land of the Moon, but the dialectic differences are such that the tribes in the east with difficulty understand their brethren in the west. The principal provinces are — Utakama to the extreme north, Usukuma on the south, —in Kinyamwezi sukuma means the north, takama the south, kiya the east, and mwere the west,—Unyanyembe in the centre, Ufyoma and Utumbara in the north-west, Unyangwira in the south-east, Usagozi and Usumbwá to the westward. The three normal divisions of the people are into Wanyamwezi, Wasukuma or northern, and Watakama or southern.

The general character of Unyamwezi is rolling ground, intersected with low conical and tabular hills, whose lines ramify in all directions. No mountain is found in the country. The superjacent stratum is clay, overlying the sandstone based upon various granites, which in some places crop out, picturesquely disposed in blocks and boulders and huge domes and lumpy masses; ironstone is met with at a depth varying from five to twelve feet, and at Kazeh, the Arab settlement in Unyanyembe, bits of coarse ore were found by digging not more than four feet in a chance spot. During the rains a coat of many-tinted greens conceals the soil; in the dry season the land is grey, lighted up by golden stubbles and dotted with wind-distorted trees, shallow swamps of emerald grass, and wide sheets of dark mud. Dwarfed stumps and charred "black-jacks" deform the fields, which are sometimes ditched or hedged in, whilst a thin forest of parachute-shaped thorns diversifies the waves of rolling land and earth-hills spotted with sun-burnt stone. The reclaimed tracts and clearings are divided from one another by strips of primæval jungle, varying from two to twelve miles in length. As in most parts of Eastern Africa, the country is dotted with "fairy mounts" — dwarf mounds, the ancient sites of trees now crumbled to dust, and the débris of insect architecture; they appear to be rich ground, as they are always diligently cultivated. The yield of the soil, according to the Arabs, averages sixty-fold, even in unfavourable seasons.

The Land of the Moon, which is the garden of
Central Intertropical Africa, presents an aspect of
peaceful rural beauty which soothes the eye like a
medicine after the red glare of barren Ugogo, and the
dark monotonous verdure of the western provinces.
The inhabitants are comparatively numerous in the
villages, which rise at short intervals above their impervious walls of the lustrous green milk-bush, with
its coral-shaped arms, variegating the well-hoed plains;
whilst in the pasture-lands frequent herds of many-
coloured cattle, plump, round-barrelled, and high-
humped, like the Indian breeds, and mingled flocks of
goats and sheep dispersed over the landscape, suggest
ideas of barbarous comfort and plenty. There are few
scenes more soft and soothing than a view of Unyamwezi in the balmy evenings of spring. As the large
yellow sun nears the horizon, a deep stillness falls upon
earth: even the zephyr seems to lose the power of rust-
ling the lightest leaf. The milky haze of midday disappears from the firmament, the flush of departing day
mantles the distant features of scenery with a lovely
rose-tint, and the twilight is an orange glow that burns
like distant horizontal fires, passing upwards through an
imperceptibly graduated scale of colours — saffron, yellow, tender green, and the lightest azure—into the dark
blue of the infinite space above. The charm of the
hour seems to affect even the unimaginative Africans,
as they sit in the central spaces of their villages, or,
stretched under the forest-trees, gaze upon the glories
around.

In Unyamwezi water generally lies upon the surface,
during the rains, in broad shallow pools, which become
favourite sites for rice-fields. These little ziwa and
mbuga — ponds and marshes — vary from two to five

feet below the level of the land; in the dry season
they are betrayed from afar by a green line of livelier
vegetation streaking the dead tawny plain.   The Arabs
seldom dig their wells deeper than six feet, and they
complain of the want of " live-water" gushing from the
rocky ground, as in their native Oman. ˙The country
contains few springs, and the surface of retentive clay
prevents the moisture penetrating to the subsoil.   The
peculiarity of the produce is its decided chalybeate
flavour.   The versant of the country varies.   The
eastern third, falling to the south-east, discharges its
surplus supplies through the Rwaha river into the
Indian Ocean ; in the centre, water seems to stagnate ;
and in the western third, the flow, turning to the north
and north-west, is carried by the Gombe nullah — a
string of pools during the dry season, and a rapid unfordable stream during the rains—into the great Malagarazi river, the principal eastern influent of the Tanganyika Lake. The levels of the country and the direction
of the waters combine to prove that the great depression of Central Africa, alluded to in the preceding chapter, commences in the district of Kigwa in Unyamwezi.

The climate of the island and coast of Zanzibar has,
it must be remembered, double seasons, which are exceedingly confused and irregular.   The lands of Unyamwezi and Uvinza, on the other hand, are as
remarkable for simplicity of division.   There eight
seasons disturb the idea of year ; here but two — a
summer and a winter.   Central Africa has, as the
Spaniards say of the Philippine Isles,

" Seis mezes de polvo,
Seis mezes de lodo."

In 1857 the Masika, or rains, commenced throughout
Eastern Unyamwezi on the 14th of November.   In the

northern and western provinces the wet monsoon begins
earlier and lasts longer. At Msene it precedes Unyanyembe about a month; in Ujiji, Karagwah, and Uganda,
nearly two months. Thus the latter countries have a
rainy season which lasts from the middle of September
till the middle of May.

The moisture-bearing wind in this part of Africa is
the fixed south-east trade, deflected, as in the great
valley of the Mississippi and in the island of Ceylon,
into a periodical south-west monsoon. As will appear
in these pages, the downfalls begin earlier in Central
Africa than upon the eastern coast, and from the latter
point they travel by slow degrees, with the northing
sun, to the north-east, till they find a grave upon the
rocky slopes of the Himalayas.

The rainy monsoon is here ushered in, accompanied,
and terminated by storms of thunder and lightning,
and occasional hail-falls. The blinding flashes of
white, yellow, or rose colour play over the firmament uninterruptedly for hours, during which no
darkness is visible. In the lighter storms thirty and
thirty-five flashes may be counted in a minute: so vivid
is the glare that it discloses the finest shades of colour,
and appears followed by a thick and palpable gloom,
such as would hang before a blind man's eyes, whilst a
deafening roar simultaneously following the flash, seems
to travel, as it were, to and fro overhead. Several
claps sometimes sound almost at the same moment, and
as if coming from different directions. The same storm
will, after the most violent of its discharges, pass over,
and be immediately followed by a second, showing the
superabundance of electricity in the atmosphere. When
hail is about to fall, a rushing noise is heard in the air,
with sudden coolness and a strange darkness from the

canopy of brownish purple clouds.   The winds are
exceedingly variable : perhaps they are most often from
the east and north-east during summer, from the north-
west and south-west in the rains ; but they are answered
from all quarters of the heavens, and the most violent
storms sail up against the lower atmospheric currents.
The Portuguese of the Mozambique attribute these terrible discharges of electricity to the quantity of mineral
substances scattered about the country ; but a steaming
land like Eastern Africa wants, during the rains, no
stronger battery.   In the rainy season the sensation is
that experienced during the equinoctial gales in the
Mediterranean, where the scirocco diffuses ·everywhere
discomfort and disease.   The fall is not, as in Western
India, a steady downpour, lasting sometimes two or
three days without a break.   In Central Africa, rain
seldom endures beyond twelve hours, and it often assumes for weeks an appearance of regularity, re-occurring
at a certain time. Night is its normal season ; the mornings are often wet, and the torrid midday is generally
dry.   As in Southern Africa, a considerable decrease
of temperature is the consequence of long-continued
rain.   Westward of Unyanyembe, hail-storms, during
the rainy monsoon, are frequent and violent; according
to the Arabs, the stones sometimes rival pigeons' eggs in
size. Throughout this monsoon the sun burns with sickly
depressing rays, which make earth reek like a garment
hung out to dry.   Yet this is not considered the unhealthy period : the inundation is too deep, and evaporation is yet unable to extract sufficient poison from
decay.

As in India and the southern regions of Africa, the
deadly season follows the wet monsoon from the middle
of May to the end of June.   The kosi or south-west

wind gives place to the kaskazi, or north-east, about
April, a little later than at Zanzibar. The cold gales
and the fervid suns then affect the outspread waters ;
the rivers, having swollen during the weeks of violent
downfall that usher in the end of the rains, begin to
shrink, and miry morasses and swamps of black vegetable mud line the low-lands whose central depths are
still under water. The winds, cooled by excessive
evaporation and set in motion by the heat, howl over
the country by night and day, dispersing through the
population colds and catarrhs, agues and rheumatisms,
dysenteries and deadly fevers. It must, however, be
remarked that many cases which in India and Sindh
would be despaired of, survived in Eastern Africa.

The hot season, or summer, lasting from the end of
June till nearly the middle of November, forms the
complement of the year. The air now becomes healthy
and temperate ; the cold, raw winds rarely blow, and
the people recover from their transition diseases. At
long intervals, during these months, but a few grateful
and refreshing showers, accompanied by low thunder-
ings, cool the air and give life to the earth. These
phenomena are expected after the change of the moon,
and not, as in Zanzibar, during her last quarter. The
Arabs declare that here, as in the island, rain sometimes
falls from a clear sky — a phenomenon not unknown to
African travellers. The drought affects the country
severely, a curious exception to the rule in the zone of
perpetual rain ; and after August whirlwinds of dust
become frequent. At this time the climate is most
agreeable to the senses ; even in the hottest nights a
blanket is welcome, especially about dawn, and it is
possible to dine at 3 or 4 P.M., when in India the exertion would be impracticable. During the day a ring-

cloud, or a screen of vapour, almost invariably tempers the solar rays; at night a halo, or a corona, generally encircles the moon. The clouds are chiefly cumulus, cumulo-stratus, and nimbus; the sky is often overcast with large white masses floating, apparently without motion, upon the milky haze, and in the serenest weather a few threads are seen pencilled upon the expanse above. Sunrise is seldom thoroughly clear, and, when so, the clouds, sublimed in other regions and brought up by the rising winds, begin to gather in the forenoon. They are melted, as it were, by the fervent heat of the sun between noon and 3 P.M., at which time also the breezes fall light. Thick mists collect about sunset, and by night the skies are seldom free from clouds. The want of heat to dilate the atmosphere at this season, and the light-absorbing vegetation which clothes the land, causes a peculiar dimness in the Galaxy and " Magellan's Clouds." The twilight also is short, and the zodiacal light is not observed. The suffocating sensation of the tropics is unknown, and at noon in the month of September — the midsummer of this region —the thermometer, defended from the wind, in a single-fold Arab tent, never exceeded 113° Fahr. Except during the rains, the dews are not heavy, as in Zanzibar, in the alluvial valleys, and in Usagara and Ujiji : the people do not fear exposure to them, though, as in parts of France, they consider dew-wetted grass unwholesome for cattle. The Arabs stand bathing in the occasional torrents of rain without the least apprehension. The temperature varies too little for the European constitution, which requires a winter. The people, however, scarcely care to clothe themselves. The flies and mosquitoes—those pests of most African countries—are here a minor annoyance.

The principal cause of disease during the summer of Unyamwezi is the east wind, which, refrigerated by the damp alluvial valleys of the first region and the tree-clad peaks and swampy plains of Usagara, sweeps the country, like the tramontanas of Italy, with a freezing cold in the midst of an atmosphere properly tepid. These unnatural combinations of extremes, causing sudden chills when the skin perspires, bring on inevitable disease; strangers often suffer severely, and the influenza is as much feared in Unyamwezi as in England. The east wind is even more dangerous in the hut than in the field : draughts from the four quarters play upon the patient, making one side of the body tremble with cold, whilst the other, defended by the wall or heated by the fire, burns with fever-glow. The gales are most violent immediately after the cessation of the rains; about the beginning of August they become warmer and fall light. At this time frequent whirlwinds sweep from the sun-parched land clouds of a fine and penetrating clay-dust, and slight shocks of earthquakes are by no means uncommon. Three were observed by the Expedition—at noon on the 14th of June, 1858; on the morning of the 13th of June; and at 5 P.M. on the 22nd of November, 1858. The motion, though mild, was distinctly perceptible; unfortunately, means of ascertaining the direction were wanted. The people of the country call this phenomenon "Tetemeka," or the trembling; and the Arabs remember a shock of a serious nature which took place at Unyanyembe in the hot season of 1852. After September, though the land is parched with drought, the trees begin to put forth their leaves; it is the coupling season of beasts, and the period of nidification and incubation for birds. The gradual lowering of the temperature, caused by the southern declination of the sun, acts like the genial warmth of an English spring. As all sudden changes from siccity to humidity are prejudicial to man, there is invariably severe disease at the end of the summer, when the rains set in.

Travellers from Unyamwezi homeward returned often represent that country to be the healthiest in Eastern and Central Africa: they quote, as a proof, the keenness of their appetites and the quantity of food which they consume. The older residents, however, modify their opinions: they declare that digestion does not wait upon appetite; and that, as in Egypt, Mazanderan, Malabar, and other hot-damp countries, no man long retains rude health. The sequelæ of their maladies are always severe; few care to use remedies, deeming them inefficacious against morbific influences to them unknown; convalescence is protracted, painful, and uncertain, and at length they are compelled to lead the lives of confirmed invalids. The gifts of the climate, lassitude and indolence, according to them, predispose to corpulence; and the regular warmth induces baldness, and thins the beard, thus assimilating strangers in body as in mind to the aborigines. They are unanimous in quoting a curious effect of climate, which they attribute to a corruption of the " humours and juices of the body." Men who, after a lengthened sojourn in these regions return to Oman, throw away the surplus provisions brought from the African coast, burn their clothes and bedding, and for the first two or three months eschew society; a peculiar effluvium rendering them, it is said, offensive to the finer olfactories of their compatriots.

The Mukunguru of Unyamwezi is perhaps the severest seasoning fever in this part of Africa. It is a bilious remittent, which normally lasts three days; it wonderfully reduces the patient in that short period, and in severe cases the quotidian is followed by a long attack of a tertian type. The consequences are severe and lasting even in men of the strongest nervous diathesis; burning and painful eyes, hot palms and soles, a recurrence of shivering and flushing fits, with the extremities now icy cold, then painfully hot and swollen, indigestion, insomnolency, cutaneous eruptions and fever sores, languor, dejection, and all the inconveniences resulting from torpidity of liver, or from an inordinate secretion of bile, betray the poison deep-lurking in the system. In some cases this fever works speedily; some even, becoming at once delirious, die on the first or the second day, and there is invariably an exacerbation of symptoms before the bilious remittent passes away.

The fauna of Unyamwezi are similar to those described in Usagara and Ugogo. In the jungles quadrumana are numerous; lions and leopards, cynhyænas and wild cats haunt the forests; the elephant and the rhinoceros, the giraffe and the Cape buffalo, the zebra, the quagga (?), and the koodoo wander over the plains; and the hippopotamus and crocodile are found in every large pool. The nyanyi or cynocephalus in the jungles of Usukuma attains the size of a greyhound; according to the people, there are three varieties of colour — red, black, and yellow. They are the terror of the neighbouring districts: women never dare to approach their haunts; they set the leopard at defiance, and, when in a large body, they do not, it is said, fear the lion. The Colobus guereza, or tippet monkey, the "polume" of Dr. Livingstone (ch. xvi.), here called mbega, is admired on account of its polished black skin and snowy-

white mane.   It is a cleanly animal, ever occupied in
polishing its beautiful garb, which, according to the
Arabs, it tears to pieces when wounded, lest the hunter
should profit by it.   The mbega lives in trees, seldom
descending, and feeds upon the fruit and the young
leaves.   The Arabs speak of wild dogs in the vicinity
of Unyanyembe, describing them as being about eighteen inches in height, with rufous-black and shaggy
coats, and long thick tails; they are gregarious, running
in packs of from 20 to 200; they attack indiscriminately man and the largest animals, and their only cry
is a howl.   About the time of our autumn the pools are
visited by various kinds of aquatic birds, widgeon,
plump little teal, fine snipe, curlew, and crane; the
ardea, or white "paddy-bird" of India, and the "lily-
trotter" (Parra Africana), are scattered over the
country; and sometimes, though rarely, the chenalopex
or common Egyptian-goose and the gorgeous-crowned
crane (Balearica pavonina), the latter a favourite dish
with the Arabs, appear.   In several parts of Unyamwezi, especially in the north, there is a large and well-
flavoured species of black-backed goose (Sakidornis
melanota): the common wild duck of England was not
seen.   Several specimens of the Buceros, the secretary-
bird (Serpentarius reptilivorus), and large vultures,
probably the condor of the Cape, were observed in Unyamwezi; the people do not molest them, holding the
flesh to be carrion.   The Cuculus indicator, called in
Kisawahili "tongoe," is common; but, its honey being
mostly hived, it does not attract attention.   Grillivori,
and a species of thrush, about the size of common larks,
with sulphur-yellow patches under the eyes, and two
naked black striæ beneath the throat, are here migratory
birds; they do good service to the agriculturist against

the locust. A variety of the Loxia or grossbill constructs nests sometimes in bunches hanging from the lower branches of the trees. The mtiko, a kind of water-wagtail (Motacilla), ventures into the huts with the audacity of a London sparrow, and the Africans have a prejudice against killing it. Swallows and martins of various kinds, some peculiarly graceful and slender, may be seen migrating at the approach of winter in regular travelling order: of these, one variety resembles the English bird. The Africans declare that a single species of hirundo, probably the sand-martin, builds in the precipitous earth-banks of the nullahs: their nests were not seen, however, as in Southern Africa, under the eaves of houses. There are a few ostriches, hawks, ravens, plovers, nightjars (Caprimulgidæ), red and blue jays of brilliant plume, muscicapæ, blackcaps or mock nightingales (Motacilla atrocapilla?), passerines of various kinds, hoopoes, bulbuls, wrens, larks, and bats. We saw but few poisonous animals. Besides the dendrophis, the only ophidia killed in the country were snakes, with slate-coloured backs, and silver bellies, resembling the harmless " mas " or " hanash " of Somaliland, the Psammophis sibilaris (L.); C. moniliger Lacépède, — according to Mr. Blyth (" Journal of the As. Soc. of Bengal," vol. xxiv., p. 306), who declares it to be not venomous — they abound in the houses and destroy the rats. The people speak of a yellow and brown-coated snake, eight feet long by five or six inches in diameter; it is probably a boa or rock-snake. Chúrá or frogs are numerous in the swamps, where the frog-concerts resemble those of the New World; and in the regions about the Tanganyika Lake a large variety makes night hideous with its croakings. Of the ranæ there are many species.

The largest is probably the "matmalelo" of S. Africa;
it is eaten by the Wagogo and other tribes. A smaller
kind is of dark colour, and with long legs, which enable it to hop great distances. A third is of a dirty
yellow, with brownish speckles. There is also a little
green tree-frog, which adheres to the broad and almost
perpendicular leaves of the thicker grasses. The leech is
found in the lakes and rivers of the interior, as well as
in Zanzibar and on both coasts of Africa; according to
the Arabs they are of two kinds, large and small. The
people neither take precautions against them when
drinking at the streams, as the Somal do, nor are they
aware of any officinal use for the animals; moreover,
it is impossible to persuade a Msawahili to collect them:
they are of P'hepo or fiendish nature, and never fail to
haunt and harm their captor. Jongo, or huge millepedes,
some attaining a length of half a foot, with shiny black
bodies and red feet, are found in the fields and forests,
especially during the rains: covered with epizoa, these
animals present a disgusting appearance, and they seem,
to judge from their spoils, to die off during the hot
weather. At certain seasons there is a great variety of
the papilionaceous family in the vicinity of waters
where libellulæ or dragon-flies also abound. The
country is visited at irregular times by flights of locusts,
here called nzige. In spring the plants are covered in
parts with the p'hánzí, a large pink and green variety,
and the destructive species depicted and described by
Salt: they rise from the earth like a glowing rose-
coloured cloud, and die off about the beginning of the
rains. The black leather-like variety, called by the
Arabs "Satan's ass," is not uncommon: it is eaten by
the Africans, as are many other edibles upon which
strangers look with disgust. The Arabs describe a fly

which infests the forest-patches of Unyamwezi : it is about the size of a small wasp, and is so fatal that cattle attacked by it are at once killed and eaten before they become carrion from its venomous effects. In parts the country is dotted with ant-hills, which, when old, become hard as sandstone : they are generally built by the termite under some shady tree, which prevents too rapid drying, and apparently the people have not learned, like their brethren in South Africa, to use them as ovens.

From Tura westward to Unyanyembe, the central district of Unyamwezi, caravans usually number seven marches, making a total of 60 rectilinear geographical miles. As far as Kigwa there is but one line of route; from that point travelling parties diverge far and wide, like ships making their different courses.

The races requiring notice in this region are two, the Wakimbu and the Wanyamwezi.

The Wakimbu, who are emigrants into Unyamwezi, claim a noble origin, and derive themselves from the broad lands running south of Unyanyembe as far westward as K'hokoro. About twenty masika, wet monsoons, or years ago, according to themselves, in company with their neighbours, the Wakonongo and the Wamia, they left Nguru, Usanga, and Usenga, in consequence of the repeated attacks of the Warori, and migrated to Kipiri, the district lying south of Tura; they have now extended into Mgunda Mk'hali and Unyanyembe, where they hold the land by permission of the Wanyamwezi. In these regions there are few obstacles to immigrants. They visit the Sultan, make a small present, obtain permission to settle, and name the village after their own chief; but the original proprietors still maintain their rights to the soil. The Wakimbu build firmly stockaded villages, tend cattle, and cultivate sorghum and maize, millet and pulse, cucumbers, and water-melons. Apparently they are poor, being generally clad in skins. They barter slaves and ivory in small quantities to the merchants, and some travel to the coast. They are considered treacherous by their neighbours, and Mapokera, the Sultan of Tura, is, according to the Arabs, prone to commit " *avanies*." They are known by a number of small lines formed by raising the skin with a needle, and opening it by points laterally between the hair of the temples and the eyebrows. In appearance they are dark and uncomely; their arms are bows and arrows, spears and knives stuck in the leathern waistbelt; some wear necklaces of curiously plaited straw, others a strip of white cowskin bound around the brow—a truly savage and African decoration. Their language differs from Kinyamwezi.

The Wanyamwezi tribe, the proprietors of the soil, is the typical race in this portion of Central Africa : its comparative industry and commercial activity have secured to it a superiority over the other kindred races.

The aspect of the Wanyamwezi is alone sufficient to disprove the existence of very elevated lands in this part of the African interior. They are usually of a dark sepia-brown, rarely coloured like diluted Indian ink, as are the Wahiao and slave races to the south, with negroid features markedly less Semitic than the people of the eastern coast. The effluvium from their skins, especially after exercise or excitement, marks their connection with the negro. The hair curls crisply, but it grows to the length of four or five inches before it-splits; it is usually twisted into many little ringlets or hanks; it hangs down like a fringe to the neck, and is combed off the forehead after the manner of the ancient Egyptians and the modern Hottentots. The beard is thin and short, there are no whiskers, and the moustachio — when not plucked out — is scant and straggling. Most of the men and almost all the women remove the eyelashes, and pilar hair rarely appears to grow. The normal figure of the race is tall and stout, and the women are remarkable for the elongation of the mammary organs. Few have small waists, and the only lean men in the land are the youths, the sick, and the famished. This race is said to be long-lived, and it is not deficient in bodily strength and savage courage. The clan-mark is a double line of little cuts, like the marks of cupping, made by a friend with a knife or razor, along the temporal fossæ from the external edges of the eyebrows to the middle of the cheeks or to the lower jaws. Sometimes a third line, or a band of three small lines, is drawn down the forehead to the bridge of the nose. The men prefer a black, charcoal being the substance generally used, the women a blue colour, and the latter sometimes ornament their faces with little perpendicular scars below the eyes. They do not file the teeth into a saw-shape as seen amongst the southern races, but they generally form an inner triangular or wedge-shaped aperture by chipping away the internal corners of the two front incisors like the Damaras, and the women extract the lower central teeth. Both sexes enlarge the lobes of the ears. In many parts of the country skins are more commonly worn than cloth, except by the Sultans and the wealthier classes. The women wear the long tobe of the coast, tightly wrapped round either above or more commonly below the breast ; the poorer classes veil the bosom with a square or softened skin ; the remainder of the dress is a kilt or short petticoat of the same material extending from

waist to knee. Maidens never cover the breast, and
children are rarely clothed ; the infant, as usual in East
Africa, is carried in a skin fastened by thongs behind
the parent's back. The favourite ornaments are beads,
of which the red coral, the pink, and the "pigeon-eggs"
made at Nuremberg are preferred. From the neck
depend strings of beads with kiwangwa, disks of shell
brought from the coast, and crescents of hippopotamus
teeth country made, and when the beard is long it is
strung with red and particoloured beads. Brass and
copper bangles or massive rings are worn upon the
wrists, the forearm bears the ponderous kitindi or coil
bracelet, and the arm above the elbow is sometimes decorated with circlets of ivory or with a razor in an ivory
étui ; the middle is girt with a coil of wire twisted
round a rope of hair or fibre, and the ankles are covered
with small iron bells and the rings of thin brass, copper,
or iron wire, called sambo. When travelling, a goat's
horn, used as a bugle, is secured over the right shoulder
by a lanyard and allowed to hang by the left side : in
the house many wear a smaller article of the same kind,
hollowed inside and containing various articles intended
as charms, and consecrated by the Mganga or medicine-
man. The arms are slender assegais with the shoulders
of the blade rounded off : they are delivered, as by the
Somal, with the thumb and forefinger after a preliminary
of vibratory motion, but the people want the force
and the dexterity of the Kafirs. Some have large
spears for thrusting, and men rarely leave the hut
without their bows and arrows, the latter unpoisoned,
but curiously and cruelly barbed. They make also the
long double-edged knives called sime, and different
complications of rungu or knob-kerries, some of them
armed with an iron lance-head upon the wooden bulge.

Dwarf battle-axes are also seen, but not so frequently
as amongst the western races on the Tanganyika Lake.
The shield in Unyamwezi resembles that of Usagara;
it is however rarely used.

There are but few ceremonies amongst the Wanyamwezi.   A woman about to become a mother retires
from the hut to the jungle, and after a few hours
returns with a child wrapped in goatskin upon her
back, and probably carrying a load of firewood on her
head.   The medical treatment of the Arabs with salt
and various astringents for forty days is here unknown.
Twins are not common as amongst the Kafir race, and
one of the two is invariably put to death; the universal
custom amongst these tribes is for the mother to wrap
a gourd or calabash in skins, to place it to sleep with,
and to feed it like, the survivor.   If the wife die without issue, the widower claims from her parents the sum
paid to them upon marriage; if she leave a child, the
property is preserved for it.   When the father can
afford it, a birth is celebrated by copious libations of
pombe.   Children are suckled till the end of the second
year. Their only education is in the use of the bow and
arrow; after the fourth summer the boy begins to learn
archery with diminutive weapons, which are gradually
increased in strength.   Names are given without ceremony; and as in the countries to the eastward, many
of the heathens have been called after their Arab
visitors. Circumcision is not practised by this people.
The children in Unyamwezi generally are the property
not of the uncle but of the father, who can sell or slay
them without blame ; in Usukuma or the northern
lands, however, succession and inheritance are claimed
by the nephews or sisters' sons.   The Wanyamwezi
have adopted the curious practice of leaving property

to their illegitimate children by slave girls or concubines, to the exclusion of their issue by wives; they
justify it by the fact of the former requiring their
assistance more than the latter, who have friends and
relatives to aid them.   As soon as the boy can walk
he tends the flocks; after the age of ten he drives the
cattle to pasture, and, considering himself independent
of his father, he plants a tobacco-plot and aspires to
build a hut for himself.   There is not a boy " which
cannot earn his own meat."

Another peculiarity of the Wanyamwezi is the position of the Wahárá or unmarried girls.   Until puberty
they live in the father's house; after that period the
spinsters of the village, who usually number from seven
to a dozen, assemble together and build for themselves
at a distance from their homes a hut where they can
receive their friends without parental interference.
There is but one limit to community in single life: if
the Mhárá or "maiden" be likely to become a mother,
her "young man" must marry her under pain of
mulct; and if she die in childbirth, her father demands
from her lover a large fine for having taken away his
daughter's life.   Marriage takes place when the youth
can afford to pay the price for a wife: it varies according to circumstances from one to ten cows.   The wife
is so far the property of the husband that he can claim
damages from the adulterer; he may not, however, sell
her, except when in difficulties.   The marriage is celebrated with the usual carouse, and the bridegroom
takes up his quarters in his wife's home, not under her
father's roof.   Polygamy is the rule with the wealthy.
There is little community of interests and apparently a
lack of family affection in these tribes.   The husband,
when returning from the coast laden with cloth, will

refuse a single shukkah to his wife, and the wife suc-
ceeding to an inheritance will abandon her husband to
starvation. The man takes charge of the cattle, goats,
sheep, and poultry; the woman has power over the
grain and the vegetables; and each must grow tobacco,
having little hope of borrowing from the other. Widows
left with houses, cattle, and fields, usually spend their
substance in supporting lovers, who are expected occasionally to make presents in return. Hence no coast
slave in Wanyamwezi is ever known to keep a shukkah
of cloth.

The usual way of disposing of a corpse in former times
was, to carry it out on the head and to throw it into
some jungle strip where the fisi or cynhyæna abounds, —
a custom which accounts for the absence of graveyards.
The Wanyamwezi at first objected to the Arabs pub-
licly burying their dead in their fields, for fear of pollution; they would assemble in crowds to close the
way against a funeral party. The merchants, however,
persevered till they succeeded in establishing a right.
When a Mnyamwezi dies in a strange country, and his
comrades take the trouble to inter him, they turn the
face of the corpse towards the mother's village, a proceeding which shows more sentiment than might be
expected from them. The body is buried standing, or
tightly bound in a heap, or placed in a sitting position
with the arms clasping the knees: if the deceased be a
great man, a sheep and a bullock are slaughtered for a
funeral feast, the skin is placed over his face, and the
hide is bound to his back. When a sultan dies in a
foreign land his body is buried upon the spot, and his
head, or what remains of it, is carried back for sepul-
ture to his own country. The chiefs of Unyamwezi
generally are interred by a large assemblage of their

subjects with cruel rites. A deep pit is sunk, with a kind of vault or recess projecting from it: in this the corpse, clothed with skin and hide, and holding a bow in the right hand, is placed sitting, with a pot of pombe, upon a dwarf stool, whilst sometimes one, but more generally three female slaves, one on each side and the third in front, are buried alive to preserve their lord from the horrors of solitude. A copious libation of pombe upon the heaped-up earth concludes the ceremony. According to the Arabs, the Wasukuma inter all their sultans in a jungle north of Unyanyembe, and the neighbouring peasants deposit before seed-time small offerings of grain at the Mzimo or Fetiss-house which marks the spot.

The habitations of the eastern Wanyamwezi are the Tembe, which in the west give way to the circular African hut ; among the poorer sub-tribes the dwelling is a mere stack of straw. The best Tembe have large projecting eaves supported by uprights : cleanliness, however, can never be expected in them. Having no limestone, the people ornament the inner and outer walls with long lines of ovals formed by pressing the finger tips, after dipping them into ashes and water for whitewash, and into red clay or black mud for variety of colour. With this primitive material they sometimes attempt rude imitations of nature — human beings and serpents. In some parts the cross appears, but the people apparently ignore it as a symbol. Rude carving is also attempted upon the massive posts at the entrances of villages, but the figures, though to appearance idolatrous, are never worshipped. The household furniture of the Tembe differs little from that described in the villages generally. The large sloping Kitanda, or bedstead of peeled tree-branch, supported by forked

sticks, and provided with a bedding of mat and cow-
hide, occupies the greater part of the outer room.   The
triangle of clay cones forming the hearth are generally
placed for light near the wall-side opposite the front door;
and the rest of the supellex consists of large stationary
bark cornbins, of gourds and bandboxes slung from the
roof, earthen-pots of black clay, huge ladles, pipes,
grass-mats, grinding-stones, and arms hung to a
trimmed and branchy tree trunk planted upright in
a corner.   The rooms are divided by party walls,
which, except when separating families, seldom reach
to the ceiling.   The fireplace acts as lamp by night,
and the door is the only chimney.

The characteristic of the Mnyamwezi village is the
" Iwánzá"— a convenience resulting probably from the
instinct of the sexes, who prefer not to mingle, and for
the greater freedom of life and manners.   Of these
buildings there are two in every settlement, generally
built at opposite sides, fronting the normal Mrimba-tree,
which sheds its filmy shade over the public court-yard.
That of the women, being a species of harem, was not
visited ; as travellers and strangers are always admitted
into the male Iwánzá, it is more readily described.   This
public-house is a large hut, somewhat more substantial
than those adjoining, often smeared with smooth clay,
and decorated here and there with broad columns of the
ovals before described, and the prints of palms dipped
in ashes and placed flat like the hands in ancient Egyptian buildings.   The roof is generally a flying thatch
raised a foot above the walls — an excellent plan for
ventilation in these regions.   Outside, the Iwánzá is
defended against the incursions of cattle by roughly-
barked trunks of trees resting upon stout uprights : in
this space men sit, converse, and smoke.   The two

doorways are protected by rude charms suspended from the lintel, hares' tails, zebras' manes, goats' horns, and other articles of prophylactic virtue. Inside, half the depth is appropriated to the Ubiri, a huge standing bedframe, formed, like the plank-benches of a civilised guard-room, by sleepers lying upon horizontal cross-bars: these are supported by forked trunks about two feet long planted firmly in the ground. The floor is of tamped earth. The furniture of the Iwánzá consists of a hearth and grinding-stone; spears, sticks, arrows, and shillelaghs are stuck to smoke in the dingy rafter ceiling, or are laid upon hooks of crooked wood depending from the sooty cross-beams: the corners are occupied by bellows, elephant-spears, and similar articles. In this " public" the villagers spend their days, and often, even though married, their nights, gambling, eating, drinking pombe, smoking bhang and tobacco, chatting, and sleeping like a litter of puppies destitute of clothing, and using one another's backs, breasts, and stomachs as pillows. The Iwánzá appears almost peculiar to Unyamwezi.

In Unyamwezi the sexes do not eat together: even the boys would disdain to be seen sitting at meat with their mothers. The men feed either in their cottages or more generally in the Iwánzá: they make, when they can, two meals during the day — in the morning, a breakfast, which is often omitted for economy, and a dinner about 3 P.M. During the interim they chew tobacco, and, that failing, indulge in a quid of clay. It probably contains some animal matter, but the chief reason for using it is apparently the necessity to barbarians of whiling away the time when not sleeping by exercising their jaws. They prefer the " sweet earth," that is to say, the clay of ant-hills: the Arabs have tried it without other effects but nausea. The custom, however, is not uncommon upon both coasts of Africa: it takes, in fact, the place of the mastic of Chios, the kat of Yemen, the betel and toasted grains of India and the farther East, and the ashes of the Somali country. The Wanyamwezi, and indeed the East-African tribes gene- rally, have some curious food prejudices. Before their closer intercourse with the Arabs they used to keep poultry, but, like the Gallas and the Somal, who look upon the fowl as a kind of vulture, they would not eat it: even in the present day they avoid eggs. Some will devour animals that have died of disease, and carrion,—the flesh of lions and leopards, elephants and rhinoceroses, asses, wild cats and rats, beetles and white ants;—others refuse to touch mutton or clean water- fowl, declaring that it is not their custom. The pre- judice has not, however, been reduced to a system, as amongst the tribes of southern Africa. They rarely taste meat except upon the march, where the prospect of gain excites them to an unusual indulgence: when a bullock is killed, they either jerk the meat, or dry it upon a dwarf platform of sticks raised above a slow and smoky fire, after which it will keep for some days. The usual food is the ugali or porridge of boiled flour: they find, however, a variety of edible herbs in the jungle, and during the season they luxuriate upon honey and sour milk. No Mnyamwezi, however, will own to repletion unless he has " sat upon pombe,"— in other words, has drunk to intoxication; and the chiefs pride themselves upon living entirely upon beef and stimulants.

The Wanyamwezi have won for themselves a repu- tation by their commercial industry. Encouraged by the merchants, they are the only professional porters of

East Africa ; and even amongst them, the Wakalaganza, Wasumbwa, and Wasukuma are the only tribes who regularly visit the coast in this capacity.   They are now no longer " honest and civil to strangers "—semi-civilisation has hitherto tended to degradation.   They seem to have learned but little by their intercourse with the Arabs.   Commerce with them is still in its infancy. They have no idea of credit, although in Karagwah and the northern kingdoms payment may be delayed for a period of two years.   They cannot, like some of their neighbours, bargain : a man names the article which he requires, and if it be not forthcoming he will take no other.   The porters, who linger upon the coast or in the island of Zanzibar, either cut grass for asses, carry stones and mortar to the town, for which they receive a daily hire of from two to eight pice, or they obtain from the larger landholders permission to reclaim and cultivate a plot of ground for vegetables and manioc.   They have little of the literature, songs and tales, common amongst barbarians ; and though they occasionally indulge in speeches, they do not, like many kindred tribes, cultivate eloquence.   On the march they beguile themselves with chanting for hours together half a dozen words eternally repeated.   Their language is copious but confused, and they are immoderately fond of simple and meaningless syllables used as interjections.   Their industry is confined to weaving coarse cloths of unbleached cotton, neatly-woven baskets, wooden milk-bowls, saddle-bags for their asses, and arms.   They rear asses and load them lightly when travelling to the coast, but they have not yet learned to ride them.   Though they carefully fence and ditch their fields, they have never invented a plough, confining themselves to ridging the land with the laborious hoe. They rarely sell one another, nor do they much encourage the desertion of slaves. The wild bondsman, when running away, is sometimes appropriated by his captor, but a Muwallid or domestic slave is always restored after a month or two. The Arabs prefer to purchase men sold under suspicion of magic; they rarely flee, fearing lest their countrymen should put them to death.

As has been said, the government of Unyamwezi is conducted by a multitude of petty chiefs. The ruling classes are thus called: Mtemi or Mwáme is the chief or sultan, Mgáwe (in the plural Wágáwe) the principal councillor, and Mánácháro, or Mnyapara (plural Wányápárá) the elder. The ryots or subjects on the other hand are collectively styled Wasengi. The most powerful chiefs are Fundikira of Unyanyembe, Masanga of Msene, and Kafrira of Kiríra. The dignity of Mtemi is hereditary. He has power of life and death over his subjects, and he seldom condescends to any but mortal punishment. His revenue is composed of additions to his private property by presents from travellers, confiscation of effects in cases of felony or magic, by the sale of subjects, and by treasure trove. Even if a man kill his own slave, the slave's effects lapse to the ruler. The villagers must give up all ivory found in the jungles, although the hunters are allowed to retain the tusks of the slaughtered animals.

A few brief remarks concerning Fundikira, the chief of Unyamwezi in 1858, may serve to illustrate the condition of the ruling class in Unyamwezi. This chief was travelling towards the coast as a porter in a caravan, when he heard of his father's death: he at once stacked his load and prepared to return home and rule. The rest of the gang, before allowing him to depart, taunted him severely, exclaiming, partly in jest, partly in earnest, "Ah! now thou art still our comrade, but presently thou wilt torture and slay, fine and flog us." Fundikira proceeding to his native country inherited, as is the custom, all his father's property and widows; he fixed himself at Ititenya, presently numbered ten wives, who have borne him only three children, built 300 houses for his slaves and dependants, and owned 2000 head of cattle. He lived in some state, declining to call upon strangers, and, though not demanding still obtaining large presents. Becoming obese by age and good living, he fell ill in the autumn of 1858, and, as usual, his relations were suspected of compassing his end by Uchawi, or black magic. In these regions the death of one man causes many. The Mganga was summoned to apply the usual ordeal. After administering a mystic drug, he broke the neck of a fowl, and splitting it into two lengths inspected the interior. If blackness or blemish appear about the wings, it denotes the treachery of children, relations and kinsmen; the backbone convicts the mother and grandmother; the tail shows that the criminal is the wife, the thighs the concubines, and the injured shanks or feet the other slaves. Having fixed upon the class of the criminals, they are collected together by the Mganga, who, after similarly dosing a second hen, throws her up into the air above the heads of the crowd and singles out the person upon whom she alights. Confession is extorted by tying the thumb backwards till it touches the wrist or by some equally barbarous mode of question. The consequence of condemnation is certain and immediate death; the mode is chosen by the Mganga. Some are speared, others are beheaded or " ammazati,"—clubbed:—a common way is to bind the cranium between two stiff pieces of wood which are gradually tightened by cords till the brain bursts out from the sutures. For women they practise a peculiarly horrible kind of impalement. These atrocities continue until the chief recovers or dies: at the commencement of his attack, in one household eighteen souls, male and female, had been destroyed; should his illness be protracted, scores will precede him to the grave, for the Mchawi or magician must surely die.

The Wanyamwezi will generally sell their criminals and captives; when want drives, they part with their wives, their children, and even their parents. For economy, they import their serviles from Ujiji and the adjoining regions; from the people lying towards the south-east angle of the Tanganyika Lake, as the Wafipa, the Wapoka, and the Wagara; and from the Nyanza races, and the northern kingdoms of Karagwah, Uganda, and Unyoro.

My Tembe near the Tanganyika.

CHAP. XIII.

AT LENGTH WE SIGHT THE LAKE TANGANYIKA, THE "SEA OF UJIJI."

THE route before us lay through a howling wilderness, once populous and fertile, but now laid waste by the fierce Watuta. Snay bin Amir had warned me that it would be our greatest trial of patience. The march began badly : Mpete, the district on the right bank of the Malagarazi River, is highly malarious, and the mosquitoes feasted right royally upon our life, even during the day-time. We bivouacked under a shady tree, within sight of the ferry, not knowing that upon the woody eminences above the valley there are usually fine kraals of dry grass and of mkora or myombo-bark. During the rainy monsoon the best encampments in these regions are made of tree-sheets: two parallel rings are cut in the bole, at a distance of six to seven feet; a perpendicular slit then connects them, the bark is easily stripped off, and the trunk, after having been left for a time to season, is filled for use.

On the 5th of February we set out betimes, across a route traversing for a short distance swampy ground along the river-side. It then stretched over jungly and wooded hill-spires, with steep rough ascents and descents, divided from neighbouring elevations by slippery mire-runs. Exposed to the full break of the rainy monsoon, and the frequent outbursts of fiery sun, I could not but admire the marvellous fertility of the soil; an impervious luxuriance of vegetation veils the lowlands, clothes the hill-sides, and caps their rounded summits. After marching five hours and twenty minutes, we found a large kraal in the district of Kinawani: the encamping ground,—partially cleared of the thick, fetid, and putrescent vegetation around, —hugs the right bank of the Malagarazi, and faces the village of Sultan Mzogera on the southern or opposite side. A small store of provisions — grain and sweet-potatoes — was purchased from the villagers of Kinawani, who flocked across the stream to trade. They were, however, fanciful in their requirements: beads, especially the coral porcelain, iron-wire, salt, and meat. The heaviness of this march caused two of the Hammals engaged at Usagozi to levant, and the remaining four to strike work. It was therefore again necessary to mount ass—ten days after an attack of " paraplegia ! "

We left Kinawani on the next morning, and striking away from the river we crossed rugged and rolling ground, divided by deep swamps of mire and grass.

To the southward ran the stream, rushing violently down a rocky bed, with tall trees lining its banks. Sailing before the morning east-wind, a huge mass of nimbus occupied the sky, and presently discharged itself in an unusually heavy downfall: during the afternoon the breeze veered as usual to the west, and the hot sunshine was for once enjoyable. After a weary trudge of five hours and twenty minutes, we entered a large and comfortable kraal, situated near a reach where the swift and turbid river foamed over a discontinuous ledge of rock, between avenues of dense and tangled jungle. No provisions were procurable at this place; man appeared to have become extinct.

The 7th of February led us over broken ground, encumbered by forest, and cut by swamps, with higher levels on the right hand, till we again fell into the marshes and fields of the river-valley. The district on the other side of the river, called Jambeho, is one of the most flourishing in Uvinza; its villages of small bird-nest huts, and its carefully hoed fields of grain and sweet-potato, affected the eye, after the dreary monotony of a jungle-march, like the glimmer of a light at the end of a night-march, or the discovery of land at the conclusion of a long sea-voyage. The village ferry was instantly put into requisition, and the chief, Ruwere, after receiving as his "dash" eight cloths, allowed us to purchase provisions. At that season, however, the harvest of grain and sweet-potatoes had not been got in, and for their single old hen the people demanded an exorbitant price. We hastened, despite all difficulties, to escape from this place of pestilence, which clouds of mosquitoes rendered as uncomfortable as it was dangerous.

The next day ushered in our departure with drizzling

rain, which drenched the slippery paths of red clay; the asses, wild with wind and weather, exposed us to accidents in a country of deep ravines and rugged boulders. Presently diverging from the Malagarazi, we passed over the brow of a low tree-clad hill above the junction of the Rusugi River, and followed the left bank of this tributary as far as its nearer ford. The Rusugi which drains the northern highlands into the Malagarazi, was then about 100 yards in width: the bottom is a red ochreish soil, the strong stream, divided in the centre by a long low strip of sand and gravel, flowed at that time breast-deep, and its banks,—as usual with rivers in these lands,—deeply cut by narrow watercourses, rendered travelling unusually toilsome. At the Rusugi Ford the road separates into a northern and a southern branch, a hill-spur forming the line of demarcation. The northern strikes off to the district of Parugerero on the left bank, where a shallower ford is found: the place in question is a settlement of Wavinza, containing from forty to fifty bee-hive huts, tenanted by salt-diggers. The principal pan is sunk in the vicinity of the river, the saline produce, after being boiled down in the huts, is piled up, and handmade into little cones. The pan affords tripartite revenue to three sultans, and it constitutes the principal wealth of the Wavinza: the salt here sold for one shukkah per masuta, or half-load, and far superior to the bitter, nitrous produce of Ugogo, finds its way throughout the heart of Africa, supplying the lands adjoining both the Tanganyika and the Nyanza Lakes.

We followed the southern line which crosses the Rusugi River at the branch islet. Fords are always picturesque. The men seemed to enjoy the washing; their numbers protected them from the crocodiles,

which fled from their shouting and splashing; and
they even ventured into deep water, where swimming
was necessary. We crossed as usual on a " unicorn " of
negroids, the upper part of the body supported by two
men, and the feet resting upon the shoulders of a third,
— a posture somewhat similar to that affected by
gentlemen who find themselves unable to pull off their
own boots. Then remounting, we ascended the grassy
rise on the right of the stream, struggled, slipped, and
slided over a muddy swamp, climbed up a rocky and
bushy ridge, and found ourselves ensconced in a ragged
and comfortless kraal upon the western slopes, within
sight of some deserted salt pans below. As evening drew
in, it became apparent that the Goanese Gaetano, the five
Wak'hutu porters, and Sarmalla, a donkey-driving son
of Ramji, had remained behind, in company with
several loads, the tent, two bags of clothes, my companion's elephant-gun, my bedding, and that of my
servant. It was certain that with this provision in the
vicinity of Parugerero they would not starve, and the
porters positively refused to halt an hour more than
necessary. I found it therefore compulsory to advance.
On the 11th February three " children " of Said bin
Salim consented, as usual, for a consideration, to return
and to bring up the laggers, and about a week afterwards they entered Ujiji without accident. The five
Wak'hutu porters, probably from the persuasions of
Muinyi Wazira, had, although sworn to fidelity with the
strongest oaths, carried into execution a long-organised
plan of desertion. Gaetano refused to march on the
day of our separation, because he was feverish, and he
expected a riding-ass to be sent back for him. He
brought up our goods safely, but blankets, towels, and
many articles of clothing belonging to his companion,

had disappeared. This difficulty was, of course, attributed to the Wak'hutu porters; probably the missing things had been sold for food by the Goanese and the son of Ramji: I could not therefore complain of the excuse.

From the Msawahili Fundi,—fattore, manciple or steward—of a small caravan belonging to an Arab merchant, Hamid bin Sulayyam, I purchased for thirty-five cloths, about thrice its value, a little single-fold tent of thin American domestics, through which sun and rain penetrated with equal facility. Like the cloth-houses of the Arab travellers generally, it was gable-shaped, six or seven feet high, about eight feet long by four broad, and so light that with its bamboo-poles and its pegs it scarcely formed a load for a man. On the 9th February, we descended from the ridge upon which the kraal was placed, and traversed a deep swamp of black mud, dotted in the more elevated parts with old salt pans and pits, where broken pottery and blackened lumps of clay still showed traces of human handiwork. Beyond this lowland, the track, striking off from the river-valley and turning to the right, entered toilsome ground. We crossed deep and rocky ravines, with luxuriant vegetation above, and with rivulets at the bottom trickling towards the Malagarazi, by scrambling down and swarming up the roughest steps of rock, boulder, and knotted tree-root. Beyond these difficulties lay woody and stony hills, whose steep and slippery inclines were divided by half a dozen waters, all more or less troublesome to cross. The porters, who were in a place of famine, insisted upon pushing on to the utmost of their strength: after six hours' march, I persuaded them to halt in the bush upon a rocky hill, where the neighbouring descent supplied water. The Fundi visited

the valley of the Rusugi River, and finding a herd of
the Mbogo or Bos Caffer, brought home a welcome addition to our well-nigh exhausted rations.

The 10th February saw us crossing the normal
sequence of jungly and stony "neat's-tongues," divided
by deep and grassy swamps, which, stagnant in the dry
weather, drain after rains the northern country to the
Malagarazi River.   We passed over by a felled tree-
trunk an unfordable rivulet, hemmed in by a dense and
fetid thicket; and the asses summarily pitched down
the muddy bank into the water, swam across and
wriggled up the slimy off-side like cats.   Thence a foul
swamp of black mire led to the Ruguvu or Luguvu
River, the western boundary of Uvinza and the eastern
frontier of Ukaranga.   This stream, which can be
forded during the dry season, had spread out after the
rains over its borders of grassy plain; we were delayed till the next morning in a miserable camping
ground, a mud-bank thinly veiled with vegetation, in
order to bridge it with branching trees.   An unusual
downfall during the night might have caused serious
consequences;—provisions had now disappeared, moreover the porters considered the place dangerous.

The 10th February began with the passage of the
Ruguvu River, where again our goods and chattels were
fated to be thoroughly sopped.   I obtained a few corn-
cobs from a passing caravan of Wanyamwezi, and charged
them with meat and messages for the party left behind.
A desert march, similar to the stage last travelled, led us
to the Unguwwe or Uvungwe River, a shallow, muddy
stream, girt in as usual by dense vegetation; and we
found a fine large kraal on its left bank.   After a cold
and rainy night, we resumed our march by fording the
Unguwwe.   Then came the weary toil of fighting through

tiger and spear-grass, with reeds, rushes, a variety of ferns, before unseen, and other lush and lusty growths, clothing a succession of rolling hills, monotonous swellings, where the descent was ever a reflection of the ascent. The paths were broken, slippery, and pitted with deep holes; along their sides, where the ground lay exposed to view, a conglomerate of ferruginous red clay — suggesting a resemblance to the superficies of Londa, as described by Dr. Livingstone—took the place of the granites and sandstones of the eastern countries, and the sinking of the land towards the Lake became palpable. In the jungle were extensive clumps of bamboo and rattan; the former small, the latter of poor quality; the bauhinia, or black-wood, and the salsaparilla vine abounded; wild grapes of diminutive size, and of the austerest flavour, appeared for the first time upon the sunny hill-sides which Bacchus ever loves, and in the lower swamps plantains grew almost wild. In parts the surface was broken into small deep hollows, from which sprang pyramidal masses of the hugest trees. Though no sign of man here met the eye, scattered fields and plantations showed that villages must be somewhere near. Sweet water was found in narrow courses of black mud, which sorely tried the sinews of laden man and beast. Long after noon, we saw the caravan halted by fatigue upon a slope beyond a weary swamp: a violent storm was brewing, and whilst half the sky was purple black with nimbus, the sun shone stingingly through the clear portion of the empyrean. But these small troubles were lightly borne; already in the far distance appeared walls of sky-blue cliff with gilded summits, which were as a beacon to the distressed mariner.

On the 13th February we resumed our travel through

screens of lofty grass, which thinned out into a straggling forest. After about an hour's march, as we entered a small savannah, I saw the Fundi before alluded to running forward and changing the direction of the caravan. Without supposing that he had taken upon himself this responsibility, I followed him. Presently he breasted a steep and stony hill, sparsely clad with thorny trees: it was the death of my companion's riding-ass. Arrived with toil,—for our fagged beasts now refused to proceed,—we halted for a few minutes upon the summit. "What is that streak of light which lies below?" I inquired of Seedy Bombay. "I am of opinion," quoth Bombay, "that that is *the* water." I gazed in dismay ; the remains of my blindness, the veil of trees, and a broad ray of sunshine illuminating but one reach of the Lake, had shrunk its fair proportions. Somewhat prematurely I began to lament my folly in having risked life and lost health for so poor a prize, to curse Arab exaggeration, and to propose an immediate return, with the view of exploring the Nyanza, or Northern Lake. Advancing, however, a few yards, the whole scene suddenly burst upon my view, filling me with admiration, wonder, and delight. It gave local habitation to the poet's fancy :—

> "Tremolavano i rai del Sol nascente
>   Sovra l' onde del mar purpuree e d' oro,
>   E in veste di zaffiro il ciel ridente
>   Specchiar parea le sue bellezze in loro.
>   D' Africa i venti fieri e d' Oriente,
>   Sovra il letto del mar, prendean ristoro,
>   E co' sospiri suoi soavi e lieti
>   Col Zeffiro increspava il lembo a Teti."

Nothing, in sooth, could be more picturesque than this first view of the Tanganyika Lake, as it lay in the lap

of the mountains, basking in the gorgeous tropical sunshine. Below and beyond a short foreground of rugged
and precipitous hill-fold, down which the foot-path
zigzags painfully, a narrow strip of emerald green, never
sere and marvellously fertile, shelves towards a ribbon
of glistening yellow sand, here bordered by sedgy rushes,
there cleanly and clearly cut by the breaking wavelets.
Further in front stretch the waters, an expanse of the
lightest and softest blue, in breadth varying from thirty
to thirty-five miles, and sprinkled by the crisp east-
wind with tiny crescents of snowy foam. The background in front is a high and broken wall of steel-
coloured mountain, here flecked and capped with pearly
mist, there standing sharply pencilled against the azure
air; its yawning chasms, marked by a deeper plum-
colour, fall towards dwarf hills of mound-like proportions, which apparently dip their feet in the wave.
To the south, and opposite the long low point, behind
which the Malagarazi River discharges the red loam
suspended in its violent stream, lie the bluff headlands
and capes of Uguhha, and, as the eye dilates, it falls
upon a cluster of outlying islets, speckling a sea-horizon.
Villages, cultivated lands, the frequent canoes of the
fishermen on the waters, and on a nearer approach the
murmurs of the waves breaking upon the shore, give a
something of variety, of movement, of life to the landscape, which, like all the fairest prospects in these regions, wants but a little of the neatness and finish of Art,
—mosques and kiosks, palaces and villas, gardens and
orchards — contrasting with the profuse lavishness
and magnificence of nature, and diversifying the unbroken *coup d'œil* of excessive vegetation, to rival, if not
to excel, the most admired scenery of the classic
regions. The riant shores of this vast crevasse ap-

peared doubly beautiful to me after the silent and spectral mangrove-creeks on the East-African sea-board, and the melancholy, monotonous experience of desert and jungle scenery, tawny rock and sun-parched plain or rank herbage and flats of black mire. Truly it was a revel for soul and sight! Forgetting toils, dangers, and the doubtfulness of return, I felt willing to endure double what I had endured; and all the party seemed to join with me in joy. My purblind companion found nothing to grumble at except the "mist and glare before his eyes." Said bin Salim looked exulting,—*he* had procured for me this pleasure, —the monoculous Jemadar grinned his congratulations, and even the surly Baloch made civil salams.

Arrived at Ukaranga I was disappointed to find there a few miserable grass-huts—used as a temporary shelter by caravans passing to and from the islets fringing the opposite coast—that clustered round a single Tembe, then occupied by its proprietor, Hamid bin Sulayyam, an Arab trader. Presently the motive of the rascally Fundi, in misleading the caravan, which, by the advice of Snay bin Amir, I had directed to march upon the Kawele district in Ujiji, leaked out. The roadstead of Ukaranga is separated from part of Kawele by the line of the Ruche River, which empties itself into a deep hollow bay, whose chord, extending from N.W. to S.E., is five or six miles in length. The strip of shelving plain between the trough-like hills and the lake is raised but a few feet above water-level. Converted by the passage of a hundred drains from the highlands, into a sheet of sloppy and slippery mire, breast deep in select places, it supports with difficulty a few hundred inhabitants: drenched with violent rain-storms and clammy dews, it is rife in fevers, and it is feared by travellers on ac-count of its hippopotami and crocodiles. In the driest season the land-road is barely practicable; during and after the wet monsoon the lake affords the only means of passage, and the port of Ukaranga contains not a single native canoe. The Fundi, therefore, wisely determined that I should spend beads for rations and lodgings amongst his companions, and be heavily mulcted for a boat by them. Moreover, he instantly sent word to Mnya Mtaza, the principal headman of Ukaranga, who, as usual with the Lakist chiefs, lives in the hills at some distance from the water, to come instanter for his Honga or blackmail, as, no fresh fish being procurable, the Wazungu were about to depart. The latter manœuvre, however, was frustrated by my securing a conveyance for the morrow. It was an open solid-built Arab craft, capable of containing thirty to thirty-five men; it belonged to an absent merchant, Said bin Usman; it was in point of size the second on the Tanganyika, and being too large for paddling, its crew rowed instead of scooping up the water like the natives. The slaves, who had named four khete of coral beads as the price of a bit of sun-dried "baccalà," and five as the hire of a foul hovel for one night, demanded four cloths—at least the price of the boat—for conveying the party to Kawele, a three hours' trip. I gave them ten cloths and two coil-bracelets, or somewhat more than the market value of the whole equipage, — a fact which I effectually used as an *argumentum ad verecundiam*.

At eight A.M., on the 14th February, we began coasting along the eastern shore of the lake in a north-westerly direction, towards the Kawele district, in the land of Ujiji. The view was exceedingly beautiful:

> " . . . the flat sea shone like yellow gold
> Fused in the sun,"

and the picturesque and varied forms of the mountains, rising above and dipping into the lake, were clad in purplish blue, set off by the rosy tints of morning. Yet, more and more, as we approached our destination, I wondered at the absence of all those features which prelude a popular settlement.   Passing the low, muddy, and grass-grown mouth of the Ruche River, I could descry on the banks nothing but a few scattered hovels of miserable construction, surrounded by fields of sorghum and sugar-cane, and shaded by dense groves of the dwarf, bright-green plantain, and the tall, sombre elæis or Guinea-palm.   By the Arabs I had been taught to expect a town, a ghaut, a port, and a bazar, excelling in size that of Zanzibar, and I had old, preconceived ideas concerning " die Stadt Ujiji," whose sire was the " Mombas Mission Map."   Presently Mammoth and Behemoth shrank timidly from exposure, and a few hollowed logs, the monoxyles of the fishermen, the wood-cutters, and the market-people, either cut the water singly, or stood in crowds drawn up on the patches of yellow sand.   About 11 A.M. the craft was poled through a hole in a thick welting of coarse reedy grass and flaggy aquatic plants to a level landing place of flat shingle, where the water shoaled off rapidly. Such was the ghaut or disembarkation quay of the great Ujiji.

Around the ghaut a few scattered huts, in the humblest bee-hive shape, represented the port-town. Advancing some hundred yards through a din of shouts and screams, tom-toms and trumpets, which defies description, and mobbed by a swarm of black beings, whose eyes seemed about to start from their heads with surprise, I passed a relic of Arab civilisation, the " Bazar." It is a plot of higher ground, cleared of grass, and

flanked by a crooked tree ; there, between 10 A.M.
and 3 P.M. — weather permitting — a mass of standing
and squatting negroes buy and sell, barter and exchange, offer and chaffer with a hubbub heard for miles,
and there a spear or dagger-thrust brings on, by no
means unfrequently, a skirmishing faction-fight. The
articles exposed for sale are sometimes goats, sheep, and
poultry, generally fish, vegetables, and a few fruits,
plantains, and melons ; palm-wine is a staple commodity,
and occasionally an ivory or a slave is hawked about :
those industriously disposed employ themselves during
the intervals of bargaining in spinning a coarse yarn
with the rudest spindle, or in picking the cotton, which
is placed in little baskets on the ground. I was led to a
ruinous Tembe, built by an Arab merchant, Hamid bin
Salim, who had allowed it to be tenanted by ticks and
slaves. Situated, however, half a mile from, and
backed by, the little village of Kawele, whose mushroom-
huts barely protruded their summits above the dense
vegetation, and placed at a similar distance from the
water in front, it had the double advantage of proxi-
mity to provisions, and of a view which at first was
highly enjoyable. The Tanganyika is ever seen to advantage from its shores: upon its surface the sight
wearies with the unvarying tintage — all shining greens
and hazy blues — whilst continuous parallels of lofty
hills, like the sides of a huge trough, close the prospect
and suggest the idea of confinement.

And now, lodged with comparative comfort, in the
cool Tembe, I will indulge in a few geographical and
ethnological reminiscences of the country lately traversed.

The fifth region includes the alluvial valley of the
Malagarazi River, which subtends the lowest spires of the

Highlands of Karagwah and Urundi, the western prolongation of the chain which has obtained, probably
from African tradition, the name of " Lunar Mountains."
In length, it extends from the Malagarazi Ferry in E.
Lat. 31° 10' to the Tanganyika Lake, in E. Long. 30° 1'.
Its breadth, from S. Lat. 3° 14', the supposed northern
limit of Urundi, to S. Lat. 5° 2'; the parallel of
Ukaranga is a distance of 108 rectilinear geographical
miles. Native caravans pass from the Malagarazi to
Ujiji in eight days, usually without halting till arrived
within a stone's throw of their destination. To a region
of such various elevations it would be difficult to assign
an average of altitude; the heights observed by thermometer never exceeded 1850 feet.

This country contains in due order, from east to west,
the lands of Uvinza, Ubuha, and Ujiji: on the northern
edge is Uhha, and on the south-western extremity
Ukaranga. The general features are those of the
alluvial valleys of the Kingani and the Mgeta Rivers.
The soil in the vicinity of the Malagarazi is a rich brown
or black loam, rank with vegetable decay. This strip
along the stream varies in breadth from one to five
miles; on the right bank it is mostly desert, but not
sterile, on the left it is an expanse of luxuriant cultivation. The northern boundary is a jagged line of hill-
spurs of primitive formation, rough with stones and
yawning with ravines: in many places the projections
assume the form of green "dogs' tails," or "neat's
tongues," projecting like lumpy ridges into the card-
table-like level of the river-land southwards. Each
mound or spur is crowned with a tufty clump, principally of bauhinias and mimosas, and often a lone,
spreading and towering tree, a Borassus or a Calabash,
ornamenting the extreme point, forms a landmark for

the caravan. The sides of these hills, composed of hornblende and gneissic rock, quartzite, quartz-grit, and ferruginous gritstone, are steep, rugged, and thickly wooded, and one slope generally reflects the other,—if muddy, muddy; and if stony, stony. Each "hanger," or wave of ground, is divided from its neighbour by a soft sedgy valley, bisected by a network of stagnant pools. Here and there are nullahs, with high stiff earthbanks for the passage of rain torrents. The grass stands in lofty screens, and the path leads over a matted mass of laid stalks which cover so closely the thick mud that loaded asses do not sink; this vegetation is burned down during the hot season, and a few showers bring up an emerald crop of young blades, sprouting phœnix-like from the ashes of the dead. The southern boundary of the valley is more regular; in the eastern parts is an almost tabular wall of rock, covered even to the crest with shrub and tree.

As is proved by the regular course of the Malagarazi River, the westward decline of the country is gentle: along the road, however, the two marches nearest to the Tanganyika Lake appear to sink more rapidly than those preceding them. The main drain receives from the northern hill-spurs a multitude of tributaries, which convey their surplus moisture into the great central reservoir.

Under the influence of the two great productive powers in nature — heat and moisture — the wondrous fertility of the soil, which puts forth where uncleared a rank jungle of nauseous odour, renders the climate dangerous. The rains divide the year into two unequal portions of eight and four months, namely, the wet monsoon, which commences with violence in September and ends in May, and the dry hot weather which rounds off the year. The showers fall, as in Zanzibar, uncontinuously, with breaks varying from a few hours to several days; unlike those of Zanzibar, they are generally accompanied by violent discharges of electricity. Lightning from the north, especially at night, is considered a sign of approaching foul weather.   It would be vain to seek in these regions of Central Africa the kaskazi and kosi, or regular north-east and south-west monsoons, those local modifications of the trade-winds which may be traced in regular progress from the centre of Equatorial Africa to the Himalayas.   The atmospheric currents deflected from the Atlantic Ocean by the coast-radiation and the arid and barren regions of Southern Africa are changed in hydrometric condition, and are compelled by the chilly and tree-clad heights of the Tanganyika Lake, and the low, cold, and river-bearing plains lying to the westward, to part with the moisture which they have collected in the broad belt of extreme humidity lying between the Ngami Lake and the equator.   When the land has become super-saturated, the cold, wet, wind, driving cold masses, surcharged with electricity, sets continually eastward, to restore the equilibrium in lands still reeking with the torrid blaze, and where the atmosphere has been rarified by from four to six months of burning suns.   At Msene, in Western Unyamwezi, the rains break about October; thence the wet monsoon, resuming its eastward course, crosses the Land of the Moon, and, travelling by slow stages, arrives at the coast in early April.   Following the northing sun, and deflected to the north-east by the rarified atmosphere from the hot, dry surface of the Eastern Horn of Africa, the rains reach Western India in June, and exhaust themselves in frequent and copious downfalls upon the southern versant of the Himalayas.   The gradual refrigeration of the ground, with the southing of the sun, produces in turn the inverse process, namely, the north-east monsoon.   About the Tanganyika, however, all is variable.   The large body of water in the central reservoir preserves its equability of temperature, while the alternations of chilly cold and potent heat, in the high and broken lands around it, cause extreme irregularity in the direction of the currents. During the rains of 1858 the prevalent winds were constantly changing: in the mornings there was almost regularly a cool north breeze drawn by the water from the heights of Urundi; in the course of the day it varied round towards the south.   The most violent storms came up from the south-east and the south-west, and as often against as with the gale.   The long and rigorous wet monsoon, broken only by a few scattered days of heat, renders the climate exceedingly damp, and it is succeeded by a burst of sunshine which dries the grass to stubble in a few days.   Despite these extremes, the climate of Ujiji has the reputation of being comparatively healthy; it owes this probably to the refreshing coolness of the nights and mornings.   The mukunguru, or seasoning-fever of this region, is not feared by strangers so much as that of Unyanyembe, yet no one expects to escape it.   It is a low bilious and aguish type, lasting from three to four days : during the attack perspiration is induced with difficulty, and it often recurs at regular times once a month.

From the Malagarazi Ferry many lines traverse the desert on the right or northern bank of the river, which is preferred to the southern, whence the Wavinza exclude travellers. Before entering this region caravans generally combine, so as to present a formidable front to possible foes.   The trunk road, called Jambeho, the most southerly of the northern routes, has been described in detail.

The district of Ukaranga extends from the Ruguvu or the Unguwwe River to the waters of the lake: on the south it is bounded by the region of Ut'hongwe, and on the north by the Ruche River. This small and sluggish stream, when near the mouth, is about forty yards in breadth, and, being unfordable at all seasons, two or three ferry-boats always ply upon its waters. The *rauque* bellow of the hippopotamus is heard on its banks, and the adjacent lowlands are infested by mosquitoes in clouds. The villages of Ukaranga are scattered in clumps over the plain—wretched hamlets, where a few households live surrounded by rare cultivation in the drier parts of the swamps. The "port of Ukaranga" is an open roadstead, which seldom shows even a single canoe. Merchants who possess boats and can send for provisions to the islands across the lake sometimes prefer, for economy, Ukaranga to Kawele; it is also made a halting-place by those *en route* to Uguhha, who would lose time by visiting Ujiji. The land, however, affords no supplies; a bazar is unknown; and the apathetic tribe, who cultivate scarcely sufficient grain for themselves, will not even take the trouble to cast a net. Ukaranga sends bamboos, rafters for building, and fire-wood, cut in the background of highlands, to Kawele and other parts of Ujiji, at which places, however, workmen must be hired.

Ukaranga signifies, etymologically, the "Land of Groundnuts." This little district may, in earlier ages, have given name to the Mocarangas, Mucarongas, or Mucarangas, a nation which, according to the Portuguese historians, from João dos Sanctos (1586-97) to Don Sebastian Xavier Botelho (1835), occupied the country within the Mozambique, from S. lat. 5° to S. lat. 25°, under subjection to the sovereign and the people of "Monomotapa." In the absence of history, analogy is the only guide. Either, then, the confusion of the Tanganyika and the Nyassa Lakes by the old geographers, caused them to extend the "Mocarangas" up to the northern water — and the grammatical error in the word "Mucaranga" justifies some suspicion as to their accuracy—or in the space of three centuries the tribe has declined from its former power and consequence, or the Wakaranga of the Tanganyika are a remnant of the mighty southern nation, which, like the Watuta tribe, has of late years been pressed by adverse circumstances to the north. Though Senhor Botelho, in his 'Memoria Estatisca,' denominates the "Monomoezi country" "Western Mucaranga," it is certain that no Mnyamwezi in the present day owns to connection with a race speaking a different dialect, and distant about 200 miles from his frontier.

The land of Ujiji is bounded on the north by the heights of Urundi, and on the south by the Ukaranga country: eastward it extends to Ubuha, and westward it is washed by the waves of the Tanganyika Lake. On its north-east lies the land of Uhha, now reduced by the predatory Watuta to a luxuriant desert.

The head-quarter village of Ujiji was in 1858 Kawele. To the westward of this settlement was the district of Gungu, facing the islet rock Bangwe. This place was deserted by travellers on account of the plundering propensities of its former chief. His son "Lurinda," however, labours to recover lost ground by courtesy and attention to strangers. South-eastwards of Kawele is the district of Ugoyye, frequented by the Arabs, who find the Sultans Habeyya and Marabu somewhat less extortionate than their neighbours. It is a sandy spot, clear of white ants, but shut out by villages and cultivation from the lovely view of the lake. To one standing at Kawele all these districts and villages are within two or three miles, and a distant glance discloses the possessions of half-a-dozen independent tribes.

Caravans entering Ujiji from the land side usually encamp in the outlying villages on the right or left bank of the Ruche, at considerable inconvenience, for some days. The origin of this custom appears to date from olden time. In East Africa, as a rule, every stranger is held to be hostile before he has proved friendly intentions, and many tribes do not admit him into their villages without a special invitation. Thus, even in the present day, the visitor in the countries of the Somal and Galla, the Wamasai and the Wakwafi, must sit under some tree outside the settlement till a deputation of elders, after formally ascertaining his purpose, escort him to their homes. The modern reason for the custom, which prevails upon the coast, as well as on the banks of the Tanganyika, is rather commercial than political. The caravan halts upon neutral ground, and the sultans or chiefs of the different villages send select messengers carrying various presents: in the interior ivory and slaves, and in the maritime regions cloth and provisions, technically called " Magubiko," and intended as an earnest of their desire to open trade. Sweet words and fair promises win the day ; the Mtongi, or head of the caravan, after a week of earnest deliberation with all his followers, chooses his host, temporary lodgings are provided for the guests, and the value of the retaining fees is afterwards recovered in Hongá and Kirembá—blackmail and customs. This custom was known in Southern Africa by the name of " marts ;"

that is, a "connection with a person belonging to another nation, so that they reside at each other's houses when visiting the place, and make mutual presents." The compulsory guest amongst the Arabs of Zanzibar and the Somal is called " Nezil."

At Ujiji terminates, after twelve stages, which native caravans generally finish in a fortnight, all halts included, the transit of the fifth region. The traveller has now accomplished a total number of 85 long, or 100 short stages, which, with necessary rests, but excluding detentions and long halts, occupy 150 days. The direct longitudinal distance from the coast is 540 geo. miles, which the sinuosities of the road prolong to 955, or in round numbers 950 statute miles. The number of days expended by the Expedition in actual marching was 100, of hours 420, which gives a rate of 2·27 miles per hour. The total time was seven and a-half months, from the 27th June, 1857, to the 18th February, 1858; thus the number of the halts exceeded by one-third the number of the marches. In practice Arab caravans seldom arrive at the Tanganyika, for reasons before alluded to, under a total period of six months. Those lightly laden may make Unyanyembe in between two and a-half and three months, and from Unyanyembe Ujiji in twenty-five stages, which would reduce their journey to four months.

Dapper ('Beschryving van Afrika,' Amst. 1671) asserts that the " blacks of Pombo, i. e. the Pombeiros, or native travellers of W. Africa, when asked respecting the distance of the lake, say that it is at least a sixty days' journey, going constantly eastwards." But the total breadth of the continent between Mbuamaji and Loanda being, in round numbers, 1560 geographical miles, this estimate would give

a marching rate of twenty-six geographical and rectilinear miles (or, allowing for deviation, thirty-six statute
miles) per diem.   When Da Couto (1565), quoting
the information procured by Francisco Barreto, during
his expedition in 1570, from some Moors (Arabs or
Wasawahili) at Patta and elsewhere, says that " from
Kilwa or Atondo (that is to say, the country of the
Watondwe) the other sea of Angola might be reached
with a journey of fifteen or twenty (150 or 200 ?)
leagues," he probably alludes to the Nyassa Lake, lying
south-westwards of Kilwa, not to the Tanganyika.   Mr.
Cooley gives one itinerary, by Mohammed bin Nasur, an
old Arab merchant, enumerating seventy-one marches
from Buromaji (Mbuamaji) to Oha (Uhha), and a total
of eighty-three from the coast to the lake ; and a second
by a native of Monomoezi, Lief bin Said (a misprint for
Khalaf bin Saíd ?) sixty-two to Ogara (Ugala), which
is placed four or five days from Oha.   In another page
he remarks that " from Buromaji, near Point Puna, to
Oha in Monomoezi is a journey of seventy-nine, or, in
round numbers, eighty days, the shores of the lake
being still six or eight days distant."   This is the
closest estimate yet made.   Mr. Macqueen, from the
itinerary of Lief bin Said, estimates the lake, from the
mouth of the river Pangani, at 604 miles, and seventy-
one days of total march.   It is evident, from the preceding pages, that African authorities have hitherto
confounded the Nyanza, the Tanganyika, and the Nyassa
Lakes.   Still, in the estimate of the distance between
the coast and Ujiji there is a remarkable and a most
deceptive coherence.

Ujiji—also called Manyofo, which appears, however,
peculiar to a certain sultanat or district—is the name
of a province, not, as has been represented, of a single

town. It was first visited by the Arabs about 1840; ten years after that they had penetrated to Unyamwezi; they found it conveniently situated as a mart upon the Tanganyika Lake, and a central point where their depôts might be established, and whence their factors and slaves could navigate the waters, and collect slaves and ivory from the tribes upon its banks. But the climate proved unhealthy, the people dangerous, and the coasting-voyages frequently ended in disaster; Ujiji, therefore, never rose to the rank of Unyanyembe or Msene. At present it is visited during the fair season, from May to September, by flying caravans, who return to Unyan-yembe as soon as they have loaded their porters.

Abundant humidity and a fertile soil, evidenced by the large forest trees and the abundance of ferns, render Ujiji the most productive province in this section of Africa: vegetables, which must elsewhere be cultivated, here seem to flourish almost spontaneously. Rice of excellent quality was formerly raised by the Arabs upon the shores of the Tanganyika; it grew luxuriantly, attaining, it is said, the height of eight or nine feet. The inhabitants, however, preferring sorghum, and wearied out by the depredations of the monkey, the elephant, and the hippopotamus, have allowed the more civilised cereal to degenerate. The principal grains are the holcus and the Indian nagli or nanchni (Eleusine coracano); there is no bajri (panicum or millet) in these regions; the pulses are phaseoli and the voandzeia, groundnuts, beans, and haricots of several different species. The manioc, egg-plant, and sweet-potato, the yam, the cucumber, an edible white fungus growing subterraneously, and the Indian variety of the Jeru-salem artichoke, represent the vegetables: the people, however, unlike the Hindus, despise, and consequently will not be at the pains to cultivate them. Sugar-cane, tobacco, and cotton are always purchasable in the bazar. The fruits are the plantain and the Guinea-palm. The mdizi or plantain-tree is apparently an aborigen of these latitudes : in certain parts, as in Usumbara, Karagwah, and Uganda, it is the staff of life : in the hilly countries there are, it is said, about a dozen varieties, and a single bunch forms a load for a man. It is found in the island and on the coast of Zanzibar, at K'hutu in the head of the alluvial valley, and, though rarely, in the mountains of Usagara. The best fruit is that grown by the Arabs at Unyanyembe : it is still a poor specimen, coarse and insipid, stringy and full of seeds, and strangers rarely indulge in it, fearing flatulence. Upon the Tanganyika Lake there is a variety called mikono t'hembu, or elephant's-hands, which is considerably larger than the Indian " horse-plantain." The skin is of a brickdust red, in places inclining to rusty-brown ; the pulp is a dull yellow, with black seeds, and the flavour is harsh, strong, and drug-like. The Elæis Guiniensis, locally called mchikichi, which is known by the Arabs to grow in the islands of Zanzibar and Pemba, and more rarely in the mountains of Usagara, springs apparently uncultivated in large dark groves on the shores of the Tanganyika, where it hugs the margin, rarely growing at any distance inland. The bright-yellow drupe, with shiny purple-black point, though nauseous to the taste, is eaten by the people. The mawezi or palm-oil, of the consistency of honey, rudely extracted, forms an article of considerable traffic in the regions about the Lake. This is the celebrated extract, whose various officinal uses in Europe have already begun to work a social reformation in W. Africa. The people of Ujiji separate, by pounding, the oily sarcocarpium from the one seed of the drupe, boil it for some hours, allow the floating substance to coagulate, and collect it in large earthen pots. The price is usually about one doti of white cotton for thirty-five pounds, and the people generally demand salt in exchange for it from caravans. This is the "oil of a red colour" which, according to Mr. Cooley, is bought by the Wanyamwezi "from the opposite or south-western side of the lake." Despite its sickly flavour, it is universally used in cooking, and it forms the only unguent and lamp-oil in the country. This fine Guinea-palm is also tapped, as the date in Western India, for toddy; and the cheapness of this tembo — the sura of West Africa — accounts for the prevalence of intoxication, and the consequent demoralisation of the Lakist tribes.

The bazar at Ujiji is well supplied. Fresh fish of various kinds is always procurable except during the violence of the rains: the people, however, invariably cut it up and clean it out before bringing it to market. Good honey abounds after the wet monsoon. By the favour of the chief, milk and butter may be purchased every day. Long-tailed sheep and well-bred goats, poultry and eggs—the two latter are never eaten by the people—are brought in from the adjoining countries: the Arabs breed a few Manilla ducks, and the people rear but will not sell pigeons. The few herds at Ujiji which have escaped the beef-eating propensities of the Watuta are a fine breed, originally, it is said, derived by the Wahha from the mountains of Karagwah. Their horns in these lands appear unusually large; their stature combines with the smallness of the hump to render them rather like English than Indian or African cattle. They are rarely sold of later days, except for enormous prices, an adult slave being the

lowest valuation of a cow.   The cattle is never stalled
or grain-fed, and the udder is little distended; the produce is about one quarter that of a civilised cow, and
the animals give milk only during the few first months
after calving.   The "tulchan" of Tibet is apparently
unknown in Central Africa; but the people are not
wanting in barbarous contrivances to persuade a stubborn animal to yield her produce.

The fauna appear rare upon the borders of the
Tanganyika: all men are hunters; every human being
loves animal food, from white ants to elephants; the
tzetze was found there, and probably the luxuriance of
the vegetation, in conjunction with the extreme humidity, tends to diminish species and individuals.   Herds
of elephants exist in the bamboo-jungles which surround
the sea, but the heaps of ivory sold in the markets of
Ujiji are collected from an area containing thousands of
square miles.   Hippopotami and crocodiles are common
in the waters, wild buffaloes in the plains.   The hyænas
are bold thieves, and the half-wild "Pariah-dogs" that
slink about the villages are little inferior as depredators.
The people sometimes make pets of them, leading them
about with cords; but they do not object to see them
shot after a raid upon the Arab's meat, butter, or milk.
These animals are rarely heard to bark; they leave
noise to the village cocks.   The huts are as usual haunted
by the grey and the musk-rat.   Of birds there is a fine
fish-eagle, about the size of a domestic cock, with snowy
head and shoulders relieving a sombre chocolate plume:
he sits majestically watching his prey upon the tall trees
overhanging the waves of the Tanganyika.   A larus, or
sea-gull, with reddish legs, lives in small colonies upon
this lake. At the end of the monsoon in 1858 these birds
were seen to collect in troops upon the sands, as they

are accustomed to do at Aden when preparing to migrate. The common kingfisher is a large bird with a white and grey plume, a large and strong black bill, and a crest which somewhat resembles that of the Indian bulbul: it perches upon the branches over the waters, and in flight and habits resembles other halcyons. A long and lank black plotus, or diver, is often seen skimming the waters, and sandpipers run along the yellow sands. The other birds are the white-breasted "parson-crow," partridges, and quails seen in Urundi; swallows in passage, curlews, motacillæ, muscicapæ, and various passerines. Ranæ, some of them noisy in the extreme, inhabit the sedges close to the lake. The termite does great damage in the sweet red soils about Kawele: it is less feared when the ground is dry and sandy. The huts are full of animal life—snakes, scorpions, ants of various kinds, whose armies sometimes turn the occupants out of doors; the rafters are hollowed out by xylophagous insects; the walls are riddled by mason-bees, hideous spiders veil the corners with thick webs, the chirp of the cricket is heard both within and out of doors, cockroaches destroy the provisions, and large brown mosquitoes and flies, ticks and bugs, assault the inhabitants.

The rise in the price of slaves and ivory has compelled Arab merchants, as will be seen in another chapter, to push their explorations beyond the Tanganyika Lake. Ujiji is, however, still the great slave-mart of these regions, the article being collected from all the adjoining tribes of Urundi, Uhha, Uvira, and Marungu. The native dealers, however, are so acute, that they are rapidly ruining this their most lucrative traffic. They sell cheaply, and think to remunerate themselves by aiding and abetting desertion. Merchants, therefore, who do not chain or cord together their gangs till they have reached the east bank of the Malagarazi River, often lose 20 per cent. The prevalence of the practice has already given Ujiji a bad name, and, if continued, will remove the market to another place, where the people are somewhat less clever and more sensible. It is impossible to give any idea of the average price of the human commodity, which varies, under the modifications of demand and supply, from two to ten doti or tobes of American domestics. Yet as these purchases sell in Zanzibar for fourteen or fifteen dollars per head, the trade realises nearly 500 per cent., and will, therefore, with difficulty be put down.

The principal tribes in this region are the Wajiji, the Wavinza, the Wakaranga, the Watuta, the Wabuha, and the Wahha.

The Wajiji are a burly race of barbarians, far stronger than the tribes hitherto traversed, with dark skins, plain features, and straight, sturdy limbs: they are larger and heavier men than the Wanyamwezi, and the type, as it approaches Central Africa, becomes rather negro than negroid.* Their feet and hands are large and flat, their voices are harsh and strident, and their looks as well as their manners are independent even to insolence. The women, who are held in high repute, resemble, and often excel, their masters in rudeness and

---

* My companion observes (in Blackwood, Nov. 1859), "It may be worthy of remark that I have always found the lighter coloured savages more boisterous and warlike than those of the dingier hue. The *ruddy black*, fleshy-looking Wazaramos and Wagogos are much *lighter* in colour (!) than any of the other tribes, and certainly have a far superior, more manly and warlike independent spirit and bearing than any of the others." The "dingiest" peoples are usually the most degraded, and therefore sometimes the least powerful; but the fiercest races in the land are the Wazaramo, the Wajiji and the Wataturu, who are at the same time the darkest.

violence; they think little in their cups of entering a
stranger's hut, and of snatching up and carrying away
an article which excites their admiration. Many of both
sexes, and all ages, are disfigured by the small-pox —
the Arabs have vainly taught them inoculation — and
there are few who are not afflicted by boils and various
eruptions; there is also an inveterate pandemic itch,
which, according to their Arab visitors, results from a
diet of putrid fish.

This tribe is extensively tattooed, probably as a protection against the humid atmosphere, and the chills of
the Lake Region. Some of the chiefs have ghastly scars
raised by fire, in addition to large patterns marked upon
their persons — lines, circles, and rays of little cupping-
cuts drawn down the back, the stomach, and the arms,
like the tattoo of the Wangindo tribe near Kilwa. Both
sexes love to appear dripping with oil; and they manifestly do not hold cleanliness to be a virtue. The head
is sometimes shaved; rarely the hair is allowed to grow;
the most fashionable coiffure is a mixture of the two;
patches and beauty-spots in the most eccentric shapes—
buttons, crescents, crests, and galeated lines — being
allowed to sprout either on the front, the sides, or the
back of the head, from a carefully-scraped scalp.
Women as well as men are fond of binding a wisp of
white tree-fibre round their heads, like the ribbon which
confines the European old person's wig. There is not
a trace of mustachio or whisker in the country; they
are removed by the tweezers, and the climate, according to the Arabs, is, like that of Unyamwezi, unfavourable
to beards. For cosmetics both sexes apply, when they
can procure such luxuries, red earth to the face, and over
the head a thick-coating of chalk or mountain-meal, which
makes their blackness stand out hideously grotesque.

The chiefs wear expensive stuffs, checks, and cottons, which they extract from passing caravans. Women of wealth affect the tobe or coast-dress, and some were seen wearing red and blue broadcloths. The male costume of the lower orders is confined to softened goat, sheep, deer, leopard, or monkey skins, tied at two corners over either shoulder, with the flaps open at one side, and with tail and legs dangling in the wind. Women who cannot afford cloth use as a succedaneum a narrow kilt of fibre or skin, and some content themselves with a tassel of fibre or a leafy twig depending from a string bound round the waist, and displaying the nearest approach to the original fig-leaf. At Ujiji, however, the people are observed, for the first time, to make extensive use of the macerated tree-bark, which supplies the place of cotton in Urundi, Karagwah, and the northern kingdoms. This article, technically termed "mbugu," is made from the inner bark of various trees, especially the mrimba and the mwale, or huge Raphia-palm. The trunk of the full-grown tree is stripped of its integument twice or thrice, and is bound with plantain-leaves till a finer growth is judged fit for manipulation. This bark is carefully removed, steeped in water, macerated, kneaded, and pounded with clubs and battens to the consistency of a coarse cotton. Palm-oil is then spirted upon it from the mouth, and it acquires the colour of chamois-leather. The Wajiji obtain the mbugu mostly from Urundi and Uvira. They are fond of striping it with a black vegetable mud, so as to resemble the spoils of leopards and wild cats, and they favour the delusion by cutting the edge into long strips, like the tails and other extremities of wild beasts. The price of the mbugu varies according to size, from six to twelve khete or strings of beads.

Though durable, it is never washed: after many months' wear the superabundance of dirt is removed by butter or ghee.

Besides the common brass-wire girdles and bracelets, armlets and anklets, masses of white-porcelain, blue-glass, and large pigeon-egg beads, and hundreds of the iron-wire circlets called sambo, which, worn with ponde-rous brass or copper rings round the lower leg, above the foot, suggest at a distance the idea of disease, the Wajiji are distinguished from tribes not on the lake by necklaces of shells — small pink bivalves strung upon a stout fibre. They have learned to make brass from the Arabs, by melting down one-third of zinc imported from the coast with two parts of the fine soft and red copper brought from the country of the Kazeembe. Like their Lakist neighbours, they ornament the throat with disks, crescents, and strings of six or seven cones, fastened by the apex, and depending to the breast. Made of the whitest ivory or of the teeth, not the tusks, of the hippopotamus, these dazzling ornaments effec-tively set off the dark and negro-like skin. Another peculiarity amongst these people is a pair of iron pincers or a piece of split wood ever hanging round the neck; nor is its use less remarkable than its presence. The Lakists rarely chew, smoke, or take snuff according to the fashion of the rest of mankind. Every man carries a little half-gourd or diminutive pot of black earthen-ware, nearly full of tobacco; when inclined to indulge, he fills it with water, expresses the juice, and from the palm of his hand sniffs it up into his nostrils. The pincers serve to close the exit, otherwise the nose must be temporarily corked by the application of finger and thumb. Without much practice it is difficult to arti-culate during the retention of the dose, which lasts a

few minutes, and when an attempt is made the words
are scarcely intelligible. The arms of the Wajiji are
small battle-axes and daggers, spears, and large bows,
which carry unusually heavy arrows. They fear the
gun and the sabre, yet they show no unwillingness to
fight. The Arabs avoid granting their demands for
muskets and gunpowder, consequently a great chief
never possesses more than two or three fire-locks.

The Lakists are an almost amphibious race, excellent
divers, strong swimmers and fishermen, and vigorous
ichthyophagists all. At times, when excited by the
morning coolness and by the prospect of a good haul,
they indulge in a manner of merriment which resembles the gambols of sportive water-fowls : standing
upright and balancing themselves in their hollow logs,
which appear but little larger than themselves, they
strike the water furiously with their paddles, skimming
over the surface, dashing to and fro, splashing one
another, urging forward, backing, and wheeling their
craft, now capsizing, then regaining their position with
wonderful dexterity. They make coarse hooks, and
have many varieties of nets and creels. Conspicuous
on the waters and in the villages is the Dewa, or "otter"
of Oman, a triangle of stout reeds, which shows the
position of the net. A stronger kind, and used for
the larger ground-fish, is a cage of open basket-work,
provided, like the former, with a bait and two entrances.
The fish once entangled cannot escape, and a log of
wood, used as a trimmer, attached to a float-rope of
rushy plants, directs the fisherman. The heaviest animals are caught by a rope-net — the likh of Oman —
weighted and thrown out between two boats. They
have circular lath frames, meshed in with a knot somewhat different from that generally used in Europe ; the

smaller variety is thrown from the boat by a single man,
who follows it into the water, — the larger, which
reaches six feet in diameter, is lowered from the bow by
cords, and collects the fish attracted by the glaring
torch-fire. The Wajiji also make large and small drag-
nets, some let down in a circle by one or more canoes,
the others managed by two fishermen, who, swimming
at each end, draw them in when ready. They have little
purse-nets to catch small fry, hoops thrust into a long
stick-handle through the reed walls that line the shore ;
and by this simple contrivance the fish are caught in
considerable quantities. The wigo or crates alluded to
as peculiar in the 'Periplus,' and still common upon
the Zanzibar coast, are found at the Tanganyika. The
common creel resembles the khún of Western India,
and is well-known even to the Bushmen of the South :
it is a cone of open bamboo-strips or supple twigs,
placed lengthways, and bound in and out by strings of
grass or tree-fibre. It is closed at the top, and at the
bottom there is a narrow aperture, with a diagonally-
disposed entrance like that of a wire rat-trap, which
prevents the fish escaping. It is placed upon its side
with a bait, embanked with mud, reeds, or sand, and
seems to answer the purpose for which it is intended.
In Uzaramo and near the coast the people narcotise fish
with the juice of certain plants, asclepias and euphorbias :
about the Tanganyika the art appears unknown.

There are many varieties of fish in the waters of this
Lake. The Mvoro is a long and bony variety, in shape
like a large mackerel ; the Sangále resembles it, but the
head and body are thicker. The Mgege, which suggests
the Pomfret of Western India, is well flavoured, but full
of bones. The Mguhe is said to attain the length of
five or six feet : it is not unlike the kheri of the Indian

rivers, and to a European palate it is the best fish that swims in these waters. The largest is the Singá, a scaleless variety, with black back, silvery belly, small fins, and long fleshy cirri : it crawls along the bottom, and is unfit for leaping or for rapid progress. This sluggish and misshapen ground-fish is much prized by the people on account of its rich and luscious fat. Like the Pallu of Sindh, it soon palls upon the European palate. Want of flavour is the general complaint made by the Arabs and coast people against the produce of the Tanganyika : they attempt to diminish the wateriness of the fish by exposing it spitted to a slow fire, and by subsequently stowing it for the night in well-closed earthen pots. Besides the five varieties above alluded to, there are dwarf eels of good flavour, resembling the Indian Bam ; Dagá'a, small fish called by the Arabs Kashu'a, minnows of many varieties, which, simply sundried, or muriated if salt can be afforded, find their way far east ; a dwarf shrimp, about one-quarter the size of the common English species ; and a large bivalve called Sinani, and identified as belonging to the genus Iridina. The meat is fat and yellow, like that of a well-fed oyster, but it is so insipid that none but a Mjiji can eat it. The shells collected upon the shores of the Tanganyika and on the land journey have been described by Mr. Samuel P. Woodward, who courteously named the species after the European members of the Expedition. To his memoir—quoted in pages 102, 103 of this volume—the reader is referred.

The Wajiji are considered by the Arabs to be the most troublesome race in these black regions. They are taught, by the example of their chiefs, to be rude, insolent, and extortionate ; they demand beads even for pointing out the road ; they will deride and imitate a

stranger's speech and manner before his face; they can
do nothing without a long preliminary of the fiercest
scolding; they are as ready with a blow as with a word;
and they may often be seen playing at "rough and
tumble," fighting, pushing, and tearing hair, in their
boats. A Mjiji uses his dagger or his spear upon a
guest with little hesitation; he thinks twice, however,
before drawing blood, if it will cause a feud. Their
roughness of manner is dashed with a curious ceremoniousness. When the sultan appears amongst his people,
he stands in a circle and claps his hands, to which all
respond in the same way. Women curtsy to one another, bending the right knee almost to the ground.
When two men meet they clasp each other's arms with
both hands, rubbing them up and down, and ejaculating
for some minutes, " Nama sanga? nama sanga?—art
thou well?" They then pass the hands down to the
forearm, exclaiming "Wákhe? wákhe?—how art thou?"
and finally they clap palms at each other, a token of
respect which appears common to these tribes of Central
Africa. The children have all the frowning and un-
prepossessing look of their parents; they reject little
civilities, and seem to spend life in disputes, biting and
clawing like wild cats. There appears to be little
family affection in this undemonstrative race. The
only endearment between father and son is a habit of
scratching and picking each other, caused probably by
the prevalence of a complaint before alluded to; as
amongst the Simiads, the intervals between pugnacity are
always spent in exercising the nails. Sometimes, also,
at sea, when danger is near, the Mjiji breaks the mourn-
ful silence of his fellows, who are all thinking of home,
with the exclamation, " Yá mgúri wánje!—O my wife!"
They are never sober when they can be drunk; perhaps

in no part of the world will the traveller more often see
men and women staggering about the village with thick
speech and violent gestures.   The favourite inebrient is
tembo or palm-toddy ; almost every one, however, even
when on board the canoe, smokes bhang, and the whoop-
ing and screaming which follow the indulgence resemble
the noise of wild beasts rather than the sounds of human
beings. Their food consists principally of holcus, manioc,
and fish, which is rarely eaten before it becomes offensive to European organs.

The great Mwami or Sultan of Ujiji in 1858-59 was
Rusimba.   Under him were several mutware (mutwale)
or minor chiefs, one to each settlement, as Kannena in
Kawele and Lurinda in Gungu.   On the arrival of a
caravan, Rusimba forwards, through his relations, a tusk
or two of ivory, thus mutely intimating that he requires
his blackmail, which he prefers to receive in beads and
kitindi or coil-bracelets, proportioning, however, his demand to the trader's means.   When this point has been
settled, the mutware sends his present, and expects a
proportionate return.   He is, moreover, entitled to a fee
for every canoe hired; on each slave the kiremba or
excise is about half the price; from one to two cloths
are demanded upon every tusk of ivory; and he will
snatch a few beads from a man purchasing provisions
for his master.   The minor headmen are fond of making
" sare " or brotherhood with strangers, in order to secure
them in case of return.   They depend for influence over
their unruly subjects wholly upon personal qualifications, bodily strength, and violence of temper.   A chief,
though originally a slave, may " win golden opinions "
by his conduct when in liquor: he assumes the most
ferocious aspect, draws his dagger, brandishes his spear,
and, with loud screams, rushes at his subjects as intent

upon annihilating them. The affairs of the nation are
settled by the mwami, the chief, in a general council of
the lieges, the wateko (in the singular mteko) or elders
presiding. Their intellects, never of the brightest, are
invariably fuddled with toddy, and, after bawling for
hours together and coming apparently to the most satisfactory conclusion, the word of a boy or of an old woman
will necessitate another lengthy palaver. The sultans,
like their subjects, brook no delay in their own affairs;
they impatiently dun a stranger half-a-dozen times a day
for a few beads, while they patiently keep him waiting
for weeks on occasions to him of the highest importance,
whilst they are drinking pombe or taking leave of their
wives. Besides the magubiko or preliminary presents,
the chiefs are bound, before the departure of a caravan
which has given them satisfaction, to supply it with
half-a-dozen masuta or matted packages of grain, and
to present the leader with a slave, who generally manages to abscond. The parting gifts are technically
called "urangozi," or guidance.

Under the influence of slavery the Wajiji have made
no progress in the art of commerce. They know nothing of bargaining or of credit: they will not barter
unless the particular medium upon which they have set
their hearts is forthcoming; and they fix a price
according to their wants, not to the value of the article.
The market varies with the number of caravans present
at the depôt, the season, the extent of supply, and a
variety of similar considerations. Besides the trade in
ivory, slaves, bark, cloth, and palm-oil, they manufacture and hawk about iron sickles shaped like the European, kengere, kiugi, or small bells, and sambo, locally
called tambi, or wire circlets, worn as ornaments round
the ankles; long double-edged knives in wooden sheaths,

neatly whipped with strips of rattan; and jembe or hoes. Of bells a dozen were purchased in March and April of 1858 for two fundo of white beads. Jembe and large sime averaged also two fundo. Of good sambo 100, and of the inferior quality 200, were procurable for a fundo. The iron is imported in a rough state from Uvira. The value of a goat was one shukkah, which here represents, as in Unyamwezi, twelve feet, or double the length of the shukkah in other regions, the single cloth being called lupande, or upande. Sheep, all of a very inferior quality, cost somewhat more than goats. A hen, or from five to six eggs, fetched one khete of samesame, or red-coral beads, which are here worth three times the quantity of white porcelain. Large fish, or those above two pounds in weight, were sold for three khete; the small fry—the white bait of this region—one khete per two pounds; and diminutive shrimps one khete per three pounds. Of plantains, a small bunch of fifteen, and of sweet potatoes and yams from ten to fifteen roots, were purchased for a khete; of artichokes, egg-plants, and cucumbers, from fifty to one hundred. The wild vegetables generically called mboga are the cheapest of these esculents. Beans, phaseoli, ground-nuts, and the voandzeia, were expensive, averaging about two pounds per khete. Rice is not generally grown in Ujiji; a few measures of fine white grain were purchased at a fancy price from one Sayfu bin Hasani, a pauper Msawahili, from the isle of Chole, settled in the country. The sugar-cane is poor and watery, it was sold in lengths of four or five feet for the khete: one cloth and two khete purchased three pounds of fine white honey. Tobacco was comparatively expensive. Of the former a shukkah procured a bag weighing perhaps ten pounds. Milk was sold at arbitrary prices, averaging about three teacups for the khete. A shukkah would procure three pounds of butter, and ghee was not made for the market. It was impossible to find sweet toddy, as the people never smoke nor clean the pots into which it is drawn; of the acid and highly intoxicating drink used by the Wajiji, from five to six teacups were to be bought with a khete. Firewood, being imported, was expensive, a khete being the price of a little faggot containing from fifty to one hundred sticks. About one pound of unclean cotton was to be purchased for three khete of samesame. It must be observed, that this list of prices, which represents the market at Kawele, gives a high average, many of the articles being brought in canoes from considerable distances, and even from the opposite coast.

The traveller in the Lake Regions loses by cloth; the people, contented with softened skins and tree-bark, prefer beads, ornaments, and more durable articles: on the other hand, he gains upon salt, which is purchased at half-price at the Parugerero Pan, and upon large wires brought from the coast. Beads are a necessary evil to those engaged in purchasing ivory and slaves. In 1858 the Wajiji rejected with contempt the black porcelains, called ububu. At first they would not receive the khanyera, or white-porcelains; and afterwards, when the Expedition had exchanged, at a considerable loss, their large stock for langiyo, or small blues, they demanded the former. The bead most in fashion was the mzizima, or large blue-glass, three khete of which were equivalent to a small cloth; the samesame, or red-corals, required to be exchanged for mzizima, of which one khete was an equivalent to three of samesame. The maguru nzige, or pink porcelains, were at par. The tobacco-stem bead, called sofi, and current at Msene, was in demand. The reader will excuse the prolixity of these wearisome details, they are necessary parts of a picture of manners and customs in Central Africa. Moreover, a foreknowledge of the requirements of the people is a vital condition of successful exploration. There is nothing to arrest the traveller's progress in this section of the African interior except the failure of his stores.

A serious inconvenience awaits the inexperienced, who find a long halt at, and a return from, Ujiji necessary. The Wanyamwezi pagazi, or porters, hired at Unyanyembe, bring with them the cloth and beads which they have received as hire for going to and coming from the lake, and lose no time in bartering the outfit for ivory or slaves. Those who prefer the former article will delay for some time with extreme impatience and daily complaints, fearing to cross Uvinza in small bodies when loaded with valuables. The purchasers of slaves, however, knowing that they will inevitably lose them after a few days at Ujiji, desert at once. In all cases, the report that a caravan is marching eastwards causes a general disappearance of the porters. As the Wajiji will not carry, the caravan is reduced to a halt, which may be protracted for months, in fact, till another body of men coming from the east will engage themselves as return porters. Moreover, the departure homewards almost always partakes of the nature of a flight, so fearful are the strangers lest their slaves should seize the opportunity to desert. The Omani Arabs obviate these inconveniences by always travelling with large bodies of domestics, whose interest it is not to abandon the master.

South of the Wajiji lie the Wakaranga, a people pre-

viously described as almost identical in development
and condition, but somewhat inferior in energy and
civilisation. Little need be said of the Wavinza, who
appear to unite the bad qualities of both the Wanyamwezi and the Ujiji. They are a dark, meagre, and ill-
looking tribe; poorly clad in skin aprons and kilts.
They keep off insects by inserting the chauri, or fly-flap,
into the waistband of their kilts: and at a distance they
present, like the Hottentots, the appearance of a race
with tails. Their arms are spears, bows, and arrows;
and they use, unlike their neighbours, wicker-work
shields six feet long by two in breadth. Their chiefs
are of the Watosi race, hence every stranger who meets
with their approbation is called, in compliment, Mtosi.
They will admit strangers into their villages, dirty
clumps of beehive huts; but they refuse to provide
them with lodging. Merchants with valuable outfits
prefer the jungle, and wait patiently for provisions
brought in baskets from the settlements. The Wavinza
seldom muster courage to attack a caravan, but stragglers are in imminent danger of being cut off by them.
Their country is rich in cattle and poultry, grain
and vegetables. Bhang grows everywhere near the
settlements, and they indulge themselves in it immoderately.

The Watuta—a word of fear in these regions—are a
tribe of robbers originally settled upon the southern
extremity of the Tanganyika Lake. After plundering
the lands of Marungu and Ufipa, where they almost
annihilated the cattle, the Watuta, rounding the eastern
side of the Lake, migrated northwards. Some years ago
they were called in by Ironga, the late Sultan of U'ungu,
to assist him against Mui' Gumbi, the powerful chief of
the Warori. The latter were defeated, after obstinate

fighting for many months. After conquering the Warori, the Watuta settled in Sultan Ironga's lands, rather by might than right, and they were expelled by his son with the greatest difficulty. From U'ungu their next step was to the southern bank of the Malagarazi River. About three years ago this restless tribe was summoned by Mzogera, the present Sultan of Uvinza, to assist him in seizing Uhha, which had just lost T'háre, its chief. The Watuta crossed the Malagarazi, laid waste the lands of Uhha and Ubuha, and desolated the northern region between the river and the lake. Shortly afterwards they attacked Msene, and were only repulsed by the matchlocks of the Arabs, after a week of hard skirmishing. In the early part of 1858 they slew Ruhembe, the Sultan of Usui, a district north of Unyanyembe, upon the road to Karagwah. In the latter half of the same year they marched upon Ujiji, plundered Gungu, and proceeded to attack Kawele. The Arab merchants, however, who were then absent on a commercial visit to Uviva, returned precipitately to defend their depôts, and with large bodies of slave musketeers beat off the invader. The lands of the Watuta are now bounded on the north by Utumbara, on the south by Msene; eastwards by the meridian of Wilyankuru, and westwards by the highlands of Urundi.

The Watuta, according to the Arabs, are a pastoral tribe, despising, like the Wamasai and the Somal, such luxuries as houses and fields; they wander from place to place, camping under trees, over which they throw their mats, and driving their herds and plundered cattle to the most fertile pasture-grounds. The dress is sometimes a mbugu or bark-cloth; more generally it is confined to the humblest tribute paid to decency by the

Kafirs of the Cape, and they have a similar objection to removing it. On their forays they move in large bodies, women as well as men, with the children and baggage placed upon bullocks, and their wealth in brass wire twisted round the horns. Their wives carry their weapons, and join, it is said, in the fight. The arms are two short spears, one in the right hand, the other in the left, concealed by a large shield, so that they can thrust upwards unawares: disdaining bows and arrows, they show their superior bravery by fighting at close quarters, and they never use the spear as an assegai. In describing their tactics, the Arabs call them "manœuvrers like the Franks." Their thousands march in four or five extended lines, and attack by attempting to envelop the enemy. There is no shouting nor war-cry to distract the attention of the combatants: iron whistles are used for the necessary signals. During the battle the sultan, or chief, whose ensign is a brass stool, sits attended by his forty or fifty elders in the rear; his authority is little more than nominal, the tribe priding itself upon autonomy. The Watuta rarely run away, and take no thought of their killed and wounded. They do not, like the ancient Jews, and the Gallas and Abyssinians of the present day, carry off a relic of the slain foe; in fact, the custom seems to be ignored south of the equator. The Watuta have still however a wholesome fear of fire-arms, and the red flag of a caravan causes them to decamp without delay. According to the Arabs they are not inhospitable, and though rough in manner they have always received guests with honour. A fanciful trait is related concerning them: their first question to a stranger will be, " Didst thou see me from afar ? " — which, being interpreted, means, Did you hear of my greatness before coming here ? — and they hold an answer in the negative to be a casus belli.

Remain for consideration the people of Ubuha and Uhha. The Wabuha is a small and insignificant tribe bounded on the north by Uhha, and on the south by the Malagarazi River: the total breadth is about three marches; the length, from the Rusugi stream of the Wavinza to the frontiers of Ujiji and Ukaranga, is in all a distance of four days. Their principal settlement is Uyonwa, the district of Sultan Mariki: it is a mere clearing in the jungle, with a few pauper huts dotting fields of sweet potatoes. This harmless and oppressed people will sell provisions, but though poor they are particular upon the subject of beads, preferring coral and blue to the exclusion of black and white. They are a dark, curly-headed, and hard-favoured race: they wear the shushah or top-knot on the poll, dress in skins and tree-barks, ornament themselves with brass and copper armlets, ivory disks, and beads, and are never without their weapons, spears and assegais, sime or daggers, and small battle-axes. Honourable women wear tobes of red broadcloth and fillets of grass or fibre confining the hair.

Uhha, written by Mr. Cooley Oha, was formerly a large tract of land bounded on the north by the mountains of Urundi, southwards and eastwards by the Malagarazi River, and on the west by the northern parts of Ujiji. As has been recounted, the Wahha dispersed by the Watuta have dispersed themselves over the broad lands between Unyanyembe and the Tanganyika, and their own fertile country, well stocked with the finest cattle, has become a waste of jungle. A remnant of the tribe, under Kanoni, their present Sultan, son of the late T'háre, took refuge in

the highlands of Urundi, not far from the principal
settlement of the mountain king Mwezí : here they find
water and pasture for their herds, and the strength of
the country enables them to beat off their enemies.
The Wahha are a comparatively fair and a not uncomely race; they are however universally held to be
a vile and servile people; according to the Arabs
they came originally from the southern regions, the
most ancient seat of slavery in E. Africa. Their
Sultans or chiefs are of Wahinda or princely origin,
probably descendants from the regal race of Unyamwezi. Wahha slaves sell dearly at Msene; an adult
male costs from five to six doti merkani, and a full-
grown girl one gorah merkani or kaniki.

Head Dresses of Wanyamwezı.

CHAP. XIV.

WE EXPLORE THE TANGANYIKA LAKE.

My first care after settling in Hamid's Tembe, was to purify the floor by pastiles of assafœtida, and fumigations of gunpowder; my second was to prepare the roof for the rainy season. Improvement, however, progressed slowly; the "children" of Said bin Salim were too lazy to work; and the Wanyamwezi porters, having expended their hire in slaves, and fearing loss by delay, took the earliest opportunity of deserting. By the aid of a Msawahili artisan, I provided a pair of cartels, with substitutes for chairs and tables. Benches of clay were built round the rooms, but they proved useless, being found regularly every morning occupied in force by a swarming, struggling colony, of the largest white ants. The roof, long overgrown with tall grass, was fortified with an extra coat of mud ; it never ceased, however, leaking like a colander ; presently the floor was covered with deep puddles, then masses of earth dropped from the sopped copings and sides of the solid walls, and, at last, during the violent showers, half the building fell in. The consequence of the extreme humidity was, that every book which had English paste in it was rendered useless by decay ; writing was rendered illegible by stains and black mildew ; moreover, during my absence, whilst exploring the Lake, Said bin Salim having neglected to keep a fire, as was ordered, constantly burning in the house, a large botanical collection was irretrievably lost. This was the more regretable as our return to the coast took place during the dry season, when the woods were bare of leaf, flower, and fruit.

On the second day after my arrival I was called upon by "Kannena," the headman of Kawele, under Rusimba, the Mwami, or principal chief of Ujiji. I had heard a bad account of the former. His predecessor, Kabeza, a great favourite with the Arabs, had died about two months before we entered Kawele, leaving a single son, hardly ten years old, and Kannena, a slave, having the art to please the widows of the deceased, and, through them, the tribe, caused himself to be elected temporary headman during the heir's minority. He was introduced habited in silk turban and broadcloth coat, which I afterwards heard he had borrowed from the Baloch, in order to put in a prepossessing first appearance. The effort, however, failed ; his aspect was truly ignoble ; a short, squat, and broad-backed figure, with natural "plumpers," a black skin cut and carved in various patterns, thick straight, stumpy, legs, and huge splay feet; his low narrow brow was ever knotted into a peevish frown, his apology for a nose much resembled the pug with which the ancients provided Silenus, and a villanous expression lurked about the depressed corners of his thick-lipped, sensual, liquorish mouth. On this occasion he behaved with remarkable civility, and he introduced, as the envoys commissioned by the great Rusimba to receive his blackmail, two gentlemen a quarter-clad in the greasiest and scantiest bark-aprons, and armed with dwarfish battle-axes. The present was finally settled at ten coil-bracelets and two fundi of coral-beads. I had no salt—the first article in demand—to spare, or much valuable merchandise might have been saved. The return was six small bundles of grain, worth, probably, one-tenth of what had been received. Then Kannena opened trade by sending us a nominal gift, a fine ivory, weighing at least seventy pounds, and worth, perhaps, one hundred pounds, or nearly two mens' loads of the white or blue-porcelain beads used in this traffic. After keeping it for a day or two, I returned it, excusing myself by saying that, having visited the Tanganyika as a "Sarkal," I could have no dealings in ivory and slaves.

This was right and proper in the character of a "Sarkal." But future adventurers are strongly advised always to assume the character of traders. In the first place, it explains the traveller's motives to the people, who otherwise lose themselves in a waste of wild conjecture. Secondly, under this plea, the explorer can push forward into unknown countries; he will be civilly received, and lightly fined, because the hosts expect to see him or his semblables again; whereas, appearing without ostensible motive amongst them, he

would be stripped of his last cloth by recurring con-
fiscations, fines, and every annoyance which greed of
gain can suggest.   Thus, as the sequel will prove, he
loses more by overcharges than by the trifling outlay
necessary to support the character of a trader.   He
travels respectably as a "Mundewa" or "Tajir" a merchant,
which is ever the highest title given by the people to
strangers; and he can avoid exciting the jealousy of
the Arabs by exchanging his tusks with them at a
trifling loss when comforts or provisions are required
for the road.

So strange an announcement on my part aroused, as
may be supposed, in the minds of the Wajiji marvel,
doubt, disbelief, ill-will.   "These are men who live
by doing nothing!" exclaimed the race commercial
as the sons of Hamburg; and they lost no time in
requesting me to quit their territory sooner than con-
venient.   To this I objected, offering, however, as compensation for the loss of their octrois and perquisites
to pay for not trading what others paid for trading.
Kannena roughly informed me that he had a claim for
Kiremba, or duties upon all purchases and sales; two
cloths, for instance, per head of slave, or per elephant's
tusk; and that, as he expected to gain nothing by
brokerage from me, he must receive as compensation, four coil-bracelets and six cotton cloths.   These
were at once forwarded to him.   He then evidenced his
ill-will in various ways, and his people were not slow
in showing the dark side of their character.   They
threatened to flog Sayfu, the old Msawahili of Chole,
for giving me hints concerning prices.   The two sur-
viving riding asses were repeatedly wounded with
spears.   Thieves broke into the outhouses by night,
and stole all the clothes belonging to the Jemadar and

to the bull-headed slave Mabruki. At first the widows of the late Kabeza, to whom the only cows in the district belonged, supplied us plentifully with milk; gradually the quantity shrank, whenever an opportunity offered it was "cut off;" and, at last, we could no longer afford the exorbitant price demanded. My companion having refused a cheese to Kannena, the dowager ladies, who owned the cows, when applied to for milk, threw away the vessel, and swore that by boiling what ought to be drunk unboiled, we were manifestly bewitching and killing their cattle. On one occasion, a young person related to Rusimba went to the huts of the Baloch, and, snatching up a fine cloth which she clasped to her bosom, defied them to recover it by force, and departed, declaring that it was a fine for bringing " whites" into the country. At first our heroes spoke of much slaughter likely to arise from such procedure, and with theatrical gesture, made " *rapière au vent;*" presently second-thoughts suggested how beautiful is peace, and thirdly, they begged so hard, that I was compelled to ransom for them the article purloined. I had unwittingly incurred the animosity of Kennena. On the day after his appearance in rich clothing he had entered unannounced with bare head, a spear or two in hand, and a bundle of wild-cats' skins by way of placket; not being recognised, he was turned out, and the ejectment mortally offended his dignity. Still other travellers fared even worse than we did. Said bin Majid, who afterwards arrived at Ujiji to trade for ivory and slaves, had two followers wounded by the Wajiji, one openly speared in the bazaar, and the other at night by a thief who was detected digging through the wall of the store-hut.

After trade was disposed of, ensued a general Bakhshish. Nothing of the kind had been contemplated or prepared for at Zanzibar, but before leaving Unyanyembe, I had found it necessary to offer an inducement, and now the promise was to be fulfilled. Moreover, most of the party had behaved badly, and in these exceptional lands, bad behaviour always expects a reward. In the first place, says the Oriental, no man misconducts himself unless he has power to offend you and you are powerless to punish him. Secondly, by "petting" the offender, he may be bribed to conduct himself decently. On the other hand, the Eastern declares, by rewarding, praising, or promoting a man who has already satisfied you, you do him no good, and you may do him great harm. The boy Faraj, who had shamelessly deserted his master, Said bin Salim, was afterwards found at Unyanyembe, in Snay bin Amir's house, handsomely dressed and treated like a guest; and his patron, forgetting all his stern resolves of condign punishment, met him with a peculiar kindness. I gave to the Baloch forty-five cloths, and to each slave, male and female, a pair. The gratification, however, proved somewhat like that man's liberality who, according to the old satirist, presented fine apparel to those whom he wished to ruin. Our people recklessly spent all their Bakhshish in buying slaves, who generally deserted after a week, leaving the unhappy ex-proprietor tantalised by all the torments of ungratified acquisitiveness.

At first the cold damp climate of the Lake Regions did not agree with us; perhaps, too, the fish diet was over-rich and fat, and the abundance of vegetables led to little excesses. All energy seemed to have abandoned us. I lay for a fortnight upon the earth, too blind to read or write, except with long intervals, too weak to

ride, and too ill to converse. My companion, who, when
arriving at the Tanganyika Lake was almost as "groggy"
upon his legs as I was, suffered from a painful ophthalmia, and from a curious distortion of face, which made
him chew sideways, like a ruminant. Valentine was
nearly blind ; and he also had a wry mouth, by no means
the properest for the process of mastication. Gaetano, who
arrived at Ujiji on the 17th February, was half-starved,
and his anxiety to make up for lost time brought on a
severe attack of fever. The Baloch complained of influenzas and catarrhs: too lazy to build huts after occu-
pying Kannena's " Traveller's Bungalow " for the usual
week, they had been turned out in favour of fresh visitors,
and their tempers were as sore as their lungs and throats.

But work remained undone ; it was necessary to awake
from this lethargy. Being determined to explore the
northern extremity of the Tanganyika Lake, whence,
according to several informants, issued a large river,
flowing northwards, and seeing scanty chance of success, and every prospect of an accident, if compelled
to voyage in the wretched canoes of the people, I at
first resolved to despatch Said bin Salim across the
water, and, by his intervention, to hire from an Arab
merchant, Hamid bin Sulayyam, the only dow, or sail-
ing-craft then in existence. But the little Arab
evidently shirked the mission, and he shirked so artistically, that, after a few days, I released him, and directed
my companion to do his best about hiring the dow,
and stocking it with provisions for a month's cruise.

Then arose the preliminary difficulties of the trip.
Kannena and all his people, suspecting that my
only object was economy in purchasing provisions,
opposed the project ; they demanded exorbitant sums,
and often when bargained down and apparently satis-

fied, they started up and rushed away, declaring that
they washed their hands of the business. At length,
Lurinda, the neighbouring headman, was persuaded to
supply a Nakhoda and a crew of twenty men. An
Arab pays on these occasions, besides rations, ten per
cent. upon merchandise; the white men were compelled
to give four coil-bracelets and eight cloths for the
canoe; besides which, the crew received, as hire, six
coil-bracelets, and to each individual provisions for
eight days, and twenty khete of large blue-glass beads,
and small blue-porcelains were issued. After many
delays, my companion set out on the 2nd of March, in
the vilest weather, and spent the first stormy day near the
embouchure of the Ruche River, within cannon shot of
Kawele. This halt gave our persecutors time to change
their minds once more, and again to forbid the journey.
I was compelled to purchase their permission by sending to Kannena an equivalent of what had been paid for
the canoe to Lurinda, viz. four coil-bracelets and eight
cloths. Two days afterwards my companion, supplied
with an ample outfit, and accompanied by two Baloch
and his men — Gaetano and Bombay — crossed the
bay of Ukaranga, and made his final departure for the
islands.

During my twenty-seven days of solitude the time
sped quickly; it was chiefly spent in eating and drinking, smoking and dozing. Awaking at 2 or 3 A.M., I
lay anxiously expecting the grey light creeping through
the door-chinks and making darkness visible; the glad
tidings of its approach were announced by the cawing
of the crows and the crowing of the village cocks.
When the golden rays began to stream over the red
earth, the torpid Valentine was called up; he brought
with him a mess of Suji, or rice-flour boiled in water,

with a little cold milk as a relish.   Then entered Muhabanya, the "slavey" of the establishment, armed with
a leafy branch to sweep the floor, and to slay the huge
wasps that riddled the walls of the tenement.   This
done he lit the fire—the excessive damp rendered this
precaution necessary—and sitting over it he bathed his
face and hands—luxurious dog !—in the pungent smoke.
Ensued visits of ceremony from Said bin Salim and the
Jemadar, who sat, stared, and, somewhat disappointed
at seeing no fresh symptoms of approaching dissolu-
tion, told me so with their faces, and went away.   From
7 A.M. till 9 A.M., the breakfast hour, Valentine was
applied to tailoring, gun-cleaning, and similar light
work, over which he groaned and grumbled, whilst I
settled down to diaries and vocabularies, a process interrupted by sundry pipes.   Breakfast was again a mess
of Suji and milk, — such civilised articles as tea, coffee,
and sugar, had been unknown to me for months.   Again
the servants resumed their labour, and they worked,
with the interval of two hours for sleep at noon, till 4
P.M.   During this time the owner lay like a log upon
his cot, smoking almost uninterruptedly, dreaming of
things past, and visioning things present, and sometimes
indulging himself in a few lines of reading and writing.

Dinner was an alternation of fish and fowl, game and
butchers' meat being rarely procurable at Ujiji.   The
fish were in two extremes, either insipid and soft, or so
fat and coarse that a few mouthfuls sufficed; most of them
resembled the species seen in the seas of Western India,
and the eels and small shrimps recalled memories of
Europe.   The poultry, though inferior to that of Unyanyembe, was incomparably better than the lean stringy
Indian chicken.   The vegetables were various and
plentiful, tomatoes, Jerusalem artichokes, sweet pota-

toes, yams, and several kinds of beans, especially a
white harricot, which afforded many a *purée*; the
only fruit procurable was the plantain, and the only
drink—the toddy being a bad imitation of vinegar—was
water.

As evening approached I made an attempt to sit under
the broad eaves of the Tembe, and to enjoy the de-
licious spectacle of this virgin Nature, and the reveries
to which it gave birth.

> " A pleasing land of drowsihed it was,
>   Of dreams that wave before the half-shut eye,
> And of gay castles in the clouds that pass,
>   For ever flushing round a summer sky."

It reminded me of the loveliest glimpses of the Mediterranean; there were the same "laughing tides," pel-
lucid sheets of dark blue water, borrowing their tints
from the vinous shores beyond; the same purple light
of youth upon the cheek of the earlier evening, the same
bright sunsets, with their radiant vistas of crimson and
gold opening like the portals of a world beyond the skies;
the same short-lived grace and loveliness of the twilight;
and, as night closed over the earth, the same cool flood
of transparent moonbeam, pouring on the tufty heights
and bathing their sides with the whiteness of virgin
snow.

At 7 P.M., as the last flush faded from the occident, the
lamp — a wick in a broken pot full of palm oil — was
brought in; Said bin Salim appeared to give the news
of the day, — how A. had abused B., and how C. had
nearly been beaten by D., and a brief conversation led to
the hour of sleep. A dreary, dismal day, you will exclaim, gentle reader; a day that

> "lasts out a night in Russia,
> When nights are longest there."

Yet it had its enjoyments. There were no post-offices, and this African Eden had other advantages, which, probably, I might vainly attempt to describe.

On the 29th of March the rattling of matchlocks announced my companion's return. The Masika had done its worst upon him. I never saw a man so thoroughly moist and mildewed ; he justified even the French phrase " wet to the bone." His paraphernalia were in a similar state; his guns were grained with rust, and his fire-proof powder-magazine had admitted the monsoon-rain. I was sorely disappointed : he had done literally nothing. About ten days before his return I had been visited by Khamis bin Jumah, an Arab merchant, who, on the part of the proprietor of the dow, gave the gratifying message that we could have it when we pleased. I cannot explain where the mismanagement lay ; it appears, however, that the wily " son of Sulayyam" detained the traveller simply for the purpose of obtaining from him gratis a little gunpowder. My companion had rested content with the promise that after three months the dow should be let to us for a sum of 500 dollars ! and he had returned without boat or provisions to report ill success. The faces of Said bin Salim and the Jemadar, when they heard the period mentioned, were indeed a study. I consoled him and myself as I best could, and applied myself to supplying certain deficiencies as regards orthography and syntax in a diary which appeared in Blackwood, of September 1859, under the title " Journal of a Cruise in the Tanganyika Lake, Central Africa." I must confess, however, my surprise at, amongst many other things, the vast horseshoe of lofty mountain placed by my companion in the map attached to that paper, near the very heart of Sir R.

Murchison's Depression. As this wholly hypothetical, or rather inventive feature,—I had seen the mountains growing upon paper under my companion's hand, from a thin ridge of hill fringing the Tanganyika to the portentous dimensions given in Blackwood (Sept. 1859), and Dr. Petermann's Mittheilungen, (No. 9, of 1859,)—wore a crescent form, my companion gravely published, with all the pomp of discovery, in the largest capitals, " This mountain range I consider to be THE TRUE MOUNTAINS OF THE MOON." * * * Thus men *do* geography! and thus discovery is stultified.

When my companion had somewhat recovered from his wetness, and from the effects of punching-in with a penknife a beetle which had visited his tympanum*, I began

---

* My companion gives in Blackwood, Sept. 1859, the following description of his untoward accident :—" This day (that of his arrival at the isle of Kivira) passed in rest and idleness, recruiting from our late exertions. At night a violent storm of rain and wind beat on my tent with such fury that its nether parts were torn away from the pegs, and the tent itself was only kept upright by sheer force. On the wind'ʀ abating, a candle was lighted to rearrange the kit, and in a moment, as though by magic, the whole interior became covered with a host of small black beetles, evidently attracted by the glimmer of the candle. They were so annoyingly determined in their choice of place for peregrinating, that it seemed hopeless my trying to brush them off the clothes or bedding, for as one was knocked aside another came on, and then another, till at last, worn out, I extinguished the candle, and with difficulty—trying to overcome the tickling annoyance occasioned by these intruders crawling up my sleeves and into my hair, or down my back and legs—fell off to sleep. Repose that night was not destined to be my lot. One of these horrid little insects awoke me in his struggles to penetrate my ear, but just too late : for in my endeavour to extract him, I aided his immersion. He went his course, struggling up the narrow channel, until he got arrested by want of passage-room. This impediment evidently enraged him, for he began with exceeding vigour, like a rabbit at a hole, to dig violently away at my tympanum. The queer sensation this amusing *measure* excited in me is past description. I felt inclined to act as our donkeys once did, when beset by a swarm of bees, who buzzed about their ears and stung their heads and eyes until they were so irritated and confused that they galloped about in the most distracted order, trying to knock them off by treading on

seriously to seek some means of exploring the northern head of the Tanganyika. Hamid bin Sulayyam had informed his late guest that he had visited the place, where, although attacked by an armada of thirty or forty hostile canoes, he had felt the influence of a large river, which drains the water northwards: in fact, he told the "lie with circumstance." By a curious coincidence, Sayfu, the Mswahili of Chole, declared that he also had sighted a stream issuing from the northern extremity of the lake—this was the " lie direct "—and he offered to accompany me as guide and interpreter. When we compared statements, we saw what was before us,—a prize for which wealth, health, and life, were to be risked.

It now became apparent that the Masika or rains, which the Arabs, whose barbarous lunar year renders untrustworthy in measurements of time, had erroneously represented as synchronous with the wet monsoon of Zanzibar, was drawing to a close, and that the season for navigation was beginning.*   After some preliminaries with Said bin

their heads, or by rushing under bushes, into houses, or through any jungle they could find. Indeed, I do not know which was worst off. The bees killed some of them and this beetle nearly did for me. What to do I knew not. Neither tobacco, oil, nor salt could be found: I therefore tried melted butter; that failing, I applied the point of a pen-knife to his back, which did more harm than good; for though a few thrusts kept him quiet, the point also wounded my ear so badly, that inflammation set in, severe suppuration took place, and all the facial glands extending from that point down to the point of the shoulder became contorted and drawn aside, and a string of bubos decorated the whole length of that region. It was the most painful thing I ever remember to have endured; but, more annoying still, I could not open my mouth for several days, and had to feed on broth alone. For many months the tumour made me almost deaf, and ate a hole between that orifice and the nose, so that when I blew it, my ear whistled so audibly that those who heard it laughed. Six or seven months after this accident happened, bits of the beetle, a leg, a wing, or parts of its body, came away in the wax."

* Not unmindful of the instructions of the Bombay Geographical Society, which called especial attention to the amount of rain-fall and evaporation in

Salim, Kannena, who had been preparing for a cruise north-wards, was summoned before me. He agreed to convey me ; but when I asked him the conditions on which he would show me the Mtoni, or river, he jumped up, dis-charged a volley of oaths, and sprang from the house like an enraged baboon. I was prepared for this difficulty, having had several warnings that the tribes on the northern shores of the Tanganyika allow no trade. But fears like Kannena's may generally be bought over. I trusted, therefore, to Fate, and resolved that at all costs, even if reduced to actual want, we should visit this mysterious stream. At length the headman yielded every point. He received, it is true, an exorbitant sum. Arabs visit-ing Uvira, the " ultima thule " of lake navigation, pay one cloth to each of the crew ; and the fare of a single passenger is a brace of coil-bracelets. For two canoes, the larger sixty feet by four, and the lesser about two-thirds that size, I paid thirty-three coil-bracelets, here equal to sixty dollars, twenty cloths, thirty-six khete of blue glass beads, and 770 ditto of white-porcelains and green-glass. I also promised to Kannena a rich reward if he acted up to his word ; and as an earnest I threw over his shoulders a six-foot length of scarlet broad-cloth, which caused his lips to tremble with joy, despite his struggles to conceal it. The Nakhoda (captain) and the crew in turn received, besides rations, eighty cloths,

a region, which abounding in lakes and rivers yet sends no supplies to the sea, I had prepared, at Zanzibar, a dish and a guage for the purpose of com-paring the hygrometry of the African with that of the Indian rainy monsoon. The instruments, however, were fated to do no work. The first portion of the Masika was spent in a journey ; ensued severe sickness, and the end of the rains happened during a voyage to the north of the Tanganyika. A few scattered observations might have been registered, but it was judged better to bring home no results, rather than imperfections which could only mislead the meteorologist.

170 khete of blue glass-beads, and forty of coral-porcelains, locally three times more valuable than whites or
greens.   Sayfu, the interpreter, was as extravagantly
paid in eight cloths and twenty-seven pounds of white
and blue-porcelains.   After abundance of dispute it was
settled that the crews should consist of fifty-five men,
thirty-three to the larger and twenty-two to the smaller
canoe.   It was an excess of at least one-half, who went
for their own profit, not for our pleasure.   When this
point was conceded, we were kindly permitted to take
with us the two Goanese, the two black gun-carriers, and
three Baloch as an escort.   The latter were the valiant
Khudabakhsh, whom I feared to leave behind; Jelai, the
mestiço-Mekrani; and, thirdly, Riza, the least mutinous
and uncivil of the party.

Before departure it will be necessary to lay before the
reader a sketch of our conveyance.   The first aspect
of these canoes made me lament the loss of Mr. Francis'
iron boat: regrets, however, were of no avail.   *Quo-
cumque modo—rem!* was the word.

The Baumrinden are unknown upon the Tanganyika
Lake, where the smaller craft are monoxyles, generally
damaged in the bow by the fishermen's fire.   The larger
are long, narrow "matumbi," or canoes, rudely hollowed
with the axe — the application of fire being still to be
invented, — in fact, a mere log of mvule, or some
other large tree which abound in the land of the Wagoma, opposite Ujiji.   The trunks are felled, scooped
out in loco, dragged and pushed by man-power down
the slopes, and finally launched and paddled over to
their destination.   The most considerable are composed
of three parts — clumsy, misshapen planks, forming,
when placed side by side, a keel and two gunwales,

the latter fastened to the centre-piece by cords of palm-fibre passing through lines of holes. The want of caulking causes excessive leakage : the crew take duty as balesmen in turns. The cry Senga! — bale out! — rarely ceases, and the irregular hollowing of the tree-trunks makes them lie lopsided in the water. These vessels have neither masts nor sails; artifices which now do not extend to this part of the African world. An iron ring, fixed in the stern, is intended for a rudder, which, however, seldom appears except in the canoes of the Arabs, steering is managed by the paddle, and a flag-staff or a fishing-rod projects jib-like from the bow. Layers of palm-ribs, which serve for fuel, are strewed over the interior to raise the damageable cargo — it is often of salt — above the bilge-water. The crew sit upon narrow benches, extending across the canoe and fastened with cords to holes in the two side-pieces; upon each bench, despite the narrowness of the craft, two men place themselves side by side. The "Karagwah," stout stiff mats used for hutting and bedding, are spread for comfort upon the seats; and for convenience of pad-dling, the sailors, when at work, incline their bodies over the sides. The space under the seats is used for stowage. In the centre there is a square place, about six feet long, left clear of benches; here also cargo is stored, passengers, cattle, and slaves litter down, the paddles, gourds, and other furniture of the crew are thrown, and the baling is carried on by means of an old gourd. The hold is often ankle-deep in water, and affords no convenience for leaning or lying down; the most comfortable place, therefore, is near the stern or the bow of the boat. The spears are planted upright amid-ships, at one or two corners of the central space so as to be ready at a moment's notice; each man usually has his dagger stuck in his belt, and on long trips all are provided with bows and arrows. These Africans cannot row; indeed they will not use oars. The paddle on the Tanganyika is a stout staff, about six feet long, and cut out at the top to admit a trefoil-shaped block the size of a man's hand:—it was described in South Africa by Captain Owen. The block, adorned with black paint in triangular patches, is lashed to the staff by a bit of whip-cord, and it seldom lasts through the day without breaking away from its frail tackling. The paddler, placing one hand on the top and the other about the middle of the staff, scoops up as it were, the water in front of him, steadying his paddle by drawing it along the side of the canoe. The eternal splashing keeps the boat wet. It is a laborious occupation, and an excessive waste of power.

The Lake People derive their modern practice of navigation, doubtless, from days of old; the earliest accounts of the Portuguese mention the traffic of this inland sea. They have three principal beats from Ujiji: the northern abuts at the ivory and slave marts of Uvira; the western conducts to the opposite shores of the Lake and the island depôts on the south-west; and the southern leads to the land of Marunga. Their canoes creep along the shores like the hollowed elders of thirty bygone centuries, and, waiting till the weather augurs fairly, they make a desperate push for the other side. Nothing but their extreme timidity, except when emboldened by the prospect of a speedy return home, preserves their cranky craft from constant accidents. The Arabs, warned by the past, rarely trust themselves to this Lake of Storms, preferring the certain peculation incurred by deputing for trading purposes agents and slaves to personal risk. Those who

must voyage on the lake build, by means of their menials
and artisans, dows, or sailing-vessels, and teach their
newly-bought gangs to use oars instead of paddles. This
is rather an economy of money than of time : they expend six months upon making the dow, whereas they can
buy the largest canoe for a few farasilah of ivory.

As my outfit was already running low, I persuaded,
before departure, two of the Baloch to return with a
down-caravan westwards, and arrived at Unyanyembe,
to communicate personally with my agent, Snay bin
Amir. They agreed so to do, but the Mtongi, or
head of the African kafilah, with true African futility, promised to take them on the next day, and set
out that night on his journey. As Said bin Majid
was about despatching a large armed party to the north
of the Lake, I then hurried on my preparations for the
voyage. Provisions and tobacco were laid in, the tent
was repaired, and our outfit, four half loads of salt—of
these two were melted in the canoe, six Gorah,—or one
load of domestics, nine coil-bracelets, the remainder of
our store, one load of blue porcelain beads, and a small
bag of the valuable red coral intended for private expenses, and " El Akibah " (the reserve), was properly
packed for concealment. Meanwhile some trifling disputes occurred with Kannena, who was in the habit of
coming to our Tembe, drunk and surly, with eyes like
two gouts of blood, knitted front, and lips viciously shot
out : when contradicted or opposed, he screamed and
gesticulated as if haunted by his P'hepo,—his fiend;—and
when very evilly disposed, he would proceed to the extreme measure of cutting down a tent. This slave-sultan
was a " son of noise :" he affected *brusquerie* of manner
and violence of demeanour the better to impressionise
his unruly subjects ; and he frightened the timid souls

around us, till at last the Jemadar's phrase was, "strength is useless here." Had I led, however, three hundred instead of thirty matchlocks, he would have crouched and cowered like a whipped cur.

At 4 P.M., on the 9th April, appeared before the Kannena in a tattered red turban donned for the occasion. He was accompanied by his ward, who was to perform the voyage as a training to act sultan, and he was followed by his sailors bearing salt, in company with their loud-voiced wives and daughters performing upon the wildest musical instruments. Of these the most noisy was a kind of shaum, a straight, long and narrow tube of wood, bound with palm-fibre and provided with an opening mouth like a clarionet; a distressing bray is kept up by blowing through a hole pierced in the side. The most monotonous was a pair of foolscap-shaped plates of thin iron, joined at the apices and connected at the bases by a solid cross-bar of the same metal; this rude tomtom is performed upon by a muffled stick with painful perseverance; the sound—how harshly it intruded upon the stilly beauty of the scenes around! —still lingers and long shall linger in my tympanum. The canoe had been moved from its usual position opposite our Tembe, to a place of known departure — otherwise not a soul could have been persuaded to embark — and ignoring the distance, I condemned myself to a hobble of three miles over rough and wet ground. The night was comfortless; the crew, who were all "half-seas over," made the noise of bedlamites; and two heavy falls of rain drenching the flimsy tent, at once spoiled the tobacco and flour, the grain and the vegetables prepared for the voyage.

Early on the next morning we embarked on board the canoes: the crews had been collected, paid, and rationed, but as long as they were near home it was impossible to keep them together. Each man thinking solely of his own affairs, and disdaining the slightest regard for the wishes, the comfort, or the advantage of his employers, they objected systematically to every article which I had embarked. Kannena had filled the canoes with his and his people's salt, consequently he would not carry even a cartel. Various points settled we hove anchor or rather hauled up the block of granite doing anchoral duty, and with the usual hubbub and strife, the orders which every man gives and the advice which no man takes, we paddled in half an hour to a shingly and grassy creek, defended by a sandpit and backed by a few tall massive trees. Opposite and but a few yards distant, rose the desert islet of Bangwe, a quoin-shaped mass of sandstone and red earth, bluff to the north and gradually shelving towards the water at the other extremity : the prolific moisture above and around had covered its upper ledge with a coat of rich thick vegetation. Landward the country rises above the creek, and upon its earth-waves, which cultivation shares with wild growth, appear a few scattered hamlets.

Boats generally waste some days at Bangwe Bay, the stage being short enough for the usual scene being encored. They load and reload, trim cargo, complete rations, collect crews, and take leave of friends and relatives, women, and palm-wine. We pitched a tent and halted in a tornado of wind and rain. Kannena would not move without the present of one of our three goats. At 4 P.M., on the 11th April, the canoes were laden and paddled out to and back from Bangwe islet, when those knowing in such matters pronounced them so heavily weighted as to be unsafe : whereupon, the youth Riza, sorely against my will, was sent back to the Kawele. On that night a furious gale carried away my tent, whilst the Goanese were, or pretended to be, out of hearing. I slept, however, comfortably enough upon the crest of a sand-wave higher than the puddles around it, and — blessings on the name of Mackintosh! — escaped the pitiless pelting of the rain.

The next morning showed a calm sea, levelled by the showers, and no pretext or desire for longer detention lingered in the hearts of the crew. At 7·20 A.M., on the 12th April, 1858, my canoe—bearing for the first time on those dark waters—

> " The flag that braved a thousand years
> The battle and the breeze,"

stood out of Bangwe Bay, and followed by my companion's turned the landspit separating the bight from the main, and made directly for the cloudy and storm-vexed north. The eastern shore of the lake, along which we coasted, was a bluff of red earth pudding'd with separate blocks of sandstone. Beyond this headland the coast dips, showing lines of shingle or golden-coloured quartzose sand, and on the shelving plain appear the little fishing-villages. They are usually built at the mouths of the gaps, combes, and gullies, whose deep gorges winding through the background of hill-curtain, become, after rains, the beds of mountain-torrents. The wretched settlements are placed between the tree clad declivities and the shore on which the waves break. The sites are far from comfortable : the ground is here veiled with thick and fetid grass ; there it is a puddle of black mud, and there a rivulet trickles through the villages. The hamlet consists of half a dozen beehive-huts, foul, flimsy, and leaky ; their only furniture is a hearth of three clods or stones, with a few mats and fishing implements. The settlements are distinguished from a

distance by their plantations of palm and plantain, and
by large spreading trees, from whose branches are suspended the hoops and the drag-nets not in actual use,
and under whose shade the people sit propped against
their monoxyles, which are drawn high up out of danger
of the surf. There was no trade, and few provisions were
procurable at Kigari. We halted there to rest, and pitching a tent in the thick grass we spent a night loud with
wind and rain.

Rising at black dawn on the 13th April, the crews
rowed hard for six hours between Kigari and another
dirty little fishing-village called Nyasanga. The settlement supplied fish-fry, but neither grain nor vegetables were offered for sale. At this place, the frontier
district between Ujiji and Urundi, our Wajiji took leave
of their fellow-clansmen and prepared with serious
countenances for all the perils of expatriation.

This is the place for a few words concerning boating
and voyaging upon the Tanganyika Lakes. The Wajiji,
and indeed all these races, never work silently or regularly. The paddling is accompanied by a long monotonous melancholy howl, answered by the yells and
shouts of the chorus, and broken occasionally by a shrill
scream of delight from the boys which seems violently to
excite the adults. The bray and clang of the horns,
shaums, and tomtoms, blown and banged incessantly
by one or more men in the bow of each canoe, made
worse by brazen-lunged imitations of these intruments
in the squeaking trebles of the younger paddlers,
lasts throughout the livelong day, exeept when terror
induces a general silence. These "Wáná Máji" —
sons of water — work in " spirts," applying lustily to
the task till the perspiration pours down their sooty
persons. Despite my remonstrances, they insisted upon

splashing the water in shovelsful over the canoe.
They make terribly long faces, however, they tremble
like dogs in a storm of sleet, and they are ready to
whimper when compelled by sickness or accident to sit
with me under the endless cold wave-bath in the hold.
After a few minutes of exertion, fatigued and worn,
they stop to quarrel, or they progress languidly till
recruited for another effort.   When two boats are
together they race continually till a bump — the signal for
a general grin — and the difficulty of using the entangled
paddles afford an excuse for a little loitering, and for the
loud chatter, and violent abuse, without which apparently this people cannot hold converse.   At times
they halt to eat, drink, and smoke : the bhang-pipe is
produced after every hour, and the paddles are taken
in whilst they indulge in the usual screaming convul-
sive whooping-cough.   They halt for their own purposes
but not for ours ; all powers of persuasion fail when
they are requested to put into a likely place for collecting shells or stones.*   For some superstitious reason

---

* THE FOLLOWING PAPER BY S. P. WOODWARD, F.G.S., COMMUNICATED BY
    PROF. OWEN, APPEARED IN THE PROCEEDINGS OF THE ZOOLOGICAL SO-
    CIETY OF LONDON, JUNE 28, 1859.

The four shells which form the subject of the present note were collected
by Captain Speke in the great freshwater lake Tanganyika in Central
Africa.

The large bivalve belongs to the genus *Iridina*, Lamarck, — a group of
river mussels, of which there are nine reputed species, all belonging to the
African continent. This little group has been divided into several sub-genera.
That to which the new shell belongs is distinguished by its broad and deeply-
wrinkled hinge-line, and is called *Pleiodon* by Conrad. The posterior slope
of this shell is encrusted with tufa, as if there were limestone rocks in the
vicinity of its habitat.

The small bivalve is a normal *Unio*, with finely sculptured valves.

The smaller univalve is concave beneath, and so much resembles a *Nerita*
or *Calyptræa* that it would be taken for a sea-shell if its history were not well
authenticated.   It agrees essentially with *Lithoglyphus*, — a genus peculiar

they allow no questions to be asked, they will not dip
a pot for water into the lake, fearing to be followed

to the Danube ; for the American shells referred to it are probably, or, I may
say, certainly distinct.   It agrees with the Danubian shells in the extreme
obliquity of the aperture, and differs in the width of the umbilicus, which in
the European species is nearly concealed by the callous columellar lip.

In the Upper Eocene Tertiaries of the Isle of Wight there are several
estuary shells, forming the genus *Globulus*, Sow., whose affinities are uncertain, but which resemble *Lithoglyphus*.

The lake Tanganyika (situated in lat. 3° to 8° S. and long. 30° E.), which
is several hundred miles in length and 30 to 40 in breadth, seems entirely
disconnected with the region of the Danube : but the separation may not always have been so complete, for there is another great lake, Nyanza, to the
northward of Tanganyika, which is believed by Speke to be the principal
source of the Nile.

The other univalve is a *Melania*, of the sub-genus *Melanella* (Swainson),
similar in shape to *M. hollandi* of S. Europe, and similar to several Eocene
species of the Isle of Wight.   Its colour, solidity, and tuberculated ribs give
it much the appearance of a small marine whelk (*Nassa*) ; and it is found in
more boisterous waters, on the shores of this great inland sea, than most of
its congeners inhabit.

1. IRIDINA (PLEIODON) SPEKII, n. sp.   (Pl. XLVII. fig. 2.)
Shell oblong, ventricose, somewhat attenuated at each end : base slightly
concave ; epidermis chestnut brown, deepening to black at the margin ; anterior slope obscurely radiated ; hinge-line compressed in front and tuberculated, wider behind and deeply wrinkled.

Length 4¾, breadth 2, thickness 1¾ inches.

Testa oblonga, tumida, extremitatibus fere attenuata, basi subarcuata ; epi-
dermide castaneo-fusca, marginem versus nigricante ; linea cardinali antice
compressa tuberculata, postice latiore, paucis rugis arata.

2. UNIO BURTONI, n. sp.   (Pl. XLVII. fig. 1.)
Shell small, oval, rather thin, somewhat pointed behind ; umbones small,
not eroded ; pale olive, concentrically furrowed, and sculptured more or less
with fine divaricating lines ; anterior teeth narrow, not prominent ; posterior
teeth laminar ; pedal scar confluent with anterior adductor.

Length 12, breadth 8⅓, thickness 5½ lines.

Testa parva, ovalis, tenuiuscula, postice subattenuata ; umbonibus parvis,
acuminatis ; epidermide pallide olivacea ; valvis lineolis divaricatis, decuss-
atum exaratis ; dentibus cardinalibus angustis, haud prominentibus.

3. LITHOGLYPHUS ZONATUS, n. sp.   (Pl. XLVII. fig. 3.)
Shell orbicular, hemispherical ; spire very small ; aperture large, very oblique ; umbilicus wide and shallow, with an open fissure in the young shell ;
lip continuous in front with the umbilical ridge ; columella callous, ultimately

and perhaps boarded by crocodiles, which are hated and dreaded by these black navigators, much as is the

covering the fissure; body-whirl flattened, pale olivaceous, with two brown bands, darker at the apex; lines of growth crossed by numerous oblique, interrupted striæ.

Diameter 5–6, height 3 lines.

Testa orbicularis, hemisphærica, late umbilicata (apud juniores rimata), spira minuta; apertura magna, valde obliqua; labio calloso (in testa adulta rimam tegente); pallide olivacea, fasciis duabus fuscis zonata; lineis incrementi striolis interruptis oblique decussatis.

4. MELANIA (MELANELLA) NASSA, n. sp.   (Pl. XLVII. fig. 4.)

Shell ovate, strong, pale brown, with (sometimes) two dark bands; spire shorter than the aperture; whirls flattened, ornamented with six brown spiral ridges crossed with a variable number of white, tuberculated, transverse ribs; base of body-whirl eight with tuberculated spiral ridges variegated with white and brown; aperture sinuated in front; outer lip simple; inner lip callous.

Length $8\frac{1}{2}$, breadth $5\frac{1}{2}$ lines.

Testa ovata, solida, pallide fusca, zonis 2 nigricantibus aliquando notata; spira apertura breviore; anfractibus planulatis, lineis 6 fuscis spiralibus et costis tuberculatis ornatis; apertura antice sinuata; labro simplici; labio calloso.

P.S. July 27th.—In addition to the foregoing shells, several others were collected by Capt. Speke, when employed, under the command of Capt. Burton, in exploring Central Africa in the years 1856-9; these were deposited in the first instance with the Geographical Society, and are now transferred to the British Museum.

A specimen of *Ampullaria (Lanistes) sinistrorsa*, Lea, and odd valves of two species of *Unio*, both smooth and olive-coloured, were picked up in the Ugogo district, an elevated plateau in lat. 6° to 7° S., long. 34° to 35° E.

A large *Achatina*, most nearly related to *A. glutinosa*, Pfr., is the "common snail" of the region between lake Tanganyika and the east coast. Fossil specimens were obtained in the Usagara district, at a place called Marora, 3000 feet above the sea, overlooking the Lufiji River, where it intersects the coast range (lat. 7° to 8° S., long. 36° to 36° E.).

Another common land snail of the same district is the well known "*Bulimus caillaudi*, Pfr.," a shell more nearly related to *Achatina* than *Bulimus*.

Captain Speke also found a solitary example of *Bulimus ovoideus*, Brug., in a musjid on the island of Kiloa (lat. 9° S., long. 39° to 40° E.). This species is identical with *B. grandis*, Desh., from the island of Nosse Bé, Madagascar, and very closely allied to *B. liberianus*, Lea, from Guinea.

shark by our seamen, and for the same cause not a
scrap of food must be thrown overboard—even the offal
must be cast into the hold. "Whittling" is here a
mortal sin: to chip or break off the smallest bit of
even a condemned old tub drawn up on the beach causes
a serious disturbance. By the advice of a kind and
amiable friend *, I had supplied myself with the desiderata for sounding and ascertaining the bottom of the
Lake: the crew would have seen me under water rather
than halt for a moment when it did not suit their purpose.
The wild men lose half an hour, when time is most
precious, to secure a dead fish as it floats past the canoe
entangled in its net. They never pass a village without
a dispute; some wishing to land, others objecting because some wish it. The captain, who occupies some
comfortable place in the bow, stern, or waist, has little
authority; and if the canoe be allowed to touch the

* Captain Balfour, H.M.I.N., who kindly supplied me with a list of necessaries for sail-making and other such operations on the Lake. I had indented upon the Engineers' Stores, Bombay, for a Massey's patent or self-
registering log, which would have been most useful had the people allowed it
to be used. Prevented by stress of business from testing it in India, I found
it at sea so thoroughly defective, that it was returned from whence it came by
the good aid of Captain Frushard, then commanding the H.E.I.C.'s sloop of
war *Elphinstone*. I then prepared at Zanzibar, a line and a lead, properly
hollowed to admit of its being armed, and this safely reached the Tanganyika Lake. It was not useless but unused: the crew objected to its being
hove, and moreover—lead and metal are never safe in Central Africa—the line,
which was originally short, was curtailed of one half during the first night
after our departure from Kawele. It is by no means easy to estimate the
rate of progress in these barbarous canoes barbarously worked. During the
"spirts" when the paddler bends his back manfully to his task, a fully-
manned craft may attain a maximum of 7 to 8 miles per hour: this exertion,
however, rarely exceeds a quarter of an hour, and is always followed by delay.
The usual pace, when all are fresh and cool, is about 4 to 5 miles, which declines through 4 and 3 to 2½, when the men are fatigued, or when the sun is
high. The medium, therefore, may be assumed at 4 miles for short, and a
little more than 2 miles an hour for long trips, halts deducted.

shore, its men will spring out without an idea of consulting aught beyond their own inclinations. Arrived at the halting-place they pour on shore; some proceed to gather firewood, others go in search of rations, and others raise the boothies. A dozen barked sticks of various lengths are planted firmly in the ground; the ends are bent and lashed together in the shape of half an orange, by strips of tree-fibre; they are then covered with the karagwah—the stiff-reed mats used as cushions when paddling—these are tightly bound on, and thus a hut is made capable of defending from rain the bodies of four or five men whose legs which project beyond the shelter are apparently not supposed to require covering. Obeying only impulse, and wholly deficient in order and purpose, they make the voyage as uncomfortable as possible; they have no regular stages and no fixed halting-places; they waste a fine cool morning, and pull through the heat of the day, or after dozing throughout the evening, at the loud cry of " Pakírá Bábá! " — pack up, hearties! —they scramble into their canoes about midnight. Outward-bound they seek opportunities for delay; when it is once " up anchor for home," they hurry with dangerous haste.

On the 14th April, a cruise of four hours conducted us to Wafanya, a settlement of Wajiji mixed with Warundi. Leaving this wretched mass of hovels on the next day, which began with a solemn warning from Sayfu — a man of melancholic temperament — we made in four hours Wafanya, the southern limit of Urundi, and the only port in that inhospitable land still open to travellers. Drawing up our canoes upon a clear narrow sandstrip beyond the reach of the surf, we ascended a dwarf earth-cliff, and pitching our tents under a spreading tree upon the summit, we made ourselves as comfortable as the noisy, intrusive, and insolent crowd, assembled to stare and to laugh at the strangers, would permit. The crew raised their boothies within a stone-throw of the water, flight being here the thought ever uppermost in their minds.

The people of this country are a noisy insolent race, addicted, like all their Lakist brethren, to drunkenness, and, when drunk, quarrelsome and violent. At Wafanya, however, they are kept in order by Kanoni, their mutware or minor chief, subject to " Mwezi," the mwami or sultan of Urundi. The old man appeared, when we reached his settlement, in some state, preceded by an ancient carrying his standard, a long wisp of white fibre attached to a spear, like the Turkish " horse-tail," and followed by a guard of forty or fifty stalwart young warriors armed with stout lance-like spears for stabbing and throwing, straight double-edged daggers, stiff bows, and heavy, grinded arrows. Kanoni began by receiving his black-mail—four cloths, two coil-bracelets, and three fundo of coral beads: the return was the inevitable goat. The climate of Wafanya is alternately a damp-cold and a "muggy" heat; the crews, however, if numerous and well armed, will delay here to feed when northward bound, and to lay in provisions when returning to their homes. Sheep and fine fat goats vary in value from one to two cloths; a fowl, or five to six eggs, costs a khete of beads; sweet potatoes are somewhat dearer than at Ujiji; there is no rice, but holcus and manioc are cheap and abundant, about 5 lbs. of the latter being sold for a single khete. Even milk is at times procurable. A sharp business is carried on in chikichi or palm-oil, of which a large earthen pot is bought for a cloth; the best paddles used by the crews are made at Wafanya; and the mbugu, or bark-cloth, is bought for four to ten khete, about one third of the market-price at Ujiji. Salt, being imported from Uvinza, is dear and scarce : it forms the first demand for barter, and beads the second. Large fish is offered for sale, but the small fry is the only article of the kind which is to be purchased fresh. The country owes its plenty, according to the guides, to almost perennial showers.

The inhospitality of the Warundi and their northern neighbours, who would plunder a canoe or insist upon a black-mail equivalent to plunder, allows neither traffic nor transit to the north of Wafanya. Here, therefore, the crews prepare to cross the Tanganyika, which is divided into two stages by the island of Ubwari.

In Ubwari I had indeed discovered "an island far away." It is probably the place alluded to by the Portuguese historian, De Barros, in this important passage concerning the great lake in the centre of Africa : " It is a sea of such magnitude as to be capable of being navigated by many sail ; and among the islands in it there is one capable of sending forth an army of 30,000 men." Ubwari appears from a distance of two days bearing north-west ; it is then somewhat hazy, owing to the extreme humidity of the atmosphere. From Wafanya it shows a clear profile about eighteen to twenty miles westward, and the breadth of the western channel between it and the mainland averages from six to seven miles. Its north point lies in south lat. 4° 7′, and the lay is N. 17° E. (corrected). From the northern point of Ubwari the eastern prolongation of the lake bears N. 3° W. and the western N. 10° W. It is the only island near the centre of the Tanganyika—a long, narrow lump of rock, twenty to twenty-five geographical miles long, by four or five of extreme breadth, with a high longitudinal spine, like a hog's back, falling towards the water — here shelving, there steep, on the sea-side—where it ends in abrupt cliffs, here and there broken by broad or narrow gorges. Green from head to foot, in richness and profuseness of vegetation it equals, and perhaps excels, the shores of the Tanganyika, and in parts it appears carefully cultivated. Mariners dare not disembark on Ubwari, except at the principal places; and upon the wooded hill-sides wild men are, or are supposed to be, ever lurking in wait for human prey.

We halted two miserable days at Wafanya. The country is peculiarly rich, dotted with numerous hamlets, which supply provisions, and even milk, and divided into dense thickets, palm-groves, and large clearings of manioc, holcus, and sweet potatoes, which mantle like a garment the earth's brown body. Here we found Kannena snugly ensconced in our sepoy's pal, or ridge-tent. He had privily obtained it from Said bin Salim, with a view to add to his and his ward's comfort and dignity. When asked to give it up—we were lodging, I under a lug-sail, brought from the coast and converted into an awning, and my companion in the wretched flimsy article purchased from the Fundi— he naively refused. Presently having seen a fat sheep, he came to me declaring that it was his perquisite: moreover, he insisted upon receiving the goat offered to us by the Sultan Kanoni. I at first demurred. His satisfactory rejoinder was: "Ngema, ndugu yango!— Well, my brother,—here we remain!" I consulted Bombay about the necessity of humouring him in every whim. "What these jungle-niggers want," quoth my counsel, "that they will have, or they will see the next month's new moon!"

The morning of the 18th April was dark and menacing. Huge purpling clouds deformed the face of the northern sky.   Having loaded the canoes, however, we embarked to cross the channel which separated us from the Ubwari island.   As the paddles were in hand, the crew, starting up from their benches, landed to bring on board some forgotten manioc.   My companion remained in his boat, I in mine.   Presently, hearing an unusual uproar, I turned round and saw the sailors arming themselves, whilst the " curtain-lion," Khuda-bakhsh, was being hustled with blows, and pushed up the little cliff by a host of black spearmen; a naked savage the while capering about, waving the Baloch's bare blade in one hand and its scabbard in the other. Kannena joined majestically in the "row," but the peals of laughter from the mob showed no signs of anger.   A Mjiji slave, belonging to Khuda-bakhsh had, it appears, taken flight, after landing unobserved with the crowd.   The brave had redemanded him of Kannena, whom he charged, moreover, with aiding and abetting the desertion.   The slave Sultan offered to refer the point to me, but the valiant man, losing patience, out with his sword, and was instantly disarmed, assaulted, and battered, as above described, by forty or fifty sailors.   When quiet was restored, I called to him from the boat.   He replied by refusing to "budge an inch," and by summoning his " brother " Jelai to join him with bag and baggage.   Kannena also used soft words, till at last, weary of waiting, he gave orders to put off, throwing two cloths to Khuda-bakhsh, that the fellow might not return home hungry. I admired his generosity till compelled to pay for it.

The two Baloch were like mules; they disliked the voyage, and as it was the Ramazan, they added to their discomforts by pretending to fast.   Their desertion was inexcusable ; they left us wholly in the power of the Wajiji, to dangers and difficulties which they themselves could not endure. Prudent Orientals, I may again observe, never commit themselves to the sole custody of Africans, even of the " Muwallid," namely those born and bred in their houses. In Persia the traveller is careful to mix the black blood with that of the higher race ; formerly, whenever the member of a family was found murdered, the serviles were all tortured as a preliminary to inves- tigation, and many stories, like the following, are re- counted. The slaves had left their master in complete security, and were sitting, in early night, merrily chat- ting round the camp fire. Presently one began to relate the list of their grievances; another proposed to end them by desertion; and a third seconded the motion, opining, however, that they might as well begin by murdering the patroon. No sooner said than done. These children of passion and instinct, in the shortest interim, act out the " dreadful thing," and as readily repent when reflection returns. The Arab, therefore, in African lands, seldom travels with Africans only ; he prefers collecting as many companions, and bringing as many hangers on as he can afford. The best escort to a European capable of communicating with and com- manding them, would be a small party of Arabs fresh from Hazramaut and untaught in the ways and tongues of Africa. They would by forming a kind of balance of power, prevent that daring pilfering for which slaves are infamous; in the long run they would save money to the explorer, and perhaps save his life.

Khudabakhsh and his comrade-deserter returned safely by land to Kawele; and when derided by the other men, he repeated, as might be expected, notable griefs. Both had performed prodogies of valour; they had however been mastered by millions. Then they had

called upon "Haji Abdullah" for assistance, to which
he had replied "My power does not extend here!" Thus
heartlessly refused aid by the only person who could
and should have afforded it, they were reduced, sorely
against their will, to take leave of him. Their tale was
of course believed by their comrades, till the crews
brought back the other version of the affair, the "camel-
hearts" then once more became the laugh and jibe of
man and woman.

After a short consultation amongst the men concerning the threatening aspect of the heavens, it was agreed
by them to defer crossing the Lake till the next day.
We therefore passed on to the northern side of the
point which limits the bay of Wafanya, and anchoring
the craft in a rushy bayou, we pitched tents in time to
protect us against a violent thunderstorm with its
wind and rain.

On the 19th April we stretched westward, towards
Ubwari, which appeared a long strip of green directly
opposite Urundi, and distant from eighteen to twenty
miles. A little wind caused a heavy chopping swell;
we were wet to the skin, and as noon drew nigh, the sun
shone stingingly, reflected by a mirrory sea. At 10 A.M.
the party drew in their paddles and halted to eat
and smoke. About 2 P.M. the wind and waves again
arose, — once more we were drenched, and the frail
craft was constantly baled out to prevent water-logging.
A long row of nine hours placed the canoes at a roadstead, with the usual narrow line of yellow sand, on the
western coast of Ubwari Island. The men landed to
dry themselves, and to cook some putrid fish which they
had caught as it floated past the canoe, with the reed
triangle that buoyed up the net. It was "strong
meat" to us, but to them its staleness was as the "taste
in his butter," to the Londoner, the pleasing toughness

of the old cock to the Arab, and the savoury "fumet" of the aged he-goat to the Baloch. After a short halt, we moved a little northwards to Mzimu, a strip of low land dividing the waters from their background of grassy rise, through which a swampy line winds from the hills above. Here we found canoes drawn up, and the islanders flocked from their hamlets to change their ivory and slaves, goats and provisions, for salt and beads, wire and cloth. The Wabwari are a peculiar, and by no means a comely race. The men are habited in the usual mbugu, tigered with black stripes, and tailed like leopard-skins : a wisp of fine grass acts as fillet, and their waists, wrists, and ankles, their knob-sticks, spears, and daggers, are bound with rattan-bark, instead of the usual wire. The women train their frizzly locks into two side-bits resembling bear's ears; they tie down the bosom with a cord, apparently for the purpose of distorting nature in a way that is most repulsive to European eyes; and they clothe themselves with the barbarous goat-skin, or the scantiest kilts of bark-cloth. The wives of the chiefs wear a load of brass and bead ornaments; and, like the ladies of Wafanya, they walk about with patriarchal staves five feet long, and knobbed at the top.

We halted for a day at Mzimu in Ubwari, where Kannena demanded seventy khete of blue-porcelain beads as his fee for safe conduct to the island. Suddenly, at 6 P.M., he informed me that he must move to other quarters. We tumbled into the boats, and after enjoying two hours of pleasant progress with a northerly current, and a splendid moonshine, which set off a scene at once wild and soft as any

"That savage Rosa dashed, or learned Poussin drew,"

we rounded the bluff northern point of the island, put into " Mtuwwa," a little bay on its western shore, pitched the tent, and slept at ease.

Another halt was required on the 22nd April. The Sultan Kisesa demanded his blackmail, which amounted to one coil-bracelet and two cloths ; provisions were hardly procurable, because his subjects wanted white beads, with which, being at a discount at Ujiji, we had not provided ourselves ; and Kannena again successfully put in a tyrannical claim for 460 khete of blueporcelains to purchase rations.

On the 23rd April we left Mtuwwa, and made for the opposite or western shore of the lake, which appeared about fifteen miles distant ; the day's work was nine hours. The two canoes paddled far apart, there was therefore little bumping, smoking, or quarrelling, till near our destination. At Murivumba the malaria, the mosquitoes, the crocodiles, and the men are equally feared. The land belongs to the Wabembe, who are correctly described in the "Mombas Mission Map" as "Menschenfresser — anthropophagi." The practice arises from the savage and apathetic nature of the people, who devour, besides man, all kinds of carrion and vermin, grubs and insects, whilst they abandon to wild growths a land of the richest soil and of the most prolific climate. They prefer man raw, whereas the Wadoe of the coast eat him roasted. The people of a village which backed the port, assembled as usual to "sow gape-seed ;" but though

"A hungry look hung upon them all,"—

and amongst cannibals one always fancies oneself considered in the light of butcher's meat,—the poor devils, dark and stunted, timid and degraded, appeared less

dangerous to the living than to the dead. In order to
keep them quiet, the bull-headed Mabruki, shortly before
dusk, fired a charge of duck-shot into the village;
ensued loud cries and deprecations to the "Murungwana," but happily no man was hurt. Sayfu the
melancholist preferred squatting through the night on
the bow of the canoe, to trusting his precious person
on shore. We slept upon a reed-margined spit of sand,
and having neglected to pitch the tent, were rained
upon to our heart's content.

We left Murivumba of the man-eaters early on the
morning of the 24th April, and stood northwards along
the western shore of the Lake : the converging trend of
the two coasts told that we were fast approaching our
destination. After ten hours' paddling, halts included,
we landed at the southern frontier of Uvira, in a place
called Mamaletua, Ngovi, and many other names.
Here the stream of commerce begins to set strong; the
people were comparatively civil, they cleared for us a
leaky old hut with a floor like iron,—it appeared to
us a palace!—and they supplied, at moderate prices,
sheep and goats, fish-fry, eggs, and poultry, grain,
manioc and bird-pepper.

After another long stretch of fifteen rainy and sunny
hours, a high easterly wind compelled the hard-worked
crews to put into Muikamba (?) of Uvira. A neighbouring hamlet, a few hovels built behind a thick wind-
wrung plantain-grove, backed a reed-locked creek,
where the canoes floated in safety and a strip of clean
sand on which we passed the night as pleasantly as the
bright moonlight and the violent gusts would permit.
On the 26th April, a paddle of three hours and a half
landed us in the forenoon at the sandy baystand, where
the trade of Uvira is carried on.

Great rejoicings ushered in the end of our outward-bound voyage.   Crowds gathered on the shore to gaze at the new merchants arriving at Uvira, with the usual concert, vocal and instrumental, screams, shouts, and songs, shaums, horns, and tom-toms.   The captains of the two canoes performed with the most solemn gravity a bear-like dance upon the mat-covered benches, which form the "quarter-decks," extending their arms, pirouetting upon both heels, and springing up and squatting down till their hams touched the mats.   The crews, with a general grin which showed all their ivories, rattled their paddles against the sides of their canoes in token of greeting, a custom derived probably from the ceremonious address of the Lakists, which is performed by rapping their elbows against their ribs.   Presently Majid and Bekkari, two Arab youths sent from Ujiji by their chief, Said bin Majid, to collect ivory, came out to meet me; they gave me, as usual, the news, and said that having laid in the store of tusks required, they intended setting out southwards on the morrow.   We passed half the day of our arrival on the bare landing-place, a strip of sand foully unclean, from the effect of many bivouacs.   It is open to the water and backed by the plain of Uvira; one of the broadest of these edges of gently-inclined ground which separate the Lake from its trough of hills.   Kannena at once visited the Mwami or Sultan Maruta, who owns a village on a neighbouring elevation; this chief invited me to his settlement, but the outfit was running low and the crew and party generally feared to leave their canoes. We therefore pitched our tents upon the sand, and prepared for the last labour, that of exploring the head of the Lake.

We had now reached the "ne plus ultra," the north-

ernmost station to which merchants have as yet been
admitted.   The people are generally on bad terms with
the Wavira, and in these black regions a traveller coming
direct from an enemy's territory is always suspected of
hostile intentions,—no trifling bar to progress.   Opposite us still rose, in a high broken line, the mountains of
inhospitable Urundi, apparently prolonged beyond the
northern extremity of the waters.   The head, which
was not visible from the plain, is said to turn N.N.
westwards, and to terminate after a voyage of two days,
which some informants, however, reduce to six hours.
The breadth of the Tanganyika is here between seven
and eight miles.   On the 28th April, all my hopes—
which, however, I had hoped against hope—were rudely
dashed to the ground.   I received a visit from the three
stalwart sons of the Sultan Maruta: they were the noblest
type of Negroid seen near the Lake, with symmetrical
heads, regular features and pleasing countenances; their
well-made limbs and athletic frames of a shiny jet black,
were displayed to advantage by their loose aprons of
red and dark-striped bark-cloth, slung, like game-bags,
over their shoulders, and were set off by opal-coloured
eyeballs, teeth like pearls, and a profusion of broad
massive rings of snowy ivory round their arms, and conical ornaments like dwarf marling-spikes of hippopotamus
tooth suspended from their necks.   The subject of the
mysterious river issuing from the Lake, was at once
brought forward.   They all declared that they had
visited it, they offered to forward me, but they unanimously asserted, and every man in the host of bystanders
confirmed their words, that the " Rusizi " enters into,
and does not flow out of the Tanganyika.   I felt sick at
heart.   I had not, it is true, undertaken to explore the
Coy Fountains by this route; but the combined asser-

tions of the cogging Shaykh and the false Msawahili had startled me from the proprieties of reason, and—this was the result!

Bombay, when questioned, declared that my companion had misunderstood the words of Hamid bin Sulayyam, who spoke of a river falling into, not issuing *from* the lake; and added his own conviction that the Arab had never sailed north of Ubwari Island. Sayfu, who at Ujiji had described, as an eye-witness, the mouth of the déversoir and its direction for two days, now owned that he had never been beyond Uvira, and that he never intended to do so. Briefly, I had been deceived by a strange coincidence of deceit.

On the 28th April, we were driven from the strip of land which we originally occupied by a S. E. gale; here a " blat," or small hurricane, which drives the foaming waters of the tideless sea up to the green margin of the land. Retiring higher up where the canoes were careened, we spread our bedding on the little muddy mounds that rise a few inches above the surface of grass-closed gutter which drains off the showers daily falling amongst the hills. I was still obliged to content myself with the lug-sail, thrown over a ridge-pole supported by two bamboo uprights, and pegged out like a tent below; it was too short to fall over the ends and to reach the ground, it was therefore a place of passage for mizzle, splash, and draught of watery wind. My companion inhabited the tent bought from the Fundi, it was thoroughly rotted, during his first trip across the Lake — by leakage in the boat, and by being " bushed " with mud instead of pegs on shore. He informed me that there was " good grub " at Uvira, and that was nearly the full amount of what I heard from or of him. Our crews had hutted themselves in the dense mass of grass

near our tents; they lived as it were under arms, and
nothing would induce them to venture away from their
only escape, the canoes, which stood ready for launching whenever required. Sayfu swore that he would
return to Ujiji rather than venture a few yards inland
to buy milk, whilst Bombay and Mabruki, who ever
laboured under the idea that every brother-African of
the jungle thirsted for their blood, upon the principle
that wild birds hate tame birds, became, when the task
was proposed to them, almost mutinous. Our nine days,
halt at Uvira had therefore unusual discomforts. The
air, however, though damp and raw, with gust, storm,
and rain, must have been pure in the extreme; appetite
and sleep — except when the bull-frogs were " making a
night of it " — were rarely wanting, and provisions
were good, cheap, and abundant.

I still hoped, however, to lay down the extreme
limits of the lake northwards. Majid and Bekkari the
Arab agents of Said bin Majid, replied to the offer of
an exorbitant sum, that they would not undertake the
task for ten times that amount. The sons of Maruta
had volunteered their escort; when I wanted to close
with them, they drew off. Kannena, when summoned
to perform his promise and reminded of the hire that
he had received, jumped up and ran out of the tent:
afterwards at Ujiji he declared that he had been willing
to go, but that his crews were unanimous in declining
to risk their lives,— which was perhaps true. Towards
the end of the halt I suffered so severely from ulceration
of the tongue, that articulation was nearly impossible,
and this was a complete stopper to progress. It is a
characteristic of African travel that the explorer may be
arrested at the very bourne of his journey, on the very
threshold of success, by a single stage, as effectually

as if all the waves of the Atlantic or the sands of Arabia lay between.

Maruta and his family of young giants did not fail to claim their blackmail; they received a total of twelve cloths, five kitindi, and thirty khete of coral beads. They returned two fine goats, here worth about one cloth each, and sundry large gourds of fresh milk — the only food I could then manage to swallow. Kannena, who had been living at Maruta's village, came down on the 5th May to demand 460 khete of blue porcelains, wherewith to buy rations for the return-voyage. Being heavily in debt, all his salt and coil-bracelets had barely sufficed for his liabilities: he had nothing to show for them but masses of Sambo — iron-wire rings — which made his ankles resemble those of a young hippopotamus. The slaves and all the fine tusks that came on board were the property of the crew.

Our departure from Uvira was finally settled for the 6th May: before taking leave of our " furthest point," I will offer a few details concerning the commerce of the place.

Uvira is much frequented on account of its cheapness; it is the great northern depôt for slaves, ivory, grain, bark-cloth, and ironware, and, in the season, hardly a day elapses without canoes coming in for merchandise or provisions. The imports are the kitindi, salt, beads, tobacco, and cotton cloth. Rice does not grow there, holcus and maize are sold at one to two fundo of common beads per masuta or small load, — perhaps sixteen pounds,—and one khete is sufficient during the months of plenty to purchase five pounds of manioc, or two and even three fowls. Plantains of the large and coarse variety are common and cheap, and one cloth is given for two goodly earthen pots full of palm-oil. Ivory

fetches its weight in brass wire : here the merchant expects for every 1000 dollars of outfit to receive 100
farasilah (3500 lbs.) of large tusks, and his profit would
be great were it not counterbalanced by the risk and by
the expense of transport.   The prices in the slave-mart
greatly fluctuate. When business is dull, boys under ten
years may be bought for four cloths and five fundo of
white and blue porcelains, girls for six shukkah, and as
a rule at these remote places, as Uvira, Ujipa, and Marungu, slaves are cheaper than in the market of Ujiji.
Adults fetch no price, they are notoriously intractable,
and addicted to desertion.   Bark-cloths, generally in the
market, vary from one to three khete of coral beads.
The principal industry of the Wavira is ironware, the
material for which is dug in the lands lying at a little
distance westward of the lake. The hoes, dudgeons, and
small hatchets, here cost half their usual price at Ujiji.
The people also make neat baskets and panniers, not
unlike those of Normandy, and pretty bowls cut out
of various soft woods, light and dark : the latter are
also found, though rarely, at Ujiji and in the western
islets.

A gale appeared to be brewing in the north — here
the place of storms — and the crews, fearing wind and
water, in the afternoon insisted upon launching their
canoes and putting out to sea at 10 A.M. on the 6th
May.   After touching at the stages before described,
Muikamba, Ngovi and Murivumba of the anthropophagi,
we crossed without other accidents but those of weather
— the rainy monsoon was in its last convulsions — the
western branch or supplementary channel separating the
Lake from the island of Ubwari.   Before anchoring at
Mzimu, our former halting-place, we landed at a steep
ghaut, where the crews swarmed up a ladder of rock, and

presently returned back with pots of the palm-oil, for which this is the principal depôt.

On the 10th May the sky was dull and gloomy, the wind was hushed, the "rain-sun" burnt with a sickly and painful heat; the air was still and sultry, stifling and surcharged, while the glimmerings of lurid lightning and low mutterings from the sable cloud-banks lying upon the northern horizon, cut by light masses of mist in a long unbroken line, and from the black arch rising above the Acroceraurian hills to the west, disturbed at times the death-like silence. Even the gulls on the beach forefelt a storm. I suggested a halt, but the crews were now in a nervous hurry to reach their homes, — impatience mastered even *their* prudence.

We left Mzimu at sunset, and for two hours coasted along the shore. It was one of those portentous evenings of the tropics — a calm before a tempest — unnaturally quiet; we struck out, however, boldly to-wards the eastern shore of the Tanganyika, and the western mountains rapidly lessened on the view. Before, however, we reached the mid-channel, a cold gust — in these regions the invariable presage of a storm — swept through the deepening shades cast by the heavy rolling clouds, and the vivid nimble lightning flashed, at first by intervals, then incessantly, with a ghastly and blinding glow, illuminating the "vast of night," and followed by a palpable obscure, and a pitchy darkness, that weighed upon the sight. As terrible was its accompaniment of rushing, reverberating thunder, now a loud roar, peal upon peal, like the booming of heavy batteries, then breaking into a sudden crash, which was presently followed by a rattling discharge like the sharp pattering of musketry. The bundles of spears planted upright amidships, like paratonnerres, seemed to invite the electric fluid into the canoes. The waves began to rise, the rain descended, at first in warning-drops, then in torrents, and had the wind steadily arisen, the cockle-shell craft never could have lived through the short, chopping sea which characterises the Tanganyika in heavy weather. The crew, though blinded by the showers, and frightened by the occasional gusts, held their own gallantly enough; at times, however, the moaning cry, " O my wife ! " showed what was going on within. Bombay, a noted Voltairian in fine weather, spent the length of that wild night in reminiscences of prayer. I sheltered myself from the storm under my best friend, the Mackintosh, and thought of the far-famed couplet of Hafiz, — with its mystic meaning I will not trouble the reader :—

" This collied night, these horrid waves, these gusts that sweep the whirling deep!
What reck they of our evil plight, who on the shore securely sleep ? "

Fortunately the rain beat down wind and sea, otherwise nothing short of a miracle could have preserved us for a dry death.

That night, however, was the last of our "sea-sorrows." After floating about during the latter hours of darkness, under the land, but uncertain where to disembark, we made at 7 A.M., on the 11th May, Wafanya, our former station in ill-famed Urundi. Tired and cramped by the night's work, we pitched tents, and escaping from the gaze of the insolent and intrusive crowd, we retired to spend a few hours in sleep.

I was suddenly aroused by Mabruki, who, rushing into the tent, thrust my sword into my hands, and exclaimed that the crews were scrambling into their boats. I went out and found everything in dire confusion. The sailors hurrying here and there, were embarking their mats and cooking-pots, some were in violent parley with Kannena, whilst a little knot was carrying a man, mortally wounded, down to the waters of the Lake.   I saw at once that the affair was dangerous.   On these occasions the Wajiji, whose first impulse is ever flight, rush for safety to their boats and push off, little heeding whom or what they leave behind.   We therefore hurried in without delay.

When both crews had embarked, and no enemy appeared, Kannena persuaded them to reland, and proving to them their superior force, induced them to demand, at the arrow's point, satisfaction of Kanoni, the chief, for the outrage committed by his subjects. During our sleep a drunken man — almost all these disturbances arise from fellows who have the "*vin méchant*"—had rushed from the crowd of Warundi, and, knobstick in hand, had commenced dealing blows in all directions.   Ensued a general mêlée.   Bombay, when struck, called to the crews to arm.   The Goanese, Valentine, being fear-crazed, seized my large " Colt " and probably fired it into the crowd ; at all events, the cone struck one of our own men below the right pap, and came out two inches to the right of the backbone. Fortunately for us he was a slave, otherwise the situation would have been desperate.   As it was, the crowd became violently excited, one man drew his dagger upon Valentine, and with difficulty I dissuaded Kannena from killing him.   As the crew had ever an eye to the "main chance," food, they at once confiscated three goats, our store for the return voyage, cut their throats, and spitted the meat upon their spears :—thus the lamb died and the wolf dined, and the innocent suffered and the plunderer was joyed, the strong showed his strength and the weak his weakness, according to the usual formula of this sublunary world.

Whilst Kannena was absent, on martial purposes
intent, I visited the sole sufferer in the fray, and after
seeing his wound washed, I forbade his friends to knead
the injured muscles, as they were doing, and to wrench
his right arm from side to side. A cathartic seemed to
have a beneficial effect. On the second day of his
accident he was able to rise. But these occurrences in
wild countries always cause long troubles. Kannena,
who obtained from Sultan Kanoni, as blood-money, a
small girl and a large sheep, declared that the man
might die, and insisted upon my forthwith depositing,
in case of such contingency, eight cloths, which, should
the wound not prove fatal, would be returned. The latter
clause might have been omitted; in these lands, *nescit*
cloth *missa reverti*. As we were about to leave Ujiji,
Kannena claimed for the man's subsistence forty cloths,
— or as equivalent, three slaves and six cloths — which
also it was necessary to pay. A report was afterwards
spread that the wretch had sunk under his wound.
Valentine heard the intelligence with all that philosophy
which distinguishes his race when mishaps occur to any
but self. His prowess, however, cost me forty-eight
dollars, here worth at least £100 in England. Still I
had reason to congratulate myself that matters had not
been worse. Had the victim been a Mjiji freeman, the
trouble, annoyances, and expense would have been interminable. Had he been a Mrundi, we should have been
compelled to fight our way, through a shower of arrows,
to the boats; war would have extended to Ujiji, and
" England," as usual, would have had to pay the expenses. When Said bin Salim heard at Kazeh a distorted account of this mishap — of course it was reported that " Haji Abdullah " killed the man — he hit
upon a notable device. Lurinda, the headman of Gungu,

had often begged the Arab to enter into "blood-bro-
therhood" with him, and this had Said bin Salim pertinaciously refused, on religious grounds, to do.   When
informed that battle and murder were in the wind, he at
once made fraternity with Lurinda, hoping to derive
protection from his spear.   His terrors afterwards persuaded him to do the same with Kannena: indeed at
that time he would have hailed a slave as "Ndugu
yango!" (my brother!)

When Kannena returned successful from his visit to
Kanoni, we prepared to leave Wafanya.   The fierce
rain and the nightly drizzle detained us, however, till
the next morning.   On the 11th May we paddled round
the southern point of Wafanya Bay to Makimoni,
a little grassy inlet, where the canoes were defended
from the heavy surf.

After this all was easy.   We rattled paddles on the
12th May, as we entered our "patrie," Nyasanga.   The
next night was spent in Bangwe Bay.   We were too
proud to sneak home in the dark; we had done something deserving a Certain Cross, we were heroes, braves
of braves; we wanted to be looked at by the fair, to be
howled at by the valiant.   Early on the morning of the
13th May we appeared with shots, shouts, and a shock-
ing noise, at the reed-lined gap of sand that forms the
ghaut of Kawele.   It was truly a triumphal entrance.
All the people of that country-side had collected to
welcome the crew, women and children, as well as men,
pressed waist-deep into the water to receive friend and
relative with becoming affection : — the gestures, the
clamour, and the other peculiarities of the excited mob
I must really leave to the reader's imagination; the
memory is too much for me.

But true merit is always modest; it aspires to Honor,
not honours.   The Wagungu, or whites, were repeatedly

" called for." I broke, however, through the sudant, strident, hircine throng, and regaining, with the aid of
Riza's strong arm, the old Tembe, was salaamed to by the
expectant Said bid Salim and the Jemadar. It felt like a
return home. But I had left, before my departure, with
my Arab chargé-d'affaires, four small loads of cloth, and
on inspecting the supplies there remained only ten
shukkah. I naturally inquired what had become of the
110 others, which had thus prematurely disappeared.
Said bin Salim replied by showing a small pile of
grain-bags, and by informing me that he had hired
twenty porters for the down-march. He volunteered,
it is true, in case I felt disposed to finish the Periplus of
the Lake, to return to Kazeh and to superintend the
transmission of our reserve supplies; as, however, he at
the same time gave me to understand that he could not
escort them back to Ujiji, I thanked him for his offer,
and declined it.

We had expended upwards of a month — from the
10th April to the 13th May, 1858 — in this voyage
fifteen days outward bound, nine at Uvira, and nine in
returning. The boating was rather a severe trial.
We had no means of resting the back ; the holds of
the canoes, besides being knee-deep in water, were
disgracefully crowded ;—they had been appropriated
to us and our four servants by Kannena, but by degrees, he introduced in addition to the sticks, spears,
broken vases, pots, and gourds, a goat, two or three
small boys, one or two sick sailors, the little slave-
girl and the large sheep. The canoes were top-
heavy with the number of their crew, and the
shipping of many seas spoilt our tents, and besides,
wetted our salt, and soddened our grain and flour; the
gunpowder was damaged, and the guns were honey-
combed with rust. Besides the splashing of the paddles

and the dashing of waves, heavy showers fell almost every day and night, and the intervals were bursts of burning sunshine.

The discomfort of the halt was not less than that of the boat. At first we pitched tents near the villages, in tall, fetid grass, upon ground never level, where stones were the succedanea for tent-pegs stolen for fuel, and where we slept literally upon mire. The temperature inside was ever in extremes, now a raw rainy cold, then a steam-bath that damped us like an April shower. The villagers, especially in the remoter districts, were even more troublesome, noisy, and inquisitive, than the Wagogo. A " notable passion of wonder " appeared in them. We felt like baited bears : we were mobbed in a moment, and scrutinised from every point of view by them ; the inquisitive wretches stood on tiptoe, they squatted on their hams, they bent sideways, they thrust forth their necks like hissing geese to vary the prospect. Their eyes, " glaring lightning-like out of their heads," as old Homer hath it, seemed to devour us ; in the ecstasy of curiosity they shifted from one Muzungu to his " brother," till, like the well-known ass between the two bundles of hay, they could not enjoy either. They were pertinacious as flies, to drive them away was only to invite a return ; whilst, worst grief of all, the women were plain, and their grotesque salutations resembled the " encounter of two dog-apes." The Goanese were almost equally honoured, and the operation of cooking was looked upon as a miracle. At last my experience in staring enabled me to categorise the infliction as follows. Firstly, is the stare furtive, when the starer would peep and peer under the tent, and its reverse, the stare open. Thirdly, is the stare curious or intelligent, which, generally accompanied with irreverent laughter regarding our

appearance. Fourthly, is the stare stupid, which
denoted the hebete incurious savage. The stare
discreet is that of sultans and great men; the stare
indiscreet at unusual seasons is affected by women and
children. Sixthly, is the stare flattering — it was
exceedingly rare, and equally so was the stare con-
temptuous. Eighthly, is the stare greedy; it was
denoted by the eyes restlessly bounding from one object
to another, never tired, never satisfied. Ninthly, is
the stare peremptory and pertinacious, peculiar to
crabbed age. The dozen concludes with the stare
drunken, the stare fierce or pugnacious, and finally the
stare cannibal, which apparently considered us as
articles of diet. At last, weary of the stare by day, and
the tent by night, I preferred inhabiting a bundle of
clothes in the wet hold of the canoe; this, at least,
saved the trouble of wading through the water, of
scrambling over the stern, and of making a way between
the two close lines of grumbling and surly blacks that
manned the paddle-benches; whenever, after a meaningless halt, some individual thought proper to scream
out "Safári!" (journey!)

Curious to say, despite all these discomforts our
health palpably improved. My companion, though
still uncomfortably deaf, was almost cured of his blindness. When that ulcerated mouth, which rendered it
necessary for me to live by suction—generally milk and
water—for seventeen days, had returned to its usual
state, my strength gradually increased. Although my feet
were still swollen by the perpetual wet and by the painful funza or entozoon, my hands partially lost their
numbness, and the fingers which before could hold the
pen only for a few minutes were once more able freely to
write and sketch. In fact, I date a slow but sensible

progress towards a complete recovery of health from the days and nights spent in the canoe and upon the mud of the Tanganyika Lake. Perhaps mind had also acted upon matter; the object of my mission was now effected, and this thought enabled me to cast off the burden of grinding care with which the imminent prospect of a failure had before sorely laden me.

The rainy monsoon broke up on the 14th May, the day after my return to Kawele, and once more, after six months of incessant storm-wind and rain, clouds and mists, we had fine, cool mornings, clear warm sun, and deliciously cold nights. The climate became truly enjoyable, but the scenery somewhat lost its earlier attractions. The faultless, regular, and uniform beauty, and the deep stillness of this evergreen land did not fail to produce that strange, inexplicable melancholy of which most travellers in tropical countries complain. In this Nature all is beautiful that meets the eye, all is soft that affects the senses; but she is a Siren whose pleasures soon pall upon the enjoyer. The mind, enfeebled perhaps by an enervating climate, is fatigued and wearied by the monotony of the charms which haunt it; cloyed with costly fare, it sighs for the rare simplicity of the desert. I have never felt this sadness in Egypt and Arabia, and was never without it in India and Zanzibar.

Our outfit, as I have observed, had been reduced to a minimum. Not a word from Snay bin Amir, my agent at Kazeh, had arrived in reply to my many missives, and old Want began to stare at us with the stare peremptory. "Wealth," say the Arabs, "hath one devil, poverty a dozen," and nowhere might a caravan more easily starve than in rich and fertile Central

Africa. Travellers are agreed that in these countries
" baggage is life :" the heartless and inhospitable race
will not give a handful of grain without return, and to
use the Moslem phrase, " Allah pity him who must beg
of a beggar ! " As usual on such occasions, the Baloch
began to clamour for more rations — they received two
cloths per diem — and to demand a bullock wherewith
to celebrate their Eed or greater Festival. There were
several Arab merchants at Kawele, but they had exhausted their stock in purchasing slaves and ivory.
None in fact were so rich as ourselves, and we were
reduced to ten shukkah, ten fundo of coral beads, and
one load of black porcelains, which were perfectly useless. With this pittance we had to engage hammals
for the hammock, to feed seventy-five mouths, and to
fee several Sultans; in fact, to incur the heavy expenses
of marching back 260 miles to Unyanyembe.

Still, with an enviable development of Hope, Said bin
Salim determined that we should reach Kazeh un-
famished. We made the necessary preparations for the
journey, patched tents and umbrella, had a grand
washing and scouring day, mended the portmanteaus,
and ground the grain required for a month's march,
hired four porters for the manchil, distributed ammunition to Said bin Salim and the Baloch, who at once
invested it in slaves, and exchanged with Said bin Majid
several pounds of lead for palm-oil, which would be an
economy at the Malagarazi Ferry. For some days past
rumours had reached here that a large caravan of
Wanyamwazi porters, commanded by an Arab merchant,
was approaching Kawele. I was not sanguine enough to
expose myself to another disappointment. Suddenly on
the 22d May, frequent musket shots announced the
arrival of strangers, and at noon the Tembe was sur-

rounded with boxes and bales, porters, slaves, and four "sons of Ramji," Mbaruko, Sangora, Khamisi, and Shehe. Shahdad the Baloch, who had been left behind at Kazeh in love, and in attendance upon his " brother," Ismail, who presently died, had charge of a parcel of papers and letters from Europe, India, and Zanzibar. They were the first received after nearly eleven months, and of course they brought with them evil tidings,—the Indian mutinies. *En revanche*, I had a kindly letter from M. Cochet, Consul of France, and from Mr. Mansfield, of the U.S., who supplied me with the local news, and added for my edification a very "low-church" Tract, the first of the family, I opine, that has yet presented itself in Central Africa. Mr. Frost reported that he had sent at once a letter apprising me of Lieut.-Colonel Hamaton's death, and had forwarded the medical supplies for which I indented from K'hutu : these, as has been explained, had not reached me. Snay bin Amir also informed me that he had retained all the packages for which he could find no porters ; that three boxes had been stolen from his "godown ;" and finally, that the second supply, 400 dollars-worth of cloth and beads, for which I had written at Inenge and had re-written at Ugogo and other places, was hourly expected to arrive.

This was an unexpected good fortune, happening at a crisis when it was really wanted. My joy was somewhat damped by inspecting the packs of the fifteen porters. Twelve were laden with ammunition which was not wanted, and with munitions *de bouche*, which were : nearly half the bottles of curry-powder, spices, and cognac were broken, tea, coffee, and sugar, had been squeezed out of their tin canisters, and much of the rice and coffee had disappeared. The three remaining loads were one of American domestics,—sixty shukkahs—and the rest contained fifteen coral bracelets and white beads. All were the refuse of their kind: the good Hindoos at Zanzibar had seized this opportunity to dispose of their flimsy, damaged, and unsaleable articles. This outfit was sufficient to carry us comfortably to Unyanyembe. I saw, however, with regret that it was wholly inadequate for the purpose of exploring the two southern thirds of the Tanganyika Lake, much less for returning to Zanzibar, viâ the Nyassa or Maravi Lake, and Kilwa, as I had once dreamed.

I received several visits from our old companion, Muhinna bin Sulayman of Kazeh, and three men of his party. He did not fail to improve the fact of his having brought up my supplies in the nick of time. He required five coil-bracelets and sixteen pounds of beads as my share of the toll taken from him by the Lord of the Malagarazi Ferry. For the remaining fifteen coil-bracelets he gave me forty cloths, and for the load and a half of white beads he exchanged 880 strings of blue porcelains — a commercial operation by which he cleared without trouble 35 per cent. Encouraged by my facility, he proposed to me the propriety of paying part of the kuhonga or blackmail claimed from new comers by Rusimba and Kannena. But facility has its limits : I quietly objected, and we parted on the best of terms.

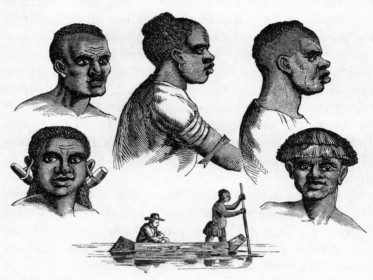

A Mnyamwezi.

A Mgogo.

A Mjiji.

Ferry Boat
on the Malagarazi River.

Mugungu Mbaya,
"the wicked white man."

A Mzaramo.

CHAP. XV.

THE TANGANYIKA LAKE AND ITS PERIPLUS.

THE Tanganyika Lake, though situated in the unexplored centre of Intertropical Africa, and until 1858
unvisited by Europeans, has a traditionary history of
its own, extending through more than three centuries.

"Accounts of a great sea in the interior of Africa obtained (partially from native travellers) at Congo and
Sofala," reached the Portuguese settlements on both
shores of the continent.* The details of de Barros

* Mr. Cooley's 'Memoir on the Geography of N'yassi,' p. 1. (Vol. XV. of
1845, Journal of the Royal Geographical Society.) The extracts from
Portuguese history in the text are entirely taken from that learned paper,

(first printed in 1852), whilst affording substantially correct details, such as the length of the Lake—100 leagues—the capability of navigation, and the one large island—Ubwari—are curiously intermingled with the errors of theoretical conclusion. Subsequently Pigafetta (1591) writing upon the authority of Portuguese inquirers, affirms that there is but one lake (the N'yassa) on the confines of Angola and Monomotapa, but that there are two lakes (the Nyassa and the Tanganyika), not lying east and west, as was supposed by Ptolemy of Alexandria, but north and south of each other, and about 400 miles asunder, which give birth to the Nile. From that epoch dates the origin of our modern misconceptions concerning the Lake Region of Central Intertropical Africa. The Nyassa and the Tanganyika were now blended, then separated, according to the theories or the information of the geographer; no explorer ventured to raise from the land of mystery the veil that invested it; and the "Mombas Mission" added the colophon by confounding, with the old confusion, the Nyanza or Ukerewe, a third lake, of which they had heard at Mombasah and elsewhere. It is not wonderful then that Dr. Vincent suspected the existence or the place of the Central Lake, or that the more ignorant popularizers of knowledge confounded the waters of the Nyassa and the Ngami.*

which in describing actualities wanted nothing but a solid foundation of data. The geographer's principal informant in 1834 was one " Khamisi bin Tani," civilised into " Khamis bin Osman," a Msawahili of Lamu who having visited the Nyassa, Maravi or Kilwa Lake, pretended that he had travelled to the Tanganyika Lake. I cannot allow this opportunity to pass without expressing my gratitude to Mr. Cooley for his courtesy in supplying me with references and other information.

* In the 'Westminster Review' (New Series, No. XX.) occurs the following passage, which sufficiently illustrates the assertion in the text ; the critic is discussing Mr. C. Andersson's 'Lake Ngami,' &c. &c. (London, 1856):

The earliest name given by theoretical writers to the hypothetical single lake appears to have been Zembére, Zémbere, Zambre, Zambri, or Zembre, probably a corruption or dialectic variety of Zambesi, that river being supposed, like the Nile, the Zaire, the Manisa, and others, to be derived from it. The word Moravi or Maravi, which still deforms our maps, is the name of a large tribe or a lordly race like the Wahinda, dwelling to the south-east and south-west of the Nyassa. In the seventeenth century Luigi Mariano, a missioner residing at the Rios de Sena, calls the Central Sea the Lake of Hemosura ; his description however applies to the Nyassa, Maravi or Kilwa Lake, and the word is probably a corruption of Rusuro or Lusuro, which in the language of Uhiao signifies a river or flowing water. In the 'Mombas Mission Map' the lake is called " See von Uniamesi," a mere misnomer, as it is separated by hundreds of miles from the Land

—" African missionaries, penetrating some little distance inland from the S.E., recently brought information, which they received second-hand from Arab travellers, of a vast fresh-water lake far in the interior, described as being of enormous dimensions — as nothing less than a great inland sea. Frequenters of the Geographical Society's meetings in Whitehall-place have observed in consequence, on the site which used to be marked in the maps as a sandy desert, a blue spot, about the size of the Caspian, and the shape of a hideous inflated leech. We trusted that a more accurate survey would correct the extreme frightfulness of the supposed form. Mr. Andersson has spared us further excitement. The lake turns out to be a mirage — a mythus with the smallest conceivable nucleus of fact. On the very spot occupied by this great blue leech — long. E. from Greenwich 23° and lat. S. 20° 21' — he found a small speck of bitter water, something more than twenty miles across, or the size of Lake Corrib in Galway. So perishes a phantom which has excited London geographers for a whole season."

Had the learned reviewer used his eyes or his judgment in Whitehall-place, he would not thus have confounded the hypothetic sea of the 'Mombas Mission Map'— a reservoir made to include the three several waters of Nyanza, Tanganyika, and Nyassa — in E. long. 24°—29°, and *S. lat.* 0° 13' —with the little Ngami explored by Dr. Livingstone and a party of friends in August, 1849, and placed by him in E. long. 23°, and in *S. lat.* 20° 20' 21'. The nearest points of the two waters are separated by an interval, in round numbers, of 700 miles.

of the Moon : the northern part is termed Ukerewe, by a confusion with the Nyanza Lake and the southern N'hánjá, for Nyassa, the old Maravi water near Kilwa. It is not a little curious, however, that Messrs. Cooley and Macqueen should both have recorded the vernacular name of the northern Lake Tangenyika, so unaccountably omitted from the 'Mombas Mission Map.' The words Tanganyenka and Tanganyenko used by Dr. Livingstone, who in places appears to confound the Lake with the Nyanza and the Nyassa, are palpable mispronunciations.

The African name for the central lake is Tanganyika, signifying an anastomosis, or a meeting place (sc. of waters,) from ku tanganyika, the popular word, to join, or meet together : the initial t being changed to ch— ku changanyika for ku tanganyika—in the lingua Franca of Zanzibar doubtless gave rise to Mr. Cooley's "Zanganyika." The word Tanganyika is universally used by the Wajiji and other tribes near and upon the Lake. The Arabs and African strangers, when speaking loosely of it, call it indifferently the Bahari or Sea, the Ziwa or Pond, and even the Mtoni or River. The "Sea of Ujiji" would, after the fashion of Easterns, be limited to the waters in the neighbourhood of that principal depot.

The Tanganyika occupies the centre of the length of the African continent, which extends from 32° N. to 33° S. latitude, and it lies on the western extremity of the eastern third of the breadth. Its general direction is parallel to the inner African line of volcanic action drawn from Gondar southwards through the regions about Kilima-ngáo (Kilimanjáro) to Mount Njesa, the eastern wall of the Nyassa Lake. The general formation suggests, as in the case of the Dead Sea, the idea of a volcano of depression—not, like the Nyanza or

Ukerewe, a vast reservoir formed by the drainage of mountains. Judging from the eye, the walls of this basin rise in an almost continuous curtain, rarely waving and infracted to 2,000 or 3,000 feet above the water-level. The lower slopes are well wooded : upon the higher summits large trees are said not to grow ; the deficiency of soil, and the prevalence of high fierce winds would account for the phenomena. The lay is almost due north and south, and the form a long oval, widening in the central portions and contracting systematically at both extremities. The length of the bed was thus calculated : From Ujiji (in S. lat. 4° 55′) to Uvira (in S. lat. 3° 25′), where the narrowing of the breadth evidences approach to the northern head, was found by exploration a direct distance of 1° 30′ = 90 miles, which, allowing for the interval between Uvira and the river Rusizi, that forms the northernmost limit, may be increased to 100 rectilinear geographical miles. According to the Arab voyagers, who have frequently rounded the lake Ujiji in eight stages from the northern, and twelve from the southern, end of the lake, the extent from Ujiji to the Marungu River, therefore, is roughly computed at 150 miles. The total of length, from Uvira, in S. lat. 30° 25′, to Marungu, in S. lat. 7° 20′, would then be somewhat less than 250 rectilinear geographical miles. About Ujiji the water appears to vary in breadth from 30 to 35 miles, but the serpentine form of the banks, with a succession of serrations and indentations of salient and re-entering angles — some jutting far and irregularly into the bed — render the estimate of average difficult. The Arabs agree in correctly stating, that opposite Ujiji the shortest breadth of the lake is about equal to the channel which divides Zanzibar from the mainland, or between 23 and 24 miles. At Uvira the breadth narrows to eight miles. Assuming, therefore, the total length at 250, and the main breadth at 20, geographical miles, the circumference of the Tanganyika would represent, in round numbers, a total of 550 miles ; the superficial area, which seems to vary little, covers about 5,000 square miles ; and the drainage from the beginning of the great Central African depression in Unyamwezi, in E. long. 33° 58', numbers from the eastward about 240 miles.

By B. P. thermometer the altitude of the Tanganyika is 1850 feet above the sea-level, and about 2000 feet below the adjacent plateau of Unyamwezi and the Nyanza, or northern lake. This difference of level, even did not high-hill ranges intervene, would preclude the possibility of that connection between the waters which the Arabs, by a conjecture natural to inexpert geographers, have maintained to the confusion of the learned. The topographical situation of the Tanganyika is thus the centre of a deep synclical depression in the continent, a long narrow trough in the southern spurs of Urundi, which, with its mountain-neighbour Karagwah, situated upon the equator, represents the Inner African portion of the Lunar Mountains. It may be observed that the parallel of the northern extremity of the Tanganyika nearly corresponds with the southern creek of the Nyanza, and that they are separated by an arc of the meridian of about 343 miles.

The water of the Tanganyika appears deliciously sweet and pure after the salt and bitter, the putrid and slimy produce of the wells, pits, and pools on the line of march. The people, however, who drink it willingly when afloat, prefer, when on shore, the little springs which bubble from its banks. They complain that it does not satisfy thirst, and contrast it unfavourably with the waters of its rival the Nyanza: it appears moreover, to corrode metal and leather with exceptional power. The colour of the pure and transparent mass has apparently two normal varieties: a dull sea-green — never, however, verdigris-coloured, as in the shoals of the Zanzibar seas, where the reflected blue of the atmosphere blends with the yellow of the sandy bottom; the other, a clear, soft blue — by day rarely deep and dark, like the ultramarine of the Mediterranean, but resembling the light and milky tints of tropical seas. Under a strong wind the waves soon rise in yeasty lines, foaming up from a turbid greenish surface, and the aspect becomes menacing in the extreme.

It was found impracticable to take soundings of the Tanganyika: the Arabs, however, agreed in asserting that with lines of several fathoms they found bottom only near the shores. The shingly sole shelves rapidly, without steps or overfalls, into blue water. Judging from the eye, the bottom is sandy and profusely strewn with worn pebbles. Reefs and washes were observed near the shores; it is impossible to form an idea of their position or extent, as the crews confine themselves to a few well-known lines, from which they cannot be persuaded to diverge. No shoals or shallows were seen at a distance from the coasts, and though islets are not unfrequent upon the margin, only one was observed or heard of near the centre.

The affluents of this lake are neither sufficiently numerous nor considerable to alter by sedimentary deposit the depth or the shape of the bed. The borders are generally low: a thick fringe of rush and reed, obviating erosion by the element, conceals the watery margin. Where the currents beat, they cut out a short and narrow strip of quartzose sand, profusely strewn

with large shingle, gravel, comminuted shells, and marine exuviæ, with a fringe of drift formed by the joint
action of wind and wave. Beyond this is a shelving
plain—the principal locality for cultivation and settlements. In some parts it is a hard clay conglomerate;
in others, a rich red loam, apparently stained with oxide
of iron ; and in others sandy, but everywhere coated
with the thickest vegetation extending up to the background of mountains. The coast is here and there
bluff, with miniature cliffs and headlands, whose formation is of sandstone strata tilted, broken, and distorted,
or small blocks imbedded in indurated reddish earth.
From the water appeared piles of a dark stone resembling angular basalt, and amongst the rock-crevices
the people find the float-clay, or mountain meal, with
which they decorate their persons and the sterns of
their canoes. The uncultivated hill summits produce
various cactaceæ; the sides are clothed with giant trees,
the mvule, the tamarind, and the bauhinia. On the
declines, more precipitous than the Swiss terraces,
manioc and cereals grow luxuriantly, whilst the lowest
levels are dark with groves of plantains and Guinea-
palms.

A careful investigation and comparison of statements
leads to the belief that the Tanganyika receives and
absorbs the whole river-system—the net-work of streams,
nullahs, and torrents—of that portion of the Central
African depression whose water-shed converges towards
the great reservoir. Geographers will doubt that such
a mass, situated at so considerable an altitude, can
maintain its level without an effluent. Moreover, the
freshness of the water would, under normal circumstances, argue the escape of saline matter washed down
by the influents from the area of drainage. But may

not the Tanganyika, situated, like the Dead Sea, as a
reservoir for supplying with humidity the winds which
have parted with their moisture in the barren and arid
regions of the south, maintain its general level by the
exact balance of supply and evaporation? And may
not the saline particles deposited in its waters be wanting
in some constituent which renders them evident to the
taste? One point concerning the versant has been
proved by these pages, namely, that the Tanganyika
cannot be drained eastward by rents in a subtending
mountain ridge, as was supposed by Dr. Livingstone
from an indiscriminately applied analogy with the
ancient head-basin of the Zambezi. Dr. Livingstone
(chap. xxiv. xxvi. et passim) informs his readers, from
report of the Arabs, that the Tanganyika is a large
shallow body of water; in fact, the residuum of a mass
anciently much more extensive. This, however, is not
and cannot be the case. In theorising upon the eastern
versant and drainage of the Tanganyika, Dr. Livingstone
seems to have been misled by having observed that the
vast inland sea of geological ages, of which Lake Ngami
and its neighbour Kumadau are now the principal
remains, had been desiccated by cracks and fissures,
caused in the subtending soils by earthquakes and
sudden upheavals, which thus opened for the waters an
exit into the Indian Ocean. This may have happened
to the Nyassa, or Southern Lake; it must not, however,
be generalized and extended to the Nyanza and the
Tanganyika.

As in Zanzibar, there is little variety of temperature
upon the Tanganyika. The violent easterly gales,
which, pouring down from the cold heights of Usagara,
acquire impetus sufficient to carry the current over
Ugogo, Unyamwezi, and Uvinza, are here less distinctly

defined. The periodical winds over the Lake—regular, but not permanent — are the south-east and the south-west, which also bring up the foulest weather. The land and sea breezes are felt almost as distinctly as upon the shores of the Indian Ocean. The breath of the morning, called by the Arabs El Barad, or the zephyr, sets in from the north. During the day are light variable breezes, which often subside, when the weather is not stormy, into calms. In the evenings a gentle afflatus comes up from the waters. Throughout the dry season the Lake becomes a wind-trap, and a heavy ground sea rolls towards the shore. In the rains there is less sea, but accidents occur from sudden and violent storms. The mountainous breakers of Arab and African informants were not seen; in fact, with a depth of three feet from ridge to dell, a wave would swamp the largest laden canoe. Wind-currents are common. Within a few hours a stream will be traversed, setting strongly to the east, and crossed by a southerly or south-westerly current. High gales, in certain localities where the waves set upon a flush, flat shore, drive the waters fifteen to twenty feet beyond the usual mark. This circumstance may partly explain the Arab's belief in a regular Madd wa Jarr—ebb and flow—which Eastern travellers always declare to have observed upon the Tanganyika and Nyassa Lakes, and which Mr. Anderson believes to exist in the little Ngami. A mass of water so large must be, to a certain extent, subject to tidal influences; but the narrowness of the bed from east to west would render their effect almost unobservable. Mr. Francis Galton referred me for the explanation of this phenomenon to a paper 'On the Seiches of Lakes,' by Colonel J. R. Jackson, F.R.G.S., published in the 'Journal of the R. G. S.,' vol. iii. of

1833, in which the learned author refers the ebb and
flow of the waters of Lake Leman, or of Geneva (and
of the lakes of Zurich, Annecy, and Constance), to "an
unequal pressure of the atmosphere on different parts
of the lake at the same time; that is, to the simul-
taneous effect of columns of air of different weight or
different elasticity, arising from temporary variations of
temperature, or from mechanical causes."

The scenery and the navigation of the Tanganyika
have been illustrated in the last chapter. Remains
only a succinct account of the physical and ethnological
features of its Periplus, carefully collected from authorities on the spot.

According to the Wajiji, from their country to the
Runangwa or Marungu River, which enters the Lake at
the southern point, there are twelve stages; this Periplus numbers 120 khambi or stations, at most of which,
however, provisions are not procurable. An extended
list of fifty-three principal points was given by the
guides; it is omitted, as it contains nothing beyond
mere names. There are, however, sixteen tribes and
districts which claim attention: of these, Ukaranga and
Ujiji have already been described.

The kingdom of Urundi, which lies north of Ujiji,
has a sea-face of about fifty miles; a low strip of exceeding fertility, backed at short distances by a band of
high green hill. This region, rising from the Lake in a
north-easterly direction, culminates into the equatorial
mass of highlands which, under the name of Karagwah,
forms the western spinal prolongation of the Lunar
Mountains. The residence of the Mwami, or chief
sultan Mwezi, is near the headstream of the Kitangure
(Kitangule), or River of Karagwah, which rises at a
place distant six days' march (sixty miles), and bearing

north-east from, the Tanganyika. His settlement, according to the Arabs, is of considerable extent; the huts are built of rattan, and lions abound in the vicinity.

Urundi differs from the lake regions generally in being a strictly monarchical country, locally governed by Watware or headmen, who transmit the customs and collections at stated periods to their suzerain. The Mwame, it is said, can gather in a short time a large host of warriors who are the terror of the neighbouring tribes. The Warundi are evidently natives of a high cold country; they are probably the "white people resembling Abyssinians," and dwelling near the Lake, of whom European geographers have heard from Zanzibar. The complexion varies from a tawny yellow, the colour of the women, to a clear dark brown, which is so brightened by the daily use of ochre mixed with palm-oil, that in few cases the real tint is discernible. The men tattoo with circles and lines like cupping-cuts; some burn up alti rilievi of large shining lumps an inch in diameter, a decoration not a little resembling large boils; others chip the fore teeth like the Wanyamwezi. Their limbs are stout and well proportioned, many stand upwards of six feet high, and they bear the appearance of a manly and martial race. Their dress is the mbugu, worn in the loosest way; their arms are heavy spears, sime, and unusually strong arrows; their ornaments are beads, brass wire, and streaks of a carmine-coloured substance, like the red farinaceous powder called in India gulal, drawn across the head and forehead. The Waganga, or priests of Urundi, wear a curious hood, a thatch of long white grass or fibre, cut away at the face and allowed to depend behind over the shoulders; their half-naked figures, occasion-

ally rattling wooden clappers, and capering cause-
lessly like madmen, present a savage and horrid appearance. Honourable women wear long tobes of
American domestics from below the arms to the ankles;
they are followed by hosts of female slaves, and preserve an exceptionally modest and decorous demeanour.
Their features are of the rounded African type of
beauty. Their necks and bosoms support a profusion
of sofi and other various-coloured beads; their fore-
heads are bound with frontlets, fillet-like bands of
white and coral porcelain, about three fingers deep, a
highly becoming ornament probably derived from Karagwah; and those who were seen by the Expedition
invariably walked about with thin staves five or six
feet long, pointed and knobbed as the walking-sticks of
ancient Egypt.

At the northern extremity of the Urundi sea-face,
and at the head of the Tanganyika, lies the land of
Uzige; it is rarely visited except by the Lakist traders.
This people, who, like their neighbours, cannot exist
without some form of traffic, have, it is said, pursued
the dows of the earlier Arab explorers with a flotilla of
small canoes; it is probable that negro traders would
be better received. In their country, according to the
guides, six rivers fall into the Tanganyika in due order
from the east : the Kuryamavenge, the Molongwe, the
Karindira, the Kariba, the Kibaiba, and westernmost
the Rusizi or Lusizi. The latter is the main drain of
the northern countries, and the best authorities, that is
to say those nearest the spot, unanimously assert that
it is an influent.

The races adjoining Uzige, namely, the Wavira on
the north-western head of the Tanganyika, and their
southern neighbours, the Wabembe cannibals, have

already been mentioned. The Wasenze inhabit the hills within or westwards of the Wabembe. Further southwards and opposite Kawele in Ujiji are the Wagoma highlanders. The lower maritime lands belonging to the Wagoma supply the gigantic mvule trees required for the largest canoes. These patriarchs of the forest are felled and shaped with little axes on the spot; when finished they are pushed and dragged down the slopes by the workmen, and are launched and paddled over to the shores of Ujiji.

South of the Wagoma are the Waguhha, who have been mentioned as the proprietors of the islets southwest of Ujiji. In their lands, according to the Arabs, is a lake or large water called Mikiziwá, whence the tribe upon its banks derives its name Wamikiziwá. Through the country of the Waguhha lies the route to Uruwwa, at present the western terminus of the Zanzibar trade. The merchant crossing the sea-arm which separates Kasenge from the mainland of the Tanganyika, strikes towards Uruwwa; the line runs over low levels shelving towards the lake, cut by a reticulation of streams unfordable after rain, and varied by hilly and rolling ground. Provisions are everywhere procurable, but the people, like the Wavinza, are considered dangerous. At Uruwwa the khete, or string of beads, is half the size of that current in other countries. The price of ivory per frasilah is 15 miranga, or 150 large khete of white, small-blue, and coarse-red porcelain beads, the latter called Lungenga; besides which a string of sungomaji (pigeon-egg beads), and a few sámesáme, or coral-beads, are thrown in. The route numbers nine long or sixteen short stages; the general direction is south-westerly. Kiyombo, the sultan of Uruwwa, is at present friendly with the Arabs; he trades in ivory, slaves, and a little copper from Katata or Katanga, a district distant fifteen marches north-west of Usenda, the now well-known capital of the great chief Kazembe. The grandfather of the present Kazembe, the "viceroy" of the country lying south-west of the Tanganyika, and feudatory to Mwátá yá Nvo, the sovereign of "Uropua," was first visited by Dr. Lacerda, governor of the Rios de Sena, in 1798-99. The traveller died, however, after being nine months in the country, without recording the name and position of the African capital; the former was supplied by the expedition sent under Major Monteiro and Captain Gamitto in 1831–32; it is variously pronounced Lucenda, Luenda, and by the Arabs Usenda, the difference being caused probably by dialect or inflexion. According to the Arabs, the Kazembe visited by the Portuguese expedition in 1831, died about 1837, and was succeeded by his son the present chief. He is described as a man of middle age, of light-coloured complexion, handsomely dressed in a Surat cap, silk coat, and embroidered loin cloth; he is rich in copper, ivory, and slaves, cloth and furniture, muskets and gunpowder. Many Arabs, probably half-castes, are said to be living with him in high esteem, and the medium of intercourse is the Kisawahili. Though he has many wives, he allows his subjects but one each, puts both adulterer and adulteress to death, and generally punishes by gouging out one or both eyes.

On the Uruwwa route caravans are composed wholly of private slaves; the races of the Tanganyika will not carry loads, and the Wanyamwezi, unmaritime savages like the Kafirs, who have a mortal dread and abhorrence of water, refuse to advance beyond Ujiji. On account of its dangers, the thriving merchants have

hitherto abandoned this line to debtors and desperate
men.

South of Uguhha lies the unimportant tribe of Wa-
t'hembwe, whose possessions are within sight of Kawele
in Ujiji. The race adjoining them is the Wakatete
or Wakadete, and the country is called by the Arabs
Awwal Marungu, on the northern frontier of Marungu.
Marungu is one of the most important divisions of the
lands about the Tanganyika. Amayr bin Said el
Shaksi, a sturdy old merchant from Oman, who, wrecked
about twelve years ago on that part of the coast, had
spent five months with the people, living on roots and
grasses, divides the region generically termed Marungu
into three distinct provinces—Marungu to the north,
Karungu in the centre, and Urungu on the south.
Others mention a western Marungu, divided from the
eastern by the Runangwa River, and they call the
former in contradistinction Marungu Tafuna, from its
sultan.

Western Marungu extends according to the Arabs in
depth from Ut'hembwe to the Wabisa, a tribe holding
extensive lands westward of the Nyassa Lake. Travellers from Unyamwezi to K'hokoro meet, near Ufipa,
caravans of the northern Wabisa *en route* to Kilwa.
Between Marungu and Usenda, the capital of the Kazembe, the road lies through the district of Kavvire,
distant seven marches; thence nine stages conduct
them to the end of the journey. There is an upper
land route through Uruwwa for those travelling from
Ujiji to Usenda, and many caravans have passed from
Unyanyembe direct through K'hokoro and Ufipa, to the
country of the Kazembe. Mr. Cooley ("Geography of
N'yassi," p. 7) conjectures that the Ambios or Imbies,
Zimbas or Muzimbas, celebrated by the old Portuguese

historians of Africa on account of an irruption, in 1570, from the north as far as the Zambezi River, "were no other than the M'Biza, or Moviza, as they are called by the Portuguese who still occupy its (the Nyassa's) south-western banks." The proper name of this well-known tribe is Wábísá (in the sing. Mbisá), not Wá-bíshá, as it is pronounced at Zanzibar, where every merchant knows "Bisha ivory." The Wábísá extend according to the Arabs from the west of the Nyassa or Kilwa Lake towards the south of the Tanganyika. They dress in bark-cloth, carry down their fine ivory to Tete and Kilimani (Quillimane); and every four or five years a caravan appears at Kilwa, where, confounding their hosts with the Portuguese, they call every Arab "muzungu," or white man. They are a semi-pastoral tribe, fond of commerce, and said to be civil and hospitable to strangers. It must be observed that those geographers are in error who connect the Wabisa with the Wanyamwezi; they are distinct in manners and appearance, habits and language. Mr. Cooley has, for instance, asserted that "the 'Moviza' and the 'Mo-nomoezi' are similar in physical character and national marks." The only mark known to the Wabisa is the kishshah, or crest of hair; not, as Khamisi Wa Tani asserted to Mr. Cooley ("Inner Africa laid Open," p. 61), a dotted line on the nose and forehead; whereas, the Wanyamwezi, as has been seen, puncture the skin. Thus Lacerda calls the "Moviza" a frizzled and peri-wigged people. The Arabs deny the assertion of Pereira, recorded by Bowdich, that the Moviza, like the Wahiao, file their teeth.

Marungu is described by the Arabs as a hilly country like Ujiji and Uvira: the precincts of the lake, however, are here less bold than the opposite shore. Off the coast lie four or five islands, two of which, according to the Arabs, are of considerable size; the only name given is Ukungwe, which appears, however, to be rather the name of the farthest point visible from Kasenge, and bearing S. 58° E. On the north-western frontier of Marungu, and about three marches from the lake, is the district called Utumbara, from Mtumbara its sultan. This Utumbara, which must not be confounded with the district of the same name in Northern Unyamwezi, is said by the Arabs to be fifteen to twenty days' march from Usenda.

Marungu, though considered dangerous, has often been visited by Arab merchants. After touching at Kasenge they coast along Uguhha for four days, not daring to land there in consequence of an event that happened about 1841–42. A large Arab caravan of 200 armed slaves, led by Mohammed bin Salih and Sulayman bin Nasir, and with four coadjutors, Abd el Al and Ibn Habib, Shiahs of Bahrayn, Nasir and Rashid bin Salim el Harisi (who soon afterwards died at Marungu) took boat to Marungu, and in due time arrived at Usenda. They completed their cargo, and were returning in a single boat, when they were persuaded by the Sultan Mtumbara to land, and to assist him in annihilating a neighbour, Sámá or Kipyoká, living at about one day's march from the Lake. The Arabs, aided by Africans, attacked a boma, or palisade, where, bursting in, they found Sámá's brother sitting upon pombe, with his wife. The villagers poured in a shower of arrows, to which the Arabs replied by shooting down the happy couple over their cups. Sámá's people fled, but presently returning they massacred the slaves of the Arabs, who were obliged to take refuge in

the grass till aid was afforded by their employer Mtumbara. Sámá, thus victorious, burned the Arab boat,
and, compelling the merchants to return to Usenda,
seized the first opportunity of slaying his rival. The
Arabs have found means of sending letters to their
friends, but they appear unable to leave the country.
Their correspondence declares them to be living in
favour with the Kazembe, who has presented them with
large rice-shambas, that they have collected ivory and
copper in large quantities, but are unable to find porters.
This being highly improbable in a land where in 1807
a slave cost five, and a tusk of ivory six or seven
squares of Indian piece-goods, and as, moreover, several
merchants, deluded by exaggerated accounts of the
Kazembe's wealth and liberality, intrusted these men
with considerable ventures, of which no tidings have as
yet reached the creditors' ears, the more acute Arabs
suspect that their countrymen are living from hand to
mouth about Usenda, and are cultivating the land with
scant prospect of quitting it.

The people of Marungu are called Wámbozwá by the
Arabs; they are subject to no king, but live under local
rulers, and are ever at war with their neighbours.
They are a dark and plain, a wild and uncomely race.
Amongst these people is observed a custom which connects them with the Wangindo, Wahiao, and the slave
races dwelling inland from Kilwa. They pierce the
upper lip and gradually enlarge the aperture till the
end projects in a kind of bill beyond the nose and chin,
giving to the countenance a peculiar duck-like appearance. The Arabs, who abhor this hideous vagary of
fashion, scarify the sides of the hole and attempt to
make the flesh grow by the application of rock-salt.
The people of Marungu, however, are little valued as

slaves; they are surly and stubborn, exceedingly de-
praved, and addicted to desertion.

Crossing the Runangwa or Marungu River, which,
draining the southern countries towards the Tanganyika,
is represented to equal the Malagarazi in volume, the
traveller passes through the districts of Marungu
Tafuna, Ubeyya, and Iwemba. Thence, turning to the
north, he enters the country of the Wapoka, between
whom and the Lake lie the Wasowwa and the Wafipa.
This coast is divided from the opposite shore by a
voyage of fourteen hours; it is a hilly expanse divided
by low plains, where men swarm according to the
natives like ants. At a short distance from the shore
lies the Mvuma group, seven rocks or islets, three of
which are considerable in size, and the largest, shaped
like a cone, breeds goats in plenty, whilst the sea around
is rich in fish. There are other islets in the neighbourhood, but none are of importance.

Ufipa is an extensive district fertilised by many
rivers. It produces grain in abundance, and the wild
rice is of excellent flavour. Cattle abounded there
before the Watuta, who held part of the country, began
a system of plunder and waste, which ended in their
emigration to the north of Uvinza; cows, formerly
purchased for a few strings of cheap white beads, are
now rare and dear. The Wafipa are a wild but kindly
people, who seldom carry arms: they have ever welcomed the merchants that visited them for slaves and
ivory, and they are subject to four or five principal
chiefs. The servile specimens seen at Unyanyembe
were more like the jungle races of the Deccan than
Africans—small and short, sooty and shrunken men, so
timid, ignorant, and suspicious, that it was found impossible to obtain from them the simplest specimen of

their dialect. Some of them, like the Wanyoro, had extracted all the lower incisors.

North of the Wafipa, according to the Arabs, lies another tribe, called Wat'hembe (?), an offshoot from the people on the opposite side of the Tanganyika. Here the lake receives a small river called the Murunguru (?). The circuit of the Tanganyika concludes with the Wat'hongwe, called from their sultan or their founder Wat'hongwe Kapana. In clear weather their long promontory is the furthest point visible from Kawele in Ujiji; and their lands extend northwards to Ukaranga and the Malagarazi River.

Such are the most important details culled from a mass of Arab oral geography : they are offered however to the reader without any guarantee of correctness. The principal authorities are the Shaykh Snay bin Amir el Harsi and Amayr bin Said el Shaksi ; the latter was an eye-witness. All the vague accounts noted down from casual informants were submitted to them for an imprimatur. Their knowledge and experience surpassing those of others, it was judged better to record information upon trust from them only, rather than to heap together reliable and unreliable details, and as some travellers do, by striking out a medium, inevitably to confuse fact with fiction. Yet it is the explorer's unpleasant duty throughout these lands to doubt everything that has not been subjected to his own eyes. The boldest might look at the " Mombas Mission Map" and tremble.

SNAY BIN AMIR'S HOUSE.

Mganga, or
medicine man.   The porter.   The Kirangozi, or
                                                                guide.
          Muinyi Kidogo.   Mother and child.

CHAP. XVI.

WE RETURN TO UNYANYEMBE.

IMMEDIATELY after the arrival of our caravan I made
preparations for quitting Ujiji. The 26th May, 1858,
was the day appointed for our departure, which was
fated to resemble a flight more than the march of a
peaceful Expedition. Said bin Salim, who had received
as "Urangozi" or retaining-fee from his two African
"brothers," Lurinda and Kannena, a boy-slave and a
youth, thought only of conveying them safely out of the
country. The Baloch, especially the Jemadar, who had
invested every cubit of cloth and every ounce of

powder in serviles, were also trembling at the prospect
of desertion.   As usual, when these barbarians see
preparations for departure, the Wajiji became more extortionate and troublesome than before.   A general
drinking-bout had followed the return of the crews from
Uvira : Kannena had not been sober for a fortnight. At
last his succession of violent and maudlin fits ended
fortunately for us in a high fever, which somewhat
tamed his vice.   Shortly after our disappearance, his
territory was attacked by the predal Watuta : and had
not the Arabs assisted in its defence, it would doubtless
have been converted into a grisly solitude, like the once
fertile and populous Uhha.   Kannena, of course, fled
into the mountains from the attack of the gallant
rascals : he had courage enough to bully, but not to
fight.   I heard of him no more : he showed no pity to
the homeless stranger, — may the world show none to
him !

I shall long remember the morning of the 26th May,
which afforded me the last sunrise-spectacle of the
Tanganyika Lake.   The charm of the scenery was
perhaps enhanced by the reflection that my eyes might
never look upon it again.   Masses of brown-purple
clouds covered the quarter of the heavens where the
sun was about to rise.   Presently the mists, ruffled like
ocean billows, and luminously fringed with Tyrian
purple, were cut by filmy rays, whilst, from behind their
core, the internal living fire shot forth its broad beams,
like the spokes of a hugh aërial wheel, rolling a flood of
gold over the light blue waters of the lake.   At last
Dan Sol, who at first contented himself with glimmering
through the cloud-mass, disclosed himself in his glory,
and dispersed with a glance the obstacles of the vapour-
ous earth : breaking into long strata and little pearly
flakes, they soared high in the empyrean, whilst the

all-powerful luminary assumed undisputed possession of earth, and a soft breeze, the breath of the morn, as it is called in the East, awoke the waters into life.

But I am not long to enjoy this mighty picture. A jarring din sings in my ears, contrasting strangely with the beautiful world before my eyes. A crowd of newly-engaged Pagazi are standing before me in the ecstasy of impatience: some poised like cranes upon the right foot, with the left sole placed against the knee, others with their arms thrown in a brotherly fashion round neigh-bours' necks, whilst others squatted in the usual Asiatic and African position, with their posteriora resting upon their calves and heels, their elbows on their thighs, and their chins propped upon their hands, gazed at me with that long longing look which in these lands evidences a something sorely wanted. Presently, from Said bin Majid's home-bound caravan, with which I had consented to travel, shots and a popping of muskets rang through the air: the restless crowd that still watched me ap-peared at the sound of this signal to lose their wits. In a moment the space before the Tembe was cleared. After a few moments, Said bin Salim ran up violently excited, declaring that his orders were of no avail, that some parties were starting with, and others without, their loads, and that no man would take up the burden assigned to him on the yesterday. I directed him to compose himself, and since he could not remain, to pre-cede me with the headstrong gang as far as the Ruche River — the first stage — whence he would send back, as soon as possible, a few men bribed to carry my ham-mock and to remove the loose loads scattered upon the ground. These, as usual on such occasions, were our own. He departed greatly delighting in the opportu-nity of escaping further trouble, and of driving off his six wild slaves in safety: true to his inconsequential

Arabo-African blood, however, neglecting the appointed
station in the eagerness of hurry, he marched on with
Said bin Majid's men to at least double the distance,
thus placing himself out of Kannena's reach, and
throwing all my arrangements into direst confusion.

Meanwhile, having breakfasted, we sat till the afternoon in the now empty and deserted Tembe, expecting
the return of the slaves. As none appeared, I was
induced by the utter misery depicted in the countenances of the Baloch, and trusting that the return-
porters would meet us on the way, to give orders for a
march about 4 P.M., to mount my manchil, and to set
out carried by only two men. Scarcely had I left the
Tembe when a small party, headed by Said bin Salim's
four children, passed by me at speed. Though summoned to halt, they sped onwards, apparently intending
to fetch the loads from the house, and thus to relieve
those left behind as a guard ; it proved afterwards that
they were bound for the bazar to buy plantains for their
patroon. Meanwhile, hurrying on with one Baloch, the
astute Gul Mohammed, Valentine, and three sons of
Ramji, as the shades of evening closed around us, we
reached, without guide or direction from the surly
villagers, the ferry of the Ruche River. Disappointed
at not finding the camp at the place proposed, we were
punted across the Styx-like stream; and for what reason
no man could say, the party took the swampy road along
the Bay of Ukaranga. The mosquitos stung like
wasps ; the loud spoutings and the hollow bursts of
bellow, snort, and grunt of the hippopotami — in these
lands they are brave as the bulls of the Spanish sierras
— and the roar of the old male crocodile startled the
party, whilst the porters had difficulty in preserving
their balance as they waded through water waist-deep,
and crept across plains of mud, mire, and sea-ooze.

As the darkness rendered the march risky, I gave the word, when arrived at a bunch of miserable huts, for a bivouac; the party, had I permitted it, would have wandered through the outer glooms without fixed purpose till permanently bogged. We spread our bedding upon the clear space between the cane-cones acting hovels, and we snatched, under a resplendent moon, and a dew that soaked through the blankets, a few hours of sleep, expecting to be aroused by a guide and porters before the end of night. Gaetano had preceded us with the provisions and the *batterie de cuisine;* we were destitute even of tobacco, and we looked forward expectantly to the march. But the dawn broke, and morning flashed over the canopy above, and the sun poured his hot rays through the cool, clear air, still we found ourselves alone. The sons of Ramji, and the others composing our party, had gradually disappeared, leaving with us only Gul Mohammed. Taking heart of grace, we then cleared out a hut, divided the bedding, lay down in the patience of expectation, and dined on goat. Our neighbour afforded us some food for the mind. Apparently an Androgyne, she had the voice, the look, and the thorax of a man, whilst the dress and the manner argued her to be a woman; it was the only approach to the dubious sex seen by me in East Africa.

About 2 P.M. appeared Ramazan and Salman, children of Said bin Said, with four porters, an insufficient supply for the long and trying march which they described. They insisted upon our enduring the heat and labour of the day so energetically, that they were turned with ignominy out of the village, and were told to send their master to escort us in the evening or on the morning of the next day. Accordingly at 9 A.M. of the 28th May appeared Said bin Salim and the Jemadar, escorted by a full gang of bearers. The former, bursting with irritation, began that loud speaking which in the East is equivalent to impertinence; he was easily silenced by a more explosive and an angrier tone of voice. Having breakfasted, we set out leisurely, and after rejoining Said bin Majid's party we advanced until evening fell upon us at the end of the first day's stage.

I have related the tale of our departure from the Tanganyika somewhat circumstantially : it was truly characteristic of Arab travelling in Eastern Africa. Said bin Salim had scant cause for hurry : slaves rarely desert on the day of departure ; knowing themselves to be watched they wait their opportunity, and find it perhaps — as our caravan discovered to its loss — a week or two afterwards. The Arab was determined to gain a few miles by passing the appointed station; he did so, and he lost two days. In his haste and dread of delay, he had neglected to lay in salt, ghee, or any other stores for the road but grain : consequently he was detained at half a dozen places to procure them. Finally, his froward children, who had done their utmost to waste time in the bazar, were not reproved, much less punished. Truly the half-caste Arab of Zanzibar is almost as futile as the slavish moiety of his ancestry.

There was little novelty in our return-march to Unyamyembe. We took the northerly route, crossing and skirting the lower spurs of the mountains which form the region of Uhha. During the first few stages, being still within the influence of that bag of Æolus, the Tanganyika trough, we endured tornados of wind and heavy rain, thunder and lightning. After the 5th March the threatening clouds drew off, the dank heavy dew diminished, and the weather became clear and hot, with a raw cold eastern wind pouring through the tepid temperature, and causing general sickness. On the 29th May we pitched at Uyonwa, a little settlement of Wabuha, who have already raised crops of sweet potatoes; if they have the sense to avoid keeping cattle, the only attraction to the robber Watuta, they may once more convert the sad waste of Uhha, a wilderness where men are now wolves to one another, into a land smiling with grains and fruits. Beyond Uyonwa we hurried over "neat-tongue" hills, separated by green swamps and black rivulets, with high woody banks, over jungle paths thick with spear and tiger grass, brambly bush and tall growths of wild arrowroot, and over a country for the most part rough and rugged, with here and there an acacia-barren, a bamboo-clump, or a lone Palmyra. Approaching the Rusugi River, which we forded on the 1st June at the upper or Parugerero passage; the regular succession of ridge and swamp gave way to a dry, stony, and thorny slope, rolling with an eastward decline. We delayed for an hour at the Salt-pass, to lay in a supply of the necessary, and the temptation to desert became irresistible. Muhabanya, the "slavey" of the establishment, ran away, carrying off his property and my hatchet. The Jemadar was rendered almost daft by the disappearance of half of his six slaves. A Mnyamwezi porter placed his burden — it was a case of Cognac and vinegar, deeply regretted!— upon the ground, and levanted. Two other porters lost their way, and disappeared for some days; their comrades, standing in awe of the Wavinza, would not venture in search of them. The Kirangozi or Mnyamwezi guide, who had accompanied the Expedition from the coast, remained behind, because his newly-purchased slave-girl had become foot-sore, and unable to advance; finding the case hopeless, he cut off her head, lest of his

evil good might come to another.   The party gave the
usual amount of trouble.   The bull-headed Mabruki
had invested his capital in a small servile, an infant
phenomenon, who, apparently under six years, trotted
manfully alongside the porters, bearing his burden of
hide-bed and water-gourd upon his tiny shoulder.   For
some days he was to his surly master as her first doll to
a young girl : when tired he was mounted upon the
back, and after crossing every swamp his feet were carefully wiped.   When the novelty, however, wore off, the
little unfortunate was so savagely beaten that I insisted
upon his being committed to the far less hard-hearted
Bombay.   The Hanmals who carried my manchil were
the most annoying of their kind.   Wanyamwezi veterans
of the way (their chief man wore a kizbao or waistcoat,
and carried an old Tower musket), originally five in
number, and paid in advance as far as Unyanyembe;
they deserted slowly and surely, till it was necessary to
raise a fresh gang.   For a short time they worked well,
then they fell off.   In the mornings when their names
were called they hid themselves in the huts, or they
squatted pertinaciously near the camp fires, or they
rushed ahead of the party.   On the road they hurried
forwards, recklessly dashing the manchil, without pity
or remorse, against stock and stone.   A man allowed
to lag behind never appeared again on that march, and
more than once they attempted to place the hammock
on the ground and to strike for increase of wages, till
brought to a sense of their duty by a sword-point applied to their ribs.   They would halt for an hour to
boil their sweet potatoes, but if I required the delay of
five minutes, or the advance of five yards, they became
half mad with fidgetiness ; they were as loud-voiced,
noisy and insolent, as turbulent and irritable, as grum-

bling, importunate, and greedy specimens of the genus
homo, species *Africanus*, as I have ever seen, even
amongst the " sons of water " in the canoes of Ujiji.
In these lands, however, the traveller who cannot utilise
the raw material that comes to hand will make but
little progress.

On the 2nd June we fell into our former route at
Jambeho, in the alluvial valley of the Malagarazi River.
The party was pitched in two places by the mismanagement of Said bin Salim; already the porters began to
raise loud cries of Posho! (provaunt!) and their dread
of the Wavinza increased as they approached the
Malagarazi Ferry. The land in the higher levels was
already drying up, the vegetation had changed from
green to yellow, and the strips of grassy and tree-clad
rock, buttressing the left bank of the river, afforded
those magnificent spectacles of conflagration which have
ever been favourite themes with the Indian muse :—

"silence profound
Enwraps the forest, save where bubbling springs
Gush from the rock, or where the echoing hills
Give back the tiger's roar, or where the boughs
Burst into crackling flame and wide extends
The blaze the Dragon's fiery breath has kindled."

WILSON'S *Uttara Rama Cheritra*, act 2.

A sheet of flame, beginning with the size of a spark,
overspread the hill-side, advancing on the wings of the
wind, with the roaring rushing sound of many hosts
where the grass lay thick, shooting huge forky tongues
high into the dark air, where tall trees, the patriarchs
of the forest, yielded their lives to the blast, smouldering
and darkening, as if about to be quenched where the
rock afforded scanty fuel, then flickering, blazing up
and soaring again till topping the brow of the hill, the
sheet became a thin line of fire, and gradually vanished

from the view, leaving its reflection upon the canopy of lurid smoke studded with sparks and bits of live braise, which marked its descent on the other side of the buttress. Resuming our march along the cold and foggy vale of the Malagarazi, and crossing on the third day the stony slabby hills that bound the fluviatile plain northward, we reached, on the 4th June, the dreaded ferry-place of the river.

The great Malagarazi still swollen, though the rains had ceased, by the surplus moisture of the sopped earth, had spread its wide heart of shallow waters, variegated with narrow veins — a deeper artery in the centre showing the main stream — far over the plain. Thus offering additional obstacles to crossing, it was turned to good account by the Mutware, the Lord of the Ferry. On arrival at the Kraal overlooking the river I summoned this Charon, who demanded as his preliminary obolus one pot of oil, seven cloths, and 300 khete of blue porcelains. Said bin Majid, our companion, paid about one-fifth the sum. But the Kraal was uncomfortable, we were stung out by armies of ants; a slight earthquake, at 11.15 A.M., on the 4th June, appeared a bad omen to Said bin Salim: briefly, I was compelled to countenance the extortion. On the next morning we set out, having been cannily preceded by Said bin Majid. Every difficulty was thrown in the way of our boxes and baggage. Often, when I refused the exorbitant sum of four and even five khete per load, the fellows quietly poled off, squatted in their canoes, and required to be summoned back by Said bin Salim with the abjectest concessions. They would not take on board a Goanese or a Baloch without extra pay, and they landed, under some pretext, Said bin Salim and the Jemadar upon a dry knoll in the waste of waters, and demanded and received a cloth before they would rescue them. In these and kindred manœuvres nearly seven hours were expended ; no accidents, however, occurred, and at 4 P.M. we saw ourselves, with hearts relieved of some load, once more at Ugogo, on the left bank of the river. I found my companion, who had preceded me, in treaty for the purchase of a little pig ; fortunately the beads would not persuade the porters to part with it, consequently my pots escaped pollution.

An eventless march of twelve days led from the Malagarazi Ferry to Unyanyembe. Avoiding the *détour* to Msene we followed this time the more direct southern route. I had expected again to find the treacle-like surface over which we had before crept, and perhaps even in a worse state; but the inundations compelled the porters to skirt the little hills bounding the swamps. Provisions—rice, holcus and panicum, manioc, cucumbers and sweet potatoes, pulse, ground-nuts, and tobacco—became plentiful as we progressed ; the arrowroot and the bhang plant flourished wild, and plantains and palmyras were scattered over the land. On the 8th June, emerging from inhospitable Uvinza into neutral ground, we were pronounced to be out of danger, and on the next day, when in the meridian of Usagozi, we were admitted for the first time to the comfort of a village. Three days afterwards we separated from Said bin Majid. Having a valuable store of tusks, he had but half loaded his porters ; he also half fed them : the consequence was that they marched like mad men, and ours followed like a flock of sheep. He would not incur the danger and expense of visiting a settlement, and he pitched in the bush, where provisions were the least obtainable. When I told him that we must part company, he deprecated the measure:

with his stock statement, viz. that at the distance of an hour's march there was a fine safe village full of provisions, and well fitted for a halt. The hour's march proved a long stage of nearly sixteen miles, over a remarkably toilsome country, a foul jungle with tsetse-haunted thorn-bushes, swamps, and inundated lands, ending at a wretched cluster of huts, which could supply nothing but a tough old hen. I was sorry to part with the Arab merchant, a civil man, and a well-informed, yet somewhat addicted to begging like all his people. His marching freaks, however, were unendurable, dawdling at the beginning of the journey, rushing through the middle, and lagging at the end. We afterwards passed him on the road, of course he had been delayed, and subsequently, during a long halt at Unyanyembe, he frequently visited me.

On the 17th June the caravan, after sundry difficulties, caused by desertion, passed on to Irora the village of Salim bin Salih, who this time received us hospitably enough. Thence we first sighted the blue hills of Unyanyembe, our destination. The next day saw us at Yombo, where, by good accident, we met a batch of seven cloth-bales and one box *en route* to Ujiji, under charge of our old enemy Salim bin Sayf of Dut'humi. My complaint against " Msopora," forwarded from Zuryomero, had, after Lieut.-Col. Hamerton's decease, on the 5th July 1857, been laid by M. Cochet, Consul de France, before H. M. the Sayyid Majid,—a fact which accounts for the readiness with which our effects were on this occasion delivered up, and for the non-appearance of the individual in person. We also received the second packet of letters which reached us during that year: as usual, they were full of evil news. Almost every one had lost some relation or friend near and dear to him : even Said bin Salim's hearth had been spoiled of its chief attraction, an only son, who, born it was supposed in consequence of my "barakat" (propitious influence), had been named Abdullah. Such tidings are severely felt by the wanderer who, living long behind the world, and unable to mark its gradual changes, lulls, by dwelling upon the past, apprehension into a belief that his home has known no loss, and who expects again to meet each old familiar face ready to smile upon his return as it was to weep at his departure.

After a day's halt to collect porters at Yombo, we marched from it on the 20th June, and passing the scene of our former miseries, the village under the lumpy hill, "Zimbili," we re-entered Kazeh. There I was warmly welcomed by the hospitable Snay bin Amir, who, after seating us to coffee, as is the custom, for a few minutes in his Barzah or ante-room, led us to the old abode, which had been carefully repaired, swept, and plastered. There a large metal tray bending under succulent dishes of rice and curried fowl, giblets and manioc boiled in the cream of the ground-nut, and sugared omelets flavoured with ghee and onion shreds, presented peculiar attractions to half-starved travellers.

Our return from Ujiji to Unyanyembe was thus accomplished in twenty-two stations, which, halts included, occupied a total of twenty-six days, from the 26th May to the 20th June 1858, and the distance along the road may be computed at 265 statute miles.

After a day's repose at Kazeh, I was called upon, as "etiquette" directs, by the few Arab merchants there present. Musa Mzuri, the Indian, was still absent at

Karagwah, and the greater part of the commercial body was scattered in trading-trips over the country. I had the satisfaction of finding that my last indent on Zanzibar for 400 dollars' worth of cloth and beads had arrived under the charge of Tani bin Sulayyam, who claimed four Gorah or pieces for safe conduct. I also recovered, though not without some display of force, the table and chair left by the escort and the slaves in the Dungomaro Nullah. The articles had been found by one Muinyi Khamisi, a peddling and not over-honest Msawahili, who demanded an unconscionable sum for porterage, and whose head-piece assumed the appearance of a coal scuttle when rewarded with the six cloths proposed by Snay bin Amir. The debauched Wazira, who had remained behind at Msene, appeared with an abundance of drunken smiles, sideling in at the doorway, which he scratched *more Africano* with one set of five nails, whilst the other was applied to a similar purpose *à posteriori*. He was ejected, despite his loud asseverations that he, and he only, could clear us through the dangerous Wagogo. The sons of Ramji, who, travelling from Msene, had entered Kazeh on the day preceding our arrival, came to the house *en masse*, headed by Kidogo, with all the jaunty and *sans-souci* gait and manner of yore. I had imagined that by that time they would have found their way to the coast. I saw no reason, however, for re-engaging them, and they at once returned to the gaieties of their capital.

During the first week following the march all paid the inevitable penalty of a toilsome trudge through a perilous jungly country, in the deadliest season of the year, when the waters are drying up under a fiery sun, and a violent *vent de bise* from the East, which pours through the tepid air like cold water into a warm bath. Again I suffered severely from swelling and numbness of the extremities, and strength returned by tantalisingly slow degrees. My companion was a martyr to obstinate deafness and to a dimness of vision, which incapacitated him from reading, writing, and observing correctly. Both the Goanese were prostrated by fever, followed by severe rheumatism and liver-pains. In the case of Valentine, who, after a few hours lay deprived of sense and sensation, quinine appearing useless — the malady only changed from a quotidian to a tertian type — I resolved to try the Tinctura Warburgii, which had been used with such effect by Lieut.-Col. Hamerton at Zanzibar. " O true apothecary ! " The result was quasi-miraculous. The anticipated paroxysm did not return ; the painful emetism at once ceased ; instead of a death-like lethargy, a sweet childish sleep again visited his aching eyes, and, chief boon of all to those so affected, the corroding thirst gave way to an appetite, followed by sound if not strong digestion. Finally, the painful and dangerous consequences of the disease were averted, and the subsequent attacks were scarcely worthy of notice. I feel bound in justice, after a personal experiment, which ended similarly, to pay this humble tribute of gratitude to Dr. Warburg's invaluable discovery. The Baloch, in their turn, yielded to the effects of malaria, many complained of ulcerations and prurigo, and their recovery was protracted by a surfeit of food and its consequences. But, under the influence of narcotics, tonics, and stimulants, we presently progressed towards convalescence ; and stronger than any physical relief, in my case, was the moral effect of success, and the cessation of the ghastly doubts and cares, and of the terrible wear and tear of mind which, from the coast to Uvira, had never been absent. I felt the proud consciousness of having done my best, under conditions from beginning to end the worst and the most unpromising, and that whatever future evils Fate might have in store for me, that it could not rob me of the meed won by the hardships and sufferings of the past.

Several Arab merchants were preparing to return coastwards for the "Mausim" (monsoon), or Indian trading-season, which, at Zanzibar, includes the months of December, January, and February, and they were not unwilling to avail themselves of my escort. But several reasons detained me at Kazeh. Some time was required to make preparations for the long down march. I had not given up the project of returning · to the seaboard *viâ* Kilwa. Moreover, it was judged advisable to collect from the Arabs details concerning the interesting countries lying to the north and south of the line traversed by the Expedition. As has been mentioned in Chap. XI., the merchants had detailed to me, during my first halt at Kazeh, their discovery of a large Bahr — a sea or lake — lying fifteen or sixteen marches to the north; and from their descriptions and bearings, my companion had laid down the water in a hand-map forwarded to the Royal Geographical Society. All agreed in claiming for it superiority of size over the Tanganyika Lake. I saw at once that the existence of this hitherto unknown basin would explain many discrepancies promulgated by speculative geographers, more especially the notable and deceptive differences of distances, caused by the confusion of the two waters.* Remained only to ascertain if the Arabs

* Mr. Erhardt, for instance, " Memoir on the Chart of East and Central Africa, compiled by J. Erhardt and J. Rebmann, London, 1856," announces the " existence of a Great Lake, called in the south Niandsha (Nyassa), in

had not, with the usual Oriental hyperbole, exaggerated the dimensions of the Northern Lake.

My companion, who had recovered strength from the repose and the comparative comfort of our head-quarters, appeared a fit person to be detached upon this duty; moreover, his presence at Kazeh was by no means desirable. To associate at the same time with Arabs and Anglo-Indians, who are ready to take offence when it is least intended, who expect servility as their due, and whose morgue of colour induces them to treat all skins a shade darker than their own as " niggers," is even more difficult than to avoid a rupture when placed between two friends who have quarrelled with each other. Moreover, in this case, the difficulty was exaggerated by the Anglo-Indian's complete ignorance of Eastern manners and customs, and of any Oriental language beyond, at least, a few words of the debased Anglo-Indian jargon.

I have dwelt upon this subject because my companion has thought proper to represent (in Blackwood, Oct. 1859) that I was "most unfortunately quite done up, but most graciously consented to wait with the Arabs and recruit health." This is far from being the fact. I had other and more important matter to work out. Writing from the spot (Unyanyembe, 2nd July 1858, and published in the Proceedings of the Royal Geographical Society, 24th Jan. 1859) my companion represents the case somewhat differently. " To diminish the disappointment, caused by the short-coming of our cloth, in not seeing the whole of the Sea Ujiji, I have proposed to take a flying trip to the unknown lake, while Captain Burton prepares for our return homewards."

the north Ukerewe, and on the coast Niasa and Bahari ya Uniamesi," makes the distance through Dschaga (Chhaga) and the Masai plains only fifty-nine marches.

On the 30th June the subject was brought forward in the presence of Said bin Salim and the Baloch. The former happily lodged at Kazeh, felt loath to tear himself from the massive arms of his charmer Halimah. He finessed as usual, giving an evasive answer, viz. that he could not decide till the last day, and he declined to influence the escort, who afterwards declared that he had done all in his power to deter them from the journey. In vain my companion threatened him with forfeiture of his reward after he returned to Zanzibar; in vain my companion told him that it was forfeited.* He held firm, and I was not over-anxious in influencing him, well knowing that though the Baloch, a stolid race, might prove manageable, the brain of the Machiavellian Arab, whose egregious selfishness never hesitated at any measure calculated to ensure its gratification, was of a somewhat too heavy metal for the article opposed to it. That Said bin Salim attempted to thwart the project I have no doubt. The Kirangozi, and the fifteen porters hired from his village with the tempting offer of five cloths per man, showed an amount of fear and shirking hardly justified by the real risks of treading so well known a tract. The Jemadar and his men at first positively refused their escort, but the meaning word " Bakhshish " slipping in reassured me. After informing them that in case of recusancy their rations should be stopped, I inquired the amount of *largesse* expected. The ten efficient men composing the guard

* I transcribe the following words from my companion's paper (Blackwood, October 1859): "I urged that it was as much his (Said bin Salim's) duty as mine to go there; and said, unless he changed his present resolution, I should certainly recommend the Government not to pay the gratuity which the consul had promised him on condition that he worked entirely to our satisfaction, in assisting the Expedition to carry out the Government's plans."

demanded fifteen cloths a piece, besides one porter each to carry their matchlocks and pervanents. The number of the porters was reduced, the cloth was procured from an Arab merchant, Sayf bin Said el Wardi, at an expense of one hundred dollars, made payable by draught upon Ladha Damha of Zanzibar: at the same time, the Baloch were warned that they must option between this and the reward conditionally promised to them after return.* Their bad example was followed by the old and faithful servant "Bombay," who required instant dismissal unless he also received cloth before the journey: he was too useful to my companion as interpreter and steward to be lightly parted with. But the granting his claim led to a similar strike and menace on the part of the bull-headed slave Mabruki, who, being merely a "head-ache" to me, at once "got the sack" till he promised, if pardoned, to shake off his fear, and not to be naughty in future. By dint of severe exertion my companion was enabled to leave Kazeh on the 10th July.

I proceed to recount the most important portion of the information — for ampler details the reader is referred to the Journal of the Royal Geographical Society — collected during my halt at Kazeh from various sources, Arab and African, especially from Snay bin Amir, concerning—

---

* So my report printed in the Proceedings Roy. Geog. Soc. loco cit. "Our asses, thirty in number, all died, our porters ran away, our goods were left behind; our black escort became so unmanageable as to require dismissal; the weakness of our party invited attacks, and our wretched Baloch deserted us in the jungle, and throughout have occasioned an infinity of trouble."

THE NORTHERN KINGDOMS : KARAGWAH, UGANDA,
AND UNYORO.

The extensive and hitherto unknown countries described in this chapter, being compact despotisms, resembling those of Ashanti and Dahomey more than the
semi-monarchies of Unyamwezi and Urundi, or the
barbarous republics of Uvinza and Ujiji, are designated
the Northern Kingdoms. It is regrettable that oral
information, and not the results of actual investigation,
are offered to the reader concerning regions so interesting as the Southern Tanganyika, the Northern Kingdoms, and the provinces south of Unyanyembe. But
absolute obstacles having interfered, it was judged
advisable to use the labours of others rather than to
omit all notice of a subject which has the importance
of novelty, because it lacked the advantages of a regular
exploration.

Informants agree in representing the northern races
as superior in civilisation and social constitution to the
other tribes of Eastern and Central Africa. Like the
subjects of the Kazembe, they have built extensive and
regular settlements, and they reverence even to worship
a single despot, who rules with a rigour which in Europe
would be called barbarity. Having thrown off the rude
equality of their neighbours, they recognise ranks in
society ; there is order amongst men, and some idea of
honour in women ; they add to commerce credit, without which commerce can hardly exist ; and they hospitably entertain strangers and guests. These accounts
are confirmed by the specimens of male and female
slaves from Karagwah and Uganda seen at Unyan-

yembe: between them and the southern races there is a marked physical difference. Their heads are of a superior cast: the regions where the reflective faculties and the moral sentiments, especially benevolence, are placed, rise high; the nose is more of the Caucasian type; the immoderate masticating apparatus which gives to the negro and the lower negroid his peculiar aspect of animality, is greatly modified, and the expression of the countenance is soft, kindly, and not deficient in intelligence.

From Unyanyembe to Kibuga, the capital of Uganda, are fifty-three stages, which are distributed into four crucial stations of Usui, Karagwah, dependent Unyoro, and Uganda. A few remarks concerning each of these divisions may not be unacceptable.

Between Unyanyembe and Usui are sixteen long, or nineteen short, stages. Though the road is for the most part rough and hilly, the marches can scarcely be reduced below ten statute, or six rectilinear geo. miles per diem; in fact, the geographer's danger when making these estimates is, that of falling, through fear of exaggeration, into the opposite and equally incorrect extreme. The general direction of the line leading from Kazeh, in Unyanyembe, to Karagwah, pointed out by Snay bin Amir, bore 345° (corrected 332°); the length of the nineteen marches would be about 115 geo. miles. The southern frontier of Usui may, therefore, be safely placed in S. lat. 3° 10′.

The route from Kazeh to Usui falls at once westward of the line leading to the Nyanza Lake; it diverges, however, but little at first, as they both traverse the small districts of Ulikampuri, Unyambewa, and Ukuni. Usonga, crossed in five short marches, is the first considerable district north of Unyanyembe. Thence the

road enters the province of Utumbara, which is flanked
on the east by Usambiro, and on the west by Uyungu,
governed by the Muhinda Sultan, Kanze. Utumbara,
as has been mentioned, was lately plundered, and
Ruhembe, its chief, was slain, by the predatory Watuta.
In Utumbara and Usambiro the people are chiefly the
Wafyoma, a tribe of Wanyamwezi : they are a commercial race, like the Wajiji — trafficking in hoes and ivory ;
and their present Sultan, Mutawazi, has often been
visited by the Arabs. Uyofu, governed by Mnyamu-
runda, is the northern boundary of Unyamwezi, after
which the route enters the ill famed territory of
Usui.

Usui is traversed in seven marches, making a sum of
twenty-six from Kazeh. According to the former computation, a total march of about 156 geo. miles would
place the southern frontier of Karagwah in S. lat. 2° 40'.
The road in several parts discloses a view of the Nyanza
Lake. Usui is described as a kind of neutral ground
between the rolling plateau of Unyamwezi and the
highlands of Karagwah : it is broken by ridges in two
places — Nyakasene the fourth, and Ruhembe the
seventh stage, where mention is also made of a small
stream. From this part of the country a wild nutmeg
is brought to Kazeh by caravans : the Arabs declare
that it grows upon the well-wooded hills, and the only
specimen shown was heavy and well flavoured, presenting a marked contrast to the poor produce of Zanzibar
island.

The Wasúí, according to the Arabs, are not Wanyamwezi. They are considered dangerous, and they
have frequently cut off the route to caravans from
Karagwah. Their principal sultan, a Muhinda named
Suwarora, demands exorbitant blackmail, and is de-

scribed as troublesome and overbearing: his bad example has been imitated by his minor chiefs.

The kingdom of Karagwah, which is limited on the north by the Kitangure or Kitangule River, a great western influent of the Nyanza Lake, occupies twelve days in traversing. The usual estimate would thus give it a depth of 72, and place the northern limit bout 228 rectilinear geo. miles from Kazeh, or in S. lat. 1° 40'. But the Kitangure River, according to the Arabs, falls into the Nyanza diagonally from south-west to north-east. Its embouchure will, therefore, not be distant from the equator. The line of road is thus described: After ascending the hills of Ruhembe the route, deflecting eastward, pursues for three days the lacustrine plain of the Nyanza. At Tenga, the fourth station, the first gradient of the Karagwah mountains is crossed, probably at low levels, where the spurs fall towards the lake. Kafuro is a large district where merchants halt to trade, in the vicinity of Weranhánjá, the royal settlement, which commands a distant view of the Nyanza. Nyakahanga, the eighth stage, is a gradient similar to that of Tenga; and Magugi, the tenth station, conducts the traveller to the northernmost ridge of Karagwah. The mountains are described as abrupt and difficult, but not impracticable for laden asses: they are compared by the Arabs to the Rubeho chain of Usagara. This would raise them about 4000 feet above the mean level of the Unyamwezi plateau and the Nyanza water, and about 8000 feet above this sea. Their surface, according to the Arabs, is alternately earth and stone, the former covered with plantains and huge timber-trees, the latter bare, probably by reason of their altitude. There are no plains, bush, or jungle, but the deep ravines and the valleys intersecting the various ridges drain the surface of the hills, and are the sites of luxuriant cultivation. The people of Karagwah, averse to the labour of felling the patriarchs of the forest, burn "*bois de vache*," like the natives of Usukuma. North of Magugi, at Katanda, a broad flat extends eastwards: the path thence descends the northern counterslope, and falls into the alluvial plain of the Kitungure River.

Karagwah is thus a mass of highlands, bounded on the north by dependent Unyoro, on the south by Usui, eastward by the tribes of Wahayya and Wapororo, upon the lacustrine plain of the Nyanza; on the south-west it inosculates with Urundi, which has been described as extending from the north-eastern extremity of the Tanganyika Lake. Its equatorial position and its altitude enable it to represent the Central African prolongation of the Lunar Mountains. Ptolemy describes this range, which he supposes to send forth the White Nile, as stretching across the continent for a distance of 10° of longitude. For many years this traditional feature has somewhat fallen into discredit: some geographers have changed the direction of the line, which, like the Himalayas, forms the base of the South African triangle from east and west to north and south, thus converting it into a formation akin to the ghauts or lateral ranges of the Indian peninsula; whilst others have not hesitated to cast ridicule upon the mythus. From the explorations of the "Mombas Mission" in Usumbara, Chhaga, and Kitui, and from the accounts of Arab visitors to the lands of Umasai and the kingdom of Karagwah, it appears that from the fifth parallel of S. lat. to the equator, an elevated mass of granite and sandstone formation crosses from the shores of the Indian Ocean to the centre of Tropical

Africa. The vast limestone band which extends from
the banks of the Burramputra to those of the Tagus
appears to be prolonged as far south as the Eastern
Horn, and near the equator to give place to sandstone formations. The line is not, however, as might
be expected from analogy with the Himalayan, a
continuous unbroken chain; it consists of insulated
mountains, apparently volcanic, rising from elevated
plains, and sometimes connected by barren and broken
ridges. The south-eastern threshold of the Lunar cor-
dillera is the highland region of Usumbara, which may
attain the height of 3000 or 4000 feet above sea-level.
It leads by a succession of mountain and valley to
Chhaga, whose apex is the "Æthiopian Olympus,"
Kilima-Ngao. From this corner-pillar the line trends
westward, and the route to Burkene passes along the
base of the principal elevations, Doengo Engai and
Endia Siriani. Beyond Burkene lies the Nyanza Lake,
in a huge gap which, breaking the continuity of the
line, drains the regions westward of Kilima-Ngao,
whilst those to the eastward, the Pangani and other
similar streams, discharge their waters to the south-
east into the Indian Ocean. The kingdom of Karagwah
prolongs the line to Urundi, upon the Tanganyika
Lake, where the south-western spurs of the Lunar
Mountains form a high continuous belt. Mr. Petherick,
of Khartum, travelling twenty-five marches, each of
twenty miles (?), in a south-south-western and due-
southerly direction from the Bahr el Ghazal, found a
granitic ridge rising, he supposes 2000 to 2500 feet
above the plain, near the equator, and lying nearly
upon the same parallel of latitude, and in about 27° E.
long. Beyond that point the land is still unexplored.
Thence the mountains may sink into the great Depres-

sion of Central Africa, or, deflected northwards of the
kingdom of Uropua, they may inosculate with the ridge
which, separating the northern negroid races of Islamised Africa from their negro brethren to the south, is
popularly known, according to Denham and Clapperton,
as el-Gibel Gumhr,—Jebel Kamar,—or Mons Lunæ.

The high woody hills of Karagwah attract a quantity
of rain. The long and copious wet monsoon divides
the year into two seasons—a winter of seven or eight,
and a summer of four or five months. The Vuli, or
lesser rains, commence, as at Zanzibar, with the Nayruz
(29th of August); and they continue with little intermis-
sion till the burst of the Masika, which lasts in Karagwah
from October to May or June. The winds, as in
Unyamwezi, are the Kaskazi, or north and north-east
gales, which shift during the heavier falls of rain to the
Kosi, the west and south-west. Storms of thunder and
lightning are frequent, and the Arabs compare the
down-pour rather to that of Zanzibar island than to the
scanty showers of Unyamwezi. The sowing season at
Karagwah, as at Msene and Ujiji, begins with the
Vuli, when maize and millet, the voandzeia, various
kinds of beans and pulse, are committed to the well-
hoed ground. Rice being unknown, the people depend
much upon holcus: this cereal, which is sown in October to prepare for the Masika in November, has, in
the mountains, a short cane and a poor insipid grain of
the red variety. The people convert it into pombe;
and they make the wine called mawa from the plantains,
which in several districts are more abundant than the
cereals. Karagwah grows according to some, according to others imports from the northern countries,
along the western margin of the Nyanza Lake, a small
wild coffee, locally called mwámí. Like all wild pro-

ductions, it is stunted and undeveloped, and the bean, which, when perfect, is about the size of a corking-pin's head, is never drunk in decoction. The berry gathered unripe is thrown into hot water to defend it from rot, or to prevent its drying too rapidly — an operation which converts the husk to a dark chocolate colour — the people of this country chew it like tobacco, and, during visits, a handful is invariably presented to the guest. According to the Arabs, it has, like the kishr of Yemen, stimulating properties, affects the head, prevents somnolency, renders water sweet to the taste, and forms a pleasant refreshing beverage, which the palate, however, never confounds with the taste of the Mocha-berry. In Karagwah a single khete of beads purchases a kubabah (from 1 lb. to 2 lbs.) of this coffee; at Kazeh and Msene, where it is sometimes brought by caravans, it sells at fancy prices. Another well-known production of all these regions is the mt'hípí-t'hípí, or Abrus precatorius, whose scarlet seeds are converted into ornaments for the head.

The cattle is a fine variety, with small humps and large horns, like that of Ujiji and Uviva. The herds are reckoned by Gundu, or stallions, in the proportion of 1 to 100 cows. The late Sultan Ndagara is said to have owned 200 Gundu, or 20,000 cows, which late civil wars have reduced to 12,000 or 13,000. In Karagwah cattle forms wealth, and everywhere in Africa wealth, and wealth only, secures defenders and dependants. The surplus males are killed for beef; this meat, with milk in its various preparations, and a little of the fine white hill-honey, forms the food of the higher classes.

The people of Karagwah, who are not, according to South African fashion, called Wakaragwah, are divided into two orders — Wahuma and Wanyambo — who seem to bear to each other the relation of patron and client, patrician and plebeian. The Wahuma comprises the rich, who sometimes possess 1000 head of cattle, and the warriors, a militia paid in the milk of cows allotted to their temporary use by the king. The Wanyambo — Fellahs or Ryots — are, it is said, treated by the nobles as slaves. The men of Karagwah are a tall stout race, doubtless from the effect of pure mountain-air and animal food. Corpulence is a beauty: girls are fattened to a vast bulk by drenches of curds and cream thickened with flour, and are duly disciplined when they refuse. The Arabs describe them as frequently growing to a monstrous size, like some specimens of female Boers mentioned by early travellers in Southern Africa. Fresh milk is the male, sour the female beverage. The complexion is a brown yellow, like that of the Warundi. The dress of the people, and even of the chiefs, is an apron of close-grained mbugu, or bark-cloth, softened with oil, and crimped with fine longitudinal lines made with a batten or pounding club. In shape it resembles the flap of an English saddle, tied by a prolongation of the upper corners round the waist. To this scarcely decent article the chiefs add a languti, or Indian-T-bandage of goat's skin. Nudity is not uncommon, and nubile girls assume the veriest apology for clothing, which is exchanged after marriage for short kilts and breast coverings of skin. Both sexes wear tiara-shaped and cravat-formed ornaments of the crimson abrus-seed, pierced and strung upon mondo, the fine fibre of the mwale or raphia-palm. The weapons are bows and arrows, spears, knobsticks, and knives ; the ornaments are beads and coil-bracelets, which, with cattle, form the marriage settlement. The huts are of the conical and circular African shape, with walls of stakes

and roofs so carefully thatched that no rain can penetrate them: the villages, as in Usagara, are scattered
upon the crests and ridges of the hills.

The Mkámá, or Sultan of Karagwah, in 1858, was
Armanika, son of Ndagara, who, although the dignity
is in these lands hereditary, was opposed by his younger
brother Rumanika. The rebel, after an obstinate
attack, was routed by Suna, the late despot af Uganda,
who, bribed by the large present of ivory, which was
advanced by Musa Mzuri of Kazeh, then trading with
Armanika, threw a large force into the field. Rumanika
was blinded and pensioned, and about four years ago
peace was restored. Armanika resides in the central
district, Weranhanja, and his settlement, inhabited only
by the royal family, contains from forty to fifty huts.
He is described as a man about thirty to thirty-five
years old, tall, sturdy, and sinewy-limbed, resembling
the Somal. His dress is, by preference, the mbugu, or
bark-cloth, but he has a large store of fine raiment
presented by his Arab visitors : in ornaments he is distinguished by tight gaiters of beads extending from
knee to ankle. His diet is meat and milk, with sometimes a little honey, plantains, and grain : unlike his
subjects, he eschews mawa and pombe. He has about
a dozen wives, an unusually moderate allowance for an
African chief, and they have borne him ten or eleven
children. The royal family is said to be a race of
centagenarians ; they are buried in their garments,
sitting and holding their weapons : when the king dies
there is a funeral feast.

Under the Mkama is a single minister, who takes the
title of Muhinda, and presides over the Wakungu,
elders and headmen, whose duty it is to collect and to
transmit to the monarch once every month his revenues,

in the shape of slaves and ivory, cattle and provisions.
Milk must be forwarded by proprietors of cows and
herds even from a distance of three days' march.
Armanika is an absolute ruler, and he governs without
squeamishness.   Adulterers are punished by heavy fines
in cattle, murderers are speared and beheaded, rebels
and thieves are blinded by gouging out the eyes with the
finger-joints of the right-hand, and severing the muscles.
Subjects are forbidden to sell milk to those who eat
beans or salt, for fear of bewitching the animals.   The
Mkama, who lives without state or splendour, receives
travellers with courtesy.   Hearing of their approach, he
orders his slaves to erect four or five tents for shelter,
and he greets them with a large present of provisions.
He demands no blackmail, but the offerer is valued
according to his offerings : the return gifts are carefully
proportioned, and for beads which suit his taste he has
sent back an acknowledgment of fifty slaves and forty
cows.   The price of adult male slaves varies from eight
to ten fundo of white, green, or blue porcelain-beads : a
woman in her prime costs two kitindi (each equal to one
dollar on the coast), and five or six fundo of mixed
beasts.   Some of these girls, being light-coloured and
well favoured, sell for sixty dollars at Zanzibar.   The
merchants agree in stating that a European would receive in Karagwah the kindest welcome, but that to
support the dignity of the white face a considerable
sum would be required.   Arabs still visit Armanika to
purchase slaves, cattle, and ivory, the whitest and
softest, the largest and heaviest in this part of Central
Africa.   The land is rich in iron, and the spears of
Karagwah, which are, to some extent, tempered, are
preferred to the rude work of the Wafyoma.   Sulphur
is found, according to the Arabs, near hot springs

amongst the mountains. A species of manatus (?) supplies a fine skin used for clothing. The simbi, or cowrie (Cypræa), is the minor currency of the country: it is brought from the coast by return caravans of Wanyamwezi.

The country of Karagwah is at present the head-quarters of the Watosi, a pastoral people who are scattered throughout these Lake Regions. They came, according to tradition, from Usingo, a mountain district lying to the north of Uhha. They refuse to carry loads, to cultivate the ground, or to sell one another. Harmless, and therefore unarmed, they are often plundered, though rarely slain, by other tribes, and they protect themselves by paying fees in cattle to the chiefs. When the Wahinda are sultans, the Watosi appear as councillors and elders; but whether this rank is derived from a foreign and superior origin, or is merely the price of their presents, cannot be determined. In appearance they are a tall, comely, and comparatively fair people; hence in some parts every "distinguished foreigner" is complimented by being addressed as "Mtosi." They are said to derive themselves from a single ancestor, and to consider the surrounding tribes as serviles, from whom they will take concubines, but to whom they refuse their daughters. Some lodges of this people were seen about Unyanyembe and Msene, where they live by selling cattle, milk, and butter. Their villages are poor, dirty, and unpalisaded; mere scatters of ragged round huts. They have some curious practices: never eat out of their own houses, and, after returning from abroad, test, by a peculiar process, the fidelity of their wives before anointing themselves and entering their houses. The Arabs declare that they are known by their black gums, which they consider a beauty.

The last feature of importance in Karagwah is the Kitangure River on its northern frontier. This stream, deriving its name from a large settlement on its banks, according to some travellers flows through a rocky trough, according to others it traverses a plain. Some, again, make it thirty yards, others 600, and even half a mile, in breadth. All these statements are reconcileable. The river issues from Higher Urundi, not far from the Malagarazi; but whilst the latter, engaged in the Depression of Central Africa, is drawn towards the Tanganyika, the former, falling into the counterslope, is directed to the north-east into the Nyanza Lake. Its course would thus lie through a mountain-valley, from which it issues into a lacustrine plain, the lowlands of Unyoro and Uganda. The dark and swift stream must be crossed in canoes even during the dry season, but, like the Malagarazi, about June or at the end of the rains, it debords over the swampy lands of its lower course.

From the Kitangure River fifteen stations conduct the traveller to Kibuga, the capital district of Uganda, and the residence of its powerful despot. The maximum of these marches would be six daily, or a total of ninety rectilinear geographical miles. Though there are no hills, the rivers and rivulets — said to be upwards of a hundred in number — offer serious obstacles to rapid travelling. Assuming then, the point where the Kitangure River is crossed to be in S. lat. 1° 14', Kibuga may be placed in S. lat. 0° 10'. Beyond Weranhanja no traveller with claims to credibility has seen the Nyanza water. North of Kibuga all is uncertain; the Arabs were not permitted by Suna, the last despot, to penetrate farther north.

The two first marches from the Kitangure River

traverse the territory of "dependent Unyoro," so called
because it has lately become subject to the Sultan of
Uganda.   In former times Unyoro in crescent-shape,
with the cusps fronting eastwards and westwards, almost
encompassed Uganda.   From dependent Unyoro the
path, crossing a tract of low jungle, enters Uganda in
the concave of the crescent.   The tributary Wahayya,
under Gaetawa, their sultan, still extend to the eastward.
North of the Wahayya, of whose territory little is
known, lies "Kittara," in Kinyoro (or Kiganda?), a word
interpreted to mean "mart," or "meeting-place."   This
is the region which supplies Karagwah with coffee.
The shrub is propagated by sowing the bean.   It attains
the height of five feet, branching out about half-way ; it
gives fruit after the third, and is in full vigour after the
fifth year.   Before almost every hut-door there is a
plantation, forming an effective feature in the landscape
of rolling and wavy hill, intersected by a network of
rivers and streams : the foliage is compared to a green
tapestry veiling the ground ; and at times, when the
leaves are stripped off by wind and rain, the plant
appears decked with brilliant crimson cherry-like
berries.   The Katonga River, crossed at Kitutu, is supposed to fall into the Nyanza, the general recipient of
the network of streams about Karagwah.   This diago-
nality may result from the compound incline produced
by the northern counterslope of the mountains of
Karagwah and the south-westward depression necessary
to form and to supply the lake.   The Katonga is a
sluggish and almost stagnant body of considerable
breadth, and when swollen it arrests the progress of
caravans.   Some portions of the river are crossed,
according to the Arabs, over a thick growth of aquatic
vegetation, which forms a kind of matwork, capable of

supporting a man's weight, and cattle are towed over in the more open parts by cords attached to their horns. Four stations lead from the Katonga River to Kibuga, the capital district of Uganda.

Kibuga is the residence of the great Mkámá or chief of Uganda. Concerning its population and peculiarities the Arabs must be allowed to tell their own tale. "Kibuga, the settlement, is not less than a day's journey in length; the buildings are of cane and rattan. The sultan's palace is at least a mile long, and the circular huts, neatly ranged in line, are surrounded by a strong fence which has only four gates. Bells at the several entrances announce the approach of strangers, and guards in hundreds attend there at all hours. They are commanded by four chiefs, who are relieved every second day: these men pass the night under hides raised upon uprights, and their heads are forfeited if they neglect to attend to the summons of the king. The harem contains about 3000 souls — concubines, slaves, and children. No male nor adult animal may penetrate, under pain of death, beyond the Barzah, a large vestibule or hall of audience where the king dispenses justice and receives his customs. This palace has often been burned down by lightning: on these occasions the warriors must assemble and extinguish the fire by rolling over it. The chief of Uganda has but two wants with which he troubles his visitors—one, a medicine against death; the other, a charm to avert the thunderbolt: and immense wealth would reward the man who could supply either of these desiderata."

Suna, the great despot of Uganda, a warlike chief, who wrested dependent Unyoro from its former possesssor, reigned till 1857. He perished in the prime of life and suddenly, as the Arabs say, like Namrud,

whilst riding " pickaback " — the state carriage of
Central Africa — upon a minister's shoulders, he was
struck by the shaft of the destroyer in the midst of
his mighty host. As is the custom of barbarous and
despotic races, the event was concealed for some months.
When the usual time had expired, one of his many
sons, exchanging his heir-elective name " Sámunjú " for
Mtesa, became king. The court usage compels the
newly elected chief to pass two years in retirement,
committing state affairs to his ministers ; little, therefore,
is yet known of him. As he will certainly tread in the
footsteps of his sire, the Arabs may again be allowed to
describe the state and grandeur of the defunct Suna ;
and as Suna was in fact the whole kingdom of Uganda,
the description will elucidate the condition of the people
in general.

" The army of Uganda numbers at least 300,000 men ;
each brings an egg to muster, and thus something like
a reckoning of the people is made. Each soldier carries
one spear, two assegais, a long dagger, and a shield,
bows and swords being unknown. When marching the
host is accompanied by women and children carrying
spare weapons, provisions, and water. In battle they
fight to the sound of drums, which are beaten with
sticks like those of the Franks : should this performance
cease, all fly the field. Wars with the Wanyoro, the
Wasoga, and other neighbours are rendered almost
chronic by the policy as well as the pleasure of the
monarch, and there are few days on which a foraging
party does not march from or return to the capital.
When the king has no foreign enemies, or when the
exchequer is indecently deficient, he feigns a rebellion,
attacks one of his own provinces, massacres the chief
men, and sells off the peasantry. Executions are

frequent, a score being often slain at a time: when remonstrated with concerning this barbarity, Suna declared that he had no other secret for keeping his subjects in awe of him, and for preventing conspiracies. Sometimes the king would accompany his army to a battue of game, when the warriors were expected to distinguish themselves by attacking the most ferocious beasts without weapons: even the elephant, borne down by numbers, yielded to the grasp of man. When passing a village he used to raise a shout, which was responded to by a loud flourish of horns, reed-pipes, iron whistles, and similar instruments. At times he decreed a grand muster of his soldiery: he presented himself sitting before his gate, with a spear in the right hand, and holding in the left the leash of a large and favourite dog resembling an Arab suluki or greyhound. The master of the hounds was an important personage. Suna took great pleasure in witnessing trials of strength, the combatants contending with a mixture of slapping and pushing till one fell to the ground. He had a large menagerie of lions, elephants, leopards, and similar beasts of disport, to whom he would sometimes give a criminal as a 'curée:' he also kept for amusement fifteen or sixteen albinos; and so greedy was he of novelty that even a cock of peculiar or uniform colour would have been forwarded by its owner to feed his eyes."

Suna when last visited by the Arabs was a "red man," aged about forty-five, tall, robust, and powerful of limb, with a right kingly presence and a warrior carriage. His head was so shaven as to leave what the Omani calls "el Kishshah," a narrow crest of hair like a cock's comb, from nape to brow; nodding and falling over his face under its weight of strung beads, it gave

him a fierce and formidable aspect. This tonsure,
confined to those about the palace, distinguishes its
officers and inmates, servile as well as free, from the
people. The Ryots leave patches of hair where they
please, but they may not shave the whole scalp under
pain of death, till a royal edict unexpectedly issued at
times commands every head to shed its honours. Suna
never appeared in public without a spear; his dress
was the national costume, a long piece of the fine
crimped mbugu or bark-cloth manufactured in these
regions, extending from the neck to the ground. He
made over to his women the rich clothes presented by
the Arabs, and allowed them to sew with unravelled
cotton thread, whereas the people under severe penalties
were compelled to use plantain fibre. No commoner
could wear domestics or similar luxuries ; and in the
presence, the accidental exposure of a limb led, according to the merchants, to the normal penalty — death.

Suna, like the northern despots generally, had a
variety of names, all expressing something bitter,
mighty, or terrible, as, for instance, Lbare, the Al-
mighty (?) ; Mbidde and Purgoma, a lion. He could
not understand how the Sultan of Zanzibar allowed
his subjects treasonably to assume the name of their
ruler ; and besides mortifying the Arabs by assuming
an infinite superiority over their prince, he shocked
them by his natural and unaffected impiety. He
boasted to them that he was the god of earth, as their
Allah was the Lord of Heaven. He murmured loudly
against the abuse of lightning; and he claimed from
his subjects divine honours, which were as readily
yielded to him as by the facile Romans to their emperors.
No Mgándá would allow the omnipotence of his sultan
to be questioned, and a light word concerning him

would have imperilled a stranger's life. Suna's domestic
policy reminds the English reader of the African peculiarities which form the groundwork of " Rasselas."
His sons, numbering more than one hundred, were
removed from the palace in early youth to separate
dungeons, and so secured with iron collars and fetters
fastened to both ends of a long wooden bar that the
wretches could never sit, and without aid could neither
rise nor lie. The heir-elective was dragged from his
chains to fill a throne, and the cadets will linger
through their dreadful lives, unless wanted as sovereigns,
until death release them. Suna kept his female children
under the most rigid surveillance within the palace : he
had, however, a favourite daughter named Nasuru,
whose society was so necessary to him that he allowed
her to appear with him in public.

The principal officers under the despot of Uganda
are, first, the Kimara Vyona (literally the " finisher of
all things ") : to him, the chief civilian of the land, the
city is committed ; he also directs the kabaka or village
headmen. The second is the Sakibobo or commander-
in-chief, who has power over the Sáwágánzí, the life-
guards and slaves, the warriors and builders of the
palace. Justice is administered in the capital by the
sultan, who, though severe, is never accused of per-
verting the law, which here would signify the ancient
custom of the country. A Mhozi — Arabised to Hoz,
and compared with the Kazi of el Islam — dispenses in
each town criminal and civil rights. The only punishments appear to be death and mulcts. Capital offenders
are beheaded or burned; in some cases they are flayed
alive; the operation commences with the face, and the
skin, which is always much torn by the knife, is stuffed
as in the old torturing days of Asia. When a criminal

absconds, the males of his village are indiscriminately slain and the women are sold — blood and tears must flow for discipline. In money suits each party begins by placing before the Mhozi a sum equivalent to the disputed claim; the object is to prevent an extensive litigiousness. Suna used to fine by fives or tens, dozens or scores, according to the offender's means; thus from a wealthy man he would take twenty male and twenty female slaves, with a similar number of bulls and cows, goats and kids, hens and even eggs. One of his favourites, who used constantly to sit by him on guard, matchlock in hand, was Isa bin Hosayn, a Baloch mercenary of H. H. Sayyid Said of Zanzibar. He had fled from his debtors, and had gradually wandered to Uganda, where the favour of the sovereign procured him wealth in ivory, and a harem containing from 200 to 300 women. " Mzagayya,"— the hairy one, as he was locally called, from his long locks and bushy beard — was not permitted, nor probably did he desire, to quit the country; after his patron's death he fled to independent Unyoro, having probably raised up, as these adventurers will, a host of enemies at Uganda.

Suna greatly encouraged, by gifts and attention, the Arab merchants to trade in his capital; the distance has hitherto prevented more than half-a-dozen caravans travelling to Kibuga; all however came away loudly praising his courtesy and hospitality. To a poor trader he has presented twenty slaves, and an equal number of cows, without expecting any but the humblest return. The following account of a visit paid to him in 1852, by Snay bin Amir, may complete his account of the despot Uganda. When the report of arrival was forwarded by word of mouth to Suna, he issued orders for the erection of as many tents as might be necessary. The guest, who was welcomed with joyful tumult by a crowd of gazers, and was conducted to the newly-built quarters, where he received a present of· bullocks and grain, plantains and sugar-canes. After three or four days for repose, he was summoned to the Barzah or audience hall, ontside of which he found a squatting body of about 2000 guards armed only with staves. Allowed to retain his weapons, he entered with an interpreter and saluted the chief, who, without rising, motioned his guest to sit down in front of him. Suna's only cushion was a mbugu ; his dress was of the same stuff ; two spears lay close at hand, and his dog was as usual by his side. The Arab thought proper to assume the posture of homage, namely, to sit upon his shins, bending his back, and, with eyes fixed on the ground — he had been cautioned against staring at the " god of earth," — to rest his hands upon his lap. The levee was full ; at a distance of fifty paces between the king and the guards sat the ministers ; and inside the palace, so placed that they could see nothing but the visitor's back, were the principal women, who are forbidden to gaze at or to be gazed at by a stranger. The room was lit with torches of a gummy wood, for Suna, who eschewed pombe, took great plea-sure in these audiences, which were often prolonged from sunset to midnight.

The conversation began with a string of questions concerning Zanzibar, the route, the news, and the other staple topics of barbarous confabulation ; when it flagged, a minister was called up to enliven it. No justice was ad-ministered nor present offered during the first audience ; it concluded with the despot rising, at which signal all dispersed. At the second visit Snay presented his blackmail, which consisted of ten cotton cloths, and one hundred fundo of coral, and other porcelain beads. The return was an offering of two ivories and a pair of serviles; every day, moreover, flesh and grain, fruit and milk were supplied without charge; whenever the wish was expressed, a string of slave-girls presently appeared bending under loads of the article in question; and it was intimated to the "king's stranger" that he might lay hands upon whatever he pleased, animate or inanimate. Snay, however, was too wise to avail himself of this truly African privilege. During the four interviews which followed, Suna proved himself a man of intelligence: he inquired about the Wazungu or Europeans, and professed to be anxious for a closer alliance with the Sultan of Zanzibar. When Snay took leave he received the usual present of provisions for the road, and 200 guards prepared to escort him, an honour which he respectfully declined: Suna offered to send with him several loads of elephants' tusks as presents to H. H. the Sayyid; but the merchant declined to face with them the difficulties and dangers of Usúí. Like all African chiefs, the despot considered these visits as personal honours paid to himself; his pride therefore peremptorily forbade strangers to pass northwards of his capital, lest the lesser and hostile chiefs might boast a similar brave. According to Snay, an European would be received with distinction, if travelling with supplies to support his dignity. He would depend, however, upon his ingenuity and good fortune upon further progress; and perhaps the most feasible plan to explore the water-shed north of the Nyanza Lake would be to buy or to build, with the permission of the reigning monarch, boats upon the nearest western shore. Suna himself, had, according to Snay, constructed a flotilla of matumbi or undecked vessels similar in shape to the Mtope or

Muntafiyah—the modern "Ploiaria Rhapta" of the Sawahili coast from Lamu to Kilwa.

Few details were given by the Arabs concerning the vulgar herd of Waganda: they are, as has been remarked, physically a finer race than the Wayamwezi, and they are as superior in character; more docile and better disciplined, they love small gifts, and show their gratitude by prostrating themselves before the donor. The specimens of slaves seen at Kazeh were, however, inferior to the mountaineers of Karagwah; the complexion was darker, and the general appearance more African. Their language is, to use an Arab phrase, like that of birds, soft and quickly spoken; the specimens collected prove without doubt that it belongs to the Zangian branch of the great South-African family. Their normal dress is the mbugu, under which, however, all wear the " languti " or Indian-T-bandage of goatskin; women appear in short kilts and breast-coverings of the same material. Both sexes decorate their heads with the tiara of abrus-seeds alluded to when describing the people of Karagwah. As sumptuary laws impede the free traffic of cloth into Uganda, the imports are represented chiefly by beads, cowries, and brass and copper wires. The wealth of the country is in cattle, ivory, and slaves, the latter often selling for ten fundo of beads, and the same sum will purchase the Wasoga and Wanyoro captives from whom the despot derives a considerable portion of his revenues. The elephant is rare in Uganda; tusks are collected probably by plunder from Usoga, and the alakah of about ninety Arab pounds is sold for two slaves, male or female. The tobacco, brought to market in leaf, as in Ujiji, and not worked, as amongst the other tribes, is peculiarly good. Flesh, sweet potatoes, and the highly nutritious plantain, which grows in groves a whole day's march long, are the chief articles of diet ; milk is drunk by women only, and ghee is more valued for unction than for cookery. The favourite inebrients are mawa and pombe ; the latter is served in neatly carved and coloured gourds, and the contents are imbibed, like sherry cobbler, through a reed.

From Kibuga the Arabs have heard that between fifteen and twenty marches lead to the Kivira River, a larger and swifter stream than the Katonga, which forms the northern limit of Uganda, and the southern frontier of Unyoro. They are unable to give the names of stations. South of Kivira is Usoga, a low alluvial land, cut by a multitude of creeks, islets, and lagoons ; in their thick vegetation the people take refuge from the plundering parties of the Waganda, whose chief built, as has been told, large boats to dislodge them. The Wasoga have no single sultan, and their only market-able commodity is ivory.

On the north, the north-west, and the west of Uganda lies, according to the Arabs, the land of Independent Unyoro. The slaves from that country vaguely de-scribe it as being bounded on the north-west by a tribe called Wakede, who have a currency of cowries, and wear tiaras of the shell ; and the Arabs have heard that on the north-east there is a " people with long daggers like the Somal," who may be Gallas (?). But whether the Nyanza Lake extends north of the equator is a question still to be decided. Those consulted at Kazeh ignored even the name of the Nyam-nyam ; nor had they heard of the Bahri and Barri, the Shilluks on the west, and the Dinkas east of the Nile, made familiar to us by the Austrian Mission at Gondokoro, and other explorers.

The Wanyoro are a distinct race, speaking a language of the Zangian family : they have suffered from the

vicinity of the more warlike Waganda, who have affixed
to the conquered the opprobrious name of widdu or
" serviles ; " and they have lost their southern possessions, which formerly extended between Karagwah and
Uganda.   Their late despot Chawambi, whose death
occurred about ten years ago, left three sons, one of
whom it is reported has fallen into the power of
Uganda, whilst the two others still rule independently.
The county is rich and fertile, and magnificent tales are
told concerning the collections of ivory, which in some
parts are planted in the ground to pen cattle.   Slaves
are cheap; they find their way to the southern markets
viâ Uganda and Karagwah.   Those seen at Kazeh and
Kirira, where the Arab traders had a large gang, appeared somewhat inferior to the other races of the
northern kingdoms, with a dull dead black colour,
flattish heads, brows somewhat retreating, prominent
eyes, and projecting lower jaws.   They were tattooed
in large burnt blotches encircling the forehead, and in
some cases the inferior excisors had been extracted.
The price of cattle in Unyoro varies from 500 to
1000 cowries.   In this country ten simbi (Cypræa)
represent one khete of beads ; they are the most esteemed currency, and are also used as ornaments for
the neck, arms, and legs, and decorations for stools and
drums.

During my companions' absence much of my spare
time was devoted to collecting specimens of the multitudinous dialects into which the great South African
family here divides itself.   After some months of desultory work I had learned the Kisawahili or coast
language, the lingua Franca of the South African coast:
it is the most useful, because the most generally known,
and because, once mastered, it renders its cognates as
easy of acquirement as Bengali or Maharatti after Hin-

dostani.   The principal obstacle is the want of instruc-
tors and books — the Kisawahili is not a written
language ; and the elementary publications put forth in
Europe gave me the preliminary trouble of composing
a grammar and a vocabulary.   Said Bin Salim, though
bred and born amongst the Wasawahili, knew but
little of the tongue, and his peculiarities of dis-
position rendered the task of instruction as wearisome
to himself as it was unsatisfactory to me.   My best
tutor was Snay Bin Amir, who had transferred to the
philology of East Africa his knowledge of Arabic grammar and syntax.   With the aid of the sons of Ramji
and other tame slaves, I collected about 1500 words
in the three principal dialects upon this line of road,
namely the Kisawahili, the Kizaramo—which includes
the Kik'hutu—and the Kinyamwezi.   At Kazeh I
found a number of wild captives, with whom I
began the dreary work of collecting specimens.   In
the languages of least consideration I contented myself
with the numerals, which are the fairest test of independence of derivation, because the most likely to be
primitive vocables.   The work was not a labour of love.
The savages could not guess the mysterious objects
of my inquiry into their names for 1, 2, and 3 ; often
they started up and ran away, or they sat in dogged
silence, perhaps thinking themselves derided.   The first
number was rarely elicited without half an hour's
"talkee-talkee" somewhat in this style:—

   "Listen, O my brother! in the tongue of the shores
(Kisawahili) we say 1, 2, 3, 4, 5"—counting the fingers
to assist comprehension.

   "Hu! hu!" replies the wild man, "*we* say fingers."

   "By no means, that's not it.   This white man wants
to know how thou speakest 1, 2, 3 ?"

" One, two, three what ? sheep, or goats, or women ? "
— expressing the numerals in Kisawahili.

" By no means, only 1, 2, 3 sheep in thine own tongue,
the tongue of the Wapoka."

" Hi! Hi! what wants the white man with the
Wapoka ? "

And so on till patience was almost impossible. But,
like the Irish shay-horse of days gone by, their tongues
once started often hobbled on without halting. The
tame slaves were more tractable, yet even in their case
ten minutes sufficed to weary out the most intellectual;
when the listless and incoherent reply, the glazed eye
gazing at vacancy, and the irresistible tendency to gape
and yawn, to nod and snooze, evidenced a feeble brain
soon overworked. Said Bin Salim would sit staring at
me with astonishment, and ejaculate, like Abba Grego-
rius, the preceptor of Ludolph, the grammarian philolo-
gist and historian of Æthiopia, " Verily in the coast-
tongue words never take root, nor do they bear
branches."

The rest of my time was devoted to preparations for
journeying. The Fundi's tent, which had accompanied
us to Uvira, was provided with an outer cover. The
Sepoys " pal," brought from Zanzibar, having been
destroyed by the ill-treatment of the villain Kannena,
I made up, with the aid of a blackguard Baghdadi,
named 'Brahim, a large tent of American domestics,
which having, however, but one cloth, and that of the
thinnest, proved a fiery purgatory on the down-march
eastwards. The canvas lug-sail was provided with an
extra double cloth, sewn round the top to increase its
dimensions: it thus became a pent-shaped affair, twelve
feet long, eight broad, and six feet high — seven would
have been better,—buttoned at the foot, which was semi-
circular, and in front provided with blue cotton cur-

tains, most useful against glare and stare. Its lightness,
combined with impenetrability, made it the model of a
tent for rapid marching. It was not, however, pegged
down close to the ground, as some explorers advise,
without the intervention of ropes ; in these lands, a tent
so pitched would rot in a week. The three tents were
fitted with solid male bamboos, and were provided
with skin-bags for their pegs, which, unless carefully
looked after, disappear almost daily. The only furniture was a kitanda or cartel: some contrivance of the
kind, a " Biddulph," or an iron bed-frame, without
joints, nuts, or screws, which are sure to break or to be
lost, is absolutely necessary in these lands, where from
Kaole to Uvira every man instinctively attempts to sit
and to sleep upon something that raises him above the
ground. Moreover, I have ever found the cartel answer
the threefold purpose of bed, chair, and table ; besides
saving weight by diminishing the quantity of bedding
required.

To the task of tent-making succeeded tailoring. We
had neglected to provide ourselves with the loose
blanket suits, served out to sailors on board men-of-war
in the tropics : they are most useful in passing through
countries where changes of climate are sudden and
marked. Besides these, the traveller should carry with
him an ample store of flannels : the material must be
shrunk before making up shirts, otherwise it will behave
as did the Little Boy's mantle when tried by the frail fair
Guinever. A red colour should moreover be avoided,
the dye soon turns dark, and the appearance excites too
much attention. Besides shirt and trousers, the only
necessary is a large " stomach-warmer " waistcoat, with
sleeves and back of similar material, without collar —
which renders sleeping in it uneasy — and provided with
four flapped pockets, to contain a compass and thermo-

mcter, a note-book, and a sketch-book, a watch and a moderate-sized knife of many uses. The latter should contain scissors, tweezers, tooth-pick, and ear-pick, needle, file, picker, steel for fire, turnscrew, watch-spring-saw, clasp blade, and pen blade : it should be made of moderate dimensions, and for safety be slung by a lanyard to the button-hole. For the cold mornings and the noon-day heats, I made up a large padded hood, bound round the head like the Arab Kufiyah. Too much cannot be said in favour of this article, which in eastward travel defends the eyes from the fiery glare, protects, when wending westwards, the carotids against the solar blaze, and, at all times, checks the intrusive staring of the crowd. I reformed my umbrella, ever an invaluable friend in these latitudes, by removing the rings and wires from the worm-eaten stick, and by mounting them on a spear, thus combining with shelter a staff and a weapon. The traveller should have at least three umbrellas, one large and water proof — white, not black — in the shape of those used by artists ; and two others of moderate size, and of the best construction, which should be covered with light-coloured calico, as an additional defence against the sun. At Kazeh I was somewhat deficient in material : my lazy " Jack of all trades," Valentine, made, however, some slippers of green baize, soled with leather, for me, overalls of American domestics for my companion, and various articles of indigo-dyed cotton for himself and his fellow-servant, who presently appeared tastefully rigged out like Paul and Virginia in " Bengal blue."

The minor works were not many. The two remaining pormanteaus of the three that had left the Coast were cobbled with goatskins, and were bound with stout thongs. The hammocks, of which half had disappeared, were patched and provided with the Nara, or Indian cotton-tape, which in these climates is better than either reims or cord. To save my eyes the spectacle of moribund fowls, suspended to a porter's pole, two light cages were made after the fashion of the country, with bent and bound withes. The metal plates, pots, and pans were furbished, and a damaged kettle was mended by a travelling tinker: the asses' saddles and halters were repaired, and, greatest luxury of all, a brace of jembe or iron hoes was converted into two pairs of solid stirrups, under the vigilant eye of Snay bin Amir. A party of slaves sent to Msene brought back fifty-four jembe, useful as return-presents and blackmail on the down-march: they paid, however, one cloth for two, instead of four. Sallum bin Hamid, the "papa" of the Arabs, sold for the sum of forty dollars a fine half-bred Zanzibar she-ass and foal — there is no surer method of procuring a regular supply of milk on Eastern journeys. My black and white beads being almost useless, he also parted with, as a peculiar favour, seventeen or eighteen pounds of pink-porcelains for forty dollars, and with a Frasibah of coffee, and a similar quantity of sugar for eighty dollars, equal to sixteen pounds sterling. On the 14th July the last Arab caravan of the season left Unyanyembe, under the command of Sayf bin Said el Wardi. As he obligingly offered to convey letters and any small articles which I wished to precede me, and knowing that under his charge effects were far safer than with our own people, I forwarded the useless and damaged surveying instruments, certain manuscripts, and various enclosures of maps, field and sketch-books, together with reports to the Royal Geographical Society.

This excitement over I began to weary of Kazeh. Snay bin Amir and most of the Arabs had set out on an expedition to revenge the murder of old Silim — an event alluded to in a former page, and the place had become dull as a mess-dinner. Said bin Salim, who was ill, who coughed and expectorated, and sincerely pitied himself because he had a cold, became more than usually unsociable: he could enjoy nothing but the society of Brahim, the bawling Baghdadi, and the crowd of ill-flavoured slavery that flocked into the vestibule. My Goanese servant, who connected my aspect with hard labour, avoided it like a pestilence. Already I was preparing to organise a little expedition to K'hokoro and the southern provinces, when unexpectedly, — in these lands a few cries and gun-shots are the only credible precursors of a caravan, — on the morning of the 25th August reappeared my companion.

At length my companion had been successful, his "flying trip" had led him to the northern water, and he had found its dimensions surpassing our most sanguine expectations. We had scarcely, however, breakfasted, before he announced to me the startling fact, that he had discovered the sources of the White Nile. It was an inspiration perhaps: the moment he sighted the Nyanza, he felt at once no doubt but that the "Lake at his feet gave birth to that interesting river which has been the subject of so much speculation, and the object of so many explorers." The fortunate discoverer's conviction was strong; his reasons were weak — were of the category alluded to by the damsel Lucetta, when justifying her penchant in favour of the "lovely gentleman," Sir Proteus :—

"I have no other but a woman's reason.
I think him so because I think him so ;" *

---

* The following extract from the Proceedings of the R. Geographical Society, May 9, 1859, will best illustrate what I mean :—

Mr. MACQUEEN, F.R.G.S., said the question of the sources of the Nile had cost him much trouble and research, and he was sure there was no material and probably his sources of the Nile grew in his mind as his Mountains of the Moon had grown under his hand.

error either in longitude or latitude in the position he had ascribed to them, namely, a little to the eastward of the meridian of 35°, and a little northward of the equator. That was the principal source of the White Nile. The mountains there were exceedingly high, from the equator north to Kaffa Enarea. All the authorities, from east, west, north, or south, now perfectly competent to form judgments upon such a matter, agreed with him; and among them were the officers commanding the Egyptian commission. It was impossible they could all be mistaken. Dr. Krapf had been within a very short distance of it; he was more than 180 miles from Mombas, and he saw snow upon the mountains. He conversed with the people who came from them, and who told him of the snow and exceeding coldness of the temperature. The line of perpetual congelation, it was well known, was 17,000 feet above the sea. He had an account of the navigation of the White Nile by the Egyptian expedition. It was then given as 3° 30′ N. lat. and 31° E. long. At this point the expedition turned back for want of a sufficient depth of water. Here the river was 1370 feet broad, and the velocity of the current *one-quarter* of a mile per hour. The journals also gave a specific and daily current, the depth and width of the river, and every thing, indeed, connected with it. Surely, looking at the current of the river, the height of the Cartoom above the level of the sea, and the distance thence up to the equator, the sources of the Nile must be 6000 or 8000 feet above the level of the sea, and still much below the line of the snow, which was 6000 or 8000 feet farther above them. He deeply regretted he was unable to complete the diagram for the rest of the papers he had given to the Society, for it was more important than any others he had previously given. It contained the journey over Africa from sea to sea, second only to that of Dr. Livingstone. But all the rivers coming down from the mountains in question, and running south-eastward, had been clearly stated by Dr. Krapf, who gave every particular concerning them. He should like to know what the natives had said was to the northward of the large lake? Did they say the rivers ran out from or into the lake? How could the Egyptian officers be mistaken?

CAPTAIN SPEKE replied. They were not mistaken; and if they had pursued their journey 50 miles farther, they would undoubtedly have found themselves at the northern borders of this lake.

MR. MACQUEEN said that other travellers, Don Angelo for instance, had been within one and a half degree of the Equator, and saw the mountain of Kimborat under the Line, and persisted in the statement, adding, that travellers had been up the river until they found it a mere brook. He felt convinced that the large lake alluded to by Captain Speke was not the source of the Nile: it was impossible it could be so, for it was not at a sufficiently high altitude.

The paper presented to the Society, when fully read in conjunction with the map, will clearly show that the Bahr-el-Abied has no connection with

The main argument in favour of the Lake representing the great reservoir of the White River was, that the "principal men" at the southern extremity ignored the extent northward. "On my inquiring about the lake's length the man (the greatest traveller in the place) faced to the north, and began nodding his head to it; at the same time he kept throwing forward his right hand, and making repeated snaps of his fingers endeavoured to indicate something immeasurable; and added, that nobody knew, but he thought it probably extended to the end of the world." Strongly impressed by this valuable statistical information, my companion therefore placed the northern limit about 4°–5° north lat., whereas the Egyptian expedition sent by the late Mohammed Ali Pacha, about twenty years ago, to explore the Coy Sources, reached 3° 22' north lat. It therefore ought to have sailed fifty miles upon the Nyanza lake. On the contrary, from information derived on the spot, that expedition placed the fountains at one month's journey—300 to 350 miles—to the south-east, or upon the northern counterslope of Mount Kenia. Whilst marching to the coast, my companion—he tells us—was assured by a "respectable Sowahili merchant, that when engaged in traffic some years previously to the northward of the line, and the westward of this lake, he had heard it commonly reported that large vessels frequented the northern extremity of these waters, in which the officers

Kilimanjaro, that it has no connection whatever with any lake or river to the south of the Equator, and that the swelling of the river Nile proceeds from the tropical rains of the northern torrid zone, as was stated emphatically to Julius Cæsar by the chief Egyptian priest Amoreis 2000 years ago.

In nearly 3° N. lat. there is a great cataract, which boats cannot pass. It is called Gherba. About half-way (50 miles) above, and between this cataract and Robego, the capital of Kuenda, the river becomes so narrow as to be crossed by a bridge formed by a tree thrown across it. Above Gherba no stream joins the river either from the south or south-west.

engaged in navigating them used sextants and kept a log, precisely similar to what is found in vessels on the ocean. Query, could this be in allusion to the expedition sent by Mohammed Ali up the Nile in former years?" (Proceedings of Royal Geographical Society, May 9, 1859.) Clearly, if Abdullah Bin Nasib, the Msawahili alluded to, had reported these words, he merely erred; the Egyptian expedition, as has been shown, not only did not find, they never even heard of a lake. But not being present at the conversation I am tempted to assign further explanation. My companion, wholly ignorant of Arabic, was reduced to depend upon "Bombay," who spoke an even more debased dialect than his master, and it is easy to see how the blunder originated. The Arabic bahr and the Kisa-wahili bahari are equally applicable in vulgar parlance to a river or sea, a lake or a river. Traditions concerning a Western Sea—the to them now unknown Atlantic—over which the white men voyage, are familiar to many East Africans; I have heard at Harar precisely the same report concerning the log and sextants. Either, then, Abdullah Bin Nasib confounded, or my companion's "interrupter" caused him to confound the Atlantic and the Lake. In the maps forwarded from Kazeh by my companion, the River Kivira was, after ample inquiry, made a western *influent* of the Nyanza Lake. In the map appended to the paper in Blackwood, before alluded to, it has become an *effluent*, and the only minute concerning so very important a modification is, " This river (although I must confess at first I did not think so) is the Nile itself!"

Beyond the assertion, therefore, that no man had visited the north, and the appearance of sextants and logs upon the waters, there is not a shade of proof *pro*.

Far graver considerations lie on the *con.* side: the reports of the Egyptian expedition, and the dates of the several inundations which—as will presently appear—alone suffice to disprove the possibility of the Nyanza causing the flood of the Nile. It is doubtless a satisfactory thing to disclose to an admiring public, of " statesmen, churchmen, missionaries, merchants, and more particularly geographers," the " solution of a problem, which it has been the first geographical desideratum of many thousand years to ascertain, and the ambition of the first monarchs in the world to unravel." (Blackwood's Magazine, October 1859.) But how many times since the days of a certain Claudius Ptolemæius surnamed Pelusiota, have not the Fountains of the White Nile been discovered and re-discovered after this fashion ?

What tended at the time to make me the more sceptical was the substantial incorrectness of the geographical and other details brought back by my companion. This was natural enough. Bombay, after misunderstanding his master's ill-expressed Hindostani, probably mistranslated the words into Kisawahili to some travelled African, who in turn passed on the question in a wilder dialect to the barbarian or barbarians under examination. During such a journey to and fro words must be liable to severe accidents. The first thing reported to me was the falsehood of the Arabs at Kazeh, who had calumniated the good Sultan Muhayya, and had praised the bad Sultan Machunda: subsequent inquiries proved their rigid correctness. My companion's principal informant was one Mansur Bin Salim, a half-caste Arab, who had been flogged out of Kazeh by his compatriots ; he pronounced Muhayya to to be a " very excellent and obliging person," and of course he was believed. I then heard a detailed account of how the caravan of Salim bin Rashid had been attacked, beaten, captured, and detained at Ukerewe, by its sultan Machunda. The Arabs received the intelligence with a smile of ridicule, and in a few days Salim bin Rashid appeared in person to disprove the report. These are but two cases of many. And what knowledge of Asiatic customs can be expected from the writer of these lines? " The Arabs at Unyanyembe had advised my donning their habit for the trip in order to attract less attention ; a vain precaution, which I believe they suggested more to gratify their own vanity in *seeing an Englishman lower himself to their position*, than for any benefit that I might receive by doing so." (Blackwood, loco cit.) This galamatias of the Arabs! — the haughtiest and the most clannish of all Oriental peoples.

But difference of opinion was allowed to alter companionship. After a few days it became evident to me that not a word could be uttered upon the subject of the Lake, the Nile, and his *trouvaille* generally without offence. By a tacit agreement it was, therefore, avoided, and I should never have resumed it had my companion not stultified the results of the Expedition by putting forth a claim which no geographer can admit, and which is at the same time so weak and flimsy, that no geographer has yet taken the trouble to contradict it.

I will here offer to the reader a few details concerning the Lake in question, — they are principally borrowed from my companion's diary, carefully corrected, however, by Snay bin Amir, Salim bin Rashid*, and other merchants at Kazeh.

---

* When my companion returned to Kazeh, he represented Ukerewe and Mazita to be islands, and, although in sight of them, he had heard nothing concerning their connection with the coast. This error was corrected by

This fresh-water sea is known throughout the African tribes as Nyanza, and the similarity of the sound to "Nyassa," the indigenous name of the little Maravi or Kilwa Lake, may have caused in part the wild confusion in which speculative geographers have involved the Lake Regions of Central Africa. The Arabs, after their fashion of deriving comprehensive names from local and minor features, call it Ukerewe, in the Kisukuma dialect meaning the "place of Kerewe" (Kelewe), an islet. As has been mentioned, they sometimes attempt to join by a river, a creek, or some other theoretical creation, the Nyanza with the Tanganyika, the altitude of the former being 3750 feet above sea-level, or 1900 feet above the latter, and the mountain regions which divide the two having been frequently travelled over by Arab and African caravans. Hence the name Ukerewe has been transferred in the "Mombas Mission Map" to the northern waters of the Tanganyika. The Nyanza, as regards name, position, and even existence, has hitherto been unknown to European geographers; but, as will presently appear, descriptions of this sea by native travellers have been unconsciously

Salim bin Rashid, and accepted by us. Yet I read in his discovery of the supposed sources of the Nile: "Mansur, and a native, the greatest traveller of the place, kindly accompanied and gave me every obtainable information. This man had traversed the island, as he called it, of Ukerewe from north to south. *But by his rough mode of describing it, I am rather inclined to think that instead of its being an actual island, it is a connected tongue of land, stretching southwards from a promontory lying at right angles to the eastern shore of the lake,* which being a wash, affords a passage to the mainland during the fine season, but during the wet becomes submerged and thus makes Ukerewe temporarily an island." The information, I repeat, was given, not by the "native," but by Salim bin Rashid. When, however, the latter proceeded to correct my companion's confusion between the well-known coffee mart Kitara and "the island of Kitiri occupied by a tribe called Watiri," he gave only offence—consequently Kitiri has obtained a local habitation in Blackwood and Petermann.

transferred by our writers to the Tanganyika of Ujiji, and even to the Nyassa of Kilwa.

M. Brun-Rollet ("Le Nil Blanc et le Soudan," p. 209) heard that on the west of the Padongo tribe, — whom he places to the S. of Mount Kambirah, or below 1° S. lat.—lies a great lake, from whose northern extremity issues a river whose course is unknown. In the map appended to his volume this water is placed between 1° S. and 3° N. lat., and about 25° 50′ E. long. (Greenwich), and the déversoir is made an in-fluent of the White Nile.

Bowdich ("Discoveries of the Portuguese," pp. 131, 132), when speaking of the Maravi Lake (the Nyassa), mentions that the "negroes or the Moors of Melinde" have mentioned a great water which is known to reach Mombaca, which the Jesuit missionaries conjectured to communicate with Abyssinia, and of which Father Lewis Marianna, who formerly resided at Tete, recommended a discovery, in a letter addressed to the government at Goa, which is still preserved among the public archives of that city. Here the confusion of the Nyanza, to which there was of old a route from Mombasah with the Nyassa, is apparent.

At the southern point, where the Muingwira River falls into the tortuous creek, whose surface is a little archipelago of brown rocky islets crowned with trees, and emerging from the blue waters, the observed lati-tude of the Nyanza Lake, is 2° 24′ S. ; the longitude by dead reckoning from Kazeh is E. long. 33° and nearly due north, and the altitude by B. P. thermometer 3750 feet above sea-level. Its extent to the north is unknown to the people of the southern regions, which rather denotes some difficulty in travelling than any great extent. They informed my companion that from

Mwanza to the southern frontier of Karagwah is a land journey of one month, or a sea voyage of five days towards the N. N. W. and then to the north. They also pointed out the direction of Unyoro N. 20° W. The Arab merchants of Kazeh have seen the Nyanza opposite Weranhanja, the capital district of Armanika, King of Karagwah, and declare that it receives the Kitangure River, whose mouth has been placed about the equator. Beyond that point all is doubtful. The merchants have heard that Suna, the late despot of Uganda, built matumbi, or undecked vessels, capable of containing forty or fifty men, in order to attack his enemies, the Wasoga, upon the creeks which indent the western shores of the Nyanza. This, if true, would protract the lake to between 1° and 1° 30′ of N. lat., and give it a total length of about 4° or 250 miles. This point, however, is still involved in the deepest obscurity. Its breadth was estimated as follows. A hill, about 200 feet above the water-level, shows a conspicuous landmark on the eastern shore, which was set down as forty miles distant. On the south-western angle of the line from the same point ground appeared; it was not, however, perceptible on the north-west. The total breadth, therefore, has been assumed at eighty miles,—a figure which approaches the traditions unconsciously chronicled by European geographers. In the vicinity of Usoga the lake, according to the Arabs, broadens out : of this, however, and in fact of all the formation north of the equator, it is at present impossible to arrive at certainty.

The Nyanza is an elevated basin or reservoir, the recipient of the surplus monsoon-rain which falls in the extensive regions of the Wamasai and their kinsmen to the east, the Karagwah line of the Lunar Mountains to the west, and to the south Usukuma or Northern

Unyamwezi.   Extending to the equator in the central
length of the African peninsula, and elevated above the
limits of the depression in the heart of the continent, it
appears to be a gap in the irregular chain which, running from Usumbara and Kilima-ngao to Karagwah,
represents the formation anciently termed the Mountains
of the Moon.   The physical features, as far as they
were observed, suggest this view.   The shores are low
and flat, dotted here and there with little hills ; the
smaller islands also are hill-tops, and any part of the
country immediately on the south would, if inundated
to the same extent, present a similar aspect.   The lake
lies open and elevated, rather like the drainage and the
temporary deposit of extensive floods than a volcanic
creation like the Tanganyika, a long narrow mountain-
girt basin.   The waters are said to be deep, and the
extent of the inundation about the southern creek
proves that they receive during the season an important
accession.   The colour was observed to be clear and
blue, especially from afar in the early morning ; after
9 A.M., when the prevalent south-east wind arose, the
surface appeared greyish, or of a dull milky white,
probably the effect of atmospheric reflection.   The tint,
however, does not, according to travellers, ever become
red or green like the waters of the Nile.   But the produce of the lake resembles that of the river in its
purity ; the people living on the shores prefer it, unlike
that of the Tanganyika, to the highest, and clearest
springs ; all visitors agree in commending its lightness
and sweetness, and declare that the taste is rather of
river or of rain-water than resembling the soft slimy
produce of stagnant muddy bottoms, or the rough
harsh flavour of melted ice and snow.

From the southern creek of the Nyanza, and beyond

the archipelago of neighbouring islets, appear the two features which have given to this lake the name of Ukerewe.   The Arabs call them " Jezirah "—an ambiguous term, meaning equally insula and peninsula — but they can scarcely be called islands.   The high and rocky Mazita to the east, and the comparatively flat Ukerewe on the west, are described by the Arabs as points terminating seawards in bluffs, and connected with the eastern shore by a low neck of land, probably a continuous reef, flooded during the rains, but never so deeply as to prevent cattle fording the isthmus. The northern and western extremities front deep water, and a broad channel separates them from the southern shore, Usukuma.   The Arabs, when visiting Ukerewe or its neighbour, prefer hiring the canoes of the Wasukuma, and paddling round the south-eastern extremity of the Nyanza, to exposing their property and lives by marching through the dangerous tribes of the coast.

Mazita belongs to a people called Makwiya.   Ukerewe is inhabited, according to some informants, by Wasukuma ; according to others, the Wakerewe are marked by their language as ancient emigrants from the highlands of Karagwah.   In Ukerewe, which is exceedingly populous, are two brother Sultans : the chief is " Machunda ;" the second, " Ibanda," rules at Wiru, the headland on the western limit.   The people collect ivory from the races on the eastern mainland, and store it, awaiting an Arab caravan.   Beads are in most request ; as in Usukuma generally, not half a dozen cloths of native and foreign manufacture will be found upon a hundred men.   The women are especially badly clad ; even the adult maidens wear only the languti of India, or the Nubian apron of aloe-fibre, strung with the pipe-stem bead called sofi, and blackened, like India-rubber, by use ; it is fastened round the waist, and depends about one foot by six or seven inches in breadth.

The Arabs who traffic in these regions generally establish themselves with Sultan Machunda, and send their slaves in canoes round the south-east angle of the lake to trade with the coast people. These races are successively from the south; the Washaki, at a distance of three marches, and their inland neighbours the Wataturu; then the Warudi, a wild tribe, rich in ivory, lying about a fortnight's distance; and beyond them the Wahumba, or Wamasai. Commercial transactions extend along the eastern shore as far as T'hiri, or Ut'hiri, a district between Ururu and Uhumba. This is possibly the origin of the island of Tiri or Kittiri, placed in my companion's map near the north-west extremity of the Nyanza Lake, off the coast of Uganda, where there is a province called Kittara, peculiarly rich in coffee. The explorer heard from the untrustworthy country people that, after a long coasting voyage, they arrived at an island where the inhabitants, a poor and naked race, live on fish, and cultivate coffee for sale. The information appears suspicious. The Arabs know of no islands upon the Nyanza which produce coffee. Moreover, if the people had any traffic, they would not be without clothing.

The savagery of the races adjacent to the Nyanza has caused accidents amongst travelling traders. About five years ago a large caravan from Tanga, on the eastern coast, consisting of 400 or 500 guns, and led by Arab merchants, at the end of a journey which had lasted nearly two years, happened to quarrel with the Wahumba or Wamasai near the lake. The subject was the burning down of some grass required for pasture by the wild men. Words led to blows; the caravan, having but two or three pounds of gunpowder, was soon dispersed; seven or eight merchants lost their lives, and a few made their escape to Unyanyembe. Before our departure from Kazeh, the slaves of Salim bin Rashid, having rescued one of the wounded survivors, who had been allowed by the Wamasai to wander into Urudi, brought him back to Kazeh. He described the country as no longer practicable. In 1858 also the same trading party, the principal authority for these statements, were relieved of several bales of cloth, during their sleep, when bivouacking upon an inhabited island near the eastern shore.

The altitude, the conformation of the Nyanza Lake, the argilaceous colour and the sweetness of its waters, combine to suggest that it may be one of the feeders of the White Nile. In the map appended to M. Brun-Rollet's volume, before alluded to, the large water west of the Padongo tribe, which clearly represents the Nyanza or Ukerewe, is, I have observed, made to drain northwards into the Fitri Lake, and eventually to swell the main stream of the White River. The details supplied by the Egyptian Expedition, which, about twenty years ago, ascended the White River to 3° 22′ N. lat., and 31° 30′ E. long., and gave the general bearing of the river from that point to its source as south-east, with a distance of one month's journey, or from 300 to 350 miles, would place the actual sources 2° S. lat., and 35° E. long., or in 2° eastward of the southern creek of the Nyanza Lake. This position would occupy the northern counterslope of the Lunar Mountains, the upper water-shed of the high region whose culminating apices are Kilima-Ngao, Kenia, and Doengo Engai. The distance of these peaks from the coast, as given by Dr. Krapf, must be considerably reduced, and little authority can be attached to his river Tumbiri.* The site, supposed by Mr. Macqueen ("Proceedings of the Geographical Society of London," January 24th, 1859), to be at least 21,000 feet above the level of the sea, and consequently 3000 or 4000 feet above the line of perpetual congelation, would admirably explain the two most ancient theories concerning the source of the White River, namely, that it arises in a snowy region, and that its inundation is the result of tropical rains.

It is impossible not to suspect that between the upper portion of the Nyanza and the watershed of the White Nile there exists a longitudinal range of elevated ground, running from east to west —a "furca" draining northwards into the Nile and southwards into the Nyanza Lake —like that which separates the Tanganyika from the Maravi or Nyassa of Kilwa. According to Don Angelo Vinco, who visited Loquéck in 1852, beyond the cataract of Garbo —supposed to be in N. lat. 2° 40′— at a distance of sixty miles lie Robego, the capital of Kuenda, and Lokoya (Logoja), of which the latter receives an affluent from the east. Beyond Lokoya the White Nile is described as a *small and rocky mountain-river*, presenting none of the features of a stream flowing

---

* The large river Tumbiri, mentioned by Dr. Krapf as flowing towards Egypt from the northern counterslope of Mount Kenia, rests upon the sole authority of a single wandering native. As, moreover, the word T'humbiri or T'humbili means a monkey, and the people are peculiarly fond of satire in a small way, it is not improbable that the very name had no foundation of fact. This is mentioned, as some geographers—for instance, Mr. Macqueen ("Observations on the Geography of Central Africa:" "Proceedings of the R. G. S. of London," May 9, 1859)—have been struck by the circumstance that the Austrian Missionaries and Mr. Werne ("Expedition to discover the sources of the White Nile, in 1840-41") gave Tubirih as the Bari name of the White Nile at the southern limit of their exploration.

from a broad expanse of water like the great Nyanza reservoir.

The periodical swelling of the Nyanza Lake, which, flooding a considerable tract of land on the south, may be supposed—as it lies flush with the basal surface of the country—to inundate extensively all the low lands that form its periphery, forbids belief in the possibility of its being the head-stream of the Nile, or the reservoir of its periodical inundation. In Karagwah, upon the western shore, the masika or monsoon lasts from October to May or June, after which the dry season sets in. The Egyptian Expedition found the river falling fast at the end of January, and they learned from the people that it would again rise about the end of March, at which season the sun is vertical over the equator. About the summer solstice (June), when the rains cease in the regions south of and upon the equator, the White Nile begins to flood. From March to the autumnal equinox (September) it continues to overflow its banks till it attains its magnitude, and from that time it shrinks through the winter solstice (December) till March. The Nile is, therefore, full during the dry season and low during the rainy season south of and immediately upon the equator. And as the northern counterslope of Kenia will, to a certain extent, be a lee-land, like Ugogo, it cannot have the superfluity of moisture necessary to send forth a first-class stream. The inundation is synchronous with the great falls of the northern equatorial regions, which extend from July to September, and is dependent solely upon the tropical rains. It is, therefore, probable that the true sources of the " Holy River " will be found to be a network of runnels and rivulets of scanty dimensions, filled by monsoon torrents, and perhaps a little swollen by melted snow on the northern water-parting of the Eastern Lunar Mountains.

Of the tribes dwelling about the Nyanza, the western have been already described. The Washaki and the Warudi are plundering races on the east, concerning whom little is known. Remain the Wahinda, a clan or class alluded to in this and a former chapter, and the Wataturu, an extensive and once powerful tribe, mentioned when treating of the regions about Tura.

The Wahinda (in the singular Muhinda) are, according to some Arabs, a foreign and ruling family, who coming from a distant country, probably in the neighbourhood of Somaliland, conquered the lands, and became Sultans. This opinion seems to rest upon physical peculiarities, — the superiority of the Wahinda in figure, stature, and complexion to their subjects suggesting a difference of origin. Others explain the word Muhinda to mean a cadet of royal family, and call the class Bayt el Saltanah, or the Kingly House. Thus, whilst Armanika is the Mkámá or Sovereign of Karagwah, his brother simply takes the title of Muhinda. These conflicting statements may be reconciled by the belief general in the country that the families of the Sultans are a foreign and a nobler race, the date of whose immigration has long fallen into oblivion. This may be credited without difficulty; the physique of the rulers —approximating more to the northern races of Arica— is markedly less negroid than that of their subjects, and the difference is too great to be explained by the effects of climate or of superior diet, comfort, and luxury.

The Wahinda are found in the regions of Usui, Karagwah, Uhha, Uvinza, Uyungu, Ujiji, and Urundi, where they live in boma—stockades—and scattered villages. Of this race are the Sultans Suwarora of the

Wasui, Armanika of Karagwah, Kanoni of Uhha, Kanze of Uyungu, Mzogera of Uvinza, Rusimba of Ujiji, Mwezi of Urundi, Mnyamurunde of Uyofo, Gaetawa of Uhayya, and Mutawazi of Utumbara. The Wahinda affect a milk diet which is exceedingly fattening, and anoint themselves plentifully with butter and ghee, to soften and polish the skin. They never sell their fellow clansmen, are hospitable and civil to strangers, seldom carry arms, fear nothing from the people, and may not be slain even in battle. Where the Wahinda reign, their ministers are the Watosi, a race which has been described when treating of their head-quarters Karagwah.

The Watataru extend from the Mángewá district, two marches northward of Tura in a north-north-westerly diagonal, to Usmáo, a district of Usukuma, at the south-east angle of the Nyanza Lake. On the north and east they are limited by the Wahumba, on the south by the people of Iramba, and there is said to be a connection between these three tribes. This wild pastoral people were formerly rich in flocks and herds; they still have the best asses in the country. About five years ago, however, they were persuaded by Msimbira, a chief of Usukuma, to aid him against his rival Mpagamo, who had called in the Arabs to his assistance. During the long and bitter contest which ensued, the Arabs, as has been related, were worsted in the field, and the Watataru suffered severe losses in cattle. Shortly before the arrival of the Expedition at Kazeh the foreign merchants had despatched to Utataru a plundering party of sixty slave-musketeers, who, however, suddenly attacked by the people, were obliged to fly, leaving behind eighteen of their number. This event was followed by a truce, and the Watataru resumed their commerce with Tura and Unyanyembe, where, in 1858, a caravan, numbering about 300 men, came in. Two small parties of this people were also met at Tura; they were small, dark, and ugly savages, almost beardless, and not unlike the "Thakur" people in Maharatta-land. Their asses, provided with neat saddle-bags of zebra skin, were better dressed than the men, who wore no clothing except the simplest hide-sandals. According to the Arabs this clan affects nudity: even adult maidens dispense with the usual skin-kilt. The men ignored bows and arrows, but they were efficiently armed with long spears, double-edged sime, and heavy hide shields. They brought calabash or monkey-bread flour—in this country, as in Ugogo, a favourite article of consumption—and a little coarse salt, collected from the dried mud of a Mbuga or swamp in the land of Iramba, to be bartered for holcus and beads. Their language sounded to the unpractised ear peculiarly barbarous, and their savage suspiciousness rendered it impossible to collect any specimens.

At Kazeh, sorely to my disappointment, it was finally settled, in a full conclave of Arabs, that we must return to the coast by the tedious path with which we were already painfully familiar. At Ujiji the state of our finances had been the sole, though the sufficient obstacle to our traversing Africa from east to west; we might— had we possessed the means—by navigating the Tanganyika southwards, have debouched, after a journey of three months, at Kilwa. The same cause prevented us from visiting the northern kingdoms of Karagwah and Uganda; to effect this exploration, however, we should have required not only funds but time. The rains there setting in about September render travelling impossible; our two years' leave of absence were drawing to a close, and even had we commanded a sufficient outfit, we were not disposed to risk the consequences of taking an extra twelve months. No course, therefore, remained but to regain the coast. We did not, however, give up hopes of making our return useful to geography, by tracing the course of the Rwaha or Rufijí River, and of visiting the coast between the Usagara Mountains and Kilwa, an unknown line not likely to attract future travellers.

SAYDUMI, A NATIVE OF UGANDA.

Mgongo Thembo, or the Elephant's Back.

CHAP. XVII.

THE DOWN-MARCH TO THE COAST.

On the 5th September 1858, Musa Mzuri — handsome
Moses, as he was called by the Africans — returned with
great pomp to Kazeh after his long residence at Karagwah. Some details concerning this merchant, who
has played a conspicuous part in the eventful "*peri-
péties*" of African discovery, may be deemed well placed.

About thirty-five years ago, Musa, a Moslem of the
Kojah sect, and then a youth, was driven by poverty
from his native Surat to follow his eldest brother
"Sayyan," who having sought fortune at Zanzibar, and
having been provided with an outfit by the Sayyid el

Laghbari, then governor of the island, made sundry journeys into the interior. About 1825, the brothers first visited the Land of the Moon, preceding the Arab travellers, who in those days made their markets at Usanga and Usenga, distant about a dozen marches to the S.S.E. of Kazeh. Musa describes Unyamwezi as richly cultivated, and he has not forgotten the hospitable reception of the people. The brothers bought up a little venture of forty Farasilah or twenty men's loads of cloth and beads, and returned with a joint stock of 800 Farasilah (800 × 35 = 28,000 lbs. avoirdupois) in ivory; as Sayyan died on the road, all fell to Musa's share. Since that time he has made five journeys to the coast and several to the northern kingdoms. About four years ago Armanika, the present Sultan of Karagwah, was besieged in a palisaded village by a rebel brother Rumanika. On this occasion Musa, in company with the king, endured great hardships, and incurred no little risk; when both parties were weary of fighting, he persuaded, by a large bribe of ivory, Suna, the powerful despot of the neighbouring kingdom of Uganda, to raise the siege, by throwing a strong force into the field. He has ever since been fraternally received by Armanika, and his last journey to Karagwah was for the purpose of recovering part of the ivory expended in the king's cause. After an absence of fifteen months he brought back about a score of splendid tusks, one weighing, he declared, upwards of 200 lbs. During his detention Salim bin Sayf, of Dut'humi, who had been entrusted by Musa with sixty-five Farasilah of ivory to barter for goods on the coast, arrived at Unyanyembe, when hearing the evil tidings, the wily Harisi appropriated the property and returned to whence he came. Like most merchants in East Africa,

Musa's business is extensive, but his gains are principally represented by outlying debts ; he cannot, therefore, leave the country without an enormous sacrifice. He is the recognised Doyen of the commercial body, and he acts agent and warehouseman ; his hall is usually full of buyers and sellers, Arab and African, and large investments of wires, beads, and cotton-cloths, some of them valuable, are regularly forwarded to him with comforts and luxuries from the coast.

Musa Mzuri is now a man of the uncertain " certain age" between forty-five and fifty, thin-bearded, tall, gaunt, with delicate extremities, and with the regular and handsome features of a high-caste Indian Moslem. Like most of his compatriots, he is a man of sad and staid demeanour, and he is apparently faded by opium, which so tyrannises over him that he carries pills in every pocket, and stores them, lest the hoard should run short, in each corner and cranny of his house. His clean new dress, perfumed with jasmine-oil and sandal-wood, his snowy skull-cap and well-fitting sandals, distinguish him in appearance from the Arabs ; and his abode, which is almost a village, with its lofty gates and its spacious courts, full of slaves and hangers-on, contrasts with the humility of the Semite tenements.

On arrival at Kazeh I forwarded to Musa the introductory letter with which H. H. the Sayyid Majid had honoured me. Sundry civilities passed between his housekeeper, Mama Khamisi, and ourselves ; she supplied the Baloch with lodgings and ourselves with milk, for which we were careful to reward her. After returning from Ujiji we found Abdullah, the eldest of Musa's two sons by different slave girls, resting at Kazeh after his down-march from Karagwah. He knew a few words of English, but he had learned no

Hindostani from his father, who curious to say, after an expatriation of thirty-five years, still spoke his mother-tongue purely and well. The youth would have become a greater favourite had he not been so hard a drinker and so quarrelsome in his cups; on more than one occasion he had dangerously cut or stabbed his servile boon-companions. Musa had spared the rod, or had used it upon him to very little purpose; after intruding himself repeatedly into the hall and begging for handsome clothes, with more instance of freedom than consisted with decorum, he was warned that if he stayed away it might be the better for his back, and he took the warning.

Musa, when rested after his weary return-march, called upon me with all due ceremony, escorted by the principal Arab merchants. I was not disappointed in finding him wholly ignorant concerning Africa and things African; Snay bin Amir had told me that such was the case. He had, however, a number of slaves fresh from Karagwah and Uganda, who confirmed the accounts previously received from Arab travellers in those regions. Musa displayed even more hospitality than his fellow-travellers. Besides the mbogoro or skinful of grain and the goat usually offered to fresh arrivals, he was ever sending those little presents of provisions which in the East cannot be refused without offence. I narrowly prevented his killing a bullock to provide us with beef, and at last I feared to mention a want before him. During his frequent visits he invariably showed himself a man of quiet and unaffected manners, dashed with a little Indian reserve, which in process of time would probably have worn off.

On the 6th September, Said bin Salim, nervously impatient to commence the march homewards, " made a khambi," that is to say, pitched our tents under a spreading tree outside and within sight of Kazeh. Although he had been collecting porters for several days, only two came to the fore ; a few refreshing showers were falling at the autumnal equinox, and the black peasantry so miscalculated the seasons that they expected the immediate advent of the great Masika. Moreover, when informed that our route would debouch at Kilwa, they declared that they must receive double pay, as they could not expect there to be hired by return caravans. That the " khambi " might assume an appearance of reality, the Baloch were despatched into " country-quarters." As they followed their usual tactic, affecting eagerness to depart but privily clinging to the pleasures of Kazeh, orders were issued definitively to " cut " their rations in case of necessity. The sons of Ramji, who had returned from Msene, without, however, intrusion or swagger, were permitted to enter the camp. Before the march I summoned them, and in severe terms recapitulated their misdeeds, warned them that they would not be re-engaged, and allowed them provisions and protection only on condition of their carrying, as the slaves of Arab merchants are expected to do, our lighter valuables, such as the digester, medicine-chest, gun-cases, camp-table and chair. They promised with an edifying humility to reform. I was compelled, however to enliven their murmuring by a few slight floggings before they would become amenable to a moral rule, and would acquire those habits of regularity which are as chains and fetters to the African man. The five Wak'hutu porters who, after robbing and deserting us on the road to Ujiji, had taken service with my old acquaintance, Salim bin Rashid—the well-informed Coast Arab merchant, originally named by H. H. the Sayyid

Majid, as my guide and caravan leader, — begged hard to be again employed. I positively refused to see them. If at this distance from home they had perjured themselves and had plundered us, what might be expected when they arrived near their native country?

As the time of departure approached, I regretted that the arrival of several travellers had not taken place a month earlier. Salim bin Rashid, whilst collecting ivory in Usukuma and to the eastward of the Nyanza Lake, had recovered a Msawahili porter, who, falling sick on the road, had been left by a caravan from Tanga amongst the wildest of the East African tribes, the Wamasai or Wahumba. From this man, who spent two years amongst those plunderers and their rivals in villany the Warudi, I derived some valuable information concerning the great northern route which spans the countries lying between the coast and the Nyanza Lake. I was also called upon by Amayr bin Said el Shaksi, a strong-framed and stout-hearted greybeard, who, when his vessel foundered in the waters of the Tanganyika, saved his life by swimming, and as he had no goods and but few of his slaves had survived, lived for five months on roots and grasses, till restored to Ujiji by an Arab canoe. A garrulous senior, fond of "venting his travels," he spent many hours with me, talking over his past adventures, and his ocular knowledge of the Tanganyika enabled me to gather many, perhaps, reliable details concerning its southern extremity. A few days before departure Hilal bin Nasur, a well-born Harisi, returned from K'hokoro; he supplied me with a list of stations and a lengthy description of his various excursions to the southern provinces.*

* For this and other purely geographical details concerning the Southern Provinces, the reader is referred to the Journal of the Royal Geographical Society, vol. xxix. 1860.

Said bin Salim, in despair that the labours of a whole fortnight spent in the jungle had produced the slenderest of results, moved from under the tree in Kazeh plain to Masui, a dirty little village distant about three miles to the east of our head-quarters. As he reported on the 25th of September that his gang was nearly completed, I sent forward all but the personal baggage. The Arab had, however, secured but three Hammals or bearers for my hammock; one a tottering old man, the other a knock-kneed boy, and the third a notorious skulk. Although supplied with meat to strengthen them, as they expressed it, they broke down after a single march. From that time, finding it useless to engage bearers for a long journey in these lands, I hired men from district to district, and dismissed them when tired. The only objection to this proceeding was its inordinate expense: three cloths being generally demanded by the porter for thirty miles. A little calculation will give an idea of the relative cost of travelling in Africa and in Europe. Assuming each man to receive one cloth, worth one dollar, for every ten miles, and that six porters are required to carry the hammock, we have in Africa an expenditure on carriage alone of nearly half a crown per mile: in most parts of Europe travel on the iron road has been reduced to one penny.

Our return from Unyanyembe to the coast was to take place during the dead season, when provisions are most expensive and are not unfrequently unprocurable. But being "Wazungu" and well provided with " African money," we might expect the people to sell to us their grain and stores, which they would have refused at tariff-prices to Arabs or Wasawahili. We carried as stock fourteen porters' loads of cloth, viz., 645 domestics, 653 blue-cottons, and 20 coloured cloths, principally Debwani, Barsati, and Subai, as presents to chiefs. The supply of beads was represented by one load of ububu or black-porcelains — afterwards thrown away as useless — half a Frasilah (17·5 pounds) of "locust-legs," or pink-porcelains, purchased from Sallum bin Hamid, and eight Kartasat or papered-bundles of the heavy and expensive "town-breakers," vermilion or coral-porcelains, amounting to seventy Fundo, each of which covered as a rule the day's minor expenses. The other stores were the fifty-four Jembe purchased at Msene, besides a few brought from Usukuma by my companion. These articles are useful in making up kuhonga or blackmail; in Ugogo and Usagara, which is their western limit, they double in value, and go even further than a white cotton-cloth. Finally, we had sixteen cows, heifers, and calves, bought in Usukuma by my companion, at the rate of six domestics per head. We expected them to be serviceable as presents, and meanwhile to add materially to our comfort by a more regular supply of milk than the villages afford. But, alas! having neglected to mark the animals, all were changed — a fact made evident by their running dry after a few days: the four calves presently died of fatigue; whenever an animal lay down upon the road its throat was summarily cut, others were left to stray and be stolen, and the last bullock preserved for a sirloin on Christmas-was prematurely lost. A small per-centage proved useful as tribute to the chiefs of Ugogo, and served as rations when grain was unprocurable. The African, however, looks upon meat, not as "Posho" — daily bread — but as kitoweyo — kitchen: two or three pounds of beef merely whet his teeth for the usual

Ugali or porridge of boiled flour. It is almost need-less to state that, despite the best surveillance and the strictest economy, we arrived at the coast almost desti-tude ; cloth and beads, hoes and cattle, all had disap-peared, and had we possessed treble the quantity, it would have gone the same way.

The 26th September, 1858, saw us on foot betimes. The hospitable Snay bin Amir, freshly recovered from an influenza which had confined him for some days to his sleeping-mat, came personally to superintend our departure. As no porters had returned for property left behind, and as all the " cooking-pots" had preceded us on the yester, Snay supplied us with his own slaves, and provided us with an Arab breakfast, well cooked, and as usual, neatly served on porcelain plates, with plaited and coloured straw dish-covers, pointed like Chinese caps. Then, promising to spend the next day with me, he shook hands and followed me out of the compound. After a march of three miles, under a white-hot sun, and through a chilling wind, to which were probably owing our subsequent sufferings, we entered the dirty little village of Masui, where a hovel had been prepared for us by Said bin Salim. There we were greeted by the caravan, and we heard with pleasure that it was ready, after a fashion, to break ground.

Early on the next morning appeared Snay bin Amir and Musa Mzuri: as I was suffering from a slight attack of fever, my companion took my place as host. The paroxysm passing off, allowed me to settle all accounts with Snay bin Amir, and to put a finishing touch to the names of stations in the journal. I then thanked these kind-hearted men for their many good deeds, and promised to report to H. H. the Sayyid Majid the hospitable reception of his Arab subjects generally, and of Snay and Musa in particular. About evening time I shook hands with Snay bin Amir — having so primed the dear old fellow with a stirrup-cup of burnt-punch, that his gait and effusion of manner were by no means such as became a staid and stately Arab Shaykh.

On the 4th October, after a week of halts and snail's marches — the insufficiency of porterage compelled me to send back men for the articles left behind at the several villages — we at last reached Hanga, our former quarters on the eastern confines of the Unyanyembe district. As long as we were within easy distance of Kazeh it was impossible to keep the sons of Ramji in camp, and their absence interfered materially with the completion of the gang. Several desertions took place, a slave given by Kannena of Ujiji to Said bin Salim, old Musangesi the Asinego, and two new purchases, male and female, made by the Baloch at Kazeh, disappeared after the first few marches. The porters were troublesome. They had divided themselves as usual into Khambi, or crews, but no regular Kirangozi having been engaged, they preferred, through mutual jealousy, following Shehe, one of the sons of Ramji. On the road, also, some heads had been broken, because the cattle-drivers had attempted to precede the line, and I feared that the fall of a chance shower might make the whole squad desert, under the impression that the sowing season had set in. In their idleness and want of excitement, they had determined to secure at Hanga the bullock claimed by down caravans at Rubuga. After four days' halt, without other labour but that of cooking, they arose under pretext of a blow given by one of the children of Said bin Salim, and packing up their goods and chattels, poured in mass, with shouts and yells, from the village, declaring that they were going home. In sore tribulation, Said bin Salim and the Jemadar begged me to take an active part, but a short experience of similar scenes amongst the Bashi-Buzuks at the Dardanelles had made me wiser than my advisers: the African, like the Asiatic, is naturally averse to the operation proverbially called "cutting off one's own nose;" but if begged not to do so, he may wax, like pinioned men, valorous exceedingly, and dare the suicidal deed. I did not move from my hut, and in half an hour everything was *in statu quo ante.* The porters had thrown the blame of the proceeding upon the blow, consequently a flogging was ordered for Said bin Salim's " child," who, as was ever the case, had been flagrantly in the wrong ; but after return, evading the point, the plaintiffs exposed the true state of affairs by a direct reference to the bullock. Thus the " child" escaped castigation, and the bullock was not given till we reached Rubuga.

At Hanga my companion was taken seriously ill. He had been chilled on the line of march by the cruel easterly wind, and at the end of the second march from Kazeh he appeared trembling as if with ague. Immediately after arrival at the foul village of Hanga — where we lodged in a kind of cow-house, full of vermin, and exposed directly to the fury of the cold gales — he complained, in addition to a deaf ear, an inflamed eye, and a swollen face, of a mysterious pain which often shifted its seat, and which he knew not whether to attribute to liver or to spleen. It began with a burning sensation, as by a branding-iron, above the right breast, and then extended to the heart with sharp twinges. After ranging around the spleen, it attacked the upper part of the right lung, and finally it settled in the region of the liver. On the 10th October, suddenly waking about dawn from a horrible dream, in which a close pack of tigers, leopards, and other beasts, harnessed with a network of iron hooks, were dragging him like the rush of a whirlwind over the ground, he found himself sitting up on the side of his bedding, forcibly clasping both sides with his hands. Half-stupefied by pain, he called Bombay, who having formerly suffered from the "Kichyoma-chyoma" — the "little irons"—raised his master's right arm, placed him in a sitting position, as lying down was impossible, and directed him to hold the left ear behind the head, thus relieving the excruciating and torturing twinges, by lifting the lung from the liver. The next spasm was less severe, but the sufferer's mind had begun to wander, and he again clasped his sides, a proceeding with which Bombay interfered.

Early on the next morning, my companion, supported by Bombay and Gaetano, staggered towards the tent. Nearing the doorway, he sent in his Goanese, to place a chair for sitting, as usual, during the toils of the day, outside. The support of an arm being thus removed, ensued a second and violent spasm of cramps and twinges, all the muscles being painfully contracted. After resting for a few moments, he called his men to assist him into the house. But neglecting to have a chair previously placed for him, he underwent a third fit of the same epileptic description, which more closely resembled those of hydrophobia than aught I had ever witnessed. He was once more haunted by a crowd of hideous devils, giants, and lion-headed demons, who were wrenching, with superhuman force, and stripping the sinews and tendons of his legs down to the ankles.

At length, sitting, or rather lying upon the chair, with limbs racked by cramps, features drawn and ghastly, frame fixed and rigid, eyes glazed and glassy, he began to utter a barking noise, and a peculiar chopping motion of the mouth and tongue, with lips protruding — the effect of difficulty of breathing — which so altered his appearance that he was hardly recognisable, and completed the terror of the beholders. When this, the third and the severest spasm, had passed away, he called for pen and paper, and fearing that increased weakness of mind and body might presently prevent any exertion, he wrote an incoherent letter of farewell to his family. That, however, was the crisis. He was afterwards able to take the proper precautions, never moving without assistance, and always ordering a resting-place to be prepared for him. He spent a better night, with the inconvenience, however, of sitting up, pillow-propped, and some weeks elapsed before he could lie upon his sides. Presently, the pains were mitigated, though they did not entirely cease: this he expressed by saying that "the knives were sheathed." Such, gentle reader, in East Africa, is the kichyoma-chyoma : either one of those eccentric after-effects of fever, which perplex the European at Zanzibar, or some mysterious manifestation of the Protean demon Miasma.

I at once sent an express to Snay bin Amir for the necessary drugs. The Arabs treat this complaint by applying to the side powdered myrrh mixed with yoke of egg, and converted into a poultice with flour of mung (Phaseolus Mungo). The material was duly forwarded, but it proved of little use. Said bin Salim meanwhile, after sundry vague hints concerning the influence of the Father of Hair, the magnificent comet then spanning the western skies, insisted, as his people invariably do on such conjunctures, upon my companion being visited by the mganga, or medicine-man of the caravan. That reverend personage, after claiming and receiving the usual fee, a fat goat, anointed with its grease two little bits of wood strung on to a tape of tree-fibre, and contented himself with fastening this Mpigi — the negroid's elixir vitæ — round my companion's waist. The ligature, however, was torn off after a few minutes, as its only effect was to press upon and pain the tenderest part.

During the forced halt which followed my companion's severe attack, I saw that, in default of physic, change of air was the most fitting restorative. My benumbed legs and feet still compelling me to use a hammock, a second was rigged up for the invalid; and by good fortune thirteen unloaded porters of a down caravan consented to carry us both for a large sum to Rubuga. The sons of Ramji were imperatively ordered to leave Kazeh under pain of dismissal, which none would incur as they had a valuable investment in slaves: with their aid the complement of porters was easily and speedily filled up.

Seedy Mubarak Bombay—in the interior the name became Mamba (a crocodile) or Pombe (small beer) — had long before returned to his former attitude, that of a respectful and most ready servant. He had, it is true, sundry uncomfortable peculiarities. A heaven-born " Pagazi," he would load himself on the march with his " T'haka-t'haka," or " chow-chow," although a porter had been especially hired for him. He had no memory: an article once taken by him was always thrown upon the ground and forgotten: in a single trip he broke my elephant gun, killed my riding-ass, and lost its bridle. Like the Eastern Africans generally, he lacked the principle of immediate action; if beckoned to for a gun in the field he would probably first delay to look round, then retire, and lastly advance. He had a curious inverted way of doing all that he did. The water-bottle was ever carried on the march either un-corked or inverted; his waistcoat was generally wound round his neck, and it appeared fated not to be properly buttoned; whilst he walked bareheaded in the sun, his Fez adorned the tufty poll of some comrade; and at the halt he toiled like a charwoman to raise our tents and to prepare them for habitation, whilst his slave, the large lazy Maktubu, a boy-giant from the mountains of Urundi, sat or dozed under the cool shade. Yet with all his faults and failures Bombay, for his unwearied activity, and especially from his undeviating honesty, — there was no man, save our "Negro Rectitude," in the whole camp who had not proved his claim to the title triliteral — was truly valuable. Said bin Salim had long forfeited my confidence by his carelessness and extravagance; and the disappearance of the outfit com-mitted to him at Ujiji, in favour, as I afterwards learned, of an Arab merchant-friend, rendered him unfit for the responsibilities of stewardship.

Having summoned Said bin Salim, I told him with all gentleness, in order to spare his "shame"— the Persian proverb says, Fell not the tree which thou hast planted —that being now wiser in Eastern African travel than before, I intended to relieve him of his troublesome duties. He heard this announcement with the wriest of faces; and his perturbation was not diminished when informed that the future distribution of cloth should be wholly in the hands of Bombay, checked by my com-panion's superintendence. The loads were accordingly

numbered and registered ; the Pagazi were forbidden,
under pain of punishment, to open or to change them
without permission ; and Said bin Salim received, like
the Baloch, a certain monthly amount of beads, besides
rations of rice for the consumption of his children.
This arrangement was persevered in till we separated
upon the seaboard : it acted well, saving outfit, time,
and a host of annoyances ; moreover, it gave us command, as the African man, like the lower animals,
respects only, if he respects anything, the hand that
gives, that feeds him.   It was wonderful to see how the
" bone of contention," cloth, having been removed, the
fierceness of those who were formerly foes melted and
merged into friendship and fraternisation.   The triad
of bitter haters, Said bin Salim, the monocular Jemadar,
and Muinyi Kidogo, now marched and sat and ate
together as if never weary of such society ; they praised
one another openly and without reserve, and if an evil
tale ever reached my ear its subject was the innocent
Bombay — its object was to ruin him in my estimation.

Acutely remembering the trouble caused by the feuds
between Said bin Salim and Kidogo upon the subject of
work, I directed the former to take sole charge of the
porters, to issue their rations, and to superintend their
loads.   The better to assist him, two disorderly sons of
Ramji were summarily flogged, and several others
who refused to carry our smaller valuables were reduced to order by the usual process of stopping rations.
" Shehe," though chosen as Kirangozi or guide from
motives of jealousy by the porters, was turned out of
office ; he persisted in demanding cloth for feeing an
Unyamwezi medicine-man, in order to provide him, a
Moslem ! with charms against the evil eye, a superstition
unknown to this part of Eastern Africa.   The Pagazi,

ordered to elect one of their number, named the youth
Twánígáná, who had brought with him a large gang.
But the plague of the party, a hideous, puckered, and
scowling old man who had called himself "Muzungu
Mbaya," or the "Wicked White," so far prevailed that
at the first halt Twanigana, with his blushing honours
in the shape of a scarlet waistcoat fresh upon him, was
found squatting solus under a tree, the rest of the party
having mutinously preceded him.   I halted at once
and recalled the porters, who, after a due interval of
murmuring, reappeared. And subsequently, by invariably siding with the newly-made Kirangozi, and by
showing myself ready to enforce obedience by any means
and every means, I gave the long-legged and weak-
minded youth, who was called "Gopa-Gopa"—"Funk-
stick"—on account of his excessive timidity, a little
confidence, and reduced his unruly followers to all the
discipline of which their race is capable.

As we were threatened with want of water on the way,
I prepared for that difficulty by packing a box with
empty bottles, which, when occasion required, might be
filled at the best springs.   The Zemzemiyah or travelling canteen of the East African is everywhere a long-
necked gourd, slung to the shoulder by a string. But
it becomes offensive after a short use, and it can never
be entrusted to servant, slave, or porter without its
contents being exhausted before a mile is measured.

By these arrangements, the result of that after-
wisdom which some have termed fools' wit, I commenced the down march under advantages, happy as a
"*bourgeois*," of trappers in the joyous *pays sauvage*.   I
have detailed perhaps to a wearisome length the preparations for the march. But the success of such expeditions mainly depends upon the measures adopted

before and immediately after departure, and this dry knowledge may be useful to future adventurers in the great cause of discovery.

The stages now appeared shorter, the sun cooler, the breeze warmer; after fourteen months of incessant fevers, the party had become tolerably acclimatised; all were now loud in praise, as they had been violent in censure, of the " water and air."   Before entering the Fiery Field, the hire for carrying the hammocks became so exorbitant that I dismissed the bearers, drew on my jack-boots, mounted the half-caste Zanzibari ass, and appeared once more as the Mtongi of a caravan.   After a fortnight my companion had convalesced so rapidly that he announced himself ready to ride.   The severe liver pains had disappeared, leaving behind them, how-ever, for a time, a harassing heart-ache and nausea, with other bilious symptoms, which developed them-selves when exposed to the burning sun of the several tirikeza.   Gradually these sequelæ ceased, sleep and appetite returned, and at K'hok'ho, in Ugogo, my com-panion had strength enough to carry a heavy rifle, and to do damage amongst the antelope and the guinea fowl. Our Goanese servants also, after suffering severely from fever)and face-ache, became different men ; Valentine, blessed with a more strenuous diathesis, carried before him a crop like a well-crammed capon.   As the porters left this country, and the escort approached their homes, there was a notable change of demeanour.   All waxed civil, even to servility, grumbling ceased, and smiles mantled every countenance.   Even Muzungu Mbaya, who in Unyamwezi had been the head and front of all offence, was to be seen in Ugogo meekly sweeping out our tents with a bunch of thorns.

We left Hanga, the dirty cow-village, on the 13th

October. The seven short marches between that place and Tura occupied fifteen days, a serious waste of time and cloth, caused by the craving of the porters for their homes. It was also necessary to march with prudence, collisions between the party and the country-people, who are unaccustomed to see the articles which they most covet carried out of the country, were frequent : in fact we flew to arms about every second day, and after infinite noise and chatter, we quitted them to boast of the deeds of " derring do," which had been consigned to the limbo of things uncreate by the fainéance of the adversary. At Eastern Tura, where we arrived on the 28th October, a halt of six days was occasioned by the necessity of providing and preparing food, at that season scarce and dear, for the week's march through the Fiery Field. The caravan was then mustered, when its roll appeared as follows. We numbered in our own party two Europeans, two Goanese, Bombay with two slaves — the child-man Nasibu and the boy-giant Maktubu — the bull-headed Mabruki, Nasir, a half-caste Mazrui Arab, who had been sent with me by the Arabs of Kazeh to save his morals, and Taufiki, a Msawahili youth, who had taken service as gun-carrier to the coast: they formed a total of 10 souls. Said bin Salim was accompanied by 12—the charmers Halimah and Zawada, his five children, and a little gang of five fresh captures, male and female. The Baloch, 12 in number, had 15 slaves and 11 porters, composing a total of 38. The sons of Ramji, and the ass-drivers under Kidogo their leader, were in all 24, including their new acquisitions. Finally 68 Wanyamwezi porters, carrying the outfit and driving the cattle, completed the party to 152 souls.

On the 3rd November, the caravan issuing from Tura

plunged manfully into the Fiery Field, and after seven
marches in as many days, halted for breath and forage at
Jiwe la Mkoa, the Round Stone.   A few rations having
been procured in its vicinity, we resumed our way on
the 12th November, and in two days exchanged, with a
sensible pleasure, the dull expanse of dry brown bush and
brushwood, dead thorn-trees, and dry Nullahs, for the
fertile red plain of Mdaburu.   After that point began the

Jiwe la Mkoa, the Round Rock.

transit of Ugogo, where I had been taught to expect accidents : they resolved themselves, however, into nothing
more than the disappearance of cloth and beads in inordinate quantities.   We were received by Magomba, the
Sultan of Kanyenye, with a charge of magic, for which
of course it was necessary to pay heavily.   The Wanyamwezi porters seemed even more timid on the down-
journey than on the up-march.   They slank about like
curs, and the fierce look of a Mgogo boy was enough

to strike a general terror. Twanigana, when safe in the mountains of Usagara, would frequently indulge me in a dialogue like the following, and it may serve as a specimen of the present state of conversation in East Africa :—

"The state, Mdula ?" (*i.e.* Abdullah, a word unpronounceable to Negroid organs.)

"The state is very! (well) and thy state ?"

"The state is very! (well) and the state of Spikka ? (my companion)."

"The state of Spikka is very ! (well.)"

"We have escaped the Wagogo (resumes Twanigana), white man O!"

"We have escaped, O my brother !"

"The Wagogo are bad."

"They are bad."

"The Wagogo are very bad."

"They are very bad."

"The Wagogo are not good."

"They are not good."

"The Wagogo are not at all good."

"They are not at all good."

"I greatly feared the Wagogo, who kill the Wanyamwezi."

"Exactly so !"

"But now I don't fear them. I call them ——s and —— s, and I would fight the whole tribe, white man O !"

"Truly so, O my brother !"

And thus for two mortal hours, till my ennui turned into marvel. Twanigana however was, perhaps, in point of intellect somewhat below the usual standard of African young men. Older and more experienced was Muzungu Mbaya, and I often listened with no small amusement to the attempts made by the Baloch to impress upon this truly African mind a respect for their revelation. Gul Mohammed was the missionary of the party: like Moslems generally, however, his thoughts had been taught to run in one groove, and if disturbed by startling objections, they were all abroad. Similarly I have observed in the European old lady, that on such subjects all the world must think with her, and I have been suspected of drawing the long-bow when describing the worship of gods with four arms, and goddesses with two heads.

Muzungu Mbaya, as the old hunks calls himself, might be sitting deeply meditative, at the end of the march, before the fire, warming his inner legs, smoking his face, and ever and anon casting pleasant glances at a small black earthen pipkin, whence arose the savoury steam of meat and vegetables. A concatenation of ideas induces Gul Mohammed to break into his favourite theme.

" And thou, Muzungu Mbaya, thou also must die ! "

"Ugh! ugh!" replies the Muzungu personally offended, " don't speak in that way ! Thou must die too."

" It is a sore thing to die," resumes Gul Mohammed.

" Hoo ! Hoo !" exclaims the other, "it is bad, very bad, never to wear a nice cloth, no longer to dwell with one's wife and children, not to eat and drink, snuff, and smoke tobacco. Hoo! Hoo! it is bad, very bad ! "

" But we shall eat," rejoins the Moslem, " the flesh of birds, mountains of meat, and delicate roasts, and drink sugared water, and whatever we hunger for."

The African's mind is disturbed by this tissue of contradictions. He considers birds somewhat low feeding, roasts he adores, he contrasts mountains of meat with his poor half-pound in pot, he would sell himself for sugar; but again he hears nothing of tobacco; still he takes the trouble to ask

"Where, O my brother?"

"There," exclaims Gul Mohammed, pointing to the skies.

This is a "chokepear" to Muzungu Mbaya. The distance is great, and he can scarcely believe that his interlocutor has visited the firmament to see the provision; he therefore ventures upon the query,

"And hast thou been there, O my brother?"

"Astaghfar ullah (I beg pardon of Allah)!" ejaculates Gul Mohammed, half angry, half amused. "What a mshenzi (pagan) this is! No, my brother, I have not exactly been there, but my Mulungu (Allah) told my Apostle*, who told his descendants, who told my father and mother, who told me, that when we die we shall go to a Shamba (a plantation), where——"

"Oof!" grunts Muzungu Mbaya, "it is good of you to tell us all this Upumbafu (nonsense) which your mother told you. So there are plantations in the skies?"

"Assuredly," replies Gul Mohammed, who expounds at length the Moslem idea of paradise to the African's running commentary of "Nenda we!" (be off!), Mama-e! (O my mother!) and "Tumbanina," which may not be translated.

Muzungu Mbaya, who for the last minute has been immersed in thought, now suddenly raises his head; and, with somewhat of a goguenard air, inquires:

"Well then, my brother, thou knowest all things!

---

* Those who translate Rasul, meaning, literally, "one sent," by prophet instead of apostle, introduce a notable fallacy into the very formula of Moslem faith. Mohammed never pretended to prophecy in our sense of foretelling future events.

answer me, is thy Mulungu black like myself, white like this Muzungu, or whity-brown as thou art?"

Gul Mohammed is fairly floored: he ejaculates sundry la haul! to collect his wits for the reply,—

" Verily the Mulungu hath no colour."

" To-o-oh! Tuh!" exclaims the Muzunga, contorting his wrinkled countenance, and spitting with disgust upon the ground. He was now justified in believing that he had been made a laughing-stock. The mountain of meat had, to a certain extent, won over his better judgment: the fair vision now fled, and left him to the hard realities of the half-pound. He turns a deaf ear to every other word; and, devoting all his assiduity to the article before him, he unconsciously obeys the advice which many an Eastern philosopher has inculcated to his disciples —

> " Hold fast the hour, though fools say nay,
>   The spheres revolve, they bring thee sorrow ;
> The wise enjoys his joy to-day,
>   The fool shall joy his joy to-morrow."

The transit of Ugogo occupied three weeks, from the 14th of November to the 5th of December. In Kanyenye we were joined by a large down-caravan of Wanyamwezi, carrying ivories; the musket-shots which announced the conclusion of certain brotherly ties between the sons of Ramji and the porters, sounded in my ears like minute-guns announcing the decease of our hopes of a return to the coast viâ Kilwa. At Kanyenye, also, we met the stout Msawahili Abdullah bin Nasib, alias Kisesa, who was once more marching into Unyamwezi: he informed me that the slaughter of Salim bin Nasir, the Bu-Saidi, and the destruction of the Rubeho settlements, after the murder of a porter, had closed our former line through Usagara. He also supplied me with valuable tea and sugar, and my companion with a quantity of valueless, or perhaps misunderstood, information, which I did not deem worth sifting. On the 6th of December, arrived at our old ground in the Ugogi Dhun, we were greeted by a freshly-arrived caravan, commanded by Jumah bin Mbwana and his two brothers, half-caste Hindi or Indian Moslems, from Mombasah.

The Hindis, after receiving and returning news with much solemnity, presently drew forth a packet of letters and papers, which as usual promised trouble. This time, however, the post was to produce the second manner of annoyance — official " wigging," — the first being intelligence of private misfortune. Imprimis, came a note from Captain Rigby, the newly-appointed successor to Lieut.-Col. Hamerton at Zanzibar, and that name was not nice in the nostrils of men. Secondly, the following pleasant announcement. I give the whole letter :

DEAR BURTON, — Go ahead! Vogel and Macguire dead—murdered. Write often to Yours truly, N. S.

And thirdly came the inevitable official wig.

Convinced, by sundry conversations with Arabs and others at Suez and Aden, during my last overland journey to India, and by the details supplied to me by a naval officer who was thoroughly conversant with the Red Sea, that, in consequence of the weakness and insufficiency of the squadron then employed, slavery still flourished, and that the numerous British subjects and protegés were inadequately protected, I had dared, after arrival at Zanzibar, privately to address on the 15th of December, 1856, a letter upon the subject to the secretary of the Royal Geographical Society. It contained an " Account of Political Affairs in the Red Sea," — to quote the words of the paper, and expressed a hope that it might be " deemed worthy to be transmitted to the Court of

Directors, or to the Foreign Office."* The only acknowledgment which I received, was the edifying information
that the Secretary to Government, Bombay, was directed
by the Right Honourable the Governor in Council,
Bombay, to state that my " want of discretion and due
regard for the authorities to whom I am subordinate, has
been regarded with displeasure by the Government."

This was hard. I have perhaps been Quixotic enough
to attempt a suggestion that, though the Mediterranean
is fast becoming a French lake, by timely measures the
Red Sea may be prevented from being converted into a
Franco-Russo-Austrian lake. But an Englishman in
these days must be proud, very proud, of his nation, and
withal somewhat regretful that he was not born of some
mighty mother of men—such as Russia and America—
who has not become old and careless enough to leave
her bairns unprotected, or cold and crusty enough to
reward a little word of wisdom from her babes and
sucklings with a scolding or a buffet.

The sore, however, had its salve. The official wig
was dated the 23rd of July, 1857. Posts are slow
in Africa. When received on the 5th of December,
1858, it was accompanied by a copy of a Bombay News-
paper, which reported that on the 30th of June, 1858,
" a massacre of nearly all the Christians took place at
Juddah, on the Red Sea," and that " it was apprehended
that the news from Juddah might excite the Arab
population of Suez to the commission of similar outrages."

At Ugogi, which, it will be remembered, is considered
the half-way station between Unyanyembe and the
coast, the sons of Ramji and the porters detained us
for a day, declaring that there was a famine upon the

* The whole correspondence, with its reply and counter-reply, are printed
in Appendix.

Mukondokwa road which we had previously traversed. At the same time they warned us that we should find the great chief, who has given a name to the Kiringa-wana route, an accomplished extortioner, and one likely to insist upon our calling upon him in person. Having given their ultimatum, they would not recede from it : for us, therefore, nothing remained but to make a virtue of necessity. We loaded on the 7th of December, and commenced the passage of the Usagara mountains by the Kiringawana line.

I must indent upon the patience of the reader by a somewhat detailed description of this southern route, which is separated from the northern by a maximum interval of forty-three miles. .The former being the more ancient, contains some settlements like Maroro and Kisanga, not unknown by report to European geographers. It is preferred by down-caravans, who have no store of cloth to be demanded by the rapacious chiefs : the up-country travellers, who have asses, must frequent the Mukondokwa, on account of the severity of the passes on the Kiringawana.

The Kiringawana numbers nineteen short stages, which may be accomplished without hardship in twelve days, at the rate of about five hours per diem. Provisions are procurable in almost every part, except when the Warori are " out;" and water is plentiful, if not good. Travel is rendered pleasant by long stretches of forest land without bush or fetid grass. The principal annoyances are the thievish propensities of the natives and the extortionate demands of the chief. A minor plague is that of mosquitoes, that haunt the rushy banks of the hill rivulets, some of which are crossed nine or ten times in the same day ; moreover, the steep and slippery ascents and descents of black earth and

mud, or rough blocks of stone, make the porters unwilling to work.

Breaking ground at 6 A.M. on the 7th December, we
marched to Murundusi, the frontier of Usagara and
Uhehe. The path lay over a rolling thorny jungle
with dottings of calabash at the foot of the Rubeho
mountains, and lumpy outliers falling on the right of
the road. After three hours' march, the sound of the
horses announced the vicinity of a village, and the
country opening out, displayed a scene of wonderful
fertility, the effect of subterraneous percolations from
the highlands. Nowhere are the tamarind, the sycamore, and the calabash, seen in such perfection; of
unusual size also are the perfumed myombo and the
mkora, the myongo, the ndabi, the chamvya, with its
edible yellowish-red berries, and a large sweet-smelling
acacia. Amidst these piles of verdure, troops of par-
roquets, doves, jays, and bright fly-catchers, find a home,
and frequent flocks and herds, a resting-place beneath
the cool shade. The earth is still sprinkled with " black-
jacks," the remains of trees which have come to an
untimely end. In the fields near the numerous villages
rise little sheds to shelter the guardians of the crops,
and cattle wander over the commons or unreclaimed
lands. Water, which is here pure and good, lies in pits
from fifteen to twenty feet deep, staged over with tree
trunks, and the people draw it in large shallow buckets,
made of gourds sewn together and strengthened with
sticks. Towards the evening, a cold east-wind brought
up with it a storm of thunder and rain, which was
pronounced by the experts to be the opening of the
rainy monsoon in Usagara.

The next day led us over an elevated undulation
cut by many jagged watercourses, and still flanked by

the outlying masses which fall westward into the waste of Mgunda M'khali. After an hour's march, we turned abruptly eastwards, and crossing a rugged stony fork, presently found a dwarf basin of red soil which supplied water. The Wahehe owners of the land have a chronic horror of the Warori; on sighting our peaceful caravan, they at once raised the war-cry, and were quieted only by the certainty that we were even more frightened than they were. At Kinganguku, the night was again wild and stormy; in fact, after leaving Ugogi, we were regularly rained upon till we had crossed the Mountains.

On the 9th December, we marched in six hours from Kinyanguku to Rudi, the principal district of Uhehe. It was an ascent plunging into the hills, which, however, on this line are easy to traverse, compared with those of the northern route; the paths were stony and rugged, and the earth was here white and glaring, there of a dull red colour. Water pure and plentiful was found in pits about fifteen feet deep, which dented the sole of a picturesque Fiumara. The people assembled to stare with the stare pertinacious; they demanded large prices for their small reserves of provisions, but they sold tobacco at the rate of two or three cakes, each weighing about one pound and a half, for a shukkah.

Passing from the settlements of Rudi, on the next morning we entered a thorn jungle, where the handiwork of the fierce Warori appeared in many a shell of smoke-stained village. We then crossed two Fiumaras exactly similar to those which attract the eye in the Somali country, broad white sandy beds, with high stiff earth-banks deeply water-cut, and with huge emerald-foliaged trees rising from a hard bare red plain. After a short march of three hours, we pitched under a

tamarind, and sent our men abroad to collect provisions. Tobacco was cheap, as at Rudi, grain and milk,
whether fresh or sour, were expensive, and two shukkahs
were demanded for a lamb or a young goat. The
people of Mporota are notorious pilferers. About noon-
tide a loud "hooroosh" and the scampering of spearmen over the country announced a squabble; presently
our people reappeared driving before them a flock
which they had seized in revenge for a daring attempt
at larceny. I directed them to retain one fine specimen
— the *lex talionis* is ever the first article of the penal
code in the East — and to return the rest. Notwith-
standing these energetic measures, the youth Taufiki
awaking in the night with a shriek like one affected by
nightmare, found that a Mhehe robber had snatched his
cloth, and favoured by the shades had escaped with impunity. The illness of Said bin Salim detained us for
a day in this den of thieves.

The 12th December carried us in three hours from
Mporota to Ikuka of Uhehe. The route wound over red
steps amongst low stony hills, the legs of the spider-
like system, and the lay of the heights was in exceeding
confusion. Belted by thorny scrub and forests of wild
fruit trees—some edible, others poisonous—were several
villages, surrounded by fields, especially rich in ground-
nuts. Beyond Ikuka the road entered stony and
rugged land, with a few sparse cultivations almost
choked by thick bushy jungle; the ragged villages contained many dogs, and a few peculiarly hideous human
beings. Thence it fell into a fine Fiumara, with pure
sweet water in pools, breaking the surface of loose white
sand; upon the banks, red soil, varying from a few
inches to 20 feet in depth, overlay bands and lines of
rounded pebbles, based on beds of granite, schiste, and

sandstone. After ascending a hill, we fell into a second watercourse, whose line was almost choked with wild and thorny vegetation, and we raised the tents in time to escape a pitiless pelting, which appeared to spring from a gap in the southern mountains. The time occupied in marching from Ikuka to Inena of Usagara was four hours, and, as usual in these short stages, there was no halt.

Two porters were found missing on the morning of the 14th December,—they had gone for provisions, and had slept in the villages, — moreover, heavy clouds hanging on the hill-tops threatened rain: a Tirikeza was therefore ordered. At 11 A.M. we set out over rises, falls, and broken ground, at the foot of the neighbouring highlands which enclose a narrow basin, the seat of villages and extensive cultivation. Small cascades flashing down the walls that hemmed us in showed the copiousness of the last night's fall. After five hours' heavy marching, we forded a rapid Fiumara, whose tall banks of stiff red clay, resting upon tilted-up strata of greenstone, enclosed a stream calf-deep, and from 10 to 12 feet broad. At this place, called Ginyindo, provisions were hardly procurable; consequently the caravan, as was its wont on such occasions, quarrelled for disport, and the Baloch, headed by " Gray-beard Musa," began to abuse and to beat the Pagazis.

The morning of the 15th December commenced with a truly African scene. The men were hungry, and the air was chill. They prepared, however, to start quietly betimes. Suddenly a bit of rope was snatched, a sword flashed in the air, a bow-horn quivered with nocked arrow, and the whole caravan rushed frantically with a fearful row to arms. As no one dissuaded the party from " fighting it out," they apparently became friends, and took up their loads.   My companion and I rode quietly forward : scarcely, however, had we emerged from the little basin in which the camp had been placed, than a terrible hubbub of shouts and yells announced that the second act had commenced.   After a few minutes, Said bin Salim came forward in trembling haste to announce that the Jemadar had again struck a Pagazi, who, running into the Nullah, had thrown stones with force enough to injure his assailant, consequently that the Baloch had drawn their sabres and had commenced a general massacre of porters.   Well understanding this misrepresentation, we advanced about a mile, and thence sent back two of the sons of Ramji to declare that we would not be delayed, and that if not at once followed, we would engage other porters at the nearest village.   This brought on a denouement : pre·sently the combatants appeared, the Baloch in a high state of grievance, the Africans declaring that they had not come to fight but to carry.   I persuaded them both to defer settling the business till the evening, when both parties well crammed with food listened complacently to that gross personal abuse, which, in these lands, represents a reprimand.

Resuming our journey, we crossed two high and steep hills, the latter of which suddenly disclosed to the eye the rich and fertile basin of Maroro.   Its principal feature is a perennial mountain stream, which, descending the chasm which forms the northern pass, winds sluggishly through the plain of muddy black soil and patches of thick rushy grass, and diffused through watercourses of raised earth, covers the land with tobacco, holcus, sweet-potato, plantains, and maize.   The cereals stood five feet high, and were already in ear : according to the people, never less than two, and often three and

THE BASIN OF MARORO.

four crops are reaped during the year. This hill-girt district is placed at one month's march from the coast. At the southern extremity, there is a second opening like the northern, and through it the " River of Maroro " sheds into the Rwaha, distant in direct line two marches west with southing.

Maroro, or Malolo, according to dialect, is the " Marorrer town" of Lt. Hardy, (Transactions of the Bombay Geographical Society, from Sept. 1841 to May 1844,) who, in 1811—12, was dispatched with Capt. Smee by the Government of Bombay to collect information at Kilwa and its dependencies, and the East African coast generally. Mr. Cooley (Inner Africa Laid Open, p. 56) writes the word Marora, and explains it to mean "trade:" the people, however, ignore the derivation. It is not a town, but a district, containing as usual on this line a variety of little settlements. The confined basin is by no means a wholesome locality, the air is warm and " muggy,", the swamp vegetation is fetid, the mosquitos venomous, and the population, afflicted with fevers and severe ulceration, is not less wretched and degraded than the Wak'hutu. Their habitations are generally Tembe, but small and poor, and their fields are dotted with dwarf platforms for the guardians of the crops. Here a cow costs twelve cloths, a goat three, whilst two fowls are procurable for a shukkah. Maroro is the westernmost limit of the touters from the Mrima; there are seldom less than 150 muskets present, and the Wasagara have learned to hold strangers in horror.

In these basins caravans endeavour, and are forced by the people, to encamp upon the further end after marching through. At the end of a short stage of three hours we forded three times the river bed, a muddy bottom, flanked by stiff rushes, and encamped under a Mkamba tree, above and to windward of the fetid

swamp.   The night was hot and rainy, clouds of mosquitos rose from their homes below, and the cynhyænas
were so numerous that it was necessary to frighten
them away with shots.   The labour of laying in provisions detained us for a day at Maroro.

On the 17th December we left the little basin
by its southern opening, which gradually winds eastward.   The march was delayed by the distribution of
the load of a porter who had fled to the Warori.   After
crossing a fourth rise, the road fell into the cultivated
valley of the Mwega River.   This is a rush-girt stream
of pure water, about 20 feet broad, and knee-deep at
the fords in dry weather; its course is S.W. to the
stream of Maroro.   Like the Mukondokwa, it spreads
out, except where dammed by the correspondence of
the salient and the re-entering angles of the hill spurs.
The road runs sometimes over this rocky and jungly
ground, horrid with thorn and cactus, fording the
stream, where there is no room for a path, and at other
times it traverses lagoon-like backwaters, garnished
with grass, rush, and stiff shrubs, based upon sun-
cracked or miry beds.   After a march of four hours we
encamped in the Mwega Basin, where women brought
down grain in baskets: cattle were seen upon the
higher grounds, but the people refused to sell milk or
meat.

The next stage was Kiperepeta; it occupied about 2
hours 30 min.   The road was rough, traversing the
bushy jungly spurs on the left bank of the rushy narrow
stream ; in many places there were steps and ladders of
detached blocks and boulders.   At last passing through
a thick growth, where the smell of jasmine loads the air,
we ascended a steep and rugged incline, whose summit
commanded a fine back view of the Maroro Basin.   A
shelving counterslope of earth deeply cracked and cut

with watercourses led us to the encamping-ground, a red patch dotted with tall calabashes, and boasting a few pools of brackish water. We had now entered the land of grass-kilts and beehive huts, built for defence upon the ridges of the hills: whilst cactus, aloe, and milk-bush showed the diminished fertility of the soil. About Kiperepeta it was said a gang of nearly 400 touters awaited with their muskets the arrival of caravans from the interior.

On the 19th December, leaving Kiperepeta, we toiled up a steep incline, cut by the sinuated channels of watercourses, to a col or pass, the water-parting of this line in Usagara: before south-westerly, the versant thenceforward trends to the south-east. Having topped the summit, we began the descent along the left bank of a mountain burn, the Rufita, which, forming in the rainy season a series of rapids and cascades, casts its waters into the Yovu, and eventually into the Rwaha River. The drainage of the hill-folds cuts, at every re-entering angle, a ragged irregular ditch, whose stony depths are impassable to heavily-laden asses. After a toilsome march of three hours, we fell into the basin of Kisanga, which, like others on this line, is an enlarged punchbowl, almost surrounded by a mass of green hills, cone rising upon cone, with tufted cappings of trees, and long lines of small haycock-huts ranged along the acclivities and ridge-lines. The floor of the basin is rough and uneven; a rich cultivation extends from the hill-slopes to the stream which drains the sole, and fine trees, amongst which are the mparamusi and the sycomore, relieve the uniformity of the well-hoed fields. Having passed through huts and villages, where two up-caravans of Wanyamwezi were halted, displaying and haggling over the cloths intended as tribute to the

Sultan Kiringawana, we prudently forded the Yovu, and placed its bed between ourselves and the enemy. The Yovu, which bisects the basin of Kisanga from N. to S. and passes by the S.E. into the Rwaha, was then about

Rufita Pass in Usagara.

four feet deep ; it flowed down a muddy bed laced with roots, and its banks, whence a putrid smell exhaled, were thick lines of sedgy grass which sheltered myriads of mosquitos. Ascending an eminence to the left of the stream, we obtained lodgings, and at once proceeded to settle kuhonga with the chief, Kiringawana.

The father, or, according to others, the grandfather of the present chief, a Mnyamwezi of the ancient Wakala-ganza tribe, first emigrated from his home in Usagozi, and, being a mighty elephant-hunter and a powerful wizard, he persuaded by arts and arms the Wasagara, who allowed him to settle amongst them, to constitute him their liege lord. The actual Kiringawana, having spent his heir-apparent days at Zanzibar, returned to Kisanga on the death of his sire, and reigned in his stead. His long residence among the Arabs has so far civilised him that he furnishes his several homes comfortably enough; he receives his tributary-visitors with ceremony, affects amenity of manner, clothes his short, stout, and sooty person in rainbow-coloured raiment, carries a Persian blade, and is a cunning diplomatist in the art of choosing cloth.

On the day of arrival I was visited by Msimbiri, the heir-apparent — kingly dignity prevented Kiringawana wading the Yovu,—who gave some information about the Rwaha river, and promised milk. The 20th of December was expended in the palaver about "dash." After abundant chaffering, the chief accepted from the Expedition, though passing through his acres on the return-march, when presents are poor, three expensive coloured cloths, and eight shukkah of domestics and Kaniki; wondering the while that the wealthy Muzungu had neglected to reserve for him something more worthy of his acceptance. He returned a fat bullock, which was instantly shot and devoured. In their indolence the caravan-men again began to quarrel; and Wulaydi, a son of Ramji, speared a porter, an offence for which he was ordered, if he failed to give satisfaction for the assault, to be turned out of camp. A march was anticipated on the next day, when suddenly, as the moon rose over the walls of the basin, a fine bonfire on the neighbouring hill and a terrible outcry announced an accident in the village occupied by the sons of Ramji. Muinyi Buyuni had left in charge of the hearth the object of his affections, a fine strapping slave-girl, whom for certain reasons he expected to sell for a premium at Zanzibar, and she had made it over to some friend, who probably had fallen asleep. The hut was soon in flames, —in these lands fires are never extinguished,—and the conflagration had extended to the nearer hovels, consuming the cloth, grain, and furniture of the inmates. Fortunately, the humans and the cattle escaped; but a delay was inevitable. The elder who owned the chief hut demanded only eighty-eight cloths, one slave, thirteen Fundo of beads, and other minor articles :—a lesser sum would have purchased the whole household. His cupidity was restrained by Kiringawana, who named as indemnity thirty cloths, here worth thirty dollars, which I gave with extreme unwillingness, promising the sons of Ramji, who appeared rather to enjoy the excitement, that they should pay for their carelessness at Zanzibar.

During the second day's halt, I attempted to obtain from Kiringawana a permission to depart from the beaten track. The noble descent of this chief gives him power over the guides of the Wanyamwezi caravans. In consequence of an agreement with the Diwans of the Mrima, he has lately closed the direct route to Kilwa, formerly regularly traversed, and he commands a little army of touters. He returned a gracious reply, which in East Africa, however, means no gracious intentions.

Resuming our march on the 22nd of December, we descended from the eminence into the basin of the Yovu River, and fought our way through a broad "Wady," declining from east to west, with thick lines of tree and bush down the centre, and everywhere else an expanse of dark and unbroken green, like a plate of spinach. Passing along the southern bank amongst wild Annonas and fine Palmyras, over a good path where there was little mud, we presently ascended rising ground through an open forest, of the rainbow hues before described, where sweet air and soft filmy shade formed, whilst the sun was low and the breath of the morning was pure and good, most enjoyable travelling. After about five hours we descended into the basin of the Ruhembe rivulet, which seems to be the " Rohambi people " of Mr. Cooley's Itinerary. (Geography of N'yassi, p. 22.) The inhabitants are Wasagara; they supply travellers with manioc, grain, and bitter egg-plants, of a scarlet colour resembling tomatos. Cultivation flourishes upon the hill-sides and in the swampy grounds about the sole of the basin, which is bisected by a muddy and apparently stagnant stream ten feet broad. We pitched tents in the open central space of a village, and met a caravan of Wasawahili from Zanzibar, who reported to Said bin Salim the gratifying intelligence that, in consequence of a rumour of his decease, his worthy brother, Ali bin Salim, had somewhat prematurely laid violent hands upon his goods and chattels.

The porters would have halted on the next day, but the excited Said exerted himself manfully; at 2 P.M. we were once more on the road. Descending from the village-eminence, we crossed in a blazing sun the fetid Ruhembe; and, after finding with some difficulty the jungly path, we struck into a pleasant forest, like that traversed on the last march. It was cut by watercourses draining south, and at these places it was necessary to dismount. At 6 P.M. appeared a clearing, with sundry villages and clumps of the Mgude tree, whose tufty summits of the brightest green, gilt by the last rays of the sun, formed a lovely picture. The porters would have rested at this spot, but they were forced forwards by the sons of Ramji. Presently we emerged upon the southern extremity of the Makata Plain, a hideous low level of black vegetable earth, peaty in appearance, and, bearing long puddles of dark scummy and stagnant rain-water, mere horse-ponds, with the additional qualities of miasma and mosquitos. The sons of Ramji had determined to reach the Makata Nullah, still distant about two hours. I called a halt in favour of the fatigued Pagazi, who heard it with pleasure, and sent to recall Wulaydi, Shehe, and Nasibu, who were acting bell-wethers. The worthies returned after a time, and revenged themselves by parading, with many grimaces, up and down the camp.

On the morning of the 24th of December, we resumed the transit of the Makata Plain, and crossed the tail of its nullah. It was here bone-dry; consequently, had we made it last night, the thirsty caravan would have suffered severely. Ensued a long slope garnished with the normal thin forest; in two places the plots of ashes, which denote the deaths of wizard and witch, apprised us that we were fast approaching benighted K'hutu. A skeleton caravan of touters, composed of six muskets and two flags, met us on the way. Presently we descended into the basin of Kikoboga, which was occupied in force by gentry of the same description. After wading four times the black, muddy, and rushy nullah, which bisects the lake, we crossed a lateral band of rough high ground, whence a further counter-slope bent down to a Khambi in a diminutive hollow, called Mwimbi. It was the ideal of a bad encamping ground. The kraal stood on the bank of a dark, miry water at the head of a narrow gap, where heat was concentrated by the funnel-shaped hillsides, and where the dark ground, strewed with rotting grass and leaves, harboured hosts of cock-roaches, beetles, and mosquitos. The supplies, a little grain, poor sugarcane, good wild vegetables, at times plantains, were distant, and the water was vile. Throughout this country, however, the Wasagara cultivators, fearing plunder should a caravan encamp near their crops, muster in force; the traveller, therefore, must not unpack except at the kraals on either edge of the cultivation.

The dawn of Christmas Day, 1858, saw us toiling along the Kikoboga River, which we forded four times. We then crossed two deep affluents, whose banks were thick with fruitless plantains. The road presently turned up a rough rise, from whose crest began the descent of the Mabruki Pass. This col may be divided into two steps: the first winds along a sharp ridge-line, a chain of well-forested hills, whose heights, bordered on both sides by precipitous slopes of earth overgrown with thorns and thick bamboo-clumps, command an extensive view of spur and subrange, of dhun and champaign, sprinkled with villages and dwarf cones, and watered by streamlets that glisten like lines of quicksilver in the blue-brown of the hazy distant landscape. Ensues, after a succession of deep and rugged watercourses, with difficult slopes, the second step; a short but sharp steep of red earth, corded with the tree-roots that have been bared by the heavy rains. Beyond this the path, spanning rough ground at the hill-base, debouches upon the course of a streamlet flowing southwards from the last heights of Usagara to the plains of Uziraha in K'hutu.

The bullock reserved for the occasion having been lost in Uhehe, I had ordered the purchase of half a dozen goats wherewith to celebrate the day; the porters, however, were too lazy to collect them. My companion and I made good cheer upon a fat capon, which acted as roast-beef, and a mess of ground-nuts sweetened with sugar-cane, which did duty as plum-pudding. The contrast of what was with what might be now, however, suggested only pleasurable sensations ; long odds were in favour of our seeing the Christmas Day of 1859, compared with the chances of things at Msene on the Christmas Day of 1857.

From Uziraha sixteen hours distributed into fourteen marches conducted us from Uziraha, at the foot of the Usagara mountains, to Central Zungomero. The districts traversed were Eastern Mbwiga, Marundwe, and Kireng-we. The road again realises the European idea of Africa in its most hideous and grotesque aspect. Animals are scarce amidst the portentous growth of herbage, not a head of black cattle is seen, flocks and poultry are rare, and even the beasts of the field seem to flee the land. The people admitted us into their villages, whose wretched straw-hovels, contrasting with the luxuriant jungle which hems them in, look like birds' nests torn from the trees: all the best settlements, however, were occupied by parties of touters. At the sight of our passing caravan the goatherd hurried off his charge, the peasant prepared to rush into the grass, the women and children slunk and hid within the hut, and no one ever left his home without a bow and a sheath of arrows, whose pitchy-coloured bark-necks denoted a fresh layer of poison.

We entered Zungomero on the 29th of December, after sighting on the left the cone at whose base rises the Maji ya W'heta, or Fontaine qui bouille. The village on the left bank of the Mgeta, which we had occupied about eighteen months before, had long been level with the ground ; we were therefore conducted with due ceremony into another settlement on the right of the stream. An army of black musketeers, in scanty but various and gaudy attire, came out to meet us, and with the usual shots and shouts conducted us to the headman's house, which had already been turned into a kind of barrack by these irregulars. They then stared as usual for half-a-dozen consecutive hours, which done they retired to rest.

After a day's repose, sending for the Kirangozi, and personally offering a liberal reward, I opened to him the subject then nearest my heart, namely, a march upon Kilwa. This proceeding probably irritated the too susceptible Said bin Salim, and caused him, if not actually to interfere, at any rate to withhold all aid towards furthering the project. Twánigana, after a palaver with his people, returned with a reply that he himself was willing, but that his men would not leave the direct track. Their reasons were various. Some had become brothers with the sons of Ramji, and expected employment from their " father." Others declared that it would be necessary to march a few miles back, which was contrary to their custom, and said that they ought to have been warned of the intention before passing the Makutaniro, or junction of the two roads. But none expressed any fear, as has since been asserted, of being sold off into slavery at Kilwa. Such a declaration would have been ridiculous. Of the many Wanyamwezi caravans that have visited Kilwa none has ever yet been seized and sold ; the coast-people are too well acquainted with their own interests to secure for themselves a permanent bad name. Seeing, however, that energetic measures were necessary to open the road, I allowed them two days for consideration, and warned them that after that time Posho or rations should be withdrawn.

On the next day I was privately informed by the Mnfumo or parson of the caravan, that his comrades intended to make a feint of desertion, and then to return, if they found us resolved not to follow them. The reverend gentleman's sister-in-law, who had accompanied us from Unyamwezi as cook and concubine to Seedy Bombay, persuaded our managing man that there was no danger of the porters traversing Uzaramo, without pay, escort, or provisions. On the 1st January, 1859, however, the gang rose to depart. I sent for the Kirangozi, who declared that though loth to leave us he must head his men : in return for which semi-fidelity I made him name his own reward; he asked two handsome cloths, a Gorah or piece of domestics, and one Fundo of coral beads — it was double his pay, but I willingly gave it, and directed Said bin Salim to write an order to that effect upon Mr. Rush Ramji, or any other Hindu who might happen to be at Kaole. But I rejected the suggestion of my companion, who proposed that half the sum agreed upon in Unyanyembe as payment to the porters—nine cloths each—should be given to them. In the first place, this donation would have been equivalent to a final dismissal. Secondly, the Arabs at Kazeh had warned me that it was not their custom to pay in part those who will not complete the journey to the coast; and I could see no reason for departing from a commercial precedent, evidently necessary to curb the Africans' alacrity in desertion.

On the day following the departure of the gang I set out to visit the Jetting Spring, and found when returning to the village shortly before noon that my companion had sent a man to recal the " Pagazi," who were said to be encamped close to the river, and to propose to them a march upon Mbuamaji. The messenger returned and reported that the Wanyamwezi had already crossed the river. Unwilling that the wretches should lose by their headstrongness, I at once ordered Said bin

Salim to mount ass and to bring back the porters by offers which they would have accepted. Some time afterwards, when I fancied that he was probably haranguing the men, he came to me to say that he had not eaten and the sun was hot. With the view of shaming him I directed Kidogo to do the work, but as he also made excuses, Khamisi and Shehe, two sons of Ramji, were despatched with cloths to buy rations for the Pagazi, and, *coûte qui coûte*, to bring them back. They set out on the 2nd January, and returned on the 7th January, never having, according to their own account, seen the fugitives.

This was a regrettable occurrence: it gave a handle to private malice under the specious semblance of public duty. But such events are common on the slave-path in Eastern Africa; of the seven gangs of porters engaged on this journey only one, an unusually small proportion, left me without being fully satisfied, and that one deserved to be disappointed.

We were detained at K'hutu till the 20th January. The airiest of schemes were ventilated by Said bin Salim and my companion. Three of the Baloch eye-sores, the "Graybeard Mohammed," the mischief-maker Khudabakhsh, and the mulatto Jelai, were sent to the coast with letters, reports, and officials for Zanzibar and home. The projectors then attempted to engage Wak'hutu porters, but after a long palaver, P'hazi Madenge, the principal chief of Uziraha, who at first undertook to transport us in person to Dut'humi, declared that he could not assist us. It was then proposed to trust for porterage to the Wazaramo; that project also necessarily fell to the ground. Two feasible plans remained: either to write to the coast for a new gang, or to await the transit of some down-caravan.

As the former would have caused an inevitable delay I preferred the latter, justly thinking that during this, the travelling-season, we should not long be detained.

On the 11th January, 1859, a large party of Wanyanwezi, journeying from the interior to the coast, bivouacked in the village. I easily persuaded Muhembe, the Mtongi or leader, to make over to me the services of nine of his men, and lest the African mind might conceive that in dismissing the last gang cloth or beads had been an object, I issued to these new porters seventy-two cloths, as much as if they had carried packs from Unyanwezi to the coast. On the 14th January, 1859, we received Mr. Apothecary Frost's letters, drugs, and medical comforts, for which we had written to him in July 1857. The next day saw us fording the warm muddy waters of the Mgeta, which was then 100 feet broad: usually knee-deep, it rises after a few showers to the breast, and during the heavy rains which had lately fallen it was impassable. We found a little village on the left bank, and there we sat down patiently to await, despite the trouble inflicted by a host of diminutive ants, who knew no rest by day or night, the arrival of another caravan to complete our gang. The medical comforts so tardily received from Zanzibar fortified us, however, to some extent against enemies and inconveniences ; we had æther-sherbet and æther-lemonade, formed by combining a wine-glass of the spirit with a *quant. suff.* of citric acid ; and when we wanted a change the villagers supplied an abundance of Pombe or small beer.

On the 17th Jan. a numerous down-caravan entered the settlement which we occupied, and it proved after inquiry to be one of which I had heard often and much. The chiefs, Sulayman bin Rashid el Riami, a coast-Arab, accompanied by a Msawahili, Mohammed bin Gharib, and others, called upon me without delay, and from them I obtained a detailed account of their interesting travel.

The merchants had left the coast for Ubena in June, 1857, and their up-march had lasted six months. They set out with a total of 600 free men and slaves, armed with 150 guns, hired on the seaboard for eight to ten dollars per head, half being advanced: they could not persuade the Wanyamwezi to traverse these regions. The caravan followed the Mbuamaji trunk-road westward as far as Maroro in Usagara, thence deflecting southwards it crossed the Rwaha River, which at the ford was knee-deep. The party travelled through the Wahehe and the Wafaji, south of and far from the stream, to avoid the Warori, who hold both banks. The sultan of these freebooters, being at war with the Wabena, would not have permitted merchants to pass on to his enemies, and even in time of peace he fines them, it is said, one half of their property for safe-conduct. On the right hand of the caravan, or to the south from Uhehe to Ubena, was a continuous chain of highlands, pouring affluents across the road into the Rwaha River, and water was procurable only in the beds of these nullahs and fiumaras. If this chain be of any considerable length, it may represent the water-parting between the Tanganyika and the Nyassa Lakes, and thus divide by another and a southerly lateral band the great Depression of Central Africa. The land was dry and barren; in fact, Ugogo without its calabashes. Scarcely a blade of grass appeared upon the whity-brown soil, and the travellers marvelled how the numerous herds obtained their sustenance. The masika or rainy monsoon began synchronously with that of Unyamwezi, but it lasted little more than half its period in the north. In the sparse cultivation, surrounded by dense bush, they were rarely able to ration oftener than once a week. They were hospitably received by Kimanu, the Jyari or Sultan of Ubena. His people, though fierce and savage, appeared pleased by the sight of strangers. The Wabena wore a profusion of beads, and resembled in dress, diet, and lodging the Warori; they were brave to recklessness, and strictly monarchical, swearing by their chief. The Warori, however, were the cleaner race; they washed and bathed, whilst the Wabena used the same fluid to purify teeth, face, and hands.

At Ubena the caravan made considerable profits in slaves and ivory. The former, mostly captured or kidnapped, were sold for four to six fundo of beads, and, merchants being rare, a large stock was found on hand. About 800 were purchased, as each Pagazi or porter could afford one at least. On the return-march, however, half of the property deserted. The ivory, which rather resembled the valuable article procured at Karagwah than the poor produce of Unyanyembe, sold at 35 to 70 fundo of yellow and other coloured beads per frasilah of 35 lbs. Cloth was generally refused, and the kitindi or wire armlets were useful only in purchasing provisions.

On its return the caravan, following for eighteen stages the right bank of the Rwaha River, met with an unexpected misfortune. They were nighting in a broad fiumara called Bonye, a tributary from the southern highlands to the main artery, when suddenly a roar and rush of waters fast approaching and the cries of men struck them with consternation. In the confusion which ensued 150 souls, for the most part slaves, and probably ironed or corded together, were carried away by the torrent, and the porters lost a great part of the ivory. A more dangerous place for encampment can scarcely be imaginod, yet the East African everywhere prefers it because it is warm at night, and the surface is soft. In the neighbourhood of the Rwaha they entered the capital district of Mui' Gumbi, the chief, after a rude reception on the frontier, where the people, mistaking them for a plundering party of Wabena, gathered in arms to the number of 4000. When the error was perceived, the Warori warmly welcomed the traders, calling them brothers, and led them to the quarters of their Sultan. Mui' Gumbi was apparently in his 70th year, a man of venerable look, tall, burly, and light-coloured, with large ears, and a hooked nose like a " moghrebi." His sons, about thirty in number, all resembled him, their comeliness contrasting strongly with the common clansmen, who are considered by their chiefs as slaves. A tradition derives the origin of this royal race from Madagascar or one of its adjoining islets. Mui' Gumbi wore a profusion of beads, many of them antiquated in form and colour, and now unknown in the market of Zanzibar: above his left elbow he had a lumpy bracelet of ivory, a decoration appropriated to chieftains. The Warori expressed their surprise that the country had not been lately visited by caravans, and, to encourage others, the Sultan offered large gangs of porters without pay to his visitors. These men never desert; such disobedience would cost them their lives. From the settlement of Mui' Gumbi to the coast the caravan travelled without accident, but under great hardships, living on roots and grasses for want of means to buy provisions.

The same caravan-traders showed me divers specimens of the Warori, and gave me the following description, which tallied with the details supplied by Snay bin Amin and the Arabs of Kazeh.

The Warori extend from the western frontier of the Wahehe, about forty marches along principally the northern bank of the Rwaha River, to the meridian of Eastern Unyanyembe.   They are a semi-pastoral tribe, continually at war with their neighbours.   They never sell their own people, but attack the Wabena, the Wakimbu, the Wahehe, the Wakonongo, and the races about Unyangwira, and drive their captives to the sea, or dispose of them to the slavers in Usagara.   The price is of course cheap; a male adult is worth from two to six shukkah merkani.   Some years ago a large plundering party, under their chief Mbangera, attacked Sultan Kalala of the Wasukuma ; they were, however, defeated, with the loss of their leader, by Kafrira of Kivira, the son-in-law of Kalala.   They also ravaged Unyanyembe, and compelled the people to take refuge on the summit of a natural rock-fortress between Kazeh and Yombo, and they have more than once menaced the dominions of Fundikira.   Those mighty boasters the Wagogo hold the Warori in awe; as the Arabs say, they shrink small as a cubit before foes fiercer than themselves. The Warori have wasted the lands of Uhehe and Unyang-wira, and have dispersed the Wakimbu and the Wamia tribes.   They have closed the main-road from the seaboard by exorbitant blackmail and charges for water, and about five years ago they murdered two coast Arab traders from Mbuamaji.   Since their late defeat by the Watuta, they have been comparatively quiet.   When the E. African Expedition, however, entered the country they had just distinguished themselves by driving the herds from Ugogi, and thus prevented any entrance into their country from that district.   Like the pastoral races generally of this portion of the peninsula, the object of their raids is cattle: when a herd falls into their hands, they fly at the beasts like hyænas, pierce them with their assegais, hack off huge slices, and devour the meat raw.

The Warori are small and shrivelled black savages. Their diminutive size is doubtless the effect of scanty food, continued through many generations: the Sultans, however, are a peculiarly fine large race of men. The slave-specimens observed had no distinguishing mark on the teeth; in all cases, however, two short lines were tattooed across the hollow of the temples. The male dress is a cloak of strung beads, weighing ten or twelve pounds, and covering the shoulders like a European cape. Some wind a large girdle of the same material round the waist. The women wear a bead-kilt extending to the knees, or, if unable to afford it, a wrapper of skin. The favourite weapon is a light, thin, and pliable assegai; they carry a sheath of about a dozen, and throw them with great force and accuracy. The bow is unknown. They usually press to close quarters, each man armed with a long heavy spear. Iron is procured in considerable quantities both in Ubena and Urori. The habitations are said to be large Tembe, capable of containing 400 to 500 souls. The principal articles of diet are milk, meat, and especially fattened dog's flesh — of which the chiefs are inordinately fond, — maize, holcus, and millet. Rice is not grown in these arid districts. They manage their intoxication by means of pombe made of grain and the bhang, which is smoked in gourd-pipes; they also mix the cannabis with their vegetable food. The Warori are celebrated for power of abstinence; they will march, it is said, six days without eating, and they require to drink but once in the twenty-four hours. In one point they resemble the Bedouins of Arabia: the chief will entertain his guests hospitably as long as they remain in his village, but he will plunder them the moment they leave it.

On the 19th January the expected down-caravan of Wanyamwezi arrived, and I found no difficulty in completing our carriage — a fair proof, be it remarked, that I had not lost the confidence of the people. The Mtongi, however, was, or perhaps pretended to be, ill ; we were, therefore, delayed for another day in a place which had no charms for us.

The 21st January enabled us to bid adieu to Zungo-mero and merrily to take the foothpath way. We made Konduchi on the 3rd February, after twelve marches, which were accomplished in fifteen days. There was little of interest or adventure in this return-line, of which the nine first stations had already been visited and described. As the Yegea mud, near Dut'humi, was throat-deep, we crossed it lower down: it was still a weary trudge of several miles through thick slabby mire, which admitted a man to his knees. In places, after toiling under a sickly sun, we crept under the tunnels of thick jungle-growth veiling the Mgazi and other streams ; the dank and fetid cold caused a deadly sensation of faintness, which was only relieved by a glass of æther-sherbet, a pipe or two of the strongest tobacco, and half an hour's repose. By degrees it was found necessary to abandon the greater part of the remaining outfit and the luggage : the Wany-amwezi, as they neared their destination, became even less manageable than before, and the sons of Ramji now seemed to consider their toils at an end. On the 25th January we forded the cold, strong, yellow stream of the Mgeta, whose sandy bed had engulfed my

elephant-gun, and we entered with steady hearts the
formerly dreaded Uzaramo. The 27th January saw us
pass safely by the village where M. Maizan came
to an untimely end. On that day Ramazan and
Salman, children of Said bin Salim, returned from
Zanzibar Island, bringing letters, clothing, and provisions for their master, who, by way of small revenge, had despatched them secretly from Zungomero.
On the 28th January we reached the Makutaniro or
anastomosis of the Kaole and Mbuamaji roads, where on
our ingress the Wazaramo had barred passage in force.
No one now ventured to dispute the way with well-
armed paupers. That evening, however, the Mtongi
indulged his men with " maneno," a harangue. Reports about fatal skirmishes between the Wazaramo and
a caravan of Wanyamwezi that had preceded us had
flown about the camp; consequently the Mtongi recommended prudence. " There would be danger to-mor-
row—a place of ambuscade—the porters must not rise
and be off too early nor too late—they must not hasten
on, nor lag behind—they had with them Wazungu, and
in case of accidents they would lose their name !" The
last sentence was frequently repeated with ever increasing emphasis, and each period of the discourse was
marked by a general murmur, denoting attention.

As I have said, there was no danger. Yet on the
next day a report arose that we were to be attacked in
a dense thicket—where no archer, be it observed, could
bend his bow—a little beyond the junction of the Mbuamaji road with that of Konduchi, our destination.
In the afternoon Said bin Salim, with important countenance, entered my tent and disclosed to me the doleful
tidings. The road was cut off. He knew it. A great
friend of his—a slave—had told him so. He remem-

bered warning me that such was the case five days ago.
I must either delay till an escort could be summoned
from the coast, or — I must fee a chief to precede me
and to reason with the enemy. It was in vain to storm,
I feared that real obstacles might be placed by the timid
and wily little man in our way, and I consented most
unwillingly to pay two coloured cloths, and one ditto of
blue-cotton, as hire to guard that appeared in the
shape of four clothless varlets, that left us after the first
quarter of an hour. The Baloch, headed by the Jemadar,
knowing that all was safe, distinguished themselves on
that night, for the first time in eighteen months, by
uttering the shouts which prove that the Oriental soldier is doing "Zam," *i.e.* is on the *qui vive*. When requested not to make so much noise they grumbled that
it was for our sake, not for theirs.

On the 30th January our natives of Zanzibar
screamed with delight at the sight of the mango-tree,
and pointed out to one another, as they appeared in
succession, the old familiar fruits, jacks and pine-apples,
limes and cocoes. On the 2nd February we greeted,
with doffed caps and with three times three and one
more, as Britons will do on such occasions, the kindly
smiling face of our father Neptune as he lay basking in
the sunbeams between earth and air. Finally, the 3rd
February 1859 saw us winding through the poles decorated with skulls—they now grin in the Royal College of
Surgeons, London—a negro Temple-bar which pointed
out the way into the little maritime village of Konduchi.

Our entrance was attended with the usual ceremony,
now familiar to the reader: the warmen danced, shot,
and shouted, a rabble of adults, youths, and boys crowded
upon us, the fair sex lulliloo'd with vigour, and a
general procession conducted their strangers to the hut

swept, cleaned, and garnished for us by old Premji, the principal Banyan of the head-quarter village, and there stared and laughed till they could stare and laugh no more.

On the evening of the same day an opportunity offered of transferring the Jemadar, the Baloch, and my *bête noire*, Kidogo, to their homes in Zanzibar Island, which lies within sight of Konduchi: as may be imagined, I readily availed myself of it. After begging powder and *et cæteras* to the last, the monocular insisted upon kissing my hand, and departed weeping bitterly with the agony of parting. By the same boat I sent a few lines to H. M. consul, Zanzibar, enclosing a list of necessaries, and requesting that a Battela, or coasting-craft, might be hired, provisioned, and despatched without delay, as I purposed to explore the Delta and the unknown course of the Rufiji River. In due time Said bin Salim and his "children," including the fair Halimah and Zawada—the latter was liberally rewarded by me for services rendered to my companion—and shortly afterwards the sons of Ramji, or rather the few who had not deserted or lagged behind, were returned to their master, and were, I doubt not, received with all the kindness which their bad conduct deserved.

We were detained at Konduchi for six days between the 3rd and 10th February. There is nothing interesting in this little African village port: instead of describing it, I will enter into a few details concerning African matters of more general importance.

The Ivory Porter, the Cloth Porter, and Woman, in Usagara.

CHAP. XVIII.

VILLAGE LIFE IN EAST AFRICA.

THE assertion may startle the reader's preconceived opinions concerning the savage state of Central Africa and the wretched condition of the slave races, negroid and negro; but is not less true that the African is in these regions superior in comforts, better dressed, fed, and lodged, and less worked than the unhappy Ryot of British India. His condition, where the slave trade is slack, may, indeed, be compared advantageously with that of the peasantry in some of the richest of European countries.

The African rises with the dawn from his couch of cow's hide. The hut is cool and comfortable during the day, but the barred door impeding ventilation at night causes it to be close and disagreeable. The hour before sunrise being the coldest time, he usually kindles a fire, and addresses himself to his constant companion,

THE BASIN OF KISANGA.

the pipe. When the sun becomes sufficiently powerful, he removes the reed-screen from the entrance, and issues forth to bask in the morning-beams. The villages are populous, and the houses touching one another enable the occupants, when squatting outside and fronting the central square, to chat and chatter without moving. About 7 A.M., when the dew has partially disappeared from the grass, the elder boys drive the flocks and herds to pasture with loud shouts and sounding applications of the quarter-staff. They return only when the sun is sinking behind the western horizon. At 8 P.M. those who have provisions at home enter the hut to refection with ugali or holcus-porridge; those who have not, join a friend. Pombe, when procurable, is drunk from the earliest dawn.

After breaking his fast the African repairs, pipe in hand, to the Iwánzá — the village "public," previously described. Here, in the society of his own sex, he will spend the greater part of the day, talking and laughing, smoking, or torpid with sleep. Occasionally he sits down to play. As with barbarians generally, gambling in him is a passion. The normal game is our "heads and tails," its implement a flat stone, a rough circle of tin, or the bottom of a broken pot. The more civilised have learned the "bao" of the coast, a kind of "tables," with counters and cups hollowed in a solid plank. Many of the Wanyamwezi have been compelled by this indulgence to sell themselves into slavery: after playing through their property, they even stake their aged mothers against the equivalent of an old lady in these lands,—a cow or a pair of goats. As may be imagined, squabbles are perpetual; they are almost always, however, settled amongst fellow-villagers with bloodless weapons. Others, instead of gambling, seek some em-

ployment which, working the hands and leaving the
rest of the body and the mind at ease, is ever a favourite
with the Asiatic and the African; they whittle wood,
pierce and wire their pipe-sticks — an art in which all
are adepts — shave one another's heads, pluck out their
beards, eyebrows, and eyelashes, and prepare and polish
their weapons.

At about 1 P.M. the African, unless otherwise employed, returns to his hut to eat the most substantial
and the last meal of the day, which has been cooked by
his women. Eminently gregarious, however, he often
prefers the Iwánzá as a dining-room, where his male
children, rélatives, and friends meet during the most
important hour of the twenty-four. With the savage
and the barbarian food is the all-in-all of life:—food is
his thought by day,—food is his dream by night. The
civilised European, who never knows hunger or thirst
without the instant means of gratifying every whim of
appetite, can hardly conceive the extent to which his
wild brother's soul is swayed by stomach; he can
scarcely comprehend the state of mental absorption in
which the ravenous human animal broods over the car-
case of an old goat, the delight which he takes in
superintending every part of the cooking process, and
the jealous eye with which he regards all who live better
than himself.

The principal articles of diet are fish and flesh, grain
and vegetables; the luxuries are milk and butter, honey,
and a few fruits, as bananas and Guinea-palm dates;
and the inebrients are pombe or millet-beer, toddy, and
mawa or plantain-wine.

Fish is found in the lakes and in the many rivers of
this well-watered land; it is despised by those who can
afford flesh, but it is a "godsend" to travellers, to

slaves, and to the poor. Meat is the diet most prized; it is, however, a luxury beyond the reach of peasantry, except when they can pick up the orts of the chiefs. The Arabs assert that in these latitudes vegetables cause heartburn and acidity, and that animal food is the most digestible. The Africans seem to have made the same discovery: a man who can afford it almost confines himself to flesh, and he considers fat the essential element of good living. The crave for meat is satisfied by eating almost every description of living thing, clean or unclean; as a rule, however, the East African prefers beef, which strangers find flatulent and heating. Like most people, they reject game when they can command the flesh of tame beasts. Next to the bullock the goat is preferred in the interior; as indeed it is by the Arabs of Zanzibar Island; whereas those of Oman and of Western Arabia abandon it to the Bedouins. In this part of Africa the cheapest and vilest meat is mutton, and its appearance — pale, soft, and braxy — justifies the prejudice against it. Of late years it has become the fashion to eat poultry and pigeons; eggs, however, are still avoided. In the absence of history and tradition, it is difficult to decide whether this aversion to eggs arises from an imported or an indigenous prejudice. The mundane egg of Hindoo mythology probably typified the physiological dogma "omne vivum ex ovo," and the mystic disciples would avoid it as representing the principle of life. In remote ages the prejudice may have extended to Africa, although the idea which gave birth to it was not familiar to the African mind. Of wild flesh, the favourite is that of the zebra; it is smoked or jerked, despite which it retains a most savoury flavour. Of the antelopes a few are deliciously tender and succulent; the greater part are black, coarse, and indigestible.

One of the inducements for an African to travel is to afford himself more meat than at home. His fondness for the article conquers at times even his habitual improvidence. He preserves it by placing large lumps upon a little platform of green reeds, erected upon uprights about eighteen inches high, and by smoking it with a slow fire. Thus prepared, and with the addition of a little salt, the provision will last for several days, and the porters will not object to increase their loads by three or four pounds of the article, disposed upon a long stick like gigantic kababs. They also jerk their stores by exposing the meat upon a rope, or spread upon a flat stone, for two or three days in the sun; it loses a considerable portion of nutriment, but it packs into a conveniently small compass. This jerked meat, when dried, broken into small pieces, and stored in gourds or in pots full of clarified and melted butter, forms the celebrated travelling provision in the East called kavurmeh: it is eaten as a relish with rice and other boiled grains. When meat is not attainable and good water is scarce, the African severs one of the jugulars of a bullock and fastens upon it like a leech. This custom is common in Karagwah and the other northern kingdoms, and some tribes, like the Wanyika, near Mombasah, churn the blood with milk.

The daily food of the poor is grain, generally holcus, maize, or bajri (panicum); wheat is confined to the Arabs, and rice grows locally, as in the Indian peninsula. The inner Africans, like the semi-civilised Arabs of Zanzibar, the Wasawahili, and the Wamrima, ignore the simple art of leavening bread by acidulated whey, sour bean-paste, and similar contrivances universally practised in Oman. Even the rude Indian chapati or scone is too artificial for them, and they have not learned to toast grain. Upon journeys the African boils his holcus unhusked in an earthen basin, drinks the water, and devours the grain, which in this state is called masango ; at home he is more particular. The holcus is either rubbed upon a stone — the mill being wholly unknown — or pounded with a little water in a huge wooden mortar ; when reduced to a coarse powder, it is thrown into an earthen pot containing boiling water sufficient to be absorbed by the flour; a little salt, when procurable, is added ; and after a few stirrings with a ladle, or rather with a broad and flat-ended stick, till thoroughly saturated, the thick mass is transferred into a porous basket, which allows the extra moisture to leak out. Such is the ugali, or porridge, the staff of life in East Africa.

During the rains vegetables are common in the more fertile parts of East Africa ; they are within reach of the poorest cultivator. Some varieties, especially the sweet potato and the mushroom, are sliced and sun-dried to preserve them through the year. During the barren summer they are boiled into a kind of broth.

Milk is held in high esteem by all tribes, and some live upon it almost exclusively during the rains, when cattle find plentiful pasture. It is consumed in three forms— " mabichi," when drunk fresh ; or converted into mabivu (butter-milk), the rubb of Arabs ; or in the shape of mtindi (curded milk), the laban of Arabia, and the Indian dahi. These Africans ignore the dudh-pinda, or ball of fresh-milk boiled down to hardness by evaporation of the serum, as practised by the Indian halwaí (confectioner) ; the indurated sour-clot of Arabia, called by the Bedouins el igt, and by the Persians the Baloch, and the Sindhians kurut, is also unknown ; and they consider cheese a miracle, and use against it their stock denunciation, the danger of bewitching cattle. The fresh produce, moreover, has few charms as a poculent amongst barbarous and milk-drinking races: the Arabs and the Portuguese in Africa avoid it after the sun is high, believing it to increase bile, and eventually to cause fever: it is certain that, however pleasant the draught may be in the cool of the morning, it is by no means so much relished during the heat of the day. On the other hand, the curded milk is everywhere a favourite on account of its cooling and thirst-quenching properties, and the people accustomed to it from infancy have for it an excessive longing. It is procurable in every village where cows are kept, whereas that newly-drawn is generally half-soured from being at once stored in the earthen pots used for curding it. These East Africans do not, however, make their dahi, like the Somal, in lumps floating upon the tartest possible serum; nor do they turn it, like the Arabs, with kid's rennet, nor like the Baloch with the solanaceous plant called panir. The best is made, as in India, by allowing the milk to stand till it clots in a pot used for the purpose, and frequently smoked for purity. Butter-milk is procurable only in those parts of the country where the people have an abundance of cattle.

Butter is made by filling a large gourd, which acts as churn, with partially-soured milk, which is shaken to and fro: it is a poor article, thin, colourless, and tainted by being stored for two or three months, without preliminary washing, in the bark-boxes called vilindo. In the Eastern regions it is converted into ghee by simply melting over the fire: it is not boiled to expel the remnant of sour milk, impurities are not removed by skimming, and finally it becomes rancid and bitter by storing in pots and gourds which have been used for the purpose during half a generation. The Arabs attempt to do away with the nauseous taste by throwing into it when boiling a little water, with a handful of flour or of unpowdered rice. Westward of Unyamwezi butter is burned instead of oil in lamps.

The common oil in East Africa is that of the karanga, bhuiphali, or ground-nut (Arachis hypogæa): when ghee is not procurable, the Arabs eat it, like cocoa-nut oil, with beans, manioc, sweet-potato and other vegetables. A superior kind of cooking is the "uto" extracted from the ufuta, simsim or sesamum, which grows everywhere upon the coast, and extends far into the interior. The process of pressing is managed by pounding the grain dry in a huge mortar; when the oil begins to appear, a little hot water is poured in, and the mass is forcibly squeezed with huge pestles; all that floats is then ladled out into pots and gourds. The viscid chikichi (palm-oil) is found only in the vicinity of the Tanganyika Lake, although the tree grows in Zanzibar and its adjacent islets. Oil is extracted from the two varieties of the castor-plant; and, in spite of its unsavoury smell, it is extensively used as an unguent by the people. At Unyanyembe and other places where the cucumber grows almost wild, the Arabs derive from its seed an admirable salad-oil, which in flavour equals, and perhaps surpasses, the finest produce of the olive. The latter tree is unknown in East Africa to the Arabs, who speak of it with a religious respect, on account of the mention made of it in the Koran.

In East Africa every man is his own maltster; and the "Iwánzá," or public-house of the village, is the common brewery. In some tribes, however, fermentation

is the essential occupation of the women. The principal inebrient is a beer without hops, called pombe.
This ποτος θειος of the negro and negroid races dates
from the age of Osiris: it is the buzah of Egypt and
the farther East, and the merissa of the Upper Nile,
the ξιθον and xythum of the West, and the oala or
boyaloa of the Kafirs and the South African races.
The taste is somewhat like soured wort of the smallest
description, but strangers, who at first dislike it exceedingly, are soon reconciled to it by the pleasurable
sensations to which it gives rise. Without violent
action, it affects the head, and produces an agreeable
narcotism, followed by sound sleep and heaviness in the
morning—as much liked by the barbarian, to whom
inebriation is a boon, as feared by the civilised man.
Being, as the Arabs say, a "cold drink," causing
hydrocele and rheumatism, it has some of the after-
effects of gin, and the drunkard is readily recognised
by his red and bleared eyes. When made thick with
the grounds or sediment of grain, it is exceedingly
nutricious. Many a gallon must be drunk by the
veteran malt-worm before intoxication; and individuals
of both sexes sometimes live almost entirely upon
pombe. It is usually made as follows: half of the
grain—holcus, panicum, or both mixed—intended for
the brew is buried or soaked in water till it sprouts;
it is then pounded and mixed with the other half, also
reduced to flour, and sometimes with a little honey. The
compound is boiled twice or thrice in huge pots, strained,
when wanted clear, through a bag of matting, and
allowed to ferment: after the third day it becomes
as sour as vinegar. The "togwa" is a favourite drink,
also made of holcus. At first it is thick and sickly,
like honeyed gruel; when sour it becomes exceedingly

heady.   As these liquors consume a quantity of grain, they are ever expensive; the large gourdful never fetches less than two khete or strings of beads, and strangers must often pay ten khete for the luxury. Some years ago an Arab taught the Wanyamwezi to distil: they soon, however, returned to their favourite fermentation.

The use of pombe is general throughout the country: the other inebrients are local.   At the island and on the coast of Zanzibar tembo, or toddy, in the West African dialects tombo, is drawn from the cocoa-tree; and in places a pernicious alcohol, called mvinyo, is extracted from it.   The Wajiji and other races upon the Tanganyika Lake tap the Guinea-palm for a toddy, which, drawn in unclean pots, soon becomes acid and acrid as the Silesian wine that serves to mend the broken limbs of the poor.   The use of bhang and datura-seed has already been alluded to.   " Máwá," or plantain-wine, is highly prized because it readily intoxicates.   The fruit when ripe is peeled and hand-kneaded with coarse green grass, in a wide-mouthed earthen pot, till all the juice is extracted : the sweet must is then strained through a *cornet* of plantain-leaf into a clean gourd, which is but partially stopped.   To hasten fermentation a handful of toasted or pounded grain is added : after standing for two days in a warm room the wine is ready for drinking.

The East Africans ignore the sparkling berille or hydromel of Abyssinia and Harar, and the mead of the Bushman race.   Yet honey abounds throughout the country, and near the villages log-hives, which from their shape are called mazinga or cannons by the people, hang from every tall and shady tree.   Bees also swarm in the jungles, performing an important part in the

vegetable economy by masculation or caprification, and
the conveyance of pollen. Their produce is of two
kinds. The cheaper resembles wasp-honey in Europe;
it is found in the forest, and stored in gourds. More
than half-filled with dirt and wood-bark, it affords but
little wax; the liquid is thin and watery, and it has a
peculiarly unpleasant flavour. The better variety, the
hive-honey, is as superior to the produce of the jungle
as it is inferior to that of India and of more civilised
lands. It is tolerable until kept too long, and it
supplies a good yellow wax, used by the Arabs to mix
with tallow in the manufacture of "dips." The best
honey is sold after the rains; but the African hoards his
store till it reddens, showing the first stage of fermentation: he will eat it after the second or third year,
when it thins, froths, and becomes a rufous-brown
fluid of unsavoury taste; and he rarely takes the
trouble to remove the comb, though the Arabs set him
the example of straining the honey through bags of
plantain-straw or matting. Decomposition, moreover,
is assisted by softening the honey over the fire to extract the wax instead of placing it in the sun. The price
varies from one to three cloths for a large gourdful.
When cheap, the Arabs make from it "honey-sugar:"
the material, after being strained and cleaned, is stored
for two or three weeks in a cool place till surface-granu-
lation takes place; the produce resembles in taste and
appearance coarse brown sugar. The "siki," a vinegar
of the country, is also made of one part honey and four
of water, left for a fortnight to acetise: it is weak and
insipid. Honey is the only sweetener in the country,
except in the places where the sugar-cane grows,
namely, the maritime and the Lakist regions. The
people chew it, ignoring the simple art of extracting

and inspissating the juice; nor do they, like the natives of Usumbara, convert it into an inebrient. Yet sugar attracts them like flies; they clap their hands with delight at the taste; they buy it for its weight of ivory; and if a thimbleful of the powder happen to fall upon the ground, they will eat an ounce of earth rather than lose a grain of it.

After eating, the East African invariably indulges in a long fit of torpidity, from which he awakes to pass the afternoon as he did the forenoon, chatting, playing, smoking, and chewing "sweet-earth." Towards sunset all issue forth to enjoy the coolness: the men sit outside the Iwánzá, whilst the women and the girls, after fetching water for household wants from the well, collecting in a group upon their little stools, indulge in the pleasures of gossipred and the pipe. This hour in the more favoured parts of the country is replete with enjoyment, which even the barbarian feels, though not yet indoctrinated into æsthetics. As the hours of darkness draw nigh, the village doors are carefully closed, and, after milking his cows, each peasant retires to his hut, or passes his time squatting round the fire with his friends in the Iwánzá. He has not yet learned the art of making a wick, and of filling a bit of pottery with oil. When a light is wanted, he ignites a stick of the oleaginous mtata, or msásá-tree — a yellow, hard, close-grained, and elastic wood, with few knots, much used in making spears, bows, and walking staves — which burns for a quarter of an hour with a brilliant flame. He repairs to his hard couch before midnight, and snores with a single sleep till dawn. For thorough enjoyment, night must be spent in insensibility, as day is in inebriety; and, though an early riser, he avoids the

" early to bed," in order that he may be able to slumber through half the day.

It is evident that these barbarians lead rather a " fast " life ; there are, however, two points that modify its evil consequences. The " damned distillation " is unknown, consequently they do not suffer from delirium tremens, its offspring. Their only brain-work is that necessitated by the simple wants of life, and by the unartificial style of gambling which they affect. Amongst the civilized, the peculiar state of the nervous system in the individual, and in society, the abnormal conditions induced by overcrowding in cities and towns, has engendered a cohort of dire diseases which the children of nature ignore.

Such is the African's idle day, and thus every summer is spent. As the wintry rains draw nigh, the necessity of daily bread suggests itself. The peasants then leave their huts at 6 or 7 A.M., often without provision, which now becomes scarce, and labour till noon, or 2 P.M., when they return home, and find food prepared by the wife or the slave-girl. During the afternoon they return to work, and sometimes, when the rains are near, they are aided by the women. Towards sunset all wend homewards in a body, laden with their implements of cultivation, and singing a kind of " dulce domum," in a simple and pleasing recitative.

When the moon shines bright the spirits of the East African are raised like the jackal's, and a furious drumming and a droning chorus summon the maidens to come out and enjoy the spectacle of a dance. The sexes seldom perform together, but they have no objection to be gazed at by each other. Their style of saltation is remarkable only for the extreme gravity which it induces — at no other time does the East

African look so serious and so full of earnest purpose.
Yet with all this thoughtfulness, " poor human nature
cannot dance of itself." The dance has already been
described as far as possible: as may be imagined, the
African Thalia is by no means free from the reproach
which caused Mohammed to taboo her to his followers.

Music is at a low ebb. Admirable timists, and no
mean tunists, the people betray their incapacity for
improvement by remaining contented with the simplest
and the most monotonous combinations of sounds. As in
everything else, so in this art, creative talent is wanting.
A higher development would have produced other
results ; yet it is impossible not to remark the delight
which they take in harmony. The fisherman will
accompany his paddle, the porter his trudge, and the
housewife her task of rubbing down grain, with song ;
and for long hours at night the peasants will sit in a
ring repeating, with a zest that never flags, the same
few notes, and the same unmeaning line. Their style
is the recitative, broken by a full chorus, and they
appear to affect the major rather than the interminable
minor key of the Asiatic. Their singing also wants
the strained upper notes of the cracked-voiced Indian
performer, and it ignores the complicated raga and
ragini or Hindu modes, which appear rather the musical
expression of high mathematics than the natural
language of harmony and melody.

The instruments of the East African are all of foreign
invention, imported from various regions, Madagascar,
and the coast. Those principally in use are the following. The zeze, or banjo, resembles in sound the
monochord Arabian rubabah, the rude ancestor of the
Spanish guitar. The sounding-board is a large hollow

gourd, open below; on the upper part, fastened by strings that pass through drilled holes, is a conical piece of gourd, cleft longitudinally to admit the arm or handle, which projects at a right angle. The arm is made of light wood, from 18 inches to 2 feet in length; the left-hand extremity has three frets formed by two notches, with intervals, and thus the total range is of six notes. A single string, made of "mondo," the

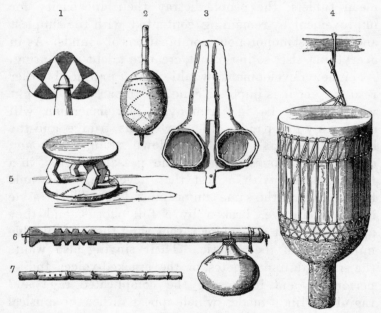

1. Paddle in East Africa.   2. The Sange or Gourd.   3. Bellows.   4. Drum.
   5. Stool.   6. The Zeze (guitar).   7. The D'hete, or Kidete.

fibre of the mwale or raphia-palm, is tied to a knob of wood projecting from the dexter extremity of the handle, thence it passes over a bridge of bent quill, which for tuning is raised or depressed, and lastly it is secured round another knob at the end beyond the frets. Sometimes, to form a bass or drone, a second string is similarly attached along the side of the arm, whilst the treble runs along the top.

The kinanda, a prototype of the psaltery and harp, the lute and lyre, and much used by the southern races in the neighbourhood of Kilwa, is of two kinds. One is a shallow box cut out of a single plank, thirteen inches long by five or six in breadth, and about two inches in depth: eleven or twelve strings are drawn tightly over the hollow. The instrument is placed in the lap, and performed upon with both hands. The other is a small bow-guitar, with an open gourd attached to the part about the handle: sometimes the bow passes through the gourd. This instrument is held in the left hand, whilst the "tocador" strikes its single cord with a thin cane-plectrum about one foot long. As in the zeze, the gourd is often adorned with black tattoo, or bright brass tacks, disposed in various patterns, amongst which the circle and the crescent figure conspicuously. A third form of the kinanda appears to be a barbarous ancestor of the Grecian lyre, which, like the modern Nubian "kisirka," is a lineal descendant from the Egyptian oryx-horn lute with the transverse bar. A combination of the zeze and kinanda is made by binding a dwarf hollow box with its numerous strings to the open top of a large circular gourd, which then acts as a sounding-board.

The wind-instruments are equally rude, though by no means so feeble as their rivals. The nai or sackbut of India, and the siwa, a huge bassoon of black wood, at least five feet long, are known only to the coast-people. The tribes of the interior use the d'hete or kidete, called by the Wasawahili zumari. It is literally the bucolic reed, a hollowed holcus-cane, pierced with four holes at the further end: the mouthpiece is not stopped in any way, and the instrument is played upon solely by the lips, a drone being sometimes supplied by the voice. Thus simple and ineffective, it has nevertheless a familiar sound to European ears. The barghumi is made by cutting an oblong hole, about the size of a man's nail, within two or three inches of the tip of a koodoo, an oryx, or a goat's horn, which, for effect and appearance, is sometimes capped with a bit of cane, whence projects a long zebra's or giraffe's tail. Like the det'he, it is played upon by the lips; and without any attempt at stops or keys, four or five notes may be produced. Its sound, heard from afar, especially in the deep silence of a tropical night, resembles not a little the sad, sweet music of the French *cor-de-chasse ;* and when well performed upon, it might be mistaken for a regimental bugle. There are smaller varieties of the barghumi, which porters carry slung over the shoulder, and use as signals on the line of march. Another curious instrument is a gourd, a few inches in circumference, drilled with many little apertures : the breath passes through one hole, and certain notes are produced by stopping others with the fingers — its loud, shrill, and ear-piercing quavers faintly resemble the European " piccolo." The only indigenous music of the pastoral African — the Somal, for instance — is whistling, a habit acquired in youth when tending the flocks and herds. This " Mu'unzi " is soft and dulcet; the ear, however, fails to detect in it either phrase or tune. For signals the East Africans practise the kik'horombwe, or blowing between the fore and the middle fingers with a noise like that of a railway whistle. The Wanyamwezi also blow over the edge of the hollow in a small antelope's horn, or through an iron tube ; and the Watuta are said to use metal-whistles as signals in battle.

The drum is ever the favourite instrument with the

African, who uses it as the alarum of war, the promise
of mirth, the token of hospitality, and the cure of diseases: without drumming his life would indeed be a
blank. The largest variety, called " ngoma ku," is the
hollowed bole of a mkenga or other soft tree, with a
cylindrical solid projection from the bottom, which holds
it upright when planted in the ground. The instrument is from three to five feet in length with a diameter
of from one to two feet : the outside is protected with a
net-work of strong cord. Over the head is stretched a
rough parchment made of calf's-skin ; and a cap of green
hide, mounted when loose, and afterwards shrunken
by exposure to fire, protects the bottom. It is vigour-
ously beaten with the fists, and sometimes with coarse
sticks. There are many local varieties of this instrument, especially the timbrel or tabret, which is about a
foot long, shaped like an hour-glass or a double " dara-
bukkah," and provided with a head of iguana-skin. The
effect of tom-toming is also produced by striking hollow
gourds and similar articles. The only cymbal is the
upatu, a flat-bottomed brass pot turned upside down,
and tapped with a bit of wood. The " sanje," a gourd
full of pebbles, is much affected in parts of the country
by women, children, and, especially, by the mganga or
rain-maker ; its use being that of the babe's rattle
amongst Europeans.

The insipidity of the African's day is relieved by frequent drinking bouts, and by an occasional hunt. For
the former the guests assemble at early dawn, and take
their seats in a circle, dividing into knots of three or
four to facilitate the circulation of the bowl. The
mwandázi, or cup-bearer, goes round the assembly,
giving scrupulous precedence to the chiefs and elders,
who are also provided with larger vessels. The sonzo,

or drinking-cup, which also serves as a travelling canteen, is made generally by the women, of a kind of grass
called mávú, or of wild palm-leaf : the split stalks are
neatly twisted into a fine cord, which is rolled up, beginning from the bottom, in concentric circles, each
joined to its neighbour by a binding of the same material : it is sometimes stained and ornamented with red
and black dyes.   The shape when finished is a trun-
cated cone, somewhat like a Turk's fez ; it measures
about six inches in diameter by five in depth, and
those of average size may contain a quart.   This cup
passes around without delay or heel-taps, and the
topers stop occasionally to talk, laugh, and snuff, to
chew tobacco, and to smoke bhang.   The scene of
sensuality lasts for three or four hours — in fact, till
the pombe prepared for the occasion is exhausted, —
when the carousers, with red eyes, distorted features,
and the thickest of voices, stagger home to doze through
the day.   Perhaps in no European country are so
many drunken men seen abroad as in East Africa.
Women also frequently appear intoxicated ; they have,
however, private " pombe," and do not drink with the
men.

The East African, who can seldom afford to gratify
his longing for meat by slaughtering a cow or a goat,
looks eagerly forward to the end of the rains, when the
grass is in a fit condition for firing ; then, armed with
bows and arrows, and with rungu or knobkerries, the
villagers have a battue of small antelopes, hares, and
birds.   During the hot season also, when the waters
dry up, they watch by night at the tanks and pools,
and they thus secure the larger kinds of game.   Elephants especially are often found dead of drought during
the hot season ; they are driven from the springs

which are haunted by the hunters, and, according to
the Arabs, they fear migrating to new seats where they
would be attacked by the herds in possession.   In many
parts the huntsmen suspend by a cord from the trees
sharpened blocks of wood, which, loosened by the
animal's foot, fall and cause a mortal wound.   This
"suspended spear," sprung by a latch, has been described
by a host of South African travellers.   It has been
sketched by Lieut. Boteler ("Narrative of a Voyage of
Discovery to Africa and Arabia," chap. iv.); and Major
Monteiro ("O Muata Cazembe," chap. v.); and described by Mr. Galton, Mr. Gordon Cumming, and Dr.
Livingstone (chap. xxviii.).   Throughout Ugogo and
upon the maritime regions large game is caught in pit-
falls, here called mtego, and in India ogi: in some
places travellers run the risk of falling into these traps.
The mtego is an oblong excavation like a great grave,
but decreasing in breadth below the surface of the
ground and it is always found single, not in pairs as
in South Africa.   The site generally chosen is near
water, and the hole is carefully masked with thin
layers of small sticks and leaves.   The Indian "sur-
rounds" and the hopo or V-shaped trap of the Bakwens
are here unknown.   The distribution of treasure-trove
would seem to argue ancient partitions and lordships,
and, in dividing the spoils of wild or tame animals,
the chief claims, according to ancient right, the breast.
This custom apparently borrowed by the Hebrews from
Africa (Leviticus, chap. vii. 30, 31), is alluded to by
almost all South-African travellers.

The elephant roams in herds throughout the country,
affecting the low grounds where stagnating water produces a plentiful vegetation: with every human being
its foe, and thousands living by its destruction, the

animal is far from becoming scarce; indeed, the greatest
number of footprints appeared near Chogwe and Tongwe,
stations of Baloch garrisons close to the town of Pangani.   The elephant hunt is with the African a solemn
and serious undertaking.   He fortifies himself with
periapts and prophylactics given by the mganga, who
also trains him to the use of his weapon.   The elephant-
spear resembles our boarding-pike rather than the light
blunt arm employed in war; it is about six feet long,
with a broad tapering head cut away at the shoulders,
and supported by an iron neck, which is planted in a
thick wooden handle, the junction being secured by a
cylinder of raw hide from a cow's tail passed over it,
and shrunk on by drying: a specimen was deposited
with the Royal Geographical Society.   The spear is invariably guarded by a mpigi or charm, the usual two bits
of wood bound together with a string or strip of skin.
It is not a little curious that the East African, though
born and bred a hunter, is, unlike almost all barbarians,
as skill-less as an European in the art of el asr, the
" spoor " or " sign."

The hunting-party, consisting of fifteen to twenty
individuals, proceeds before departure to sing and dance,
to drink and drum for a consecutive week.   The women
form line and perambulate the village, each striking an
iron jembe or hoe with a large stone, which forms an
appropriate accompaniment to the howl and the vigele-
gele, "lullilooing," or trills of joy.   At every step the
dancer sways herself elephant-like from side to side,
and tosses her head backwards with a violence threatening dislocation of the atlas.   The line, led by a fugle-
woman by the right, who holds two jembe in one hand,
but does not drum, stops facing every Arab house
where beads may be expected, and performs the most

hideous contortions, whirling the arms round the shoulder-socket, kneeling, and imitating the actions of various animals. The labour done, the ladies apply to their pombe, and reappear after four or five hours with a telltale stagger and a looseness of limb which adds a peculiar charm to their gesticulations. The day concludes with a "fackeltanz" of remarkable grotesqueness. This merrymaking is probably intended as a consolation for the penance which the elephant-hunter's wife performs during the absence of her mate; she is expected to abstain from good food, handsome cloth, and fumigation: she must not leave the house, and for an act of infidelity the blame of failure in the hunt will fall heavily upon her. Meanwhile the men—at least as "far gone" as the women—encircle with a running jumping gait, and with the grace and science of well-trained bears, a drum or a kilindo,—the normal bark bandbox,—placed with open mouth upon the ground, and violently beaten with sticks and fists or rubbed and scraped with stones. It forms also a sounding-board for a kinanda or bow-guitar, one end of which is applied to it, whilst a shrill fife of goat's horn gives finish and completeness to the band. Around the drum are placed several elephants' tails, possibly designed to serve the purpose of the clay-corpse introduced into the feasts of ancient Egypt.

When thoroughly drenched with drink, the hunters set out early in the morning, carrying live brands lest fire should fail them in the jungle, and applying them to their mouths to keep out the cold air. These trampers are sometimes dangerous to stragglers from caravans, especially in countries where the robber or the murderer expects to escape with impunity. In some places hunting-huts have been erected; they are, however, seldom used when elephants are sought, as a herd once startled does not readily return to the same pasture-grounds. The great art of the African muinzi or elephant-hunter is to separate a tusker from the herd without exciting suspicion, and to form a circle round the victim. The mganga, then rising with a shout, hurls or thrusts the first spear, and his example is followed by the rest. The weapons are not poisoned : they are fatal by a succession of small wounds. The baited beast rarely breaks, as might be expected, through the frail circle of assailants : its proverbial obstinacy is excited; it charges one man, who slips away, when another, with a scream, thrusts the long stiff spear into its hind quarters, which makes it change intention and turn fiercely from the fugitive to the fresh assailant. This continues till the elephant, losing breath and heart, attempts to escape; its enemies then redouble their efforts, and at length the huge prey, overpowered by pain and loss of blood trickling from a hundred gashes, bites the dust. The victors, after certain preliminaries of singing and dancing, carefully cut out the tusks with small, sharp axes, and the rich marrow is at once picked from the bamboo and devoured upon the spot, as the hare's liver is in Italy. The hunt concludes with a grand feast of fat and garbage, and the hunters return home in triumph, laden with ivory, with ovals of hide for shields, and with festoons of raw and odorous meat spitted upon long poles.

Throughout East Africa the mouse, as the saying is, travels with a staff : the education of youth and the exercises of manhood are confined to the practice of weapons. Yet the people want the expertness of the Somal of the North and the Kafirs of the South; their internal feuds perpetuate the necessity of offensive measures, and of the presence of arms, but their agricultural state, rendering them independent of the chase, prevents their reliance upon their skill for daily food. In consequence of being ever armed, the African like the Asiatic is nothing without his weapons; he cannot use his strength, and when he comes to blows he fights like a woman. Thus the habitual show of arms is a mere substitute for courage; in dangerous countries, as in Ugogo, the Wanyamwezi do not dare to carry them for fear of provocation, whereas at home and in comparative safety they never appear without spear or knobstick.

The weapons universally carried are the spear and the assegai. The bow and arrow, the knobkerry, the dagger, and the battle-axe are confined to certain tribes, whilst the musket and the sword are used beyond the coast only by strangers. The shield is seldom seen.

The lance of the European, Arab, and Indian is unknown to these unequestrian races. The bravest tribes prefer the stabbing-spear, which brings them to close quarters with the enemy. The weapon indeed cannot make the man, but by reaction it greatly modifies his manliness. Thus the use of short weapons generally denotes a gallant nation; the old Roman gladius, the French briquet, and the Afghan charay would be useless in the hands of a timid people. Under the impression that the further men stand from their enemies the less is to be expected from them, the French knights not inaptly termed the " villanous saltpetre " the " grave of honour," whilst their English rivals called the gun a " hell-born murderer," and an " instrument hateful in the sight of God and man." The Africans have also acted upon this idea. A great Kafir chief did

what Plutarch relates of Camillus: he broke short the
assegais of his "magnificent savages" when he sent
them to war, and forbade each warrior to return without having stained his stick with blood; the consequence was, that, instead of "dumb-shooting" at a
distance, they rushed in and won.

The mkuki, farárá, or spear, is more generally used
for stabbing than throwing. It has a long narrow blade
of untempered iron, so soft that it may be bent with
the fingers; it is capable, however, of receiving a fine
edge. The shoulders are rounded off, and one or two
lines extend lengthways along the centre from socket to
point. At the socket where the shaft is introduced, it
its covered with a bit of skin from the tail of some
animal drawn on like a stocking, and sometimes the iron
is forced on when heated, so as to adhere by contraction of
the metal. The shaft, which is five to six feet long, is
a branch of the dark-brown mkole or the light-yellow
mtata-tree, chosen because close-grained, tough, pliable,
and free from knots ; it is peeled, straightened in hot
ashes, pared down to the heart, smoothed with a knife,
carefully oiled or greased, without which it soon becomes
brittle, and polished with the leaves of the mkuba-tree.
The wood is mostly ornamented with twists of brass
and copper wire ; it is sometimes plated with zinc or tin,
and it is generally provided with an iron heel for plant-
ing in the ground. Some tribes—the northern Wagogo
and their neighbours the Wamasai for instance—have
huge spear-heads like shovels, unfit for throwing. The
best weapons for war are made in Karagwah.

The kikuki, assegai, or javelin, is much used by the
Warori and other fighting tribes, who enter action with
a sheaf of those weapons. Nowhere, however, did the
East African appear possessed of the dexterity de-

scribed by travellers amongst the southern races. The
assegai resembles the spear in all points, except that the
head is often barbed, and it is more lightly timbered ;
the shaft is rarely more than four feet in length, and it
tapers to the thinness of a man's little finger. It is laid
upon the palm of the right hand, and balanced with a
vibratory motion till the point of equilibrium is found,
when it is delivered with little exertion of the muscles
beyond the run or spring, and as it leaves the hand it
is directed by the forefinger and thumb. Sometimes,
to obviate breaking, the assegai is made like the Indian
" sang," wholly of iron.

The East African is a " good archère and a fayre."
The cubit-high Armiger begins as soon as he can walk
with miniature weapons, a cane bow and reed bird-
bolts tipped with wood, to practise till perfect at gourds
and pumpkins ; he considers himself a man when he
can boast of iron tips. With many races " pudor est
nescire sagittas." The bravest, however, the Wamasai
and the Wakwafi, the Warori and the Watuta, ignore
the practice ; with them—

> " No proof of manhood, none
> Of daring courage, is the bow ;"

and the Somali abandons it to his Midgan or servile.
The bow in East Africa is invariably what is called a
" self-bow," that is to say, made of a single piece,
and backed weapons are unknown. It is uncommonly
stiff, and the strongest archer would find it difficult to
" draw up a yard ; " of this nature probably was the
bow sent to Cambyses by the Æthiopian monarch,
with the taunting message that he had better not
attack men who could bend such weapons. When
straight it may measure five feet from tip to tip. It is
made with the same care as the spear, from a branch of

the mumepweke or the mtata-tree, laboriously cut and scraped so as to taper off towards the horns, and smeared with oil or grease, otherwise it is easily sprung, and it is sometimes adorned with plates of tin and zinc, with copper or brass wire and tips.   The string is made of hide, gut, the tendons of a bullock's neck or hock, and sometimes of tree-fibre; it is nearly double the bow in length, the extra portion being whipped for strength as well as contingent use round the upper horn.   In shooting the bow is grasped with the left hand, but the thumb is never extended along the back; the string is drawn with the two bent forefingers, though sometimes the shaft is held after the Asiatic fashion with the thumb and index.   The bow is pulled with a jerk as amongst the Somal, and not let fly as by Europeans with a long steady loose.   The best bows are made by the tribes near the Rufiji River.

The arrow is about two feet in length; the stele or shaft is made of some light wood, and often of reed. Its fault is want of weight: to inflict damage upon an antelope it must not be used beyond point-blank, fifteen to twenty paces; and a score will be shot into a bullock before it falls.   The musketeer, despising the arrow at a distance, fears it at close quarters, knowing that for his one shot the archer can discharge a dozen.   From the days of Franklin to the era of Silistria, Citate, and Kars, fancy-tacticians have advocated the substituti on of the bow or the addition of it to the "queen of weapons," the musket.   Their reasons for a revival of the obsolete arm are its lightness, its rapidity of discharge, and its silent action.   They forget, however, the saying of Xenophon, that it is impiety in a man who has not learned archery from his childhood to ask such boon of the easy gods.

The East Africans ignore the use of red-hot arrows; and the poisoned shaft, an unmanly weapon, unused by the English and French archers even in their deadliest wars, is confined to the Wanyika of Mombasah, the Wazaramo, the Wak'hutu, the Western Wasagara, and the people of Uruwwa. The Wazaramo and Wak'hutu call the plant from which the poison is extracted Mkandekande. They sold at somewhat an exorbitant price a leaf full of the preparation, but avoided pointing out to the expedition the plant, which from their description appears to be a variety of euphorbia. M. Werne ("Sources of the White Nile," chap. viii.) says that the river tribe prepare their arrow-poison from a kind of asclepias, whose milky sap is pressed out between two stones and allowed to thicken. Dr. Livingstone (chap. viii.) mentions the use of the n'gwa caterpillar amongst the Bushmen, who also poison waters with the Euphorbia arborescens; and Mr. Andersson (chap. vii.) specifies the Euphorbia candelabrum amongst the Ovaherero and the Hill Damaras. In East Africa the poison-leaves are allowed to distil their juices into a pot, which for inspissation is placed over a slow fire; becoming thick and slab, the contents are applied with a stick to the arrow, and are smoothed between the hands. When finished, the part behind the barb is covered with a shiny brown-black coat, not unlike pitch, to the extent of four or five inches. After drying it is renewed by the application of a fresh layer, the old being removed by exposure to the fire. The people fear this poison greatly; they wash their hands after touching it, and declare that a wounded man or beast loses sense, "moons about," and comes to the ground before running a quarter of a mile. Much exaggeration, however, must be expected upon the subject of toxicology amongst barbarians: it acts like the Somali arrow-poison, as a strong narcotic, and is, probably, rarely fatal, even when freshly applied.

Fearing the action of the wind upon such light shafts if unfledged, the archer inserts into the cloven end three or four feathers, the cockfeather being as in Europe perpendicular when the arrow is nocked. The pile or iron head is curiously and cruelly barbed with long waving tails; the neck is toothed and edged by dinting the iron when hot with an axe, and it is sometimes half-sawed that it may break before extraction. The East Africans also have forkers or two-headed shafts, and bird-bolts or blunt arrows tipped with some hard wood, used when the weapon is likely to be lost. Before loosing an arrow the archer throws into the air a pinch of dust, not to find out the wind, but for good luck, like the Tartars of Tibet before discharging their guns. In battle the heavy-armed man holds his spear and a sheaf of spare arrows in the bow-hand, whilst a quiver slung to the left side contains reserve missiles, and a little axe stuck in the right side of the girdle is ready when the rest fail. The ronga or quiver is a bark-case, neatly cut and stained. It is of two forms, full-length, and provided with a cover for poisoned, and half-length for unpoisoned, arrows.

The rungu or knobkerry is the African club or mace; it extends from the Cape to the negroid and the Somal tribes north of the equator. The shape varies in almost every district: the head is long or round, oval or irregular, and sometimes provided on one side with an edge; it is cut out of the hardest wood, and generally from one piece. In some cases the knob is added to the handle, and in others it is supplied with a spear-head. The handle is generally two feet long, and it is cut thin enough to make the weapon top-heavy. The Mnyamwezi is rarely seen abroad without this weapon; he uses it in the chase, and in battle against the archer: he seems to trust it in close quarters rather than the feather-weight arrow or the spear that bends like gutta-percha, and most murders are committed with it. The East people do not, like the Kafirs, use the handle of the knobkerry as a dibble.

The sime or dudgeon is the makeshift for the Arab jambiyah and the Persian khanjar. The form of this weapon differs in almost every tribe. The Wahumba or Wamasai use blades about four feet long by two fingers in breadth; the long, round, and guardless hilt is ribbed for security of grasp, and covered with leather; their iron is of excellent quality, and the shape of the weapon has given rise to the report that "they make swords on the model of those of the Knights Templars." The Wazegura and the Wagogo use knives not unlike the poniard of the Somal. In some tribes it is 3·5 feet long, with a leathern sheath extending half-way up the blade. Generally it is about half that size, straight, pointed, and double-edged, or jagged with teeth. The regions about the Lake manufacture and export great numbers of these weapons varying from a finger's length to full dimensions.

The shoka or battle-axe is much used by the tribes around the Tanganyika. It has a blade of triangular shape, somewhat longer and thinner than that used as a working tool, which is passed through the bulging head of a short handle cut out of the bauhinia or some other hard tree. Amongst the Wasagara the peculiar mundu or bill often serves for the same purpose.

The targes of the Wasagara and the Wanyamwezi have already been described; the Wavinza make a shield of basket-work. six feet by two, and much resembling that of the southern Kafirs, and the Wa'ungu carry large pavoises of bull's hide. It is probable that the exceeding humidity of the climate, so ruinous to leather, prevents the general adoption of the shield; on the march it is merely an encumbrance, and the warrior must carry it on his head beyond the reach of the dewy grass.

The maritime races, the Wazegura, and others opposite the island of Zanzibar, have imprudently been allowed to purchase fire-arms, which they employ in obstructing caravans and in kidnapping-commandos against their weaker neighbours. A single German house has, it is said, sold off 13,000 Tower muskets in one year. The arms now preferred are those exported by Hamburg and America; they fetch 4 dollars each; the French single-barrel is somewhat cheaper, averaging 3 dollars 50 cents. In the interior fire-arms are still fortunately rare—the Arabs are too wise to arm the barbarians against themselves. In Unyamwezi an old gun is a present for a chief, and the most powerful rulers seldom can boast of more than three. Gunpowder is imported from Zanzibar in kegs of 10 and 25 lbs., bearing the American mark; it is of the description used in blasting, and fouls the piece after a few discharges. The price varies at Zanzibar from 3 dollars 50 cents to 7 dollars, and upon the coast from 5 to 10 dollars per small keg; in Unyamwezi ammunition is exchanged for ivory and slaves, and some Arab merchants keep as many as thirty kegs in the house, which they retail to factors and traders at the rate of 1 to 2 shukkahs per lb.

Swords in East Africa are used only by strangers. The Wasawahili and the slave-factors prefer the kittareh, a curved sabre made in Oman and Hazramaut, or, in its stead, an old German cavalry-blade. The Arabs carry as a distinction the "faranji," a straight, thin, double-edged, guardless, and two-handed sword, about four feet long, and sharp as a carving-knife; the price varies from 10 to 100 dollars.

The negroid is an unmechanical race; his industry has scarcely passed the limits of savage invention. Though cotton abounds in the interior, the Wanyam-wezi only have attempted a rude loom; and the working of iron and copper is confined to the Wafyoma and the Lakist races. The gourd is still the principal succeda-neum for pottery. The other branches of industry which are necessary to all barbarians are mats and baskets, ropes and cords.

Carpentering amongst the East Africans is still in its rudest stage; no Dædalus has yet taught them to jag their knives into saws. It is limited to making the cots and cartels upon which the people invariably sleep, and to carving canoes, mortars, bowls, rude platters, spoons stools, and similar articles of furniture. The tree, after being rung and barked to dry the juices, is felled by fire or the axe; it is then cut up into lengths of the re-quired dimensions, and hacked into shape with slow and painful toil. The tools are a shoka, or hatchet of puerile dimensions, perhaps one-fifth the size of our broad axes, yet the people can use it to better advantage than the admirable implement of the backwoodsman. The mbizo or adze is also known in the interior, but none except the Fundi and the slaves trained upon the coast have ever seen a hand-saw, a centre-bit, or a chisel.

Previous to weaving, cotton is picked and cleaned with the hand; it is then spun into a coarse thread. Like the Paharis of India, the East Africans ignore the distaff; they twist the material round the left wrist. The mlavi, or spindle, is of two forms; one is a short stick, in-

serted in a hole practised through a lump of lead or burnt
clay, like the Indian bhaunri; the other is a thin bit of
wood, about 1·5 ft. long, with a crescent of the same
material on the top, and an iron hook to hold the thread.
The utanda, or loom-frame differs from the vertical-
shaped article of West Africa.   Two side-poles about
twelve feet long, and supported at the corners by four
uprights, are placed at an angle, enabling the workman to
stand to his work; and the oblong is completed by two
cross-bars, round which the double line of the warp, or
longitudinal threads of the woven tissue, are secured.
The dimensions of the web vary from five to six feet
in length, by two to three broad. The weft, or transverse
thread, is shot with two or three thin laths, or spindles,
round which the white and coloured yarns are wound,
through the doubled warp, which is kept apart by
another lath passing between the two layers, and the
spindle is caught with the left hand as it appears at the
left side.   Lastly, a lath, broader and flatter than the
others, is used to close the work, and to beat the thread
home.   As the workman deems three hours per diem
ample labour, a cloth will rarely be finished under a
week.   Taste is shown in the choice of patterns: they
are sometimes checks with squares, alternately black and
white, or in stripes of black variegated with red dyes
upon a white ground: the lines are generally broad in
the centre, but narrow along the edges, and the texture
not a little resembles our sacking. The dark colour is
obtained from the juice of the mzima-tree; it stains the
yarn to a dull brown, which becomes a dark mulberry,
or an Indian-ink black, when buried for two or three
days in the vegetable mud of the ponds and pools. The
madder-red is produced by boiling the root and bark of
a bush called mda'a; an ochreish tint is also extracted

from the crimson matter that stains the cane and the leaves of red holcus. All cloths have the tambua or fringe indispensable in East Africa. Both weaving and dyeing are men's not women's work in these lands.

The cloth is a poor article: like the people of Ashanti, who from time immemorial have woven their own cottons, the East African ever prefers foreign fabrics. The loose texture of his own produce admits wind and rain; when dry it is rough and unpleasant, when wet heavy, comfortless as leather, and it cannot look clean, as it is never bleached. According to the Arabs, the yarn is often dipped into a starch made from grain, for the purpose of thickening the appearance of the texture: this disappears after the first washing, and the cloth must be pegged down to prevent its shrinking to half-size. The relative proportion of warp and weft is unknown, and the woolly fuzzy quality of the half-wild cotton now in use impoverishes the fabric. Despite the labour expended upon these cloths, the largest size may be purchased for six feet of American domestics, or for a pair of iron hoes: there is therefore little inducement to extend the manufacture.

Iron is picked up in the state called Utundwe, or gangue, from the sides of low sandstone hills: in places the people dig pits from two to four feet deep, and, according to the Arabs, they find tears, nodules, and rounded lumps. The pisolithic iron, common in the maritime regions, is not worked. The mhesi or blacksmith's art is still in its infancy. The iron-stone is carried to the smithy, an open shed, where the work is done: the smelting-furnace is a hole in the ground, filled with lighted charcoal, upon which the utundwe is placed, and, covered with another layer of fire, it is allowed to run through the fuel. The blast is produced by mafukutu (bellows): they are two roughly rounded troughs, about three inches deep by six in diameter, hewn out of a single bit of wood and prolonged into a pair of parallel branches, pierced for the passage of the wind through two apertures in the walls of the troughs. The troughs are covered with skin, to which are fixed two long projecting sticks for handles, which may be worked by a man sitting. A stone is placed upon the bellows for steadiness, and clay nozzles, or holcus-canes with a lateral hole, are fixed on to the branches to prevent them from charring. Sometimes as many as five pairs are worked at once, and great is the rapidity required to secure a continuous outdraught. Mr. Andersson ("Lake Ngami," chap. xvi.) gives a sketch of a similar contrivance amongst the South Africans: the clay-tubes, however, are somewhat larger than those used in Unyamwezi by "blacksmiths at work." The ore is melted and remelted several times, till pure; tempering and case-hardening are unknown, and it is stored for use by being cast in clay-moulds, or made up into hoes. The hammer and anvil are generally smooth stones. The principal articles of ironmongery are spears, assegais, and arrow-heads, battle-axes, hatchets, and adzes, knives and daggers, sickles and razors, rings and sambo, or wire circlets. The kinda is a large bell, hung by the ivory-porter to his tusk on the line of the march: the kengere or kiugi a smaller variety which he fastens to his legs. Pipes, with iron bowls and stems, are made by the more ingenious, and the smoker manufactures for himself small pincers or pliers which, curious to say, are unknown even by name to the more civilised people of Zanzibar.

Copper is not found upon this line in East Africa.

From the country of the Kazembe, however, an excellent red and heavy, soft and bright variety, not unlike that of Japan, finds its way to Ujiji, and sometimes to the coast. It is sold in bars from one to two feet long. At Ujiji, where it is cheap, four to five pounds are procurable for two doti, there worth about four dollars. Native copper, therefore, is almost as expensive as that imported from Europe. It is used in making the rude and clumsy bangles affected by both sexes, sambo, and ornaments for the spear and bow, the staff and the knobkerry.

The art of ceramics has made but little progress in East Africa; no Anacharsis has yet arisen to teach her

Gourds.

sons the use of the wheel. The figuline, a greyish-brown clay, is procured from river-beds, or is dug up in the country; it is subjected to the preliminary operations of pounding, rubbing dry upon a stone, pulversiing, and purifying from stones and pebbles. It is then worked into a thick mass, with water, and the potter fashions it with the hand, first shaping the mouth; he adds an inch to it when dry, hardens it in the sun, makes another addition, and thus proceeds till it is finished. Lines and other ornaments having been traced, the pots are baked in piles of seven or eight, by burning grass—wood-fire would crack them—consequently the material always remains half-raw. Usually the colour becomes lamp-black ; in Usagara, however, the potter's clay burns red, like the soil—the effect of iron. A cunning workman will make in a day four of these pots, some of them containing several gallons, and their perfect regularity of form, and often their picturequeness of shape, surprise the stranger. The best are made in Ujiji, Karagwah, and Ugunda : those of Unyamwezi are inferior, and the clay of Zanzibar is of all the worst.

There are many kinds of pots which not a little resemble the glazed jars of ancient Egypt. The ukango, which acts as vat in fermenting liquor, is of the greatest dimensions. The mtungi is a large water-vessel with a short and narrow neck, and rounded at the bottom so as to be conveniently carried on the head. The chungu, or cooking-pot, has a wide and open mouth ; it is of several varieties, large and small. The mkungu is a shallow bowl, precisely like those made at the tomb of Moses, and now familiar to Europe. At Ujiji and on the Lake they also manufacture smaller vessels, with and without spouts.

In a country where pottery is scarce and dear, the buyu or Cucurbita lagenaria supplies every utensil except those used for cooking ; its many and various adaptations render it a valuable production. The people train it to grow in the most fantastic shapes, and ornament it by tatooing with dark paint, and by patterns worked in brass tacks and wires ; where it splits, it is artistically sewn together. The larger kinds serve as well-buckets, water-pots, travelling-canteens, churns, and the sounding-boards of musical instrument : a hookah, or water-pipe, is made by distorting the neck, and the smaller varieties are converted into snuff-boxes,

medicine-cases, and unguent-pots. The fruit of the
calabash-tree is also called buyu : split and dried it is
used as ladles, but it is too small to answer all the
purposes of the gourd.

The East Africans excel in the manufacture of
mtemba or bori—pipe-heads. These are of two kinds.
One is made from a soft stone, probably steatite, found
in Usonga, near Utumbara, and on the road to Karagwah : it is, however, rare, and about ten times the price
of the clay bowls, because less liable to break. The
other is made of a plastic or pipe-clay, too brittle to
serve for pots, and it invariably cracks at the shank,
unless bound with wire. Both are hand-made, and are
burned in the same rough way as the pottery. At
Msene, where the clay pipe is cheapest, the price of the
bowl is a khete, or double string of white or blue beads.
The pipe of Unyamwezi is of graceful shape, a cone
with the apex downwards ; this leaves but little of the
hot, oily, and high-smelling tobacco at the bottom,
whereas in Europe the contrary seems to be the rule.
In Ujiji the bowl is small, rounded, and shallow ; it is,
moreover, very brittle. The most artful " mtemba " is
made by the people of Uvira : black inside, like other
pottery, its exterior is coloured a greyish-white, and is
adorned with red by means of the Indian geru (Colco-
thar or Crocus Martis). Bhang is always, and tobacco
is sometimes, smoked in a water-pipe : the bowl is of
huge size, capable of containing at least half a pound,
and its upper half is made to incline towards the
smoker's face. The Lakist tribes have a graceful
variety, like the Indian " chillam," very different from
the awkward, unwieldy, and distorted article now
fashionable in Unyamwezi and the Eastern countries.
The usual pipe-stem is a tube of about 1·5 feet long,

generally a hollow twig of the dwarf melewele-tree. As it is rudely bored with hot wire, it must be made air-tight by wax and a coating of brass or copper wire ; a strap of hairy skin prevents the pipe-shank parting from the stick. Iron and brass tubes are rare and highly prized; the fortunate possessor will sometimes ask for a single specimen two shukkahs.

Basket-making and mat-weaving are favourite occupations in East Africa for both sexes and all ages ; even the Arabs may frequently be seen absorbed in an employment which in Oman would be considered derogatory to manliness. The sengo, or common basket, from the coast to the Lake, is an open, shallow, and pan-shaped article, generally made of mwanzi, or bamboo-bark, reddened in parts and stained black in others by the root of the Mkuruti and other trees, and white where the outer coat has been removed from the bamboo. The body, which resembles a popular article in ancient Egypt, is neatly plaited, and the upper ends are secured to a stout hoop of the same material. The kanda (in the plural makanda) acts in the interior as matting for rooms, and is converted into bags for covering bales of cloth, beads, and similar articles. It is made from the myara (myala) or Chamærops humilis; the leaf is peeled, sun-dried, and split with a bit of iron into five or six lengths, joined at the base, which is trimmed for plaiting. The Karagwah, the only mat made in the interior of Africa, is used as bedding and carpeting; on journeys the porters bivouac under it; it swells with the wet, and soon becomes impervious to rain or heavy dew. It is of two kinds: one of rushes growing in the vicinity of water, the other of grass rolled up into little bundles. A complicated stitch runs along the whole length in double lines. The best description of mat is called mkeke. It is made at Zanzibar and the coast, from the young fronds of the ukhindu or brab, neatly stained with various dyes. Women of family pride themselves upon their skill in making the mkeke, which still attains a price of four dollars. Amongst the maritime races none but the chiefs have a right to sit upon it; there are no such distinctions in the interior, where these mats are carried for sale by the slaves. From the brab also are made neat strainers to purify honey, pombe, and similar articles. They are open-mouthed cylinders, from one to two feet long, and varying in diameter from three to six inches. The bottom is narrowed by whipping fibre round the loose ends of the leaves. The fishing-nets have been described when treating of the Tanganyika. The luávo, or hand-net, is made of calabash or other fibre, with coarse wide meshes; it is affixed to two sticks firmly planted in the ground, and small animals are driven into it by beaters.

The basts or barks and fibrous substances in East Africa are cheap and abundant, but labour and conveyance being difficult and expensive, they would require to be shipped from Zanzibar in the condition of half-stuff. The best and most easily divisible into pliant and knot-tying fibres are, upon the coast the pineapple, and in the interior the plantain. The next in value are the integuments of the calabash and the myombo tree. These fibres would produce a good article were it not for the artlessness of African manipulation. The bark is pounded or chewed, and, in lieu of spinning, is twisted between the hands; the largest ropes are made in half an hour, and break after a few minutes of hard work. A fine silky twine, used for fishing, is made from the aloetic plants called by the Wasawahili mkonge, and by the

Arabs bag, masad and kideh: it is the hig or haskul of Somaliland, where it affects the poorest ground, cannot be burnt down, and is impassable to naked legs and cattle. The leaves are stripped of their coats, and the ends being tightly bound between two pieces of wood, the mass of fibre is drawn out like a sword from its sheath. Fatilah, or matchlock matches, are made in Zanzibar of cotton, and in the interior of calabash fibre.

As might be expected among a sparse population leading a comparatively simple life, the vast variety of diseases which afflict more civilised races, who are collected in narrow spaces, are unknown in East Africa even by name. Its principal sporadic is fever, remittent and intermittent, with its multitudinous secondaries, concerning which notices have been scattered through the preceding pages. The most dangerous epidemic is its aborigen, the small-pox, which, propagated without contact or fomites, sweeps at times like a storm of death over the land. For years it has not left the Arab colony at Kazeh, and, shortly before the arrival of the Expedition, in a single month 52 slaves died out of a total of 800. The ravages of this disease amongst the half-starved and over-worked gangs of caravan porters have already been described; as many as a score of these wretches have been seen at a time in a single caravan; men staggering along blinded and almost insensible, jostling and stumbling against every one in their way; and mothers carrying babes, both parent and progeny in the virulent stage of the fell disease. The Arabs have partially introduced the practice of inoculating, anciently known in South Africa; the pus is introduced into an incision in the forehead between the eyebrows. The people have no remedy for small-pox: they trust entirely to the vis medicatrix. There is a milder form of the malady, called shúrúá, resembling the chicken-pox of Europe; it is cured by bathing in cold water and smearing the body with ochreish earth. The Arab merchants of Unyanyembe declare that, when they first visited Karagwah, the people were decimated by the táún, or plague. They describe correctly the bubo under the axillæ, the torturing thirst, and the rapid fatality of the disease. In the early part of 1859 a violent attack of cholera, which extended from Maskat along the eastern coast of Arabia and Africa, committed terrible ravages in the island of Zanzibar and throughout the maritime regions. Of course, no precautions of quarantine or cordon militaire were taken, yet the contagion did not extend into the interior.

Strangers in East Africa suffer from dysenteries and similar disorders consequent upon fever; and, as in Egypt, few are free from hæmorrhoids, which in Unyamwezi are accompanied by severe colics and umbilical pains. Rheumatism and rheumatic fever, severe catarrhs and influenzas, are caused by the cold winds, and, when crossing the higher altitudes, pneumonia and pleurisis abound in the caravan. On the coast many settlers, Indian and Arab, show upon the skin whitish leprous spots, which are treated with various unguents. In the interior, though well provided with fresh meat and vegetables, travellers are attacked by scurvy, even in the absence of its normal exciting causes, damp, cold, and poor diet. This phenomenon has often been observed upon the upper course of the Nile; Europeans have been prostrated by it even in the dry regions westward of the Red Sea, and the Portuguese officers who explored Usenda of the Kazembe suffered tortures from the complaint.

Common diseases among the natives are umbilical hernia and prolapsus : the latter is treated by the application of powdered bhang, dry or mixed with ghee. They are subject to kihindu-hindu — in Arabic, sara — the epilepsy, which they pretend to cure by the marrow of rhinoceros' shank. Of the many fits and convulsions which affect them, the kichyoma-chyoma is the most dreaded. The word, which means the " little irons," describes the painful sensations, the cramps and stitches, the spasms and lancinations, which torment the sufferer. Many die of this disease. It is not extraordinary that the fits, convulsions, and contortions which it suddenly induces should lead the people to consider it in the light of possession, and the magician to treat it with charms. Madness and idiocy are not uncommon : of the patient it is said, " Ana wazimo " — " he has fiends." In most parts the people, after middle age, are tender-eyed from the effects of smoke within, glare without, exposure and debauchery. Not a few samples of acute ophthalmic disease were seen.

In the lower and more malarious spots, desquamations, tumours, and skin diseases are caused by suddenly suppressed perspiration. The terrible kidonda or helcoma of the maritime regions and the prurigo of Ujiji have already been alluded to. The " chokea " is a hordeolum or large boil, generally upon the upper eyelid. The " funza " is supposed to result from the bite of a large variety of fly. It begins with a small red and fiery swelling, which bursts after a time and produces a white entozoon about half an inch in length. " Kumri " are common blains, and " p'hambazi " malignant blind-boils, which leave a deep discoloured scar ; when the parts affected are distant from the seat of circulation, the use of the limb is sometimes lost. For most of these sores tutiya or murtutu, blue-stone, is considered a specific.

As might be expected amongst an ignorant and debauched race coming in direct contact with semi-civilisation, the lues has found its way from the island of Zanzibar to Ujiji and into the heart of Africa. It is universally believed both by the natives and by the Arabs, who support the assertion with a host of proofs, to be propagated without contact. Such, indeed, is the general opinion of the Eastern world, where perhaps its greater virulence may assimilate it to the type of the earlier attacks in Europe. The disease, however, dies out, and has not taken root in the people as amongst the devoted races of North America and the South Sea islands. Although a malignant form was found extending throughout the country, mutilation of the features and similar secondaries were not observed beyond the maritime region. Except blue-stone, mineral drugs are unknown, and the use of mercury and ptyalism have not yet exasperated the evil. The minor form of lues is little feared and yields readily to simples; the consequences, however, are strangury, cystitis, chronic nephritic disease, and rheumatism.

" Polypharmacy " is not the fault of the profession in East Africa, and the universal belief in possession tends greatly to simplify the methodus modendi. The usual cathartic is the bark of a tree called kalákalá, which is boiled in porridge. There is a great variety of emetics, some so violent that several Arabs who have been bold enough to swallow them, barely escaped with life. The actual cautery — usually a favourite counter-irritant amongst barbarous people—is rarely practised in East Africa ; in its stead powder of blue-stone is applied to the sore or wound, which has been carefully scraped, and the patient howls with pain for twenty-four hours. They bleed frequently as Italians, who even after being startled resort to a mild phlebotomy, and they cut down straight upon the vein with a sharp knife. They prefer the cucurbitula cruenta, like the Arabs, who say,—

> " Few that cup repent ;
> Few that bleed, rejoice."

A favourite place is the crown of the head. The practitioner, after scarifying the skin with a razor or a dagger, produces a vacuum by exhausting the air through a horn applied with wetted edges; at the point is a bit of wax, which he closes over the aperture with his tongue or teeth, as the hospital " singhi " in India uses a bit of leather. Cupping — called ku hu míká or kumíká — is made highly profitable by showing strange appearances in the blood. They cure by excision the bite of snakes, which, however, are not feared nor often fatal in these lands. They cannot reduce dislocations, and they never attempt to set or splint a broken bone.

The mganga or medicine-man, in his character of " doctor," is a personage of importance. He enters the sick-room in the dignity of antelope-horn, grease, and shell-necklace, and he sits with importance upon his three-legged stool. As the devil saves him the trouble of diagnosis, he begins by a prescription, invariably ordering something edible for the purpose, and varying it, according to the patient's means, from a measure of grain to a bullock. He asserts, for instance, that a pound of fat is required for medicine ; a goat must be killed, and his perquisite is the head or breast—a preliminary to a more important fee. Then the price of prescription—a *sine quâ non* to prescribing—is settled upon and paid in advance. After certain questions, invariably suggesting the presence of poison, the medical practitioner proceeds to the cure; this is generally a charm or periapt bound round the part affected. In common diseases, however, like fever, the mganga will condescend to such profane processes as adhibiting sternutatories and rubbing the head with vegetable powders. If the remedies prove too powerful or powerless, he at once decamps; under normal circumstances he incapacitates himself for performing his promise of calling the next day by expending his fee in liquor. The Africans have in one point progressed beyond Europeans: there are as many women physicians as men.

A Mnyamwezı.   A Mheha.

CHAP. XIX.

THE CHARACTER AND RELIGION OF THE EAST AFRICANS; THEIR GOVERNMENT, AND SLAVERY.

THE study of psychology in Eastern Africa is the study of man's rudimental mind, when, subject to the agency of material nature, he neither progresses nor retrogrades. He would appear rather a degeneracy from the civilised man than a savage rising to the first step, were it not for his apparent incapacity for improvement. He has not the ring of the true metal; there is no rich nature, as in the New Zealander, for education to cultivate. He seems to belong to one of those childish races which, ɪ.ever rising to man's estate, fall like worn-out links from the great chain of animated nature. He unites the incapacity of infancy with the unpliancy of age; the futility of childhood, and the credulity of youth, with the scepticism of the adult and the stubbornness and bigotry of the old. He has "beaten lands" and seas. For centuries he has been in direct intercourse with the more advanced people of the eastern coast, and though few have seen an European, there are not many who have not cast eyes upon an Arab. Still he has stopped short at the threshold of progress; he shows no signs of development; no higher and more varied orders of intellect are called into being. Even the simple truths of El Islam have failed to fix the thoughts of men who can think, but who, absorbed in providing for their bodily wants, hate the trouble of thinking. His mind, limited to the objects seen, heard, and felt, will not, and apparently cannot, escape from the circle of sense, nor will it occupy itself with aught but the present. Thus he is cut off from the pleasures of memory, and the world of fancy is altogether unknown to him. Perhaps the automaton which we call spiritual suffers from the inferiority of the mechanism by which it acts.

The East African is, like other barbarians, a strange mixture of good and evil: by the nature of barbarous society, however, the good element has not, whilst the evil has, been carefully cultured.

As a rule, the civilised or highest type of man owns the sway of intellect, of reason; the semi-civilised — as are still the great nations of the East — are guided by sentiment and propensity in a degree incomprehensible to more advanced races; and the barbarian is the slave of impulse, passion, and instinct, faintly modified by sentiment, but ignorant of intellectual discipline. He appears, therefore, to the civilised man a paralogic being, — a mere mass of contradictions; his ways are not our ways, his reason is not our reason. He deduces effects from causes which we ignore; he compasses his ends by contrivances which we cannot comprehend; and his artifices and polity excite, by their shallowness and "inconsequence," our surprise and contempt. Like that Hindu race that has puzzled the plain-witted Englishman for the century closing with the massacres of Delhi and Cawnpore, he is calculated to perplex those who make conscience an instinct which elevates man to the highest ground of human intelligence. He is at once very good-tempered and hard-hearted, combative and cautious; kind at one moment, cruel, pitiless, and violent at another ; sociable and unaffectionate ; superstitious and grossly irreverent ; brave and cowardly, servile and oppressive ; obstinate, yet fickle and fond of changes; with points of honour, but without a trace of honesty in word or deed ; a lover of life, though addicted to suicide ; covetous and parsimonious, yet thoughtless and improvident; somewhat conscious of inferiority, withal unimprovable.   In fact, he appears an embryo of the two superior races.   He is inferior to the active-minded and objective, the analytic and perceptive European, and to the ideal and subjective, the synthetic and reflective Asiatic.   He partakes largely of the worst characteristics of the lower Oriental types — stagnation of mind, indolence of body, moral deficiency, superstition, and childish passion ; hence the Egyptians aptly termed the Berbers and negroes the " perverse race of Kush."

The main characteristic of this people is the selfishness which the civilised man strives to conceal, because publishing it would obstruct its gratification. The barbarian, on the other hand, displays his inordinate egotism openly and recklessly; his every action discloses those unworthy traits which in more polished races chiefly appear on public occasions, when each man thinks solely of self-gratification. Gratitude with him is not even a sense of prospective favours; he looks upon a benefit as the weakness of his benefactor and his own strength; consequently, he will not recognise even the hand that feeds him. He will, perhaps, lament for a night the death of a parent or a child, but the morrow will find him thoroughly comforted. The name of hospitality, except for interested motives, is unknown to him: "What will you give me?" is his first question. To a stranger entering a village the worst hut is assigned, and, if he complain, the answer is that he can find encamping ground outside. Instead of treating him like a guest, which the Arab Bedouin would hold to be a point of pride, of honour, his host compels him to pay and prepay every article, otherwise he might starve in the midst of plenty. Nothing, in fact, renders the stranger's life safe in this land, except the timid shrinking of the natives from the "hot-mouthed weapon" and the necessity of trade, which induces the chiefs to restrain the atrocities of their subjects. To travellers the African is, of course, less civil than to merchants, from whom he expects to gain something. He will refuse a mouthful of water out of his abundance to a man dying of thirst; utterly unsympathising, he will not stretch out a hand to save another's goods, though worth thousands of dollars. Of his own property, if a ragged cloth or a lame slave be lost, his violent excitement is ridiculous to behold. His egotism renders him parsimonious even in self-gratification; the wretched curs, which he loves as much as his children, seldom receive a mouthful of food, and the sight of an Arab's ass feeding on grain elicits a prolonged "Hi! hi!" of extreme surprise. He is exceedingly improvident, taking no thought for the morrow — not from faith, but rather from carelessness as to

what may betide him ; yet so greedy of gain is he that
he will refuse information about a country or the direction of a path without a present of beads.   He also invariably demands prepayment : no one keeps a promise
or adheres to an agreement, and, if credit be demanded
for an hour, his answer would be, " There is nothing in
my hand."   Yet even greed of gain cannot overcome
the levity and laxity of his mind.   Despite his best interests, he will indulge the mania for desertion caused
by that mischievous love of change and whimsical desire
for novelty that characterise the European sailor.   Nor
can even lucre prevail against the ingrained indolence
of the race — an indolence the more hopeless as it is the
growth of the climate.   In these temperate and abundant lands Nature has cursed mankind with the abundance of her gifts ; his wants still await creation, and
he is contented with such necessaries as roots and herbs,
game, and a few handfuls of grain — consequently improvement has no hold upon him.

In this stage of society truth is no virtue.   The
" mixture of a lie " may " add to pleasure" amongst
Europeans ; in Africa it enters where neither pleasure
nor profit can arise from the deception.   If a Mnyamwezi guide informs the traveller that the stage is short,
he may make up his mind for a long and weary march,
and *vice versâ*.   Of course, falsehood is used as a defence by the weak and oppressed ; but beyond that, the
African desires to be lied to, and one of his proverbs is,
" 'Tis better to be deceived than to be undeceived."
The European thus qualifies the assertion,

> " For sure the pleasure is as great
> In being cheated as to cheat."

Like the generality of barbarous races, the East

Africans are wilful, headstrong, and undisciplinable : in point of stubbornness and restiveness they resemble the lower animals. If they cannot obtain the very article of barter upon which they have set their mind, they will carry home things useless to them; any attempt at bargaining is settled by the seller turning his back, and they ask according to their wants and wishes, without regard to the value of goods. Grumbling and dissatisfied, they never do business without a grievance. Revenge is a ruling passion, as the many rancorous fratricidal wars that have prevailed between kindred clans, even for a generation, prove. Retaliation and vengeance are, in fact, their great agents of moral control. Judged by the test of death, the East African is a hardhearted man, who seems to ignore all the charities of father, son, and brother. A tear is rarely shed, except by the women, for departed parent, relative, or friend, and the voice of the mourner is seldom heard in their abodes. It is most painful to witness the complete inhumanity with which a porter seized with small-pox is allowed by his friends, comrades, and brethren to fall behind in the jungle, with several days' life in him. No inducement—even beads—can persuade a soul to attend him. Every village will drive him from its doors; no one will risk taking, at any price, death into his bosom. If strong enough, the sufferer builds a little bough-hut away from the camp, and, provided with his rations—a pound of grain and a gourdful of water—he quietly expects his doom, to feed the hyæna and the raven of the wild. The people are remarkable for the readiness with which they yield to fits of sudden fury; on these occasions they will, like children, vent their rage upon any object, animate or inanimate, that presents itself. Their temper is characterised by a nervous, futile impatience; under delay or disappointment they become madmen. In their own country, where such displays are safe, they are remarkable for a presump- tuousness and a violence of manner which elsewhere disappears. As the Arabs say, there they are lions, here they become curs. Their squabbling and clamour pass description: they are never happy except when in dispute. After a rapid plunge into excitement, the brawlers alternately advance and recede, pointing the finger of threat, howling and screaming, cursing and using terms of insult which an inferior ingenuity—not want of will—causes to fall short of the Asiatic's model vituperation. After abusing each other to their full, both " parties " usually burst into a loud laugh or a burst of sobs. Their tears lie high; they weep like Goanese. After a cuff, a man will cover his face with his hands and cry as if his heart would break. More furious shrews than the women are nowhere met with. Here it is a great truth that " the tongues of women cannot be governed." They work off excitement by scolding, and they weep little compared with the men. Both sexes delight in " argument," which here, as elsewhere, means two fools talking foolishly. They will weary out of patience the most loquacious of the Arabs. This de- velopment is characteristic of the East African race, and " maneno marefu ! "—long words ! — will occur as a useless reproof half a dozen times in the course of a single conversation. When drunk, the East African is easily irritated; with the screams and excited gestures of a maniac he strides about, frantically flourishing his spear and agitating his bow, probably with notched arrow ; the spear-point and the arrow-head are often brought perilously near, but rarely allowed to draw blood. The real combat is by pushing, pulling hair, and slapping with a will, and a pair thus engaged require to be torn asunder by half a dozen friends. The settled tribes are, for the most part, feeble and unwarlike barbarians; even the bravest East African, though, like all men, a combative entity, has a valour tempered by discretion and cooled by a high development of cautiousness. His tactics are of the Fabian order: he loves surprises and safe ambuscades; and in common frays and forays the loss of one per cent. justifies a *sauve qui peut*. This people, childlike, is ever in extremes. A man will hang himself from a rafter in his tent, and kick away from under him the large wooden mortar upon which he has stood at the beginning of the operation with as much sang-froid as an Anglo-Saxon in the gloomy month of November; yet he regards annihilation, as all savages do, with loathing and ineffable horror. " He fears death," to quote Bacon, " as children fear to go in the dark; and as that natural fear in children is increased with tales, so is the other." The African mind must change radically before it can " think upon death, and find it the least of all evils." All the thoughts of these negroids are connected with this life. " Ah !" they exclaim, " it is bad to die ! to leave off eating and drinking ! never to wear a fine cloth !" As in the negro race generally, their destructiveness is prominent ; a slave never breaks a thing without an instinctive laugh of pleasure ; and however careful he may be of his own life, he does not value that of another, even of a relative, at the price of a goat. During fires in the town of Zanzibar, the blacks have been seen adding fuel, and singing and dancing, wild with delight. On such occasions they are shot down by the Arabs like dogs.

It is difficult to explain the state of society in which

the civilised " social evil " is not recognised as an evil.
In the economy of the affections and the intercourse
between the sexes, reappears that rude stage of society
in which ethics were new to the mind of now en-
lightened man.   Marriage with this people—as amongst
all barbarians, and even the lower classes of civilised races—is a mere affair of buying and selling.
A man must marry because it is necessary to his comfort, consequently the woman becomes a marketable
commodity.   Her father demands for her as many
cows, cloths, and brass-wire bracelets as the suitor can
afford; he thus virtually sells her, and she belongs to
the buyer, ranking with his other live stock.   The
husband may sell his wife, or, if she be taken from him
by another man, he claims her value, which is ruled by
what she would fetch in the slave-market.   A strong
inducement to marriage amongst the Africans, as
with the poor in Europe, is the prospective benefit to
be derived from an adult family; a large progeny
enriches them.   The African—like all barbarians, and,
indeed, semi-civilised people—ignores the dowry by
which, inverting Nature's order, the wife buys the
husband, instead of the husband buying the wife.   Marriage, which is an epoch amongst Christians, and an
event with Moslems, is with these people an incident of
frequent recurrence.   Polygamy is unlimited, and the
chiefs pride themselves upon the number of their wives,
varying from twelve to three hundred.   It is no disgrace
for an unmarried woman to become the mother of a
family; after matrimony there is somewhat less laxity.
The mgoni or adulterer, if detected, is punishable by a
fine of cattle, or, if poor and weak, he is sold into
slavery; husbands seldom, however, resort to such
severities, the offence, which is considered to be against

vested property, being held to be lighter than petty larceny. Under the influence of jealousy, murders and mutilations have been committed, but they are rare and exceptional. Divorce is readily effected by turning the spouse out of doors, and the children become the father's property. Attachment to home is powerful in the African race, but it regards rather the comforts and pleasures of the house, and the unity of relations and friends, than the fondness of family. Husband, wife, and children have through life divided interests, and live together with scant appearance of affection. Love of offspring can have but little power amongst a people who have no preventive for illegitimacy, and whose progeny may be sold at any time. The children appear undemonstrative and unaffectionate, as those of the Somal. Some attachment to their mothers breaks out, not in outward indications, but by surprise, as it were: " Mámá! mámá!" — mother! mother! — is a common exclamation in fear or wonder. When childhood is passed, the father and son become natural enemies, after the manner of wild beasts. Yet they are a sociable race, and the sudden loss of relatives sometimes leads from grief to hypochondria and insanity, resulting from the inability of their minds to bear any unusual strain. It is probable that a little learning would make them mad, like the Widad, or priest of the Somal, who, after mastering the reading of the Koran, becomes unfit for any exertion of judgment or common sense. To this over-development of sociability must be ascribed the anxiety always shown to shift, evade, or answer blame. The "ukosa," or transgression, is never accepted; any number of words will be wasted in proving the worse the better cause. Hence also the favourite phrase, "Mbáyá we!" — thou art bad! — a pet mode of reproof which sounds simple and uneffective to European ears.

The social position of the women—the unerring test of progress towards civilisation—is not so high in East Africa as amongst the more highly organised tribes of the south. Few parts of the country own the rule of female chiefs. The people, especially the Wanyamwezi, consult their wives, but the opinion of a brother or a friend would usually prevail over that of a woman.

The deficiency of the East African in constructive power has already been remarked. Contented with his haystack or beehive hut, his hemisphere of boughs, or his hide acting tent, he hates and has a truly savage horror of stone walls. He has the conception of the " Madeleine," but he has never been enabled to be delivered of it. Many Wanyamwezi, when visiting Zanzibar, cannot be prevailed upon to enter a house.

The East African is greedy and voracious; he seems, however, to prefer light and frequent to a few regular and copious meals. Even the civilised Kisawahili has no terms to express the breakfast, dinner, and supper of other languages. Like most barbarians, the East African can exist and work with a small quantity of food, but he is unaccustomed, and therefore unable, to bear thirst. The daily ration of a porter is 1 kubabah ($=$ 1·5 lbs.) of grain; he can, with the assistance of edible herbs and roots, which he is skilful in discovering in the least likely places, eke out this allowance for several days, though generally, upon the barbarian's impulsive principle of mortgaging the future for the present, he recklessly consumes his stores. With him the grand end of life is eating; his love of feeding is inferior only to his propensity for intoxication. He drinks till he can no longer stand, lies down to sleep, and awakes to drink again. Drinking-bouts are solemn things, to which the most important business must yield precedence. They celebrate with beer every event—the traveller's return, the birth of a child, and the death of an elephant—a labourer will not work unless beer is provided for him. A guest is received with a gourdful of beer, and, amongst some tribes, it is buried with their princes. The highest orders rejoice in drink, and pride themselves upon powers of imbibing: the proper diet for a king is much beer and a little meat. If a Mnyamwezi be asked after eating whether he is hungry, he will reply yea, meaning that he is not drunk. Intoxication excuses crime in these lands. The East African, when in his cups, must issue from his hut to sing, dance, or quarrel, and the frequent and terrible outrages which occur on these occasions are passed over on the plea that he has drunk beer. The favourite hour for drinking is after dawn,— a time as distasteful to the European as agreeable to the African and Asiatic. This might be proved by a host of quotations from the poets, Arab, Persian, and Hindu. The civilised man avoids early potations because they incapacitate him for necessary labour, and he attempts to relieve the headache caused by stimulants. The barbarian and the semi-civilised, on the other hand, prefer them, because they relieve the tedium of his monotonous day; and they cherish the headache because they can sleep the longer, and, when they awake, they have something to think of. The habit once acquired is never broken: it attaches itself to the heartstrings of the idle and unoccupied barbarian.

In morality, according to the more extended sense of the word, the East African is markedly deficient. He has no benevolence, but little veneration—the negro race is ever irreverent — and, though his cranium rises high in the region of firmness, his futility prevents his being firm. The outlines of law are faintly traced upon his heart. The authoritative standard of morality fixed by a revelation is in him represented by a vague and varying custom, derived traditionally from his ancestors; he follows in their track for old-sake's sake. The accusing conscience is unknown to him. His only fear after committing a treacherous murder is that of being haunted by the angry ghost of the dead; he robs as one doing a good deed, and he begs as if it were his calling. His depravity is of the grossest: intrigue fills up all the moments not devoted to intoxication.

The want of veneration produces a savage rudeness in the East African. The body politic consists of two great members, masters and slaves. Ignoring distinctions of society, he treats all men, except his chief, as his equals. He has no rules for visiting: if the door be open, he enters a stranger's house uninvited; his harsh, barking voice is ever the loudest; he is never happy except when hearing himself speak; his address is imperious, his demeanour is rough and peremptory, and his look "sfacciato." He deposits his unwashed person, in his greasy and tattered goat-skin or cloth, upon rug or bedding, disdaining to stand for a moment, and he always chooses the best place in the room. When travelling he will push forward to secure the most comfortable hut: the chief of a caravan may sleep in rain or dew, but, if he attempt to dislodge his porters, they lie down with the settled purpose of mules—as the Arabs say, they "have no shame." The curiosity of these people, and the little ceremony with which they gratify it, are at times most troublesome. A stranger must be stared at; total apathy is the only remedy: if the victim lose his temper, or attempt to dislodge them, he will find it like disturbing a swarm of bees. They will come for miles to "sow gape-seed:" if the tent-fly be closed, they will peer and peep from below, complaining loudly against the occupant, and, if further prevented, they may proceed to violence. On the road hosts of idlers, especially women, boys, and girls, will follow the caravan for hours; it is a truly offensive spectacle—these un-couth figures, running at a "gymnastic pace," half clothed except with grease, with pendent bosoms shaking in the air, and cries that resemble the howls of beasts more than any effort of human articulation. This offensive ignorance of the first principles of social inter-course has been fostered in the races most visited by the Arabs, whose national tendency, like the Italian and the Greek, is ever and essentially republican. When strangers first appeared in the country they were re-ceived with respect and deference. They soon, however, lost this vantage-ground: they sat and chatted with the people, exchanged pleasantries, and suffered slights, till the Africans found themselves on an equality with their visitors. The evil has become inveterate, and no greater contrast can be imagined than that between the man-ners of an Indian Ryot and an East African Mshenzi.

In intellect the East African is sterile and incult, ap-parently unprogressive and unfit for change. Like the uncivilised generally, he observes well, but he can deduce nothing profitable from his perceptions. His intelligence is surprising when compared with that of an uneducated English peasant; but it has a narrow bound, beyond which apparently no man may pass. Like the Asiatic, in fact, he is stationary, but at a much lower level. Devotedly fond of music, his love of tune has invented nothing but whistling and the whistle: his instruments are all borrowed from the coast people. He delights in singing, yet he has no metrical songs: he contents himself with improvising a few words without sense or rhyme, and repeats them till they nauseate: the long, drawling recitative generally ends in " Ah! ha^n! " or some such strongly-nasalised sound. Like the Somal, he has tunes appropriated to particular occasions, as the elephant-hunt or the harvest-home. When mourning, the love of music assumes a peculiar form: women weeping or sobbing, especially after chastisement, will break into a protracted threne or dirge, every period of which concludes with its own particular groan or wail: after venting a little natural distress in a natural sound, the long, loud improvisation, in the highest falsetto key, continues as before. As in Europe the " laughing-song " is an imitation of hilarity somewhat distressing to the spirits of the audience, so the "weeping-song " of the African only tends to risibility. His wonderful loquacity and volubility of tongue have produced no tales, poetry, nor display of eloquence; though, like most barbarians, somewhat sententious, he will content himself with squabbling with his companions, or with repeating some meaningless word in every different tone of voice during the weary length of a day's march. His language is highly artificial and musical: the reader will have observed that the names which occur in these pages often consist entirely of liquids and vowels, that consonants are unknown at the end of a word, and that they never are double except at the beginning. Yet the idea of a syllabarium seems not to have occurred to the negroid mind. Finally, though the East African delights in the dance, and is an excellent timist—a thousand heels striking the ground simultaneously sound like one—his performance is as uncouth as perhaps was ever devised by man. He delights in a joke, which manages him like a Neapolitan; yet his efforts in wit are of the feeblest that can be conceived.

Though the general features of character correspond throughout the tribes in East Africa, there are also marked differences. The Wazaramo, for instance, are considered the most dangerous tribe on this line: caravans hurry through their lands, and hold themselves fortunate if a life be not lost, or if a few loads be not missing. Their neighbours, the Wasagara of the hills, were once peaceful and civil to travellers: the persecutions of the coast-people have rendered them morose and suspicious; they now shun strangers, and, never knowing when they may be attacked, they live in a constant state of agitation, excitement, and alarm. After the Wazaramo, the tribes of Ugogo are considered the most noisy and troublesome, the most extortionate, quarrelsome and violent on this route: nothing restrains these races from bloodshed and plunder but fear of retribution and self-interest. The Wanyamwezi bear the highest character for civilisation, discipline, and industry. Intercourse with the coast, however, is speedily sapping the foundations of their superiority : the East African Expedition suffered more from thieving in this than in any other territory, and the Arabs now depend for existence there not upon prestige, but sufferance, in consideration of mutual commercial advantage. In proportion as the traveller advances into the interior, he finds the people less humane, or rather less human. The Wavinza, the Wajiji, and the other Lakist tribes, much resemble one another: they are extortionate, violent, and revengeful barbarians ; no Mnyamwezi dares to travel alone through their territories, and small parties are ever in danger of destruction.

In dealing with the East African the traveller cannot

do better than to follow the advice of Bacon — " Use savages justly and graciously, with sufficient guard nevertheless." They must be held as foes; and the prudent stranger will never put himself in their power, especially where life is concerned. The safety of a caravan will often depend upon the barbarian's fear of beginning the fray: if the onset once takes place, the numbers, the fierce looks, the violent gestures, and the confidence of the assailants upon their own ground, will probably prevail. When necessary, however, severity must be employed; leniency and forbearance are the vulnerable points of civilised policy, as they encourage attack by a suspicion of fear and weakness. They may be managed as the Indian saw directs, by a judicious mixture of the " Narm " and " Garm " — the soft and hot. Thus the old traders remarked in Guinea, that the best way to treat a black man was to hold out one hand to shake with him, while the other is doubled ready to knock him down. In trading with, or even when dwelling amongst this people, all display of wealth must be avoided. A man who would purchase the smallest article avoids showing anything beyond its equivalent.

The ethnologist who compares this sketch with the far more favourable description of the Kafirs, a kindred race, given by travellers in South Africa, may suspect that only the darker shades of the picture are placed before the eye. But, as will appear in a future page, much of this moral degradation must be attributed to the working, through centuries, of the slave-trade : the tribes are no longer as nature made them; and from their connection with strangers they have derived nothing but corruption. Though of savage and barbarous type, they have been varnished with the semi-civilisation of trade and commerce, which sits ridiculously upon their minds as a rich garment would upon their persons.

Fetissism — the word is derived from the Portuguese feitiço, "a doing,"— scil. of magic, by euphuism — is still the only faith known in East Africa. Its origin is easily explained by the aspect of the physical world, which has coloured the thoughts and has directed the belief of man: he reflects, in fact, the fantastical and monstrous character of the animal and vegetable productions around him. Nature, in these regions rarely sublime or beautiful, more often terrible and desolate, with the gloomy forest, the impervious jungle, the tangled hill, and the dread uniform waste tenanted by deadly inhabitants, arouses in his mind a sensation of utter feebleness, a vague and nameless awe. Untaught to recommend himself for protection to a Superior Being, he addresses himself directly to the objects of his reverence and awe: he prostrates himself before the sentiment within him, hoping to propitiate it as he would satisfy a fellow-man. The grand mysteries of life and death, to him unrevealed and unexplained, the want of a true interpretation of the admirable phenomena of creation, and the vagaries and misconceptions of his own degraded imagination, awaken in him ideas of horror, and people the invisible world with ghost and goblin, demon and spectrum, the incarnations, as it were, of his own childish fears. Deepened by the dread of destruction, ever strong in the barbarian breast, his terror causes him to look with suspicion upon all around him: "How," inquires the dying African, " can I alone be ill when others are well, unless I have been bewitched?" Hence the belief in magical and supernatural powers in man, which the stronger minded have turned to their own advantage.

Fetissism is the adoration, or rather the propitiation, of natural objects, animate and inanimate, to which certain mysterious influences are attributed. It admits neither god, nor angel, nor devil; it ignores the very alphabet of revealed or traditionary religion — a creation, a resurrection, a judgment-day, a soul or a spirit, a heaven or a hell. A modified practical atheism is thus the prominent feature of the superstition. Though instinctively conscious of a being above them, the Africans have as yet failed to grasp the idea: in their feeble minds it is an embryo rather than a conception — at the best a vague god, without personality, attributes, or providence. They call that being Mulungu, the Uhlunga of the Kafirs, and the Utika of the Hottentots. The term, however, may mean a ghost, the firmament, or the sun; a man will frequently call himself Mulungu, and even Mulungu Mbaya, the latter word signifying bad or wicked. In the language of the Wamasai "Ai," or with the article "Engai" — the Creator — is feminine, the god and rain being synonymous.

The Fetiss superstition is African, but not confined to Africa. The faith of ancient Egypt, the earliest system of profane belief known to man, with its Triad denoting the various phases and powers of nature, was essentially fetissist; whilst in the Syrian mind dawned at first the idea of "Melkart," a god of earth, and his Baalim, angels, viceregents, or local deities. But generally the history of religions proves that when man, whether degraded from primal elevation or elevated from primal degradation, has progressed a step beyond atheism—the spiritual state of the lowest savagery—he advances to the modification called Fetissism, the condition of the infant mind of humanity. According to the late Col. Van Kennedy; " such expressions as

the love and fear of God never occur in the sacred
books of the Hindus." The ancient Persians were
ignicolists, adoring ethereal fire. Confucius owned that
he knew nothing about the gods, and therefore preferred
saying as little as possible upon the subject. Men, still
without tradition or training, confused the Creator with
creation, and ventured not to place the burden of providence upon a single deity. Slaves to the agencies of
material nature, impressed by the splendours of the
heavenly bodies, comforted by fire and light, persuaded
by their familiarity with the habits of wild beasts that
the brute creation and the human claimed a mysterious
affinity, humbled by the terrors of elemental war, and
benefitted by hero and sage, —

> " Quicquid humus, pelagus, cœlum mirabile gignunt,
>   Id duxere deos."

The barbarian worshipped these visible objects not as
types, myths, divine emanations, or personifications of
a deity: he adored them for themselves. The modern
theory, the mode in which full-grown man explains
away the follies of his childhood, making the interpretation precede the fable, fails when tested by experience.
The Hindu, and, indeed, the ignorant Christian, still
adore the actual image of man and beast; it is unreasonable to suppose that they kneel before and worship
with heart and soul its metaphysics; and an attempt to
allegorise it, or to deprive it of its specific virtues,
would be considered, as in ancient Greece and Rome,
mere impiety.

By its essence, then, Fetissism is a rude and sensual
superstition, the faith of abject fear, and of infant races
that have not risen, and are, perhaps, incapable of rising
to theism—the religion of love and the belief of the

highest types of mankind.   But old creeds die hard, and error, founded upon the instincts and feelings of human nature borrows the coherence and uniformity of truth.   That Fetissism is a belief common to man in the childhood of his spiritual life, may be proved by the frequent and extensive remains of the faith which the cretinism of the Hamitic race has perpetuated amongst them to the present day, still sprouting like tares even in the fair field of revealed religion.   The dread of ghosts, for instance, which is the mainstay of Fetissism, is not inculcated in any sacred book, yet the belief is not to be abolished.   Thus the Rakshasa of the Hindus is a disembodied spirit, doing evil to mankind; and the ghost of the prophet Samuel, raised by the familiar of the Witch of Endor, was the immortal part of a mortal being, still connected with earth, and capable of return- ing to it.   Through the Manes, the Umbra, and the Spectrum of the ancients, the belief has descended to the moderns, as the household words ghost, goblin, and bogle, revenant, polter-geist, and spook, Duh, Dusha, and Dukh attest.   Precisely similar to the African ghost-faith is the old Irish belief in Banshees, Pookas, and other evil entities ; the corporeal frame of the dead forms other bodies, but the spirit hovers in the air, watching the destiny of friends, haunting houses, killing children, injuring cattle, and causing disease and de- struction.   Everywhere, too, their functions are the same: all are malevolent to the living, and they are seldom known to do good.   The natural horror and fear of death which may be observed even in the lower animals has caused the dead to be considered vindictive and destructive.

Some missionaries have detected in the habit, which prevails throughout Eastern and Western Africa, of

burying slaves with the deceased, of carrying provisions
to graves, and of lighting fires on cold nights near the
last resting-places of the departed, a continuation of
relations between the quick and the dead which points
to a belief in a future state of existence. The wish is
father to that thought: the doctrine of the soul, of
immortality, belongs to a superior order of mind, to a
more advanced stage of society. The belief, as its
operations show, is in presentity, materialism, not in
futurity, spiritualism. According to the ancients, man
is a fourfold being:—

> "Bis duo sunt homini, manes, caro, spiritus, umbra:
> Quatuor hæc loci bis duo suscipiunt
> Terra tegit carnem, tumulum circumvolitat umbra,
> Manes Orcus habet, spiritus astra petit."

Take away the Manes and the astral Spirit, and remains
the African belief in the εἴδωλον or Umbra, spiritus, or
ghost. When the savage and the barbarian are asked
what has become of the "old people" (their ancestors),
over whose dust and ashes they perform obsequies, these
veritable secularists only smile and reply Wáme-kwisha,
"they are ended." It proves the inferior organisation
of the race. Even the North American aborigines,
a race which Nature apparently disdains to preserve,
decided that man hath a future, since even Indian corn
is vivified and rises again. The East African has
created of his fears a ghost which never attains the
perfect form of a soul. This inferior development has
prevented his rising to the social status of the Hindu,
and other anciently civilised races, whom a life wholly
wanting in purpose and occupation drove from the
excitement necessary to stimulate the mind towards
a hidden or mysterious future. These wild races seek

otherwise than in their faith a something to emotionise and to agitate them.

The East African's Credenda—it has not arrived at the rank of a system, this vague and misty dawning of a creed—are based upon two main articles. The first is demonology, or, rather, the existence of Koma, the spectra of the dead; the second is Uchawi, witchcraft or black magic, a corollary to the principal theorem. Few, and only the tribes adjacent to the maritime regions, have derived from El Islam a faint conception of the one Supreme. There is no trace in this country of the ancient and modern animal-worship of Egypt and India, though travellers have asserted that vestiges of it exist amongst the kindred race of Kafirs. The African has no more of Sabæism than what belongs to the instinct of man: he has a reverence for the sun and moon, the latter is for evident reasons in higher esteem, but he totally ignores star-worship. If questioned concerning his daily bread, he will point with a devotional aspect towards the light of day; and if asked what caused the death of his brother, will reply Jua, or Rimwe, the sun. He has not, like the Kafir, a holiday at the epoch of new moon: like the Moslem, however, on first seeing it, he raises and claps his hands in token of obeisance. The Mzimo, or Fetiss hut, is the first germ of a temple, and the idea is probably derived from the Kurban of the Arabs. It is found throughout the country, especially in Uzaramo, Unyamwezi, and Karagwah. It is in the shape of a dwarf house, one or two feet high, with a thatched roof, but without walls. Upon the ground, or suspended from the roof, are handfuls of grain and small pots full of beer, placed there to propitiate the ghosts, and to defend the crops from injury.

A prey to base passions and melancholy godless fears,

the Fetissist, who peoples with malevolent beings the invisible world, animates material nature with evil influences. The rites of his dark and deadly super- stition are all intended to avert evils from himself, by transferring them to others: hence the witchcraft and magic which flow naturally from the system of demon- ology. Men rarely die without the wife or children, the kindred or slaves, being accused of having com- passed their destruction by " throwing the glamour over them;" and, as has been explained, the trial and the conviction are of the most arbitrary nature. Yet witchcraft is practised by thousands with the firmest convictions in their own powers; and though frightful tortures await the wizard and the witch who have been condemned for the destruction of chief or elder, the vindictiveness of the negro drives him readily to the malevolent practices of sorcery. As has happened in Europe and elsewhere, in the presence of torture and the instant advance of death, the sorcerer and sorceress will not only confess, but even boast of and believe in, their own criminality. "Verily I slew such a one! — I brought about the disease of such another!"—these are their demented vaunts, the offspring of mental imbecility, stimulated by traditional hallucination.

In this state of spiritual death there is, as may be imagined, but little of the fire of fanaticism: polemics are as unknown as politics to them; their succedaneum for a god is not a jealous god. But upon the subjects of religious belief and revelation all men are equal: Davus becomes Œdipus, the fool is as the sage. What the " I " believes, that the " Thou " must acknowledge, under the pains and penalties of offending Self-esteem. Whilst the African's faith is weakly catholic, he will not admit that other men are wiser on this point than

himself.   Yet he will fast like a Moslem, because doing
something seems to raise him in the scale of creation.
His mind, involved in the trammels of his superstition,
and enchained by custom, is apparently incapable of
receiving the impressions of El Islam.   His Fetissism,
unspiritualised by the philosophic Pantheism and Poly-
theism of Europe and Asia, has hitherto unfitted him
for that belief which was readily accepted by the more
Semitic maritime races, the Somal, the Wasawahili, and
the Wamrima.   To a certain extent, also, it has been
the policy of the Arab to avoid proselytising, which
would lead to comparative equality: for sordid lucre
the Moslem has left the souls of these Kafirs to eternal
perdition.   According to most doctors of the saving
faith, an ardent proselytiser might convert by the sword
whole tribes, though he might not succeed with individuals, who cannot break through the ties of society.   The
" Mombas Mission," however, relying upon the powers
of persuasion, unequivocally failed, and pronounced
their flock to be " not behind the greatest infidels and
scoffers of Europe: they blaspheme, in fact, like children."   With characteristic want of veneration they
would say, " Your Lord is a bad master, for he does
not cure his servants."   When an early convert died,
the Wanyika at once decided that there is no Saviour,
as he does not prevent the decease of a friend.   The
sentiment generally elicited by a discourse upon the
subject of the existence of a Deity is a desire to
see him, in order to revenge upon him the deaths of
relatives, friends, and cattle.*

* That the Western African negro resembles in this point his negroid
brother, the following extract from an amusing and truthful little volume,
entitled " Trade and Travels in the Gulf of Guinea and Western Africa "
(London : Simpkin and Marshall, 1851), will prove :—

Fetissism supplies an abundance of professionally holy men. The "Mfumo" is translated by the Arabs

Always anxious, — says Mr. J. Smith, the author, — to get any of them (the Western Africans) to talk about God and religion, I said, "What have you been doing King Pepple?"

"All the same as you do, — I tank God."

"For what?"

"Every good ting God sends me."

"Have you seen God?"

"Chi! no; — suppose man see God, he must die one minute." (He would die in a moment.)

"When you die won't you see God?"

With great warmth, "I know no savvy. (I don't know.) How should I know? Never mind. I no want to hear more for that palaver." (I want no more talk on that subject.)

"What way?" (Why?)

"It no be your business, you come here for trade palaver."

I knew — resumes Mr. Smith — it would be of no use pursuing the subject at that time, so I was silent, and it dropped for the moment.

In speaking of him dying, I had touched a very tender and disagreeable chord, for he looked very savage and sulky, and I saw by the rapid changes in his countenance that he was the subject of some intense internal emotion. At length he broke out, using most violent gesticulations, and exhibiting a most inhuman expression of countenance, "Suppose God was here, I must kill him, one minute!"

"You what? you kill God?" followed I, quite taken aback, and almost breathless with the novel and diabolical notion; "You kill God? why, you talk all some fool" (like a fool); "you cannot kill God; and suppose it possible that God could die, everything would cease to exist. He is the Spirit of the universe. But he can kill you."

"I know I cannot kill him; but suppose I could kill him, I would."

"Where does God live?"

"For top."

"How?" He pointed to the zenith.

"And suppose you could, why would you kill him?"

"Because he makes men to die."

"Why, my friend," in a conciliatory manner, "you would not wish to live for ever, would you?"

"Yes, I want to stand" (remain for ever).

"But you will be old by and by, and if you live long enough, will become very infirm, like that old man," pointing to a man very old for an African and thin, and lame, and almost blind, who had come into the court during the foregoing conversation, to ask for some favour (I wonder he had not been destroyed),—" and like him you will become lame, and deaf, and

Bassar, a seer or clairvoyant.   The Mchawi is the Sahhar, magician, or adept in the black art.   Amongst the Wazegura and the Wasagara is the Mgonezi, a word Arabised into Rammal or Geomantist.   He practises the Miramoro, or divination and prediction of fray and famine, death and disease, by the relative position of small sticks, like spilikins, cast at random on the ground. The "rain-maker," or "rain-doctor" of the Cape, common throughout these tribes, and extending far north of the equator, is called in East Africa Mganga, in the plural Waganga: the Arabs term him Tabib, doctor or physician.

The Mganga, in the central regions termed Mfumo, may be considered as the rude beginning of a sacerdotal order.   These drones, who swarm throughout the land, are of both sexes: the women, however, generally confine themselves to the medical part of the profession. The calling is hereditary, the eldest or the cleverest son begins his neoteric education at an early age, and succeeds to his father's functions.   There is little mystery in the craft, and the magicians of Unyamwezi have not refused to initiate some of the Arabs.   The power of the Mganga is great: he is treated as a sultan, whose word is law, and as a giver of life and death.   He is

blind, and will be able to take no pleasure; would it not be better, then, for you to die when this takes place, and you are in pain and trouble, and so make room for your son, as your father did for you?"

"No, it would not; I want to stand all same I stand now."

"But supposing you should go to a place of happiness after death and ——"

"I no savvy nothing about that, I know that I now live, and have too many wives, and niggers (slaves), and canoes," (he did not mean what he said, in saying he had too many wives, &c., it is their way of expressing a great number,) "and that I am king, and plenty of ships come to my country. I know no other ting, and I want to stand."

I offered a reply, but he would hear no more, and so the conversation on that subject ceased; and we proceeded to discuss one not much more agreeable to him — the payment of a very considerable debt which he owed me.

addressed by a kingly title, and is permitted to wear the chieftain's badge, made of the base of a conical shell.   He is also known by a number of small greasy and blackened gourds, filled with physic and magic, hanging round his waist, and by a little more of the usual grime—sanctity and dirt being connected in Africa as elsewhere.   These men are sent for from village to village, and receive as obventions and spiritual fees sheep and goats, cattle and provisions.   Their persons, however, are not sacred, and for criminal acts they are punished like other malefactors.   The greatest danger to them is an excess of fame.   A celebrated magician rarely, if ever, dies a natural death: too much is expected from him, and a severer disappointment leads to consequences more violent than usual.   The Arabs deride their pretensions, comparing them depreciatingly to the workers of Simiya, or conjuration, in their own country.   They remark that the wizard can never produce rain in the dry, or avert it in the wet season. The many, however, who, to use a West African phrase, have "become black" from a long residence in the country, acquire a sneaking belief in the Waganga, and fear of their powers.   The well-educated classes in Zanzibar consult these heathen, as the credulous of other Eastern countries go to the astrologer and geomantist, and in Europe to the clairvoyant and the tireuse de cartes. In one point this proceeding is wise: the wizard rarely wants wits; and whatever he has heard secretly or openly will inevitably appear in the course of his divination.

It must not be supposed, however, that the Mganga is purely an impostor.   To deceive others thoroughly a man must first deceive himself, otherwise he will be detected by the least discerning.   This is the simple secret of so many notable successes, achieved in the most unpromising causes by self-reliance and enthusiasm, the parents of energy and consistence. These barbarians are more often sinned against by their own fears and fooleries of faith, than sinners against their fellow-men by fraud and falsehood.

The office of Uganga includes many duties. The same man is a physician by natural and supernatural means, a mystagogue or medicine-man, a detector of sorcery, by means of the Judicium Dei or ordeal, a rain-maker, a conjuror, an augur, and a prophet.

As a rule, all diseases, from a boil to marasmus senilis, are attributed by the Fetissist to P'hepo, Hubub, or Afflatus. The three words are synonymous. P'hepo, in Kisawahili, is the plural form of upepo (a zephyr), used singularly to signify a high wind, a whirlwind ("devil"), and an evil ghost, generally of a Moslem. Hubub, the Arabic translation, means literally the blowing of wind, and metaphorically "possession." The African phrase for a man possessed is "ana p'hepo," "he has a devil." The Mganga is expected to heal the patient by expelling the possession. Like the evil spirit in the days of Saul, the unwelcome visitant must be charmed away by sweet music; the drums cause excitement, and violent exercise expels the ghost, as saltation nullifies in Italy the venom of the tarantula. The principal remedies are drumming, dancing, and drinking, till the auspicious moment arrives. The ghost is then enticed from the body of the possessed into some inanimate article, which he will condescend to inhabit. This, technically called a Keti, or stool, may be a certain kind of bead, two or more bits of wood bound together by a strip of snake's skin, a lion's or a leopard's claw, and other similar articles, worn round the head, the arm, the wrist, or the ankle. Paper is still considered great medicine by the Wasukuma and other tribes, who will barter valuable goods for a little bit : the great desideratum of the charm, in fact, appears to be its rarity, or the difficulty of obtaining it. Hence also the habit of driving nails into and hanging rags upon trees. The vegetable itself is not worshipped, as some Europeans who call it the " Devil's tree " have supposed : it is merely the place for the laying of ghosts, where by appending the Keti most acceptable to the spectrum, he will be bound over to keep the peace with man. Several accidents in the town of Zanzibar have confirmed even the higher orders in their lurking superstition. Mr. Peters, an English merchant, annoyed by the slaves who came in numbers to hammer nails and to hang iron hoops and rags upon a " Devil's tree " in his courtyard, ordered it to be cut down, to the horror of all the black beholders, of whom no one would lay an axe to it. Within six months five persons died in that house — Mr. Peters, his two clerks, his cooper, and his ship's carpenter. This superstition will remind the traveller of the Indian Pipul (Ficus religiosa), in which fiends are supposed to roost, and suggest to the Orientalist an explanation of the mysterious Moslem practices common from Western Africa to the farthest East. The hanging of rags upon trees by pilgrims and travellers is probably a relic of Arab Fetissism, derived in the days of ignorance from their congeners in East Africa. The custom has spread far and wide : even the Irish peasantry have been in the habit of suspending to the trees and bushes near their " holy wells " rags, halters, and spancels, in token of gratitude for their recovery, or that of their cattle.

There are other mystical means of restoring the sick

to health; one specimen will suffice. Several little sticks, like matches, are daubed with ochre, and marks are made with them upon the patient's body. A charm is chanted, the possessed one responds, and at the end of every stave an evil spirit flies from him, the signal being a stick cast by the Mganga upon the ground. Some unfortunates have as many as a dozen haunting ghosts, each of which has his own periapt: the Mganga demands a distinct honorarium for the several expulsions. Wherever danger is, fear will be; wherever fear is, charms and spells, exorcisms and talismans of portentous powers will be in demand; and wherever supernaturalisms are in requisition, men will be found, for a consideration, to supply them.

These strange rites are to be explained upon the principle which underlies thaumaturgy in general: they result from conviction in a gross mass of exaggerations heaped by ignorance, falsehood, and credulity, upon the slenderest foundation of fact — a fact doubtless solvable by the application of natural laws. The African temperament has strong susceptibilities, combined with what appears to be a weakness of brain, and great excitability of the nervous system, as is proved by the prevalence of epilepsy, convulsions, and hysteric disease. According to the Arab, El Sara, epilepsy, or the falling sickness, is peculiarly common throughout East Africa; and, as we know by experience in lands more civilised, the sudden prostration, rigidity, contortions, &c. of the patient, strongly suggest the idea that he has been taken and seized ($\dot{\epsilon}\pi\iota\lambda\eta\phi\theta\epsilon\tilde{\iota}\varsigma$) by, as it were, some external and invisible agent. The negroid is, therefore, peculiarly liable to the epidemical mania called "Phantasmata," which, according to history, has at times of great mental agitation and popular disturbance broken out in different parts of Europe, and which, even in this our day, forms the basework of " revivals." Thus in Africa the objective existence of spectra has become a tenet of belief. Stories that stagger the most sceptical are told concerning the phenomenon by respectable and not unlearned Arabs, who point to their fellow-countrymen as instances. Salim bin Rashid, a half-caste merchant, well known at Zanzibar, avers, and his companions bear witness to his words, that on one occasion, when travelling northwards from Unyanyembe, the possession occurred to himself. During the night two female slaves, his companions, of whom one was a child, fell, without apparent cause, into the fits which denote the approach of a spirit. Simultaneously, the master became as one intoxicated; a dark mass, material, not spiritual, entered the tent, and he felt himself pulled and pushed by a number of black figures, whom he had never before seen. He called aloud to his companions and slaves, who, vainly attempting to enter the tent, threw it down, and presently found him in a state of stupor, from which he did not recover till the morning. The same merchant circumstantially related, and called witnesses to prove, that a small slave-boy, who was produced on the occasion, had been frequently carried off by possession, even when confined in a windowless room, with a heavy door carefully bolted and padlocked. Next morning the victim was not found, although the chamber remained closed. A few days afterwards he was met in the jungle wandering absently like an idiot, and with speech too incoherent to explain what had happened to him. The Arabs óf Oman, who subscribe readily to transformation, deride these tales ; those of African blood believe them. The transformation-belief, still so common in Maskat, Abyssinia, Somaliland, and the Cape, and anciently an almost universal superstition, is, curious to say, unknown amongst these East African tribes. The Wahiao, lying between Kilwa and the Nyassa Lake, preserve, however, a remnant of the old creed in their conviction, that a malevolent magician can change a man after death into a lion, a leopard, or a hyæna. On the Zambezi the people, according to Dr. Livingstone (chap. xxx.), believe that a chief may metamorphose himself into a lion, kill any one he chooses, and then return to the human form. About Tete (chap. xxxi.) the negroids hold that, " while persons are still living, they may enter into lions and alligators, and then return again to their own bodies." Travellers determined to find in Africa counterparts of European and Asiatic tenets, argue from this transformation a belief in the " transmigration of souls." They thus confuse material metamorphosis with a spiritual progress, which is assuredly not an emanation from the Hamitic mind. The Africans have hitherto not bewildered their brains with metaphysics, and, ignoring the idea of a soul, which appears to be a dogma of the Caucasian race, they necessarily ignore its immortality.

The second, and, perhaps, the most profitable occupation of the Mganga, is the detection of Uchawi, or black magic. The fatuitous style of conviction, and the fearful tortures which, in the different regions, await those found guilty, have already been described, as far as description is possible. Amongst a people where the magician is a police detector, ordeals must be expected to thrive. The Baga or Kyapo of East Africa — the Arabs translate it El Halaf, or the Oath — is as cruel,

absurd, and barbarous, as the red water of Ashanti, the
venoms of Kasanji (Cassange), the muavi of the Banyai
tribes of Monomotapa, the Tangina poison of the Mala-
gash, the bitter water of the Jews, the " saucy-water"
of West Africa, and the fire tests of mediæval Europe.
The people of Usumbara thrust a red-hot hatchet into
the mouth of the accused. Among the south-eastern
tribes a heated iron spike, driven into some tender part
of the person, is twice struck with a log of wood. The
Wazaramo dip the hand into boiling water, the Waganda
into seething oil; and the Wazegura prick the ear with
the stiffest bristles of a gnu's tail. The Wakwafi have
an ordeal of meat that chokes the guilty. The Wanyamwezi pound with water between two stones, and
infuse a poisonous bark called " Mwavi: " it is first
administered by the Mganga to a hen, who, for the
nonce, represents the suspected. If, however, all parties
be not satisfied with such trial, it is duly adhibited to
the accused.

In East Africa, from Somaliland to the Cape, and
throughout the interior amongst the negroids and negroes
north as well as south of the equator, the rain-maker or
rain-doctor is a personage of consequence; and he does not
fail to turn the hopes and fears of the people to his own
advantage. A season of drought causes dearth, disease, and
desolation amongst these improvident races, who therefore connect every strange phenomenon with the object
of their desires, a copious wet monsoon. The enemy
has medicines which disperse the clouds. The stranger
who brings with him heavy showers is regarded as a
being of good omen; usually, however, the worst is expected from the novel portent; he will, for instance, be
accompanied and preceded by fertilising rains, but the
wells and springs will dry up after his departure, and

the result will be drought or small-pox. These rumours which may account for the Lybian stranger-sacrifices in the olden time, are still dangerous to travellers. The Mganga must remedy the evil. His spells are those of fetissists in general, the mystic use of something foul, poisonous, or difficult to procure, such as the album græcum of hyænas, snakes' fangs, or lions' hair; these and similar articles are collected with considerable trouble by the young men of the tribe for the use of the rain-maker. But he is a weatherwise man, and rains in tropical lands are easily foreseen. Not unfrequently, however, he proves himself a false prophet; and when all the resources of cunning fail he must fly for dear life from the victims of his delusion.

The Mganga is also a predictor and a soothsayer. He foretels the success or failure of commercial undertakings, of wars, and of kidnapping-commandos; he foresees famine and pestilence, and he suggests the means of averting calamities. He fixes also, before the commencement of any serious affair, fortunate conjunctions, without which a good issue cannot be expected. He directs expiatory offerings. His word is ever powerful to expedite or to delay the march of a caravan; and in his quality of augur he considers the flight of birds and the cries of beasts, like his prototype of the same class in ancient Europe and in modern Asia.

The principal instrument of the Mganga's craft is one of the dirty little buyu or gourds which he wears in a bunch round his waist; and the following is the usual programme when the oracle is to be consulted. The magician brings his implements in a bag of matting; his demeanour is serious as the occasion; he is carefully greased, and his head is adorned with the diminutive antelope-horns fastened by a thong of leather above the forehead. He sits like a sultan upon a dwarf stool in front of the querist, and begins by exhorting the highest possible offertory. No pay, no predict. Divination by the gourd has already been described; the Mganga has many other implements of his craft. Some prophesy by the motion of berries swimming in a cup full of water, which is placed upon a low stool surrounded by four tails of the zebra or the buffalo lashed to sticks planted upright in the ground. The Kasanda is a system of folding triangles not unlike those upon which plaything soldiers are mounted. Held in the right hand, it is thrown out, and the direction of the end points to the safe and auspicious route; this is probably the rudest appliance of prestidigitation. The shero is a bit of wood about the size of a man's hand, and not unlike a pair of bellows, with a dwarf handle, a projection like a nozzle, and in the circular centre a little hollow. This is filled with water, and a grain or fragment of wood, placed to float, gives an evil omen if it tends towards the sides, and favourable if it veers towards the handle or the nozzle. The Mganga generally carries about with him to announce his approach a kind of rattle called "sánje." This is a hollow gourd of pine-apple shape, pierced with various holes, prettily carved and half filled with maize, grains, and pebbles; the handle is a stick passed through its length and secured by cross-pins.

The Mganga has many minor duties. In elephant hunts he must throw the first spear and endure the blame if the beast escapes. He marks ivory with spots disposed in lines and other figures, and thus enables it to reach the coast without let or hindrance. He loads the kirangozi or guide with charms and periapts to defend him from the malice which is ever directed

at a leading man, and sedulously forbids him to
allow precedence even to the Mtongi, the commander
and proprietor of the caravan.   He aids his tribe by
magical arts in wars, by catching a bee, reciting over it
certain incantations, and loosing it in the direction of the
foe, when the insect will instantly summon an army of its
fellows and disperse a host, however numerous.   This
belief well illustrates the easy passage of the natural
into the supernatural.   The land being full of swarms,
and man's body being wholly exposed, many a caravan
has been dispersed like chaff before the wind by a bevy
of swarming bees.   Similarly in South Africa the
magician kicks an ant-hill and starts wasps which put
the enemy to flight.   And in the books of the Hebrews
we read that the hornet sent before the children of
Israel against the Amorite was more terrible than sword
or bow.   (Joshua, xxiv.)

The several tribes in East Africa present two forms
of government, the despotic and the semi-monarchical.

In the despotic races, the Wakilima or mountaineers
of Chhaga, for instance, the subjects are reduced to the
lowest state of servility.   All, except the magicians and
the councillors, are " Wasoro "—soldiers and slaves to
the sultan, mangi, or sovereign.   The reader will bear
in mind that the word " sultan" is the Arabic term applied generically by traders to all the reguli and roitelets,
the chiefs and headmen, whose titles vary in every region.
In Uzaramo the Sultan is called p'hazi; in Khutu, p'hazi
or mundewa; in Usagara, mundewa; in Ugogo, mteme;
in Unyamwezi, mwami; in Ujiji and Karagwah, mkama.
" Wazir " is similarly used by the Arabs for the principal
councillor or minister, whose African name in the several
tribes is mwene goha, mbáhá, mzágírá, magáwe, mhángo,
and muhinda.   The elders are called throughout the

country Wagosi and Wányáp'hárá; they form the council of the chief. All male children are taken from their
mothers, are made to live together, and are trained to
the royal service, to guarding the palace, to tilling the
fields, and to keeping the watercourses in order. The
despot is approached with fear and trembling; subjects
of both sexes must stand at a distance, and repeatedly
clap their palms together before venturing to address
him. Women always bend the right knee to the earth,
and the chief acknowledges the salutation with a nod.
At times the elders and even the women inquire of the
ruler what they can do to please him : he points to a
plot of ground which he wishes to be cleared, and this
corvée is the more carefully performed, as he fines them
in a bullock if a weed be left unplucked. In war female
captives are sold by the king, and the children are kept
to swell the number of his slaves. None of the Wasoro
may marry without express permission. The king has
unlimited power of life and death, which he exercises
without squeamishness, and a general right of sale over
his subjects; in some tribes, as those of Karagwah,
Uganda, and Unyoro, he is almost worshipped. It is a
capital offence to assume the name of a Sultan ; even a
stranger so doing would be subjected to fines and other
penalties. The only limit to the despot's power is the
Ada, or precedent, the unwritten law of ancient custom,
which is here less mutable than the codes and pandects
of Europe. The African, like the Asiatic, is by nature
a conservative, at once the cause and the effect of his
inability to rise higher in the social scale. The king
lives in a manner of barbarous state. He has large
villages crowded with his families and slaves. He never
issues from his abode without an armed mob, and he
disdains to visit even the wealthiest Arabs. The monar-

chical tribes are legitimists of the good old school, disdaining a *novus homo ;* and the consciousness of power
invests their princes with a certain dignity and majesty
of demeanour.   As has been mentioned, some of the
Sultans whose rule has the greatest prestige, appear, from
physical peculiarities, to be of a foreign and a nobler
origin.

In the aristocratical or semi-monarchical tribes, as the
Wanyamwezi, the power of the Sultan depends mainly
upon his wealth, importance, and personal qualifications
for the task of rule.   A chief enabled to carry out a
" fist-right" policy will raise himself to the rank of a
despot, and will slay and sell his subjects without mercy.
Though surrounded by a council varying from two to a
score of chiefs and elders, who are often related or
connected with him, and who, like the Arab shayks,
presume as much as possible in ordering this and forbid-
ding that, he can disregard and slight them.   More
often, however, his authority is circumscribed by a rude
balance of power ; the chiefs around him can probably
bring as many warriors into the field as he can.   When
weak, the sultan has little more authority than the
patell of an Indian village or the shaykh of a Bedouin
tribe.   Yet even when the chief cannot command in his
own clan, he is an important personage to travelling
merchants and strangers.   He can cause a quarrel, an
advance, or an assassination, and he can quiet brawls
even when his people have been injured.   He can open
a road by providing porters, or bar a path by deterring
a caravan from proceeding, or by stopping the sale of
provisions.   Thus it is easy to travel amongst races
whose chiefs are well disposed to foreigners, and the
utmost circumspection becomes necessary when the
headmen are grasping and inhospitable.   Upon the whole,

the chiefs are wise enough to encourage the visits of traders.

A patriarchal or purely republican form of government is unknown in East Africa. The Wasagara, it is true, choose their chief like the Banyai of "Monomotapa," but, once elected, he becomes a monarch. Loyalty—or, to reduce it to its elements, veneration for the divinity that hedges in a king—is a sentiment innate in the African mind. Man, however, in these regions is not a political animal; he has a certain instinctive regard for his chief and a respect for his elders. He ignores, however, the blessings of duly limited independence and the natural classification of humanity into superior and inferior, and honours — the cheap pay of nations — are unknown. He acknowledges no higher and lower social strata. His barbarism forbids the existence of a learned oligarchy, of an educated community, or of a church and state, showing the origin of the connection between the soul and body of society. Man being equal to man, force being the only law and self the sole consideration, mutual jealousy prevents united efforts and deadens all patriotic spirit. No one cares for the public good; the welfare of the general must yield to the most contemptible individual interests; civil order and security are therefore unknown, and foreign relations cannot exist.

In the lowest tribes the chieftain is a mere nonentity, " a Sultan," as the Arabs say, " within his own walls." His subjects will boast, like the Somal, that he is " *tanquam unus ex nobis ;*" and they are so sensible of restraint that "girdles and garters would be to them bonds and shackles" metaphorically as well as literally. The position of these Sultans is about equal to that of the diwans of the Mrima; their dignity is confined to sitting upon a dwarf three-legged stool, to wearing more brass wire than beads, and to possessing clothes a little better than those of their subjects. The "regulus" must make a return present to strangers after receiving their offerings, and in some cases must begin with gifts. He must listen to the words of his councillors and elders, who, being without salary, claim a portion of the presents and treasure-trove, interfere on all occasions of blackmail, fines, and penalties, demand, from all petitioners gifts and bribes to secure interest, and exert great influence over the populace.

Legitimacy is the rule throughout the land, and the son, usually the eldest, succeeds to the father, except amongst the Wasukuma of N. Unyamwezi, where the line of descent is by the sister's son — the "surer side" — for the normal reason, to secure some of the blood royal for ruling. Even the widows of the deceased become the property of the successor. This truly African practice prevails also amongst the Bachwana, and presents another of those curious points of resemblance between the Hamite and Semite races which have induced modern ethnologists to derive the Arab from Africa. The curious custom amongst the Wanyamwezi of devising property to illegitimate children is not carried out in the succession to power. Where there are many sons, all, as might be expected, equally aspire to power; sometimes, however, of two brothers, one will consent to hold authority under the other. In several tribes, especially in Usukuma, the widow of a chief succeeds to his dignity in default of issue.

Punishments are simple in East Africa. The sar, vendetta or blood-feud, and its consequence, the diyat or weregeld, exist in germ, unreduced, as amongst the more civilised Arabs, to an artful and intricate system.

But these customs are founded, unlike ours, upon barbarous human nature. Instinct prompts a man to slay the slayer of his kith and kin; the offence is against the individual, not the government or society. He must reason to persuade himself that the crime, being committed against the law, should be left to the law for notice; he wants revenge, and he cares nought for punishment or example for the prevention of crime. The Sultan encourages the payment of blood-money to the relatives of the deceased, or, if powerful enough, claims it himself, rather than that one murder should lead to another, and eventually to a chronic state of bloodshed and confusion. Thus, in some tribes the individual revenges himself, and in others he commits his cause to the chief. Here he takes an equivalent in cattle for the blood of a brother or the loss of a wife; there he visits the erring party with condign punishment. The result of such deficiency of standard is a want of graduation in severity; a thief is sometimes speared and beheaded, or sold into slavery after all his property has been extorted by the chief, the councillors, and the elders, whilst a murderer is perhaps only fined.

The land in East Africa is everywhere allodial; it does not belong to the ruler, nor has the dawn of the feudal system yet arisen there. A migratory tribe gives up its rights to the soil, contrary to the mortmain system of the Arab Bedouins, and, if it would return, it must return by force. The Sultan, however, exacts a fee from all immigrants settling in his territory.

The sources of revenue in East Africa are uncertain, desultory, and complicated. The agricultural tribes pay yearly a small per centage of grain; this, however, is the office of the women, who are expert in fraud. Neither sowing nor harvest can take place without the chief's permission, and the issue of his order is regulated by his own interests. Amongst the hunting tribes, slain elephants become the hunter's property, but the Sultan claims as treasure-trove a tusk of any animal found wounded or dead in his dominions, and in all cases the spoils of dead lions are crown property. The flesh of game is distributed amongst the elders and the ruling family, who also assert a claim to the cloth or beads purchased by means of the ivory from caravans. Some have abditaria and considerable stores of the articles most valued by barbarians. Throughout the slave-paths the chiefs have learned to raise revenue from the slaves, who thus bribe them to forbear from robbery. But whilst the stronger require large gifts without return, the weaker make trifling presents, generally of cattle or provisions, and expect many times the value in brass wire, cloth, and beads. The stranger may refuse these offerings; it is, however, contrary to custom, and as long as he can afford it he should submit to the imposition. Fiscs and fines are alarmingly frequent. If the monsoon-rains delay, the chief summons a Mganga to fix upon the obstructor; he is at once slain, and his property is duly escheated. The Sultan claims the goods and chattels of all felons and executed criminals, even in the case of a servant put to death by his master. In the more republican tribes the chief lives by the sweat of his slaves. Briefly, East Africa presents an instructive study of human society in its first stage after birth.

I will conclude this uninteresting chapter—attribute its dulness, gentle reader, to the effects of the climate and society of Konduchi—with a subject which strikes home to the heart of every Englishman, slavery.

The origin of slavery in East Africa is veiled in the

glooms o the past. It is mentioned in the Periplus (chap. iii.), as an institution of the land, and probably it was the result of the ancient trade with southern Arabia. At present it is almost universal: with the exceptions of the Wahinda, the Watosi, and the Wagogo, all the tribes from the eastern equatorial coast to Ujiji and the regions lying westward of the Tanganyika Lake may be called slave-races. An Arab, Msawahili, and even a bondsman from Zanzibar, is everywhere called Murungwana or freeman. Yet in many parts of the country the tribes are rather slave-importers than exporters. Although they kidnap others, they will not sell their fellows, except when convicted of crime— theft, magic, murder, or cutting the upper teeth before the lower. In times of necessity, however, a man will part with his parents, wives, and children, and when they fail he will sell himself without shame. As has been observed, amongst many tribes the uncle has a right to dispose of his nephews and nieces.

Justice requires the confession that the horrors of slave-driving rarely meet the eye in East Africa. Some merchants chain or cord together their gangs for safer transport through regions where desertion is at a premium. Usually, however, they trust rather to soft words and kind treatment; the fat lazy slave is often seen stretched at ease in the shade, whilst the master toils in the sun and wind. The "property" is well fed and little worked, whereas the porter, belonging to none but himself, is left without hesitation to starve upon the road-side. The relationship is rather that of patron and client than of lord and bondsman; the slave is addressed as Ndugu-yango, "my brother," and he is seldom provoked by hard words or stripes. In fact, the essence of slavery, compulsory unpaid labour, is perhaps more prevalent in independent India than in East Africa; moreover, there is no adscriptus glebæ, as in the horrid thraldom of Malabar. To this general rule there are terrible exceptions, as might be expected amongst a people with scant regard for human life. The Kirangozi, or guide, attached to the Expedition on return from Ujiji, had loitered behind for some days because his slave girl was too footsore to walk. When tired of waiting he cut off her head, for fear lest she should become gratis another man's property.

In East Africa there are two forms of this traffic, the export and the internal trade. For the former slaves are collected like ivories throughout the length and breadth of the land. They are driven down from the principal dêpots, the island of Kasenge, Ujiji, Unyanyembe, and Zungomero to the coast by the Arab and Wasawahili merchants, who afterwards sell them in retail at the great mart, Zanzibar. The internal trade is carried on between tribe and tribe, and therefore will long endure.

The practice of slavery in East Africa, besides demoralising and brutalising the race, leads to the results which effectually bar increase of population and progress towards civilisation. These are commandos, or border wars, and intestine confusion.

All African wars, it has been remarked, are for one of two objects, cattle-lifting or kidnapping. Some of the pastoral tribes—as the Wamasai, the Wakwafi, the Watuta, and the Warori—assert the theory that none but themselves have a right to possess herds, and that they received the gift directly from their ancestor who created cattle; in practice they covet the animals for the purpose of a general gorge. Slaves, however, are much more frequently the end and aim of

feud and foray. The process of kidnapping, an inveterate custom in these lands, is in every way agreeable
to the mind of the man-hunter. A *"multis utile bellum,"*
it combines the pleasing hazards of the chase with the
exercise of cunning and courage; the battue brings
martial glory and solid profit, and preserves the barbarian from the listlessness of life without purpose.
Thus men date from foray to foray, and pass their days
in an interminable blood-feud and border war. A poor
and powerful chief will not allow his neighbours to rest
wealthier than himself; a quarrel is soon found, the
stronger attacks the weaker, hunts and harries his
cattle, burns his villages, carries off his subjects and
sells them to the first passing caravan. The inhabitants
of the land have thus become wolves to one another;
their only ambition is to dispeople and destroy, and the
blow thus dealt to a thinly populated country strikes at
the very root of progress and prosperity.

As detrimental to the public interests as the border
wars is the intestine confusion caused by the slave trade.
It perpetuates the vile belief in Uchawi or black magic:
when captives are in demand, the criminal's relations
are sold into slavery. It affords a scope for the
tyranny of a chief, who, if powerful enough, will enrich
himself by vending his subjects in wholesale and retail.
By weakening the tie of family, it acts with deadly
effect in preventing the increase of the race.

On the coast and in the island of Zanzibar the slaves
are of two kinds—the Muwallid or domestic, born in
captivity, and the wild slave imported from the interior.

In the former case the slave is treated as one of the
family, because the master's comfort depends upon the
man being contented; often also his sister occupies the

dignified position of concubine to the head of the house
These slaves vary greatly in conduct. The most
tractable are those belonging to the Diwans and the
Wasawahili generally, who treat them with the utmost
harshness and contempt. The Arabs spoil them by a
kinder usage; few employ the stick, the salib, or cross
—a forked pole to which the neck and ankles are lashed
—and the makantale or stocks, for fear of desertion.
Yet the slave if dissatisfied silently leaves the house,
lets himself to another master, and returns after perhaps
two years' absence as if nothing had occurred. Thus
he combines the advantages of freedom and slavery.
Moreover, it is a proverb among the Arabs that a slave
must desert once in his life, and he does so the more
readily as he betters his condition by so doing. The
worst in all points are those belonging to the Banyans,
the Indians, and other European subjects; they know
their right to emancipation, and consult only their own
interests and inclinations. The Muwallid or domestic
slave is also used like the Pombeiro of West Africa.
From Unyamwezi and Ujiji he is sent to traffic in the
more dangerous regions—the master meanwhile dwelling amongst his fellow countrymen in some comfortable
Tembe. This proceeding has greatly injured the commerce of the interior, and necessitates yearly lengthening
journeys. The slave intrusted with cloth and beads
suddenly becomes a great man; he is lavish in supporting the dignity of a fundi or fattore, and consulting nothing but his own convenience, he will loiter
for six months at a place where he has been sent for a
week. Thus it is that ivory sold in Unyamwezi but a
dozen years ago at 10 lbs. for 1 lb. of beads now fetches
nearly weight for weight. And this is a continually
increasing evil. No caravan, however, can safely tra-

verse the interior without an escort of slave-musketeers. They never part with their weapons, even when passing from house to house, holding that their lives depend upon their arms; they beg, borrow, or steal powder and ball; in fact they are seldom found unready. They will carry nothing but the lightest gear, the master's writing-case, bed, or praying-mat; to load them heavily would be to ensure desertion. Contrary to the practice of the free porter, they invariably steal when they run away; they are also troublesome about food, and they presume upon their weapons to take liberties with the liquor and the women of the heathen.

The imported slaves again are of two different classes. Children are preferred to adults; they are Islamised and educated so as to resemble the Muwallid, though they are even somewhat less tame. Full-grown serfs are bought for predial purposes; they continue indocile, and alter little by domestication. When not used by the master they are left to plunder or to let themselves out for food and raiment, and when dead they are cast into the sea or into the nearest pit. These men are the scourge of society; no one is safe from their violence; and to preserve a garden or an orchard from the depredations of the half-starved wretches, a guard of musketeers would be required. They are never armed, yet, as has been recounted, they have caused at Zanzibar servile wars, deadly and lasting as those of ancient Rome.

Arabs declare that the barbarians are improved by captivity—a partial theory open to doubt. The servum pecus retain in thraldom that wildness and obstinacy which distinguish the people and the lower animals of their native lands; they are trapped, but not tamed; they become captives, but not civilised. However trained, they are probably the worst servants in the world; a slave-household is a model of discomfort. The wretches take a trouble and display an ingenuity in opposition and disobedience, in perversity, annoyance, and villany, which rightly directed would make them invaluable. The old definition of a slave still holds good—"an animal that eats as much and does as little as possible." Clumsy and unhandy, dirty and careless, he will never labour unless ordered to do so, and so futile is his nature that even the inducement of the stick cannot compel him to continue his exertions; a whole gang will barely do the work of a single servant. He "has no end," to use the Arab phrase: that is to say, however well he may begin, he will presently tire of his task; he does not and apparently he will not learn; his first impulse, like that of an ass, is not to obey; he then thinks of obeying; and if fear preponderate he finally may obey. He must deceive, for fraud and foxship are his force; when detected in some prodigious act of rascality, he pathetically pleads, "Am I not a slave?" So wondrous are his laziness and hate of exertion, that despite a high development of love of life he often appears the most reckless of mortals. He will run away from the semblance of danger; yet on a journey he will tie his pipe to a leaky keg of gunpowder, and smoke it in that position rather than take the trouble to undo it. A slave belonging to Musa, the Indian merchant at Kazeh, unwilling to rise and fetch a pipe, opened the pan of his musket, filled it with tobacco and fire, and beginning to inhale it from the muzzle blew out his brains. Growing confident and impudent from the knowledge of how far he may safely go, the slave presumes to the utmost. He steals instinctively, like a magpie: a case is quoted in which the gold spangles were stripped from an officer's sword-belt whilst dining with the Prince of Zanzibar. The slave is almost always half-naked; whatever clothes he obtains from the master are pawned or sold in the bazar; hence he must pilfer and plunder almost openly for the means of gratifying his lowest propensities, drinking and intrigue. He seems to acquire from captivity a greater capacity for debauchery than even in his native wilds; he has learned irregularities unknown to his savage state: it is the brutishness of negroid nature brought out by the cheap and readily attainable pleasures of semi-civilisation. Whenever on moonlight nights the tapping of the tomtom responds to the vile squeaking of the fife, it is impossible to keep either a male or female slave within doors. All rendezvous at the place, and, having howled and danced themselves into happiness, conclude with a singularly disorderly scene. In the town of Zanzibar these "Ngoma" or dances were prohibited for moral reasons by the late Sayyid. The attachment of a slave to his master is merely a development of selfishness; it is a greater insult to abuse the Ahbab (patroon), than, according to Eastern fashion, the father and mother, the wife and sister. No slave-owner, however, praises a slave or relies upon his fidelity. The common expression is, "There is no good in the bondsman."

Like the Somal, a merry and light-hearted race in foreign countries, but rendered gloomy and melancholy by the state of affairs at home, the negroid slaves greatly improve by exportation: they lose much of the surliness and violence which distinguish them at Zanzibar, and are disciplined into a kind of respect for superiors. Thus, "Seedy Mubarak" is a prime favourite on board an Indian steamer; he has also strength and courage enough to make himself respected. But "Seedy

Mubarak " has tasted the intoxicating draught of liberty, he is in high good humour with himself and with all around him, he is a slave merely in origin, he has been adopted into the great family of free men, and with it he has identified all his interests.   Eastern history preserves instances of the valour and faithfulness of bondsmen, as the annals of the West are fond of recording the virtues of dogs.   Yet all the more civilised races have a gird at the negro.   In the present day the Persians and other Asiatics are careful, when bound on distant or dangerous journeys, to mix white servants with black slaves; they hold the African to be full of strange childish caprices, and to be ever at heart a treacherous and bloodthirsty barbarian.   Like the "bush-negroes" of Surinam, once so dangerous to the Dutch, the runaway slaves from Zanzibar have formed a kind of East African Liberia, between Mount Yombo and the Shimba section of the Eastern Ghauts.   They have endangered the direct caravan-road from Mombasah to Usumbara; and though trespassing upon the territory of the Mwasagnombe, a sub-clan of the Wadigo, and claimed as subjects by Abdullah, the son of Sultan Kimwere, they have gallantly held their ground.   According to the Arabs there is another servile republic about Gulwen, near Brava.   Travellers speak with horror of the rudeness, violence, and cruelty of these self-emancipated slaves; they are said to be more dangerous even than the Somal, who for wanton mischief and malice can be compared with nothing but the naughtiest schoolboys in England.

The serviles at Zanzibar have played their Arab masters some notable tricks.   Many a severe lord has perished by the hand of a slave.   Several have lost their eyes by the dagger's point during sleep.   Curious tales are told of ingenious servile conspiracy.   Mohammed bin Sayf, a Zanzibar Arab, remarkable for household discipline, was brought to grief by Kombo, his slave, who stole a basket of nutmegs from the Prince, and, hiding them in his master's house, denounced him of theft. Fahl bin Nasr, a travelling merchant, when passing through Ugogo, nearly lost his life in consequence of a slave having privily informed the people that his patroon had been killing crocodiles and preserving their fat for poison. In both these cases the slaves were not punished; they had acted, it was believed, according to the true instincts of servile nature, and chastisement would have caused desertion, not improvement.

As regards the female slaves, the less said about them, from regard to the sex, the better: they are as deficient in honour as in honesty, in modesty and decorum as in grace and beauty. No man, even an Arab, deems the mother of his children chaste, or believes in the legitimacy of his progeny till proved.

Extensive inquiries into the subject lead to a conviction that it is impossible to offer any average of the price of slaves. Yet the question is of importance, as only the immense profit causes men thus to overlook all considerations of humanity. A few general rules may be safely given. There is no article, even horseflesh, that varies so much in market-value as the human commodity: the absolute worth is small compared with the wants of the seller and the requirements and the means of the purchaser. The extremes range from six feet of unbleached domestics or a few pounds of grain in time of famine, to seventy dollars, equal to 15l. The slaves are cheapest in the interior, on account of the frequency of desertion: about Unyamwezi they are dearer, and most expensive in the island of Zanzibar.

At the latter place during the last few years they have doubled in price: according to the Arabs, who regard the abolition of slavery with feelings of horror, this increase results from the impediments thrown in the way by the English; a more probable explanation may be found in the greater cheapness of money. At Zanzibar the price of a boy under puberty is from fifteen to thirty dollars. A youth till the age of fifteen is worth a little less. A man in the prime of life, from twenty-five to forty, fetches from thirteen to twenty dollars; after that age he may be bought from ten to thirteen. Educated slaves, fitted for the work of factors, are sold from twenty-five to seventy dollars, and at fancy prices. The price of females is everywhere about one-third higher than that of males. At Zanzibar the ushur or custom-dues vary according to the race of the slave: the Wahiao, Wangindo, and other serviles imported from Kilwa, pay one dollar per head, from the Mrima or maritime regions two dollars, and from Unyamwezi, Ujiji, and the rest of the interior three dollars. At the central depôt, Unyanyembe, where slaves are considered neither cheap nor dear, the value of a boy ranges between eight and ten doti or double cloths; a youth from nine to eleven; a man in prime, from five to ten; and past his prime from four to six. In some parts of the interior men are dearer than children under puberty. In the cheapest places, as in Karagwah and Urori, a boy costs three shukkahs of cloth, and three fundo or thirty strings of coral beads; a youth from ten to fifteen fundo; a man in prime from eight to ten; and no one will purchase an old man. These general notes must not, however, be applied to particular tribes: as with ivory and other valuable commodities, the amount and the description of the circulating medium vary at almost every march.

It was asserted by the late Colonel Hamerton, whose local knowledge was extensive, that the average of yearly import into the island of Zanzibar was 14,000 head of slaves, the extremes being 9000 and 20,000. The loss by mortality and desertion is 30 per cent. per annum; thus, the whole gang must be renewed between the third and fourth year.

By a stretch of power slavery might readily be abolished in the island of Zanzibar, and in due time, after the first confusion, the measure would doubtless be found as profitable as it is now unpalatable to the landed proprietors, and to the commercial body. A " sentimental squadron," like the West African, would easily, by means of steam, prevent any regular exportation to the Asiatic continent. But these measures would deal only with effects, leaving the causes in full vigour; they would strike at the bole and branches, the root retaining sufficient vitality to resume its functions as soon as relieved of the pressure from without. Neither treaty nor fleet would avail permanently to arrest the course of slavery upon the seaboard, much less would it act in the far realms of the interior. At present the African will not work: the purchase of predial slaves to till and harvest for him is the great aim of his life. When a more extensive intercourse with the maritime regions shall beget wants which compel the barbarian, now contented with doing nothing and having nothing, to that individual exertion and that mutual dependency which render serfdom a moral impossibility in the more advanced stages of human society,—when man, now valueless except to himself, shall become more precious by his labour than by his sale, in fact an article so expensive that strangers cannot afford to buy him,—then we may expect to witness the extinction of the evil. Thus, and thus only can " Rachel, still weeping for her children," in the evening of her days, be made happy.

Meanwhile, the philanthropist, who after sowing the good seed has sense and patience to consign the gathering of the crop to posterity, will hear with pleasure that the extinction of slavery would be hailed with delight by the great mass throughout the length and breadth of Eastern Africa. This people, "robbed and spoiled" by their oppressors, who are legionary, call themselves "the meat," and the slave-dealers "the knife:" they hate and fear their own demon Moloch, but they lack unanimity to free their necks from his yoke. Africa still "lies in her blood," but the progress of human society, and the straiter bonds which unite man with man, shall eventually rescue her from her old pitiable fate.

The Bull-headed Mabruki.   African standing position.

CONCLUSION.

ON the 9th February the Battela and the stores required for our trip arrived at Konduchi from Zanzibar, and the next day saw us rolling down the coast, with a fair fresh breeze, towards classic Kilwa, the Quiloa of De Gama, of Camoens, and of the Portuguese annalists. I shall reserve an account of this most memorable shore for a future work devoted especially to the seaboard of Zanzibar — coast and island : — in the present tale of adventure the details of a *cabotage* would be out of place. Suffice it to say that we lost nearly all our crew by the cholera, which, after ravaging the eastern coast of Arabia and Africa, and the islands of Zanzibar and Pemba, had almost depopulated the southern settlements on the mainland. We were unable to visit the course of the great Rufiji River, a counterpart of the Zambezi in the south, and a water-road which appears destined to become the highway of nations into Eastern equatorial Africa. No man dared to take service on board the infected vessel; the Hindu Banyans, who directed the Copal trade of the river regions aroused against us the chiefs of the interior; moreover, the stream was in flood, overflowing its banks, and its line appeared marked by heavy purple clouds, which discharged a deluge of rain. Convinced that the travelling season was finished, I turned the head of the Battela northwards, and on the 4th March, 1859, after a succession of violent squalls and pertinacious calms, we landed once more upon the island of Zanzibar.

Sick and way-worn I entered the house connected in memory with an old friend, not without a feeling of sorrow for the change — I was fated to regret it even more.   The excitement of travel was succeeded by an utter depression of mind and body: even the labour of talking was too great, and I took refuge from society in a course of French novels *à vingt sous la pièce.*

Yet I had fallen upon stirring times: the little state, at the epoch of my return, was in the height of confusion.   His Highness the Sayyid Suwayni, Suzerain of Maskat, seizing the pretext of a tribute owed to him by his cadet brother of Zanzibar, had embarked, on the 11th February, 1859, a host of Bedouin brigands upon four or five square-rigged ships and many Arab craft: with this power he was preparing a hostile visit to the island.   The Baloch stations on the mainland were drained of mercenaries, and 7000 muskets, with an amount of ammunition, which rendered the town dangerous, were served out to slaves and other ruffians. Dows from Hadramaut brought down armed adventurers, who were in the market to fight for the best pay. The turbulent Harisi chiefs of Zanzibar were terrified into siding with his Highness the Sayyid Majid by the influence of H. M. consul, Captain Rigby.   But the representatives of the several Christian powers could not combine to preserve the peace, and M. Ladislas Cochet, Consul de France, an uninterested spectator of the passing events, thought favourably of his Highness the Sayyid Suwayni's claim, he believed that the people if consulted would prefer the rule of the elder brother, and he could not reconcile his conscience to the unscrupulous means — the *force majeure* — which his opponent brought into the field.   The Harisi, therefore, with their thousands of armed retainers — in a single review I saw about 2200 of them — preserved an armed neutrality, which threatened mischief to the weaker of the rival brothers: trade was paralysed, the foreign merchants lost heavily, and no less than eighty native vessels were still at the end of the season due from Bombay and the north. To confuse confusion, several ships collecting negro "emigrants" and "free labourers," *per fas et nefas*, even kidnapping them when necessary, were reported by the Arab local authorities to be anchored and to be cruising off the coast of Zanzibar.

After a fortnight of excitement and suspense, during which the wildest rumours flew through the mouths of men, it was officially reported that H. M.'s steamer *Punjaub*, Captain Fullerton, H.M.I.N., commanding, had, under orders received from the government of Bombay, met his Highness the Sayyid Suwayni off the eastern coast of Africa and had persuaded him to return.

Congratulations were exchanged, salutes were fired, a few Buggalows belonging to the enemy's fleet, which was said to have been dispersed by a storm, dropped in and were duly captured, the negroes drank, sang, and danced for a consecutive week, and with the least delay armed men poured in crowded boats from the island towards their several stations on the mainland. But the blow had been struck, the commercial prosperity of Zanzibar could not be retrieved during the brief remnant of the season, and the impression that a renewal of the attempt would at no distant time ensure similar disasters seemed to be uppermost in every man's mind.

His Highness the Sayyid Majid had honoured me with an expression of desire that I should remain until the expected hostilities might be brought to a close. I did so willingly in gratitude to a prince to whose good-will my success was mainly indebted. But the consulate was no longer what it was before. I felt myself too conversant with local politics, and too well aware of what was going on to be a pleasant companion to its new tenant. At last, on the 15th March, when concluding my accounts with Ladha Damha, the collector of customs at Zanzibar, that official requested me, with the usual mystery, to be the bearer of despatches, privately addressed by his prince, to the home government. I could easily guess what they contained. Unwilling, however, to undertake such a duty when living at the consulate, and seeing how totally opposed to official *convenance* such a procedure was, I frankly stated my objections to Ladha Damha, and repeated the conversation to Captain Rigby. As may be imagined, this little event did not diminish his desire to see me depart.

Still I was unwilling to leave the field of my labours while so much remained to be done. As my health appeared gradually to return under the influence of repose and comparative comfort, I would willingly have delayed at the island till the answer to an application for leave of absence, and to a request for additional funds could be received from the Government of Bombay and the Royal Geographical Society. But the evident anxiety of my host to disembarrass himself of his guest, and the nervous impatience of my companion — who could not endure the thought of losing an hour — compelled me, sorely against my wish, to abandon my intentions.

Said bin Salim, the Ras Kafilah, called twice or thrice at the consulate. I refused, however, to see him, and explained the reason to Captain Rigby. That gentleman agreed with me at the time that the Arab had been more than sufficiently rewarded by the sum advanced to him by Lieut.-Colonel Hamerton : but — perhaps he remembers the cognomen by which he was known in days of yore amongst his juvenile *confrères* at Addiscombe?—he has since thought proper to change his mind. The Jemadar and the Baloch attended me to the doorway of the prince's darbar: I would not introduce them to their master or to the consul, as such introduction would have argued myself satisfied with their conduct, nor would I recommend them for promotion or reward. Ladha Damha put in a faint claim for salary due to the sons of Ramji; but when informed of the facts of the case he at once withdrew it, and I heard no more of it at Zanzibar. As regards the propriety of these severe but equitable measures, my companion was, I believe, at that time of the same opinion as myself: perhaps Captain Speke's prospect of a return to East Africa, and of undertaking a similar exploration, have caused him since that epoch to think, and to think that he then thought, otherwise.

The report of the success of the *Punjaub's* mission left me at liberty to depart. With a grateful heart I bade adieu to a prince whose kindness and personal courtesy will long dwell in my memory, and who at the parting interview had expressed a hope to see me again, and had offered me a passage homeward in one of his ships-of-war. At the time, however, a clipper-built barque, the *Dragon of Salem*, Captain M'Farlane commanding, was discharging cargo in the harbour, preparatory to sailing with the S.W. monsoon for Aden. The captain consented to take us on board: Captain Rigby, however, finding his boat too crowded, was compelled to omit accompanying us—a little mark of civility not unusual in the East. His place, however, was well filled up by Seedy Mubarak Bombay, whose honest face appeared at that moment, by contrast, peculiarly attractive.

On the 22nd March, 1859, the clove-shrubs and the cocoa-trees of Zanzibar again faded from my eyes. After crossing and re-crossing three times the tedious line, we found ourselves anchored, on the 16th April, near the ill-omened black walls of the Aden crater.

The crisis of my African sufferings had taken place during my voyage upon the Tanganyika Lake: the fever, however, still clung to me like the shirt of Nessus. Mr. Apothecary Frost, of Zanzibar, had advised a temporary return to Europe: Dr. Steinhaeuser, the civil surgeon, Aden, also recommended a lengthened period of rest. I bade adieu to the coal-hole of the East on the 28th April, 1859, and in due time greeted with becoming heartiness the shores of my native land.

FINIS CORONAT OPUS!

The Elephant Rock ('Ακρωτήριον 'Ελέφας, Periplus II. راس الفيل), seen from fifteen miles at sea, direction S.W.

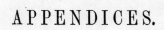

APPENDICES.

APPENDIX I.

COMMERCE, IMPORTS AND EXPORTS.

COMMERCE has for ages been a necessity to the East African, who cannot be contented without his clothing and his ornaments, which he receives in barter for the superfluity of his country. Against its development, however, serious obstacles have hitherto interposed. On the seaboard and in the island the Banyans, by monopolizing the import traffic, do injury to the internal trade. In the interior the Wasawahili excite, with all the animosity of competition, the barbarians against Arab interlopers, upon the same sordid and short-sighted principle that the latter display when opposing the ingress of Europeans. Finally, the Arabs, according to their own confession, have by rapacity and imprudence impoverished the people without enriching themselves. Their habit of sending fundi on trading trips is, as has been explained, most prejudicial both to seller and buyer; the prices of provisions as well as of merchandise increase almost visibly; and though the evil might be remedied by a little combination, solidarity of interests being unknown, that little is nowhere found. All, Banyans, Wasawahili, and Arabs, like semi-civilised people generally, abhor and oppose a free trade, which they declare would be as injurious to themselves as doubtless advantageous to the country. Here, as in Europe, the battle of protection has still to be fought; and here, unlike Europe, the first step towards civilisation, namely, the facility of intercourse between the interior and the coast, has yet to be created.

The principal imports into East Africa are domestics and piece goods, plain and unbleached cotton cloths, beads, and brass wire. The minor items for the native population are prints, coloured cloths Indian and Arabian, broadcloth, calicos, caps, ironware, knives and needles, iron and copper wires for ornaments, and in some regions trinkets and ammunition. A small trade, chiefly confined to the Arabs, is done in provisions, spices, drugs, and other luxuries.

The people of East Africa when first visited were satisfied
with the worst and flimsiest kaniki or indigo-dyed Indian cotton.
This they presently gave up for the "merkani," American
"domestics," or unbleached shirting and sheeting, which now
supplies the markets from Abyssinia to the Mozambique.   But
the wild men are losing predilection for a stuff which is neither
comfortable nor durable, and in many regions the tribes, satisfied
with goat-skins and tree-barks, prefer to invest their capital in
the more attractive and durable beads and wire.   It would evidently be advantageous if England or her Indian colonies would
manufacture an article better suited to the wants of the country
than that at present in general use; but, under existing circumstances, there is little probability of this being done.

The "domestics" from the mills near Salem, Lawrence,
Manchester, and others, called in the island of Zanzibar wilaiti
("foreign"), or khami (the "raw"), is known throughout the
inner country as "merkani" or American.   These unbleached
cottons are of two kinds: the wilaiti mpana (broad) or sheeting,
sold in pieces about 30 yards long and 36 to 38 inches broad,
and the wilaiti kabibu (narrow) or shirting, of the same length
but less in breadth, from 32 to 34 inches.   In the different
mills the lengths vary, the extremes being 24 and 36 yards.
The cloth measures in use throughout the country are the
following : —

2½ Fitr (short spans)	= 1 Mukono, Ziraá, or cubit.
2 Mikono, or Ziraá (cubits)	= 1 Half-Shukkah (*i.e.* 3 feet of domestics).
2 Half-Shukkah	= 1 Shukkah, Mwenda, Upande, or Lupande, the Portuguese Braça(*i.e.* 6 feet of domestics).
2 Shukkahs	= 1 Tobe (Ar. Saub), Doti, Unguo ya ku shona (washing cloth), or simply Unguo (12 ft.)
2 Doti	= 1 Takah.
7 to 11 Doti	= 1 Jurah or Gorah, the piece.

The fitr or short span is from the extended end of the forefinger to the thumb; the shibr or long span is from the thumb
to the little finger; of these, two go to that primitive measure
the cubit or elbow length.   Two cubits in long measure compose the war or yard, and two wár the ba'a or fathom.

The price of domestics greatly varies in dear years and cheap
years.   At Zanzibar it sometimes falls to 2 dols. per gorah or
piece, and it often rises to 2·75 dols.   When the dollar is
alluded to, the Maria Theresa crown is always meant.   The
price in Bombay is from 213 to 215 Co.'s rs. per cent.   At
Zanzibar the crown is divided like the rupee into 16 annas, and
each anna into 9 or 8 pice; of these the full number is 128 to

the dollar, but it is subject to incessant fluctuations. Merchants usually keep accounts in dollars and cents. The Arabs divide the dollar as follows : --

4 Ruba baisah (the " pie ")'= Baisah (in the plur. Biyas), the Indian Paisa.
8 Biyas = 1 Anna.
2 Annas, or 16 Pice = 1 Tumun or eighth.
4 Annas, or 32 Pice, or 25 Cents = 1 Ruba, Rubo or Quarter-dollar, the Indian Paola.
2 Ruba, or 64 Pice, or 50 Cents = 1 Nusu or Half-dollar.
2 Nusu = Dollar.

The Spanish or pillar dollar is called by the Arabs abu madfa, and by the Wasawahili riyal mazinga (the " cannon dollar "), In the East generally it is worth from 6 to 8 per cent. more than the Maria Theresa, but at Zanzibar, not being a legal tender. the value is unfixed. The only subdivision of this coin generally known is the seringe, pistoline, or " small quarter dollar," which is worth only 10 pice and 2 pies, whereas the ruba, or quarter of the Maria Theresa, is 32 pice. The French 5-franc piece, raised in value by a somewhat arbitrary process from 114 to 110 per 100 " piastres d'Espagne " by M. Guillain in 1846, has no currency, though the Banyans attempt to pass them off upon strangers at 108 for 100 Maria Theresas. In selling, the price ranges from 15 to 22 shukkahs, each of which, assuming the dollar or German crown to be worth 4s. 2d., will be worth upon the island from 6d. to 8d. The shukkah is, as has been said, the shilling and florin of East Africa, and it is assuredly the worst circulating medium ever invented by mankind. The progress of its value as it recedes from the seaboard, and other details concerning it, which may be useful to future travellers, have been treated of in the preceding pages.

First in importance amongst the cloths is the kaniki or kiniki; its names and measures are made to differ by the traders according to the fashion of semi-civilised people, who seek in confusion and intricacy facilities for fraud and chicanery. The popular divisions are—

4 Mikono, Ziraá, or cubits = 1 Shukkah.
2 Shukkah = 1 Doti or Tobe.
2 Doti = 1 Jurah, Gorah, or Takah.
2 Takah = 1 Korjah, Kori, or score.

Of this indigo-dyed cotton there are three kinds : the best, which is close and neatly made, is seldom exported from Zanzibar. The gorah or piece of 16 cubits, 45 inches in breadth, is worth about 1 dollar. The common variety, 40 inches broad, supplied to the markets of the interior, costs about half that sum; and the worst kind, which averages in breadth 36 inches, represents a little less. The value of the korjah or score fluctuates between 8 and 13 dollars. Assuming, therefore, the average at 10 dollars, and the number of shukkahs contained in the gorah at 80, the price of each will represent 6d. Thus it is little inferior in price to the merkani or domestics when purchased upon the seaboard: its progress of value in the interior, however, is by no means in proportion, and by some tribes it is wholly rejected.

The lucrative bead trade of Zanzibar is now almost entirely in the hands of the Banyan capitalists, who, by buying up ships' cargoes, establish their own prices, and produce all the inconveniences of a monopoly. In laying in a stock the traveller must not trust himself to these men, who seize the opportunity of palming off the waste and refuse of their warehouses: he is advised to ascertain from respectable Arab merchants, on their return from the interior, the varieties requisite on the line of march. Any neglect in choosing beads, besides causing daily inconvenience, might arrest an expedition on the very threshold of success: towards the end of these long African journeys, when the real work of exploration commences, want of outfit tells fatally. The bead-monopolisers of Zanzibar supplied the East African expedition with no less than nine men's loads of the cheapest white and black beads, some of which were thrown away, as no man would accept them at a gift. Finally, the utmost economy must be exercised in beads: apparently exhaustless, a large store goes but a little way: the minor purchases of a European would average 10 strings or necklaces per diem, and thus a man's load rarely outlasts the fifth week.

Beads, called by the Arabs kharaz, and by the Wasawahili ushanga, are yearly imported into East Africa by the ton—in quantities which excite the traveller's surprise that so little is seen of them. For centuries there has been a regular supply of these ornaments; load after load has been absorbed; but although they are by no means the most perishable of substances, and though the people, like the Indians, carry their wealth upon their persons, not a third of the population wears any considerable quantity. There are about 400 current varieties, of which each has its peculiar name, value, and place of preference; yet, being fabricated at a distance from the spot, they lack the perpetual change necessary to render them thoroughly attractive. In Urori and Ubena, antiquated marts, now nearly neglected, there are varieties highly prized by the people: these might be imitated with advantage.

For trading purposes a number of different kinds must be laid in,—for travellers, the coral or scarlet, the pink porcelain, and the large blue glass bead, are more useful than other colours. Yet in places even the expensive coral bead has been refused.

Beads are sold in Zanzibar island by the following weights:

16 Wakiyyah (ounces, each=1 dollar in weight)=1 Ratl (or pound; in the plural, Artál).
3 Ratl, or 48 Wakiyyah = 1 Man (Maund).
12 Amnan (Maunds) = 1 Frasilah (35 to 36 pounds).
60 Artál (pounds) = 1 Frasilah.
20 to 22 Farásilah (according to the article purchased)=1 Kandi (Candy).

The Zanzibar lb. is the current English avoirdupois. The Arabs use a ratl without standard, except that it should be equal to sixteen Maria Theresa dollars. According to M. Guillain, it is four grammes (each 22·966 grs. avoir.) less than the English lb., and when reduced to seven grammes it is considered under weight. The "man" or maund is the general measure: there are, however, three varieties. The "man" of Zanzibar consists of three ratl, that of Maskat contains nine, and that of Oman generally 0·25 less than the Zanzibar maund. The frasilah (in the plur. farásilah) may roughly be assumed as one-third of the cwt.: the word probably gave rise to the English coffee-weight called a "frail."

The measures of beads are as complicated and arbitrary as those of cloth. The following are the terms known throughout the interior, but generally unintelligible at Zanzibar, where this merchandise is sold by weight:

4 Bitil (each a single length from index tip to wrist) = 1 Khete.
10 Khete (each a doubled length round the throat, or round the thumb, to the elbow-bone.") = 1 Fundo (i.e. a "knot.")
10 Fundo (in the plural, Mafundo) = 1 Ugoyye, or Ugoe.
10 Ugoyye (or 60 Fundo) = 1 Miranga, or Gana.

Of these bead measures there are local complications. In the central regions, for instance, the khete is of half size, and the fundo consists of five, not of ten khete.

Beads are purchased for the monopolisers of Zanzibar unstrung, and before entering the country it is necessary to measure and prepare the lengths for barter. The string, called "ut'hembwe" (in the plural "t'hembwe"), is generally made of palm-fibre, and much depends for successful selling, especially in the larger kinds of beads, upon the regularity and attractiveness of the line. It will be remembered that beads in East

Africa represent the copper and smaller silver coins of
European countries ; it is, however, impossible to reduce the
khete, the length most used in purchases, to any average: it
varies from a halfpenny to three-pence.   The average value of
the khete in Zanzibar coin is three pice, and about 100 khete
are included in the man or maund.   The traveller will find
the bitil used as our farthing, the khete is the penny, the
shukkah kaniki is the sixpence and shilling, the shukkah
merkani and the fundo represent the halfcrown and crown,
whilst the Barsati cloth, the kitindi or coil bracelet, and the
larger measures of beads, form the gold money.   The following
varieties are imported in extensive outfits.   Nos. 1, 2, and 3,
are the expensive kinds; Nos. 4, 5, and 6, are in local demand,
cheap in the maritime, and valuable in the central regions, and
the rest are the more ordinary sorts.   All those that are round
and pierced are called indifferently by the Arabs madruji, or
the " drilled."

1. Samsam (Ar.) sámesáme (Kis.), kimara-p'hamba (food-
finishers), joho (scarlet cloth), and kifungá-mgi (town-breakers,
because the women are mad for them), are the various names
for the small coral bead, a scarlet enamelled upon a white
ground.   They are known at Zanzibar as kharaz-kartasi—
paper beads—because they are sent into the country ready
strung, and packed in paper parcels, which ought to weigh 4
pounds each, but are generally found to vary from 8 to 10
fundo or knots.   Of this bead there are 15 several sizes, and
the value of the frasilah is from 13 to 16 dollars at Zanzibar.   In Unyamwezi, where the sámesáme is in greatest
demand, one fundo is equivalent to 1 shukkah merkani, and
6 khete to the shukkah kaniki.

2. Next in demand to the sámesáme, throughout the country,
except at Ujiji, where they lose half their value, are the pink
porcelain, called gulabi (the rosy), or máguru lá nzige (locust's
feet).   The price in Zanzibar varies from 12 to 15 dollars per
frasilah.

3. The blue porcelain, called in Venice ajerino, and in East
Africa langiyo or murtutu (blue vitriol) is of three several
sizes, and the best is of the lightest colour.   The larger variety,
called langiyo mkuba, fetches, at Zanzibar, from 6 to 12
dollars per frasilah, and the p'heke, or smaller, from 7 to 9
dollars.   In Usagara and Unyamwezi, where from 3 to 4
fundo are equivalent to the shukkah merkani, and 1 to 2 to the
shukkah kaniki, it is used for minor purchases, where the
sámesáme would be too valuable.   It is little prized in other

parts, and between Unyamwezi and Ujiji it falls to the low level
of the white porcelain.

4. A local variety, current from Msene to the Tanganyika
Lake, where, in the heavier dealings, as the purchase of slaves
and ivory, a few strings are always required to cap the bargain,
is called mzizima, mtunda, balghami, and jelabi, the ringel
perle of Germany. It is a large flat bead of glass; the khete
contains about 150, and each item acts as a copper coin. The
mzizima is of two varieties; the more common is a dark blue,
the other is of a whitish and opaline tint. At Zanzibar the
frasilah costs from 7 to 9 dollars. In Unyamwezi 3 fundo are
equivalent to 1 shukkah merkani, and 1 fundo to 1 shukkah
kaniki.

5. Another local variety is the balghami mkuba, popularly
called sungomaji, a bead made at Nuremberg (?). It is a porcelain, about the size of a pigeon's egg, and of two colours,
white and light blue. The sungomaji, attached to a thin cord
or twine, is worn singly or in numbers as an ornament round
the neck, and the people complain that the polish soon wears
off. At Zanzibar the price per 1000 is from 15 to 20 dollars,
but it is expected to decline to 10 dollars. This bead is useful
in purchasing ivory in Ugogo and Unyamwezi, and in hiring
boats at Ujiji: its relative value to cloth is 19 per shukkah
merkani, and 15 per shukkah kaniki.

6. The sofi, called in Italian cannettone, resembles bits of
broken pipe-stems, about two-thirds of an inch in length. It is
of various colours, white, brick-red, and black. Each bead is
termed masaro, and is used like pice in India: of these the
khete contains from 55 to 60. The price varies, at Zanzibar,
from 2 to 3 dollars per frasilah; in the interior, however, the
value greatly increases, on account of insufficient importation.
This bead, in 1858, was in great demand throughout Usagara,
Unyamwezi, and the western regions, where it was as valuable
as the sámesáme. Having neglected to lay in a store at
Zanzibar, the East African Expedition was compelled to exchange cloth for it at Msene and Ujiji, giving 1 shukkah
merkani for 30 to 35 khete, and 1 shukkah kaniki for 15 to
25. In Ujiji, however, many of the purchases were rejected
because the bits had become small by wear, or had been
chipped off by use.

7. The staple of commerce is a coarse porcelain bead, of
various colours, known in Zanzibar by the generic name of
háfizi. There are three principal kinds. The khanyera or
ushanga waupa (white beads) are common throughout the

country.   The average value, at Zanzibar, is 6 dollars per frasilah: in Unyamwezi, 4 fundo were equivalent to the shukkah merkani, and 2 to 3 to the kaniki; but the people, glutted with this bead (as many as 20,000 strings were supplied to the East African Expedition by the Banyans of Zanzibar), preferred 1 khete of sámesáme to 3 of khanyera.   The kidunduguru is a dull brick-red bead, worth at Zanzibar from 5 to 7 dollars per frasilah, but little prized in the interior, where it is derisively termed khanyera ya mk'hundu.   Another red variety of háfizi is called merkani: it is finely made to resemble the sámesáme, and costs from 7 to 11 dollars per frasilah.   Of this bead there are four several subdivisions.   The uzanzawírá or samuli (ghee-coloured) is a bright yellow porcelain worth, at Zanzibar, from 7 to 9 dollars per frasilah.   It is in demand throughout Chhaga and the Masai country, but is rarely seen on the central line.

8.   The sukoli are orange-coloured or rhubarb-tinted porcelain, which average, at Zanzibar, from 7 to 9 dollars.   They are prized in Usagara and Ugogo, but are little worn in other places.

9.   The nílí (green), or ukutí wa mnazi (coco-leaves), are little beads of transparent green glass; they are of three sizes, the smallest of which is called kíkítí.   The Zanzibar price is from 6 to 11 dollars.   In Ujiji they are highly valued, and are readily taken in small quantities throughout the central line.

10.   The ghubari (dust-coloured), or nya kifu (?) is a small dove-coloured bead, costing, in Zanzibar, from 7 or 8 dollars. It is used in Uzaramo, but its dulness of aspect prevents it being a favourite.

11.   The lungenya or lak'hio is a coarse red porcelain, valued at 5 to 6 dollars in Zanzibar, and now principally exported to Uruwwa and the innermost regions of Central Africa.

12.   The bubu (ububu?), also called ukumwi and ushanga ya vipande, are black Venetians, dull dark procelain, ranging, at Zanzibar, from 5 to 7 dollars.   They are of fourteen sizes, large, medium, and small; the latter are the most valued.   These beads are taken by the Wazaramo.   In East Usagara and Unyamwezi they are called khuni or firewood, nor will they be received in barter except when they excite a temporary caprice.

The other beads, occasionally met with, are the sereketi, ovals of white or garnet-red, prized in Khutu; choroko or mágiyo, dull green porcelains; undriyo maupe (?), mauve-coloured, round or oval; undriyo mausi (?), dark lavender; asmani, sky-coloured glass; and pusange, blue Bohemian glass beads, cut into facets. The people of the coast also patronise a variety of large fancy articles, flowered, shelled, and otherwise ornamented; these, however, rarely find their way into the interior.

After piece goods and beads, the principal articles of traffic, especially on the northern lines and the western portion of the central route, are masango (in the singular sango), or brass wires, called by the Arabs hajúlah. Nos. 4 or 5 are preferred. They are purchased in Zanzibar, when cheap, for 12 dollars, and when dear for 16 dollars per frasilah. When imported up country the frasilah is divided into three or four large coils, called by the Arabs daur, and by the Africans khata, for the convenience of attachment to the banghy-pole. Arrived at Unyanyembe they are converted by artizans into the kitindi, or coil-bracelets, described in the preceding pages. Each daur forms two or three of these bulky ornaments, of which there are about 11 to the frasilah, and the weight is thus upwards of three pounds. The charge for the cutting, cleaning, and twisting into shape is about 1 doti of domestics for 50 kitindis. The value of the kitindi, throughout Unyamwezi, in 1858, was 1 doti merkani; at Ujiji, where they are in demand for slaves and ivory, the price was doubled. Thus, the kitindi, worth one dollar each—when cheap, nine are bought for ten dollars — in Zanzibar, rises to five dollars in the lake regions. Kitindi were formerly made of copper wire; it has fallen into disuse on account of its expense, — at Zanzibar from 15 to 20 dollars per frasilah. Large iron wires, called senyenge, are confined to Ugogo and the northern countries inhabited by the Wamasai. The East Africans have learned to draw fine wire, which they call uzi wa shaba (brass thread); they also import from the coast Nos. 22 to 25, and employ them for a variety of decorative purposes, which have already been alluded to. The average price of this small wire at Zanzibar is 12 dollars per frasilah. As has been mentioned, sat or zinc, called by the Africans bati (tin), is imported by the Wajiji.

The principal of the minor items are coloured cloths, called by the people "cloths with names:" of these, many kinds are imported by every caravan. In some regions, Ugogo for instance, the people will not sell their goats and more valuable provisions for plain piece-goods; their gross and gaudy tastes lead them to despise sober and uniform colours. The sultans invariably demand for themselves and their wives showy goods, and complete their honga or blackmail with domestics and indigo-dyed cottons, which they divide amongst their followers. Often, too, a bit of scarlet broadcloth, thrown in at the end of a lengthened haggle, opens a road and renders impossibilities possible.

The coloured cloths may be divided into three kinds,—woollens, cottons, and silks mixed with cotton. Of the former, the principal varieties now imported are Joho or broadcloth; of the second, beginning with the cheapest, are Barsati, Dabwani, Jamdani, Bandira, Shít (chintz), Khuzarangi, Ukaya, Sohari, Shali, Taujiri, Msutu, Kikoi, and Shazar or Mukunguru; the mixed and most expensive varieties are the Subai, Dewli, Sabuni, Khesi, and Masnafu. Travelling Arabs usually take a piece of baftah or white calico as kafan or shrouds for themselves or their companions in case of accidents. At Zanzibar the value of a piece of 24 yds. is 1 dollar 25 cents. Blankets were at first imported by the Arabs, but being unsuited to the climate and to the habits of the people they soon became a drug in the market.

Joho (a corruption of the Arabic Johh) is a coarse article, either blue or scarlet. As a rule, even Asiatics ignore the value of broadcloth, estimating it, as they do guns and watches, by the shine of the exterior: the African looks only at the length of the pile and the depth of the tint. The Zanzibar valuation of the cheap English article is usually 50 cents (2s. 1d.) per yard; in the interior rising rapidly through double and treble to four times that price, it becomes a present for a prince. At Ujiji and other great ivory-marts there is a demand for this article, blue as well as red; it is worn, like the shukkah merkani, round the loins by men and round the bosom by women, who, therefore, require a tobe or double length. At Unyanyembe there are generally pauper Arabs or Wasawahili artisans who can fashion the merchants' supplies into the kizbao or waistcoats affected by the African chiefs in imitation of their more civilised visitors.

Of the second division the cheapest is the Barsati, called by the Africans kitambi; it is a blue cotton cloth, with a broad red stripe extending along one quarter of the depth, the other three-quarters being dark blue; the red is either of European or Cutch dye. The former is preferred upon the coast for the purchase of copal. Of this Indian stuff there are three kinds, varying in size, colour, and quality; the cheapest is worth at Zanzibar (where, however, like dabwani, it is usually sold by the gorah of two uzar or loin-cloths) from 5 to 7 dollars per score; the second 10 dollars 50 cents; and the best 14 to 15 dollars. The barsati in the interior represents the doti or tobe of Merkani. On the coast it is a favourite article of wear with the poorer freemen, slaves, and women. Beyond the maritime regions the chiefs will often refuse a barsati, if of small dimensions and flimsy texture. Formerly, the barsati was made of silk, and cost 7 dollars per loin-cloth. Of late years the Wanyamwezi have taken into favour the barsati or kitambi banyani; it is a thin white long cloth, called in Bombay kora (Corah, or cotton piece-goods), with a narrow reddish border of madder or other dye stamped in India or at Zanzibar. The piece of 39 yards, which is divided into 20 shukkah, costs at Bombay 4·50 Co.'s rs.; at Zanzibar 2 dollars 50 cents; and the price of printing the edge is 1 dollar 75 cents.

The dabwani is a kind of small blue and white check made at Maskat; one fourth of its breadth is a red stripe, edged with white and yellow. This stuff, which from its peculiar stiffening of gum appears rather like grass-cloth than cotton, is of three kinds: the cheapest, dyed with Cutch colours, is much used in the far interior; it costs at Zanzibar 12 dols. 50 cents per score of pieces, each two and a half yards long;—the medium quality, employed in the copal trade of the coast, is stained with European dye, and superior in work; the score of pieces, each 3 yards long, costs 30 dols.;—and the best, which is almost confined to the island of Zanzibar, ranges from 40 to 45 dols. per kori. The dabwani is considered in the interior nearly double the value of the barsati, and it is rarely rejected unless stained or injured.

The jamdani is a sprigged or worked muslin imported from India: though much prized for turbans by the dignitaries of the maritime races, it is rarely carried far up the country. At Zanzibar the price of 10 yards is 1 dol., and the piece of 20 lengths, each sufficient for a turban, may be purchased for 15 dols.

The bandira (flag stuff) is a red cotton bunting imported from Bombay. It is prized in the interior by women. At Zanzibar the price of this stuff greatly varies; when cheap the piece of 28 yards may be obtained for 2 dols. 50 cents, when dear it rises to 3 dols. 50 cents. It is sold by gorah of $7\frac{1}{2}$ shukkahs.

Shít, or chintz, is of many different kinds. The common English is a red cotton, striped yellow and dark green; it fetches from 1 dol. 50 cents to 2 dols. per piece of 28 yards, and is little prized in the interior. Those preferred, especially in Unyamwezi and Ujiji, are the French and Hamburg; the former is worth at Zanzibar from 4 dols. 50 cents per piece of 35 yards, to 5 dols. 50 cents per gorah of 10 shukkahs, and the latter from 5 dols. to 5 dols. 50 cents. The most expensive is the "ajemi," that used by the Persians as lining for their lambswool caps; the price is from 50 cents to 1 dol. per yard, which renders it a scarce article even in Zanzibar island.

The khuzarangi, a European cotton dyed a reddish nankeen, with pomegranate rind and other colouring matters, at Maskat, is almost confined to the Arabs, who make of it their normal garment, the long and sleeved shirt called el dishdashah, or in Kisawahili khanzu. It is the test of foreign respectability and decorum when appearing amongst the half-clad African races, and the poorest of pedlars will always carry with him one of these nightgown-like robes. The price of the ready-made dishdashah ranges from 50 cents to 2 dols. 50 cents, and the uncut piece of 16 yards costs from 2 dols. to 2 dols. 50 cents.

The ukaya somewhat resembles the kaniki, but it is finer and thinner. This jaconnet, manufactured in Europe and dyed in Bombay, is much used by female slaves and concubines as head veils. The price of the piece of 20 yards, when of inferior quality, is 2 dollars 50 cents; it ranges as high as 12 dollars.

The sohari, or ridia, made at Maskat, is a blue and white check with a red border about 5 inches broad, with smaller stripes of red, blue, and yellow; the ends of the piece are checks of a larger pattern, with red introduced. There are many varieties of this cloth, which, considered as superior to the dabwani as the latter is superior to the barsati, forms an acceptable present to a chief. The cheapest kind, much used in Unyamwezi, costs 16 dollars 25 cents per kori, or score. The higher sorts, of which however only 1 to 40 of the inferior is imported into the country, ranges from 22 to 30 dollars.

The shali, a corruption of the Indian shal (shawl), is a common English imitation shawl pattern of the poorest cotton. Bright yellow or red grounds, with the pear pattern and similar ornaments, are much prized by the chiefs of Unyamwezi. The price of the kori, or score, is 25 dollars.

The taujiri (from the Indian taujír burá) is a dark blue cotton stuff, with a gaudy border of madder-red or tumeric-yellow, the former colour preferred by the Wahiao, the latter by the Wanyamwezi. The price per score varies from 8 to 17 dollars.

The msutu is a European cotton dyed at Surat, indigo blue upon a madder-red ground, spotted with white. This print is much worn by Arab and Wasawahili women as a nightdress and morning wrapper; in the interior it becomes a robe of ceremony. At Zanzibar the piece of 20 lengths, each 2·25 yards long and 40 inches broad (two breadths being sown together), costs 19 dollars. The kisutu, an inferior variety, fetches, per kori of pieces 2·50 yards long, 13 dollars.

The kikoi is a white cotton, made at Surat, coarse and thick, with a broad border of parallel stripes, red, yellow, and indigo blue: per kori of pieces 2 yards long, and sewn in double breadths, the price is 5 dollars. A superior variety is made principally for the use of women, with a silk border, which costs from 1 to 4 dollars.

The shazar, called throughout the interior mukunguru, is a Cutch-made cotton plaid, with large or small squares, red and white, or black and blue ; this cloth is an especial favourite with the Wamasai tribes.   The score of pieces, each 2 yards, costs 6 dollars 25 cents.   There is a dearer variety, of which each piece is 3 yards long, costing 16 dollars per kori, and therefore rarely sold.

Of the last division of " cloths with names," namely those of silk and cotton mixed, the most popular is the subaí.   It is a striped stuff, with small checks between the lines, and with a half-breadth of border, a complicated pattern of red, black, and yellow.   This cloth is used as an uzar, or loin-cloth, by the middle classes of Arabs ; the tambua, taraza, or fringe, is applied to the cloth with a band of gold thread at Zanzibar, by Wasa-wahili.   The subai, made at Maskat of Cutch cotton, varies greatly in price : the cheapest, of cotton only, may be obtained for 2 dollars ; the medium, generally preferred for presents to great chiefs, is about 5 dollars 50 cents ; whilst the most expensive, inwoven with gold thread, ranges from 8 to 30 dollars.

The dewli is the Indian lungi, a Surat silk, garnished with a border of gold thread and a fringe at Zanzibar.   It is a red, yellow, or green ground, striped in various ways, and much prized for uzar.   The price of the cheap piece of 3·50 yards is 7 dollars, besides the fringe, which is 2 dollars more ; the best, when adorned with gold, rise to 80 dollars.

The sabuni uzar, made in Maskat, is a silk-bordered cotton, a small blue and white check ; the red and yellow edging which gives it its value is about one-fifth of its breadth.   The score of pieces, each 2·50 yards long, varies from 25 to 50 dollars ; the more expensive, however, rarely find their way into the interior.

The khesi is a rare importation from Bombay, a scarlet silk, made at Tannah ; the piece sold at Bombay for 10 Co.'s rs. fetches at Zanzibar 5 dols. 50 cents to 6 dollars ; this kind is preferred by the Wanyamwezi chiefs ; when larger, and adorned with gold stripes, it rises to 35 Co.'s rs., or 19 dollars, and is prized by the Banyans and Hindis of Zanzibar.

The masnafu is rare like the khesi ; it is a mixed silk and cotton cloth, of striped pattern, made at Maskat.   The cheapest is a piece of 1·75 yards, costing from 2 to 5 dollars, and highly regarded in Unyamwezi ; the larger kinds, of 2·50 yards, rise from 5 to 6 dollars, and the Arabs will pay from 20 to 25 dollars for those worked with gold thread.

These notes upon the prices of importations into Central Africa rest upon the authority of the Hindus, and principally of Ladha Damha, the collector of customs at Zanzibar. Specimens of the cloths were deposited with the Royal Geographical Society of London, and were described by the kindness of Mr. Alderman Botterill, F.R.G.S.

Remain for consideration the minor and local items of traffic.

The skull-caps are of two kinds. One is a little fez, locally called kummah. It is made in France, rarely at Bagdad, and sells at Zanzibar for 5 dols. 50 cents to 9 dollars per dozen. The cheaper kind is preferred in Unyamwezi; it is carried up from the coast by Arab slaves and Wasawahili merchants, and is a favourite wear with the sultan and the mtongi. At Unyanyembe the price of the fez rises to 1 dollar. The "alfiyyah" is the common Surat cap, worked with silk upon a cotton ground; it is affected by the Diwans and Shomwis of the coasts. The "vis-gol," or 20-stitch, preferred for importation, cost 8 dollars per score; the "tris-gol," or 30-stich, 13 dollars; and the "chalis-gol," or 40-stitch, 18 dollars.

Besides these articles, a little hardware finds its way into the country. Knives, razors, fish-hooks, and needles are useful, especially in the transit of Uzaramo. As an investment they are useless; the people, who make for themselves an article which satisfies their wants, will not part with valuables to secure one a little better. They have small axes and sharp spears, consequently they will not buy dear cutlery; they have gourds, and therefore they care little for glass and china. The Birmingham trinkets and knicknacks, of which travellers take large outfits to savage and barbarous countries, would in East Africa be accepted by women and children as presents, but unless in exceptional cases they would not procure a pound of grain; mirrors are cheap and abundant at Zanzibar, yet they are rarely imported into the interior. The people will devise new bijouterie for themselves, but they will not borrow it from strangers. In the maritime regions, where the tribes are more civilised, they will covet such foreign contrivances, as dollars, blankets, snuff-boxes, and tin cylinders which can be converted into tobacco pouches: the Wanyamwezi would not regard them. Similarly in Somaliland, a case of Birmingham goods carried through the country returned to Aden almost full.

Coffee, sugar, and soap may generally be obtained in small quantities from the Arabs of Unyanyembe. At Zanzibar the price of common coffee is 3 dollars 75 cents, and of Mocha 5 dollars 50 cents per frasilah. Sugar is of three kinds: the

buluji, or loaf-sugar, imported from America, averages 6 annas;
sukkari za mawe, or sugar-candy, fetches upon the island 5
dollars 50 cents per frasilah; and the bungálá, or sukkari za
mchanga (brown Bengal sugar), costs 3 dollars 50 cents; gur,
or molasses, sells at Zanzibar for 1 dollar 25 cents per frasilah.
Soap is brought to Zanzibar island by the Americans, French,
and India merchants.

The other articles of importation into Zanzibar, which, however, so rarely find their way into the interior, that they do not
merit detailed notice, are—rice and other cereals from Bombay
and Western India; shipping materials, canvas, rigging, hempen
cord, planks and boards, paint, pitch, turpentine, linseed-oil,
bees'-wax, and tar, from America and India; metals from Europe
and India; furniture from Europe and America, China and
Bombay; carpets and rugs from Turkey and Persia; mats from
Madagascar; made-up clothes from Maskat and Yemen; glass-
ware from Europe and America; pottery, paper, and candles
from Europe and Bombay; kuzah (water-jars) from the Persian
Gulf; woods and timber from Madagascar, the Mozambique,
and the coast as far north as Mombasah; skins and hides from
the Banadir; salt-fish (shark and others) from Oman, Hazramaut, and the Benadir; brandy, rum, peppermint, eau de
Cologne, syrups and pickles, tobacco, cigars, and tea, from
Bombay, France, and the Mauritius; rose-water from the Gulf;
attar of rose and of sandal from Bombay; dates, almonds, and
raisins from Arabia and the Gulf; gums and ambergris from
Madagascar, the Mozambique, and the " Sayf-Tawil" (the long
low coast extending from Ras Awath, in N. lat. 5° 33', to Ras
el-Khayl, N. lat. 7° 44'); aloes and dragon's-blood from Socotra;
incense, gum Arabic, and myrrh from the Somali country and
the Benadir; turmeric, opium, ginger, nutmegs, colombo-root,
cardamoms, cinnamon, aniseed, camphor, benzoin, assafœtida,
saltpetre, potash, blue vitriol, alum, soda, saffron, garlic, fenu-
greek, and other drugs and spices from Bombay and Western
India.

The staple articles of the internal trade throughout the regions
extending from the coast of the Indian Ocean to the lakes of
Central Africa are comprised in slaves and cattle, salt, iron, tobacco, mats and strainers, and tree-barks and ropes. Of these,
all except salt have been noticed in detail in the preceding pages.

Salt is brought down during the season from East Arabia to
Zanzibar by Arab dows, and is heaped up for sale on a strip of
clear ground under the eastern face of the gurayza or fort.   It
is of two kinds: the fine rock salt sells at 6 annas per frasilah,

and the inferior, which is dark and sandy, at about half that price. On the coast the principal ports and towns supply themselves with sea-salt evaporated in the rudest way. Pits sunk near the numerous lagoons and backwaters allow the saline particles to infiltrate; the contents, then placed in a pierced earthen pot, are allowed to strain into a second beneath. They are inspissated by boiling, and are finally dried in the sun, when the mass assumes the form of sand. This coarse salt is sold after the rains, when it abounds, for its weight of holcus; when dear, the price is doubled. In the interior there are two great markets, and the regularity of communication enables the people to fare better as regards the luxury than the more civilised races of Abyssinia and Harar, where of a millionnaire it is said, " he eateth salt." An inferior article is exported from Ugogo, about half-way between the East Coast and the Tanganyika Lake. A superior quality is extracted from the pits near the Rusugi River in Western Uvinza, distant but a few days from Ujiji. For the prices and other conditions of sale the reader is referred to Chapters V. and VII.

The subject of exports will be treated of at some length; it is not only interesting from its intrinsic value, but it is capable of considerable development, and it also offers a ready entrance for civilisation. The African will never allow the roads to be permanently closed—none but the highly refined amongst mankind can contemplate with satisfaction a life of utter savagery. The Arab is too wise to despise " protection," but he will not refuse to avail himself of assistance offered by foreigners when they appear as capitalists. Hitherto British interests have been neglected in this portion of the African continent, and the name of England is unknown in the interior. Upon the island of Zanzibar, in 1857-8, there was not an English firm; no line of steamers connected it with India or the Cape, and, during the dead season, nine months have elapsed before the answer to a letter has been received from home.

The reader is warned that amongst the East Africans the " bay o shara "—barter or round trade—is an extensive subject, of which only the broad outlines and general indications can be traced. At present, the worthlessness of time enables both buyer and seller to haggle *ad libitum*, and the superior craft of the Arab, the Banyan, the Msawahili, and the more civilised slave, has encumbered with a host of difficulties the simplest transactions. It is easy to be a merchant and to buy wholesale at Zanzibar, but a lengthened period of linguistic study and of conversancy with the habits and customs of the people must be spent by the stranger who would engage in the task of retail-buying in the interior.

The principal article of export from the Zanzibar coast is copal, from the interior ivory. The minor items are hippopotamus teeth, rhinoceros horns, cattle, skins, hides, and horns, the cereals, timbers, and cowries. Concerning the slaves, who in East Africa still form a considerable item of export, details have been given in the preceding pages. The articles which might be exploited, were means of carriage supplied to the people, are wax and honey, orchella-weed, fibrous substances, and a variety of gums.

The copal of Zanzibar, which differs materially from that of the Western Coast of Mexico and the cowaee (Australian dammar?) of New Zealand, is the only article convertible into the fine varnishes now so extensively used throughout the civilised world.

As the attention of the Expedition was particularly directed to the supplies of copal in East Africa by Dr. G. Buist, LL.D., Secretary to the Bombay branch of the R. G. Society, many inquiries and visits to the copal diggings were made. In the early part of 1857 specimens of the soils and subsoils, and of the tree itself, were forwarded to the Society.

The copal-tree is called by the Arabs shajar el sandarús, from the Hindostani chhandarus; by the Wasawahili msandarusi; and by the Wazaramo and other maritime races mnángú. The tree still lingers on the island and the mainland of Zanzibar. It was observed at Mombasah, Saadani, Muhonyera, and Mzegera of Uzaramo; and was heard of at Bagamoyo, Mbuamaji, and Kilwa. It is by no means, as some have supposed, a shrubby thorn; its towering bole has formed canoes 60 feet long, and a single tree has sufficed for the kelson of a brig. The average size, however, is about half that height, with from 3 to 6 feet girth near the ground; the bark is smooth, the lower branches are often within reach of a man's hand, and the tree frequently emerges from a natural ring-fence of dense vegetation. The trunk is of a yellow-whitish tinge, rendering the tree conspicuous amid the dark African jungle-growths; it is dotted with exudations of raw gum, which is found scattered in bits about the base; and it is infested by ants, especially by a long ginger-coloured and semi-transparent variety, called by the people maji-m'oto, or " boiling water," from its fiery bite. The copal wood is yellow tinted, and the saw collects from it large flakes; when dried and polished it darkens to a honey-brown, and, being well veined, it is used for the panels of doors. The small and pliable branches, freshly cut, form favourite "bakur," the kurbaj or bastinadoing instrument of these regions; after long keeping they become brittle. The modern habitat of the tree is the alluvial sea-plain and the anciently raised beach: though extending over the crest of the latter formation, it ceases to be found at any distance beyond the landward counterslope, and it is unknown in the interior.

The gum copal is called by the Arabs and Hindus sandarus, by the Wasawahili sandarusi, and by the Wanyamwezi—who employ it like the people of Mexico and Yucatan as incense in incantations and medicinings—sirokko and mámnángu. This semi-fossil is not "washed out by streams and torrents," but "crowed" or dug up by the coast clans and the barbarians of the maritime region. In places it is found when sinking piles for huts, and at times it is picked up in spots overflowed by the high tides. The East African seaboard, from Ras Gomani in S. lat. 3° to Ras Delgado in 10° 41', with a medium depth of 30 miles, may indeed be called the "copal coast;" every part supplies more or less the gum of commerce. Even a section of this line, from the mouth of the Pangani River to Ngao (Monghou), would, if properly exploited, suffice to supply all our present wants.

The Arabs and Africans divide the gum into two different kinds. The raw copal (copal vert of the French market) is called sandarusi za miti, "tree copal," or chakází, corrupted by the Zanzibar merchant to "jackass" copal. This chakazi is either picked from the tree or is found, as in the island of Zanzibar, shallowly imbedded in the loose soil, where it has not remained long enough to attain the phase of bitumenisation. To the eye it is smoky or clouded inside, it feels soft, it becomes like putty when exposed to the action of alcohol, and it viscidises in the solution used for washing the true copal. Little valued in European technology, it is exported to Bombay, where it is converted into an inferior varnish for carriages and palanquins, and to China, where the people have discovered, it is said, for utilising it, a process which, like the manufacture of rice paper and of Indian ink, they keep secret. The price of chakazi varies from 4 to 9 dollars per frasilah.

The true or ripe copal, properly called sandarusi, is the produce of vast extinct forests, overthrown in former ages either by some violent action of the elements, or exuded from the roots of the tree by an abnormal action which exhausted and destroyed it. The gum, buried at depths beyond atmospheric influence, has, like amber and similar gum-resins, been bitumenised in all its purity, the volatile principles being fixed by moisture and by the exclusion of external air. That it is the produce of a tree is proved by the discovery of pieces of gum embedded in a touch-wood which crumbles under the fingers; the "goose-skin," which is the impress of sand or gravel, shows that it was buried in a soft state; and the bees, flies, gnats, and other insects which are sometimes found in it delicately preserved, seem to disprove a remote geologic antiquity. At the end of the rains it is usually carried ungarbled to Zanzibar. When garbled upon the coast it acquires an additional value of 1 dollar per frasilah. The Banyan embarks it on board his own boat, or pays a freight varying from 2 to 4 annas, and the ushur or government tax is 6 annas per frasilah with half an anna for charity. About 8 annas per frasilah are deducted for "tare and tret." At Zanzi-bar, after being sifted and freed from heterogeneous matter, it is sent by the Banyan retailer to the Indian market or sold to the foreign merchant. It is then washed in solutions of various strengths: the lye is supposed to be composed of soda and other agents for softening the water; its proportions, however, are kept a profound secret. European technologists have, it is said, vainly proposed theoretical methods for the delicate part of the operation which is to clear the goose-skin of dirt. The Americans exported the gum uncleaned, because the operation is better performed at Salem. Of late years they have begun to prepare it at Zanzibar, like the Hamburg traders. When taken from the solution, in which from 20 to 37 per cent. is lost, the gum is washed, sun-dried for some hours, and cleaned with a hard brush, which must not, however, injure the goose skin; the dark "eyes," where the dirt has sunk deep, are also picked out with an iron tool. It is then carefully garbled with due regard to colour and size. There are many tints and peculiarities known only to those whose interests compel them to study and to observe copal, which, like cotton and Cashmere shawls, requires years of experience. As a rule, the clear and semi-transparent are the best; then follow the numerous and almost imperceptible varieties of dull white, lemon colour, amber yellow, rhubarb yellow, bright red, and dull red. Some specimens of this vegetable fossil appear by their dirty and blackened hue to have been subjected to the influence of fire; others again are remarkable for a tender grass-green colour. According to some authorities, the gum, when long kept, has been observed to change its tinge. The sizes are fine, medium, and large, with many subdivisions; the pieces vary from the dimensions of small pebbles to 2 or 3 ounces; they have been known to weigh 5 lbs., and, it is said, at Salem a piece of 35 lbs. is shown.   Lastly, the gum is thrown broad-cast into boxes and exported from the island.   The Hamburg merchants keep European coopers, who put together the cases whose material is sent out to them.   It is almost impossible to average the export of copal from Zanzibar.   According to the late Lieutenant-Colonel Hamerton, it varies from 800,000 to 1,200,000 lbs. per annum, of which Hamburg absorbs 150,000 lbs., and Bombay two lacs' worth.   The refuse copal used for-merly to reach India as " packing," being deemed of no value in commerce; of late years the scarcity of the supply has rendered merchants more careful.   The price, also, is subject to incessant fluctuations, and during the last few years it has increased from 4 dol. 50 cents to a maximum of 12 dollars per frasilah.

According to the Arabs, the redder the soil the better is the copal.   The superficies of the copal country is generally a thin coat of white sand, covering a dark and fertilising humus, the vestiges of decayed vegetation, which varies from a few inches to a foot and a half in depth.   In the island of Zanzibar, which produces only the chakazi or raw copal, the subsoil is a stiff blue clay, the raised sea-beach, and the ancient habitat of the coco. It becomes greasy and adhesive, clogging the hoe in its lower bed; where it is dotted with blood-coloured fragments of ochreish earth, proving the presence of oxidising and chalybeate efficients, and with a fibrous light-red matter, apparently decayed coco-roots.   At a depth of from 2 to 3 feet water oozes from the greasy walls of the pit.   When digging through these formations, the gum copal occurs in the vegetable soil overlying the clayey subsoil.

A visit to the little port of Saadani afforded different results. After crossing 3 miles of alluvial and maritime plain, covered with a rank vegetation of spear grass and low thorns, with occa-sional mimosas and tall hyphænas, which have supplanted the coco, the traveller finds a few scattered specimens of the living tree and pits dotting the ground.   The diggers, however, ge-nerally advance another mile to a distinctly formed sea-beach, marked with lateral bands of quartzose and water-rolled pebbles, and swelling gradually to 150 feet from the alluvial plain.   The thin but rich vegetable covering supports a luxuriant thicket, the subsoil is red and sandy, and the colour darkens as the excavation deepens.   After 3 feet, fibrous matter appears, and below this copal, dusty and comminuted, is blended with the red ochreish earth.   The guides assert that they have never hit upon the subsoil of blue clay, but they never dig lower than a man's waist, and the pits are seldom more than 2 feet in depth.   Though the soil is red, the copal of Saadani is not highly prized, being of a dull white colour; it is usually designated as " chakazi."

On the line inland from Bagamoyo and Kaole the copal-tree was observed at rare intervals in the forests, and the pits extended as far as Muhonyera, about 40 miles in direct distance from the coast.   The produce of this country, though not first-rate, is considered far superior to that about Saadani.

Good copal is dug in the vicinity of Mbuamaji, and the diggings are said to extend to 6 marches inland.   The Wadenkereko, a wild tribe, mixed with and stretching southwards of the Wazaramo, at a distance of two days' journey from the sea, supply a mixed quality, more often white than red.   The best gums are procured from Hunda and its adjacent districts.   Frequent feuds with the citizens deter the wild people from venturing out of their jungles, and thus the Banyans of Mbuamaji find two small dows sufficient for the carriage of their stores.   At that port the price of copal varies from 2 dol. 50 cents to 3 dol. per frasilah.

The banks of the Rufiji River, especially the northern district of Wánde, supply the finest and best of copal; it is dug by the Wawande tribe, who either carry it to Kikunya and other ports, or sell it to travelling hucksters.   The price in loco is from 1 dol. 50 cents to 2 dollars per frasilah; on the coast it rises to 3 dol. 50 cents.   At all these places the tariff varies with the Bombay market, and in 1858 little was exported owing to the enlistment of " free labourers."

In the vicinity of Kilwa, for four marches inland, copal is dug up by the Mandandu and other tribes; owing to the facility of carriage and the comparative safety of the country it is somewhat dearer than that purchased on the banks of the Rufiji.   The copal of Ngao (Monghou) and the Lindi creek is much cheaper than at Kilwa; the produce, however, is variable in quality, being mostly a dull white chakazi.

Like that of East African produce generally, the exploitation of copal is careless and desultory.   The diggers are of the lowest classes, and hands are much wanted.   Near the seaboard it is worked by the fringe of Moslem negroids called the Wamrima or Coast clans; each gang has its own mtu mku or akida'ao (mucaddum—headman), who, by distributing the stock, contrives to gain more and to labour less than the others. In the interior it is exploited by the Washenzi or heathen, who work independently of one another.   When there is no blood-feud they carry it down to the coast, otherwise they must await the visits of petty retail dealers from the ports, who enter the country with ventures of 10 or 12 dollars, and barter for it cloth, beads, and wire.   The kosi—south-west or rainy monsoon—is the only period of work ; the kaskazi, or dry season, is a dead time.   The hardness of the ground is too much for the energies of the people : moreover, "kaskazi copal" gives trouble in washing on account of the sand adhering to its surface, and the flakes are liable to break.   As a rule, the apathetic Moslem and the futile heathen will not work whilst a pound of grain remains in their huts.   The more civilised use a little jembe or hoe, an implement about as efficient as the wooden spade with which an English child makes dirt-pies.

The people of the interior "crow" a hole about six inches in diameter with a pointed stick, and scrape out the loosened earth with the hand as far as the arm will reach.   They desert the digging before it is exhausted ; and although the labourers could each, it is calculated, easily collect from ten to twelve lbs. per diem, they prefer sleeping through the hours of heat, and content themselves with as many ounces.   Whenever upon the coast there is a blood-feud—and these are uncommonly frequent—a drought, a famine, or a pestilence, workmen strike work, and cloth and beads are offered in vain.   It is evident that the copal-mine can never be regularly and efficiently worked as long as it continues in the hands of such unworthy miners.   The energy of Europeans, men of capital and purpose, settled on the sea-board with gangs of foreign workmen, would soon remedy existing evils; but they would require not only the special permission, but also the protection of the local government. And although the intensity of the competition principle amongst the Arabs has not yet emulated the ferocious rivalry of civilisa-tion, the new settlers must expect considerable opposition from those in possession.   Though the copal diggings are mostly situated beyond the jurisdiction of Zanzibar, the tract labours under all the disadvantages of a monopoly: the diwans, the heavy merchants, and the petty traders of the coast derive from it, it is supposed, profits varying from 80 to 100 per cent.   Like other African produce, though almost dirt-cheap, it becomes dear by passing through many hands, and the frasilah, worth from 1 to 3 dollars in the interior, acquires a value of from 8 to 9 dollars at Zanzibar.

Zanzibar is the principal mart for perhaps the finest and largest ivory in the world.   It collects the produce of the lands lying between the parallels of 2° N. lat. and 10° S. lat., and the area extends from the coast to the regions lying westward of the Tanganyika Lake.   It is almost the only legitimate article of traffic for which caravans now visit the interior.

An account of the ivory markets in Inner Africa will remove sundry false impressions.   The Arabs are full of fabulous reports concerning regions where the article may be purchased for its circumference in beads, and greed of gain has led many of them to danger and death.   Wherever tusks are used as cattle-pens or to adorn graves, the reason is that they are valueless on account of the want of conveyance.

The elephant has not wholly disappeared from the maritime regions of Zanzibar.   It is found, especially during the rainy monsoon, a few miles behind Pangani town: it exists also amongst the Wazegura, as far as their southern limit, the Gama River.   The Wadoe hunt the animal in the vicinity of Shakini, a peak within sight of Zanzibar.   Though killed out of Uzaramo, and K'hutu, it is found upon the banks of the Kingani and the Rufiji rivers.   The coast people now sell their tusks for 30 to 35 dollars' worth of cloth, beads, and wire per frasilah.

In Western Usagara the elephant extends from Maroro to Ugogi.   The people, however, being rarely professional hunters, content themselves with keeping a look-out for the bodies of animals that have died of thirst or of wounds received elsewhere. As the chiefs are acquainted with the luxuries of the coast, their demands are fantastic.   They will ask, for instance, for a large tusk—the frasilah is not used in inland sales—a copper caldron worth 15 dollars; a khesi, or fine cloth, costing 20 dollars; and a variable quantity of blue and white cottons: thus, an ivory, weighing perhaps 3 frasilah, may be obtained for 50 dollars.

Ugogo and its encircling deserts are peculiarly rich in elephants.   The people are eminently hunters, and, as has been remarked, they trap the animals, and in droughty seasons they find many dead in the jungles.   Ivory is somewhat dearer in Ugogo than in Unyamwezi, as caravans rarely visit the coasts.   It is generally bartered to return caravans for slaves brought from the interior; of these, five or six represent the value of a large tusk.

The ivory of Unyamwezi is collected from the districts of Mgunda Mk'hali, Usukuma, Umanda, Usagozi, and other adjacent regions.   When the " Land of the Moon " was first visited by the Arabs, they purchased, it is said, 10 farasilah of ivory with 1 frasilah of the cheap white or blue porcelains.   The price is now between 30 and 35 dollars per frasilah in cloth, beads, and wire.   The Africans, ignoring the frasilah, estimate the value of the tusk by its size and quality; and the Arabs ascertain its exact weight by steelyards.   Moreover, they raise the weight of what they purchase to 48 lbs., and diminish that which they sell to 23·50 lbs., calling both by the same name, frasilah. When the Arab wishes to raise an outfit at Unyanyembe he can always command three gorahs of domestics (locally worth 30 dollars) per frasilah of ivory. Merchants visiting Karagwah, where the ivory is of superior quality, lay in a stock of white, pink, blue, green, and coral beads, and brass armlets, which must be made up at Unyanyembe to suit the tastes of the people. Cloth is little in demand. For one frasilah of beads and brass wire they purchase about one and a half of ivory. At K'hokoro the price of tusks has greatly risen; a large specimen can scarcely be procured under 40 doti of domestics, one frasilah of brass wire, and 100 fundo of coloured beads. The tusks collected in this country are firm, white, and soft, sometimes running 6 farasilah (210 lbs.) The small quantity collected in Ubena, Urori, and the regions east of the Tanganyika Lake, resembles that of K'hokoro.

The ivory of Ujiji is collected from the provinces lying around the northern third of the lake, especially from Urundi and Uvira. These tusks have one great defect; though white and smooth when freshly taken from the animal, they put forth after a time a sepia-coloured or dark brown spot, extending like a ring over the surface, which gradually spreads and injures the texture. Such is the "Jendai" or "Gendai" ivory, well known at Zanzibar: it is apt to flake off outside, and is little prized on account of its lightness. At Ujiji tusks were cheap but a few years ago, now they fetch an equal weight of porcelain or glass beads, in addition to which the owners—they are generally many—demand from 4 to 8 cloths. Competition, which amongst the Arabs is usually somewhat unscrupulous, has driven the ivory merchant to regions far west of the Tanganyika, and geography will thrive upon the losses of commerce.

The process of elephant-hunting, the complicated division of the spoils, and the mode of transporting tusks to the coast, have already been described. A quantity of ivory, as has appeared, is wasted in bracelets, armlets, and other ornaments. This would not be the case were the imports better calculated to suit the tastes of the people. At present the cloth-stuffs are little prized, and the beads are not sufficiently varied for barbarians who, eminently fickle, require change by way of stimulant. The Arabs seek in ivory six qualities: it must be white, heavy, soft, thick—especially at the point—gently curved—when too much curved it loses from 10 to 14 per cent.—and it must be marked with dark surface-lines, like cracks, running longitudinally towards the point. It is evident from the preceding details that the Arab merchants gain but little beyond a livelihood in plenty and dignity by their expeditions to the interior. An investment of 1,000 dollars rarely yields more than 70 farasilah (2450 lbs.) Assuming the high price of Zanzibar at an average of 50 dollars per farasilah, the stock would be worth 3500 dollars—a net profit of 1050 dollars. Against this, however, must be set off the price of porterage and rations—equal to at least five dollars per frasilah—the enormous interest upon the capital, the wastage of outfit, and the risk of loss, which, upon the whole, is excessive. Though time, toil, and sickness, not being matters of money, are rarely taken into consideration by the Eastern man, they must be set down on the loss side of the account. It is therefore plain that commercial operations on such a scale can be remunerative only to a poor people, and that they can be rendered lucrative to capitalists only by an extension and a development which, depending solely upon improved conveyance, must be brought about by the energy of Europeans. For long centuries past and for centuries to come the Semite and the Hamite have been and will be contented with human labour. The first thought which suggests itself to the sons of Japhet is a tramroad from the coast to the Lake regions.

The subject of ivory as sold at Zanzibar is as complicated as that of sugar in Great Britain or of cotton in America. A detailed treatise would here be out of place, but the following notices may serve to convey an idea of the trade.

The merchants at Zanzibar recognise in ivory, the produce of these regions, three several qualities. The best, a white, soft, and large variety, with small "bamboo," is that from the Banadir, Brava, Makdishu, and Marka. A somewhat inferior kind, on account of its hardness, is brought from the countries of Chaga, Umasai, and Nguru. The Wamasai often spoil their tusks by cutting them, for the facility of transport; and, like the people of Nguru and other tribes, they stain the exterior by sticking the tooth in the sooty rafters of their chimneyless huts, with the idea that so treated it will not crack or split in the sun. This red colour, erroneously attributed at Zanzibar to the use of ghee, is removed by the people with blood, or cowdung mixed with water. Of these varieties the smaller tusks fetch from 40 to 50 dollars; when they attain a length of 6 feet, the price would be 12l.; and some choice specimens 7½ feet long fetch 60l. A lot of 47 tusks was seen to fetch 1500l.; the average weight of each was 95 lbs., 80 being considered moderate, and from 70 to 75 lbs. poor.

The second quality is that imported from the regions about

the Nyassa Lake, and carried to Kilwa by the Wabisa, the Wahiao, the Wangindo, the Wamakua, and other clans. The " Bisha ivory " formerly found its way to the Mozambique, but the barbarians have now learned to prefer Zanzibar; and the citizens welcome them, as they sell their stores more cheaply than the Wahiao, who have become adepts in coast arts. The ivory of the Wabisa, though white and soft, is generally small, the full length of a tusk being 7 feet. The price of the " bab kalasi "—scrivellos or small tusks, under 20 lbs.—is from 24 to 25 dollars; and the value increases at the rate of somewhat less than 1 dollar per lb. The " bab gujrati or kashshi," the bab kashshi, is that intended for the Cutch market. The tusk must be of middling size, little bent, very bluff at the point as it is intended for rings and armlets ; the girth must be a short span and three fingers, the bamboo shallow and not longer than a hand. Ivory fulfilling all these conditions will sell as high as 70 dollars per frasilah,—medium size of 20 to 45 lbs.—fetches 56 to 60 dollars. The " bab wilaiti," or " foreign sort," is that purchased in European and American markets. The largest size is preferred, which ranging from 45 to 100 lbs., may be purchased for 52 dollars per frasilah.

The third and least valued quality is the western ivory, the Gendai, and other varieties imported from Usagara, Uhehe, Urori, Unyamwezi, and its neighbourhood. The price varies according to size, form, and weight, from 45 to 56 dollars per frasilah.

The transport of ivory to the coast, and the profits derived by the maritime settlers, Arab and Indian, have been described. When all fees have been paid, the tusk, guarded against smuggling by the custom-house stamp, is sent to Zanzibar. On the island scrivellos under 6 lbs. in weight are not registered. According to the late Lieutenant-Colonel Hamerton, the annual average of large tusks is not less than 20,000. The people of the country make the weight range between 17,000 and 25,000 frasilah. The tusk is larger at Zanzibar than elsewhere. At Mozambique, for instance, 60 lbs. would be considered a good average for a lot. Monster tusks are spoken of. Specimens of 5 farasilah are not very rare, and the people have traditions that these wonderful armatures have extended to 227 lbs., and even to 280 lbs. each.

Amongst the minor articles of export from the interior, hippopotamus teeth have been enumerated. Beyond the coast, however, they form but a slender item in the caravan load. In the inner regions they are bought in retail; the price ranges between 1 and 2 fundo of beads, and at times 3 may be procured for a shukkah. On the coast they rise, when fine, to 25 dollars per frasilah. At Zanzibar a large lot, averaging 6 to 8 lbs. in weight (12 lbs. would be about the largest), will sell for 60 dollars; per frasilah of 5 lbs. from 40 to 45 dollars: whilst the smallest fetch from 5 to 6 dollars. Of surpassing hardness, they are still used in Europe for artificial teeth. In America porcelain bids fair to supplant them.

The gargatan (karkadan?), or small black rhinoceros with a double horn, is as common as the elephant in the interior. The price of the horn is regulated by its size; a small specimen is to be bought for 1 jembe or iron hoe. When large the price is doubled. Upon the coast a lot fetches from 6 to 9 dollars per frasilah, which at Zanzibar increases to from 8 to 12 dollars. The inner barbarians apply plates of the horn to helcomas and ulcerations, and they cut it into bits, which are bound with twine round the limb, like the wooden mpigii or hirizi. Large horns are imported through Bombay to China and Central Asia, where it is said the people convert them into drinking-cups, which sweat if poison be administered in them: thus they act like the Venetian glass of our ancestors, and are as highly prized as that eccentric fruit the coco de mer. The Arabs of Maskat and Yemen cut them into sword-hilts, dagger-hafts, tool-handles, and small boxes for tobacco, and other articles. They greatly prize, and will pay 12 dollars per frasilah, for the spoils of the kobaoba, or long-horned white rhinoceros, which, however, appears no longer to exist in the latitudes westward of Zanzibar island.

Black cattle are seldom driven down from the interior, on account of the length and risk of the journey. It is evident, however, that the trade is capable of extensive development. The price of full-grown bullocks varies, according to the distance from the coast, between 3 and 5 doti; whilst that of cows is about double. When imported from the mainland ports, 1 dollar per head is paid as an octroi to the government, and about the same sum for passage-money. As Banyans will not allow this traffic to be conducted by their own craft, it is confined to the Moslem population. The island of Zanzibar is supplied with black cattle, chiefly from the Banadir and Madagascar, places beyond the range of this description. The price of bullocks varies from 5 to 8 dollars, and of cows from 6 to 9 dollars. Goats and sheep abound throughout Eastern Africa. The former, which are preferred, cost in the maritime regions from 8 to 10 shukkah merkani; in Usagara, the most distant province which exports them to Zanzibar, they may be bought for 4 to 6 shukkah per head. The Wasawahili conduct a small trade in this live stock, and sell them upon the island for 4 to 5 dollars per head. From their large profits, however, must be deducted the risk of transport, the price of passage, and the octroi, which is 25 cents per head.

The exceptional expense of man-carriage renders the exportation of hides and horns from the far interior impossible. The former are sold with the animal, and are used for shields, bedding, saddle-bags, awnings, sandals, and similar minor purposes. Skins, as has been explained, are in some regions almost the only wear; consequently the spoils of a fine goat command, even in far Usukuma, a doti of domestics. The principal wild hides, which, however, rarely find their way to the coast, are those of the rhinoceros—much prized by the Arabs for targes—the lion and the leopard, the giraffe and the buffalo, the zebra and the quagga. Horns are allowed to crumble upon the ground. The island of Zanzibar exports hides and skins, which are principally those of bullocks and goats brought from Brava, Marka, Makdishu, and the Somali country. The korjah or score of the former has risen from 10 to 24 dollars; and the people have learned to mix them with the spoils of wild animals, especially the buffalo. When taken from the animal the hides are pinned down with pegs passed through holes in the edges; thus they dry without shrinking, and become stiff as boards. When thoroughly sun-parched they are put in soak and are pickled in sea-water for forty-eight hours; thus softened, they are again stretched and staked, that they may remain smooth : as they are carelessly removed by the natives, the meat fat, flippers, ears, and all the parts likely to be corrupted, or, to prevent close stowage, are cut off whilst wet. They are again thoroughly sun-dried, the grease which exudes during the operation is scraped off, and they are beaten with sticks to expel the dust. The Hamburg merchants paint their hides with an arsenical mixture, which preserves them during the long months of magazine-storing and sea-voyage. The French and American traders omit this operation, and their hides suffer severely from insects.

Details concerning the growth of cereals in the interior have occurred in the preceding pages. Grain is never exported from the lands lying beyond the maritime regions : yet the disforesting of the island of Zanzibar and the extensive plantations of clove-trees rendering a large importation of cereals necessary to the Arabs, an active business is carried on by Arab dows from the whole of the coast between Tanga and Ngao (Monghou), and during the dear season, after the rains, considerable profits are

realised. The corn measures used by the Banyans are as
follows:—

    2 Kubabah (each from 1·25 to 1·50 lbs., in fact, our "quart") =1 Kisaga.
    3 Kubabah =1 Pishi (in Khutu the Pishi=2 Kubabah).
    4 Kubabah=1 Kayla (equal to 2 Man).
  24 Kayla   =1 Frasilah.
  60 Kayla   =1 Jizlah, in Kisawahili Mzo.
  20 Farasilah =1 Kandi (candy).

As usual in these lands, the kubabah or unit is made to be
arbitrary; it is divided into two kinds, large and small. The
measure is usually a gourd.

The only timber now utilised in commerce is the mukanda'a
or red and white mangrove, which supplies the well-known bordi
or "Zanzibar rafters." They are the produce of the fluviatile
estuaries and the marine lagoons, and attain large dimensions
under the influence of potent heat and copious rains. The best
is the red variety, which, when thrown upon the shore, stains
the sand; it grows on the soft and slimy bank, and anchors
itself with ligneous shoots to the shifting soil. The white mangrove, springing from harder ground, dispenses with these supports; it is called mti wa muytu ("wild wood"), and is quickly
destroyed by worms. Indeed, all the bordi at Zanzibar begin
to fail after the fifth year if exposed to the humid atmosphere;
at Maskat it is said they will last nearly a century. The rafter
trade is conducted by Arab dows: the crews fell the trees, after
paying 2 or 3 dollars in cloth by way of ada or present to the
diwan, who permits them to hire labourers. The korjah or
score of cut and trimmed red mangrove rafters formerly cost at
Zanzibar 1 dollar; the price has now risen to 2 and 3 dollars.
This timber finds its way to Aden and the woodless lands of
Eastern and Western Arabia; at Jeddah they have been known
to fetch 1 dollar each.

The maritime regions also supply a small quantity of the
"grenadille wood," called by the people, who confound it with
real ebony (Diospyros ebenus), abnus and pingú. It is not so
brittle as ebony; it is harder than lignum-vitæ (G. officinalis),
spoiling the common saw, and is readily recognised by its
weight. As it does not absorb water or grease, it is sent to
Europe for the mouth-pieces and flanges of instruments, and
for the finer parts of mills. The people use it in the interior for
pipe-bowls.

The mpira or caoutchouc-tree (Ficus elastica) grows abun-
dantly throughout the maritime regions. A few lumps of the
gum were brought to Zanzibar at the request of a merchant,

who offered a large sum for a few tons, in the vain hope of
stimulating the exploitation of this valuable article.   The
specimens were not, however, cast in moulds as by the South
American Indians; they were full of water, and even fouler
than those brought from Madagascar.   To develop the trade
European supervision would be absolutely necessary during the
season for tapping the trees.

A tree growing upon the coast and common in Madagascar
produces, when an incision has been made in the bark, a juice
inspissating to the consistency of soft soap, and much resembling
the Indian "kokam."   This "kanya" is eaten by Arabs and
Africans, with the idea that it "moistens the body:" in cases
of stiff joints, swellings of the extremities, and contractions of
the sinews, it is melted over the fire and is rubbed into the
skin for a fortnight or three weeks.

The produce and the value of the coco and areca palms have
already been noted.   Orchella-weed (Rocilla fuciformis?) a
lichen most valuable in dyeing, is found, according to the late
Lieut.-Colonel Hamerton, growing on trees and rocks throughout the maritime regions.   The important growths of the interior are the frankincense and bdellium, the coffee and nutmeg
—which, however, are still in a wild state—the tamarind, and
the sisam or black wood.   The largest planks are made of the
mtimbati (African teak?) and the mvule; they are now exported from the coast to the island, where they have almost died
out.   As the art of sawing is unknown, a fine large tree is invariably sacrificed for a single board.   It was the opinion of the
late Lieut.-Colonel Hamerton that a saw-mill at the mouth of
the Pangani River would, if sanctioned by the local government, be highly remunerative.

Cowries, called by the Arabs kaure, in Kisawahili khete,
and in the interior simbi, are collected from various places in
the coast-region between Ras Hafun and the Mozambique.
This trade is in the hands of Moslem hucksters; the Banyan
who has no objection to the valuable ivory or hippopo-
tamus-tooth, finds his religion averse to the vile spoils of the
Cypræa.   Cowries are purchased on the mainland by a curious
specimen of the "round-trade;" money is not taken, so the
article is sold measure for measure of holcus grain.   From
Zanzibar the cowrie takes two directions.   As it forms the currency of the regions north of the "Land of the Moon," and is
occasionally demanded as an ornament in Unyamwezi, the
return African porters, whose labour costs them nothing, often
partly load themselves with the article; the Arab, on the other

hand, who seldom visits the northern kingdoms, does not find compensation for porterage and rations. The second and principal use of cowries is for exportation to the West African coast, where they are used in currency—50 strings, each of 40 shells, or a total of 2000, representing the dollar. This, in former days a most lucrative trade, is now nearly ruined. Cowries were purchased at 75 cents per jizlah, which represents from 3 to 3½ sacks, of which much, however, was worthless. The sacks in which they were shipped cost in Zanzibar 1 dollar 44 cents, and fetched in West Africa 8 or 9 dollars. The shells sold at the rate of 80l. (60l. was the average English price) per ton ; thus the profits were estimated at 500 per cent., and a Hamburg house rose, it is said, by this traffic, from 1 to 18 ships, of which 7 were annually engaged in shipping cowries. From 75 cents the price rose to 4 dollars, it even attained a maximum of 10 dollars, the medium being 6 and 7 dollars per jizlah, and the profits necessarily declined.

Cotton is indigenous to the more fertile regions of Eastern as well as of Western Africa. The specimens hitherto imported from Port Natal and from Angola have given satisfaction, as they promise, with careful cultivation, to rival in fineness, firmness, and weight the medium-staple cotton of the New World. On the line between Zanzibar and the Tanganyika Lake the shrub grows almost wild, with the sole exception of Ugogo and its two flanks of wilderness, where the ground is too hard and the dry season too prolonged to support it. The partial existence of the same causes renders it scarce and dear in Unyamwezi. A superior quality was introduced by the travelling Arabs, but it soon degenerated. Cotton flourishes luxuriantly in the black earths fat with decayed vegetation, and on the rich red clays of the coast regions, of Usumbara, Usagara, and Ujiji, where water underlies the surface. These almost virgin soils are peculiarly fitted by atmospheric and geologic conditions for the development of the shrub, and the time may come when vast tracts, nearly half the superficies of the lands, here grass-grown, there cumbered by the primæval forest, may be taught to bear crops equalling the celebrated growths of Egypt and Algeria, Harar and Abyssinia. At present the cultivation is nowhere encouraged, and it is limited by the impossibility of exportation to the scanty domestic requirements of the people. It is grown from seed sown immediately after the rains, and the only care given to it is the hedging requisite to preserve the dwarf patches from the depredations of cattle. In some parts the shrub is said to wither after the third year, in others to be perennial.

Upon the coast the cotton grown by the Wasawahili and Wamrima is chiefly used as lamp-wicks and for similar domestic purposes; Zanzibar Island is supplied from Western India. The price of raw uncleaned cotton in the mountain regions is about 0·25 dollar per maund of 3 Arab lbs. In Zanzibar, where the msufi or bombax abounds, its fibrous substance is a favourite substitute for cotton, and costs about half the price. In Unyamwezi it fetches fancy prices; it is sold in handfuls for salt, beads, and similar articles. About 1 maund may be purchased for a shukkah, and from 1 to 2 oz. of rough home-spun yarn for a fundo of beads. At Ujiji the people bring it daily to the bazar and spend their waste time in spinning yarn with the rude implements before described. This cotton, though superior in quality, as well as quantity, to that of Unyanyembe, is but little less expensive.

Tobacco grows plentifully in the more fertile regions of East Africa. Planted at the end of the rains, it gains strength by sun and dew, and is harvested in October. It is prepared for sale in different forms. Everywhere, however, a simple sun-drying supplies the place of cocking and sweating, and the people are not so fastidious as to reject the lower or coarser leaves and those tainted by the earth. Usumbara produces what is considered at Zanzibar a superior article: it is kneaded into little circular cakes four inches in diameter by half an inch deep: rolls of these cakes are neatly packed in plantain-leaves for exportation. The next in order of excellence is that grown in Uhiáo: it is exported in leaf or in the form called kambari, "roll-tobacco," a circle of coils each about an inch in diameter. The people of Khutu and Usagara mould the pounded and wetted material into discs like cheeses, 8 or 9 inches across by 2 or 3 in depth, and weighing about 3 lbs.; they supply the Wagogo with tobacco, taking in exchange for it salt. The leaf in Unyamwezi generally is soft and perishable, that of Usukuma being the worst: it is sold in blunt cones, so shaped by the mortars in which they are pounded. At Karagwah, according to the Arabs, the tobacco, a superior variety, tastes like musk in the water-pipe. The produce of Ujiji is better than that of Unyamwezi; it is sold in leaf, and is called by the Arabs hamúmí, after a well-known growth in Hazramaut. It is impossible to assign an average price to tobacco in East Africa; it varies from 1 khete of coral beads per 6 oz. to 2 lbs.

Tobacco is chewed by the maritime races, the Wasawahili, and especially the Zanzibar Arabs, who affect a religious scruple about smoking. They usually insert a pinch of nurah or coral-lime into their quids,—as the Somal introduces ashes,—to make them bite; in the interior, where calcareous formations are deficient, they procure the article from cowries brought from the coast, or from shells found in the lakes and streams. About Unyamwezi all sexes and ages enjoy the pipe. Farther eastward snuff is preferred. The liquid article in fashion amongst the Wajiji has already been described. The dry snuff is made of leaf toasted till crisp and pounded between two stones, mixed with a little magádí or saltpetre, sometimes scented with the heart of the plantain-tree and stored in the tumbakira or gourd-box.

The other articles exported from the coast to Zanzibar are bees'-wax and honey, tortoiseshell and ambergris, ghee, tobacco, the sugar-cane, the wild arrowroot, gums, and fibrous substances; of these many have been noticed, and the remainder are of too trifling a value to deserve attention.

To conclude the subject of commerce in East Africa. It is rather to the merchant than to the missionary that we must look for the regeneration of the country by the development of her resources. The attention of the civilized world, now turned towards this hitherto neglected region, will presently cause slavery to cease; man will not risk his all in petty and passionless feuds undertaken to sell his weaker neighbour; and commerce, which induces mansuetude of manners, will create wants and interests at present unknown. As the remote is gradually drawn nigh, and the difficult becomes accessible, the intercourse of man — strongest instrument of civilisation in the hand of Providence — will raise Africa to that place in the great republic of nations from which she has hitherto been unhappily excluded.

Already a line of steam navigation from the Cape of Good Hope to Aden and the Red Sea, touching at the various important posts upon the mainland and the islands of East Africa, has been proposed. This will be the first step towards material improvement. The preceding pages have, it is believed, convinced the reader that the construction of a tramroad through a country abounding in timber and iron, and where only one pass of any importance presents itself, will be attended with no engineering difficulties. As the land now lies, trade stagnates, loanable capital remains idle, produce is depreciated, and new seats of enterprise are unexplored. The specific for existing evils is to be found in facilitating intercourse between the interior and the coast, and that this will in due season be effected we may no longer doubt.

APPENDIX II.

1.

"East India House, 13th September, 1856.

" Sir,—I am commanded by the Court of Directors of the East India Company to inform you, that, in compliance with the request of the Royal Geographical Society, you are permitted to be absent from your duties as a regimental officer whilst employed with an Expedition, under the patronage of Her Majesty's Government, to be despatched into Equatorial Africa, for the exploration of that country, for a period not exceeding two years. I am directed to add, that you are permitted to draw the pay and allowances of your rank during the period of your absence, which will be calculated from the date of your departure from Bombay.

" I am, Sir,

" Your most obedient humble Servant,
" (Signature illegible.)

" Lieutenant R. Burton."

2.

"East India House, 24th October, 1856.

" Sir,—In consequence of a communication from the office of the Secretary of State for War, intimating that you are required as a witness on the trial by Court-Martial now pending on Colonel A. Shirley, I am desired to convey to you the commands of the Court of Directors that you instantly return to London for that purpose. In obeying this order, you are required to proceed, not through France, but by the steamer direct from Alexandria to Southampton. You will report yourself to the Secretary of State for War immediately on your arrival. The agent for the East India Company in Egypt has received instructions by this mail to supply you with the necessary funds for your passage.

" I am, Sir,

" Your most obedient humble Servant,
" (Signed) JAMES MELVILLE.

" Lieutenant Burton."

3.

" The Military Secretary, East India House.

" Sir,—I have the honour to acknowledge your official letter of the 24th October, conveying to me the commands of the Court of Directors to return instantly to London by the steamer direct from Alexandria to Southampton.

" The steamer in question left Alexandria on November 6th, at about 10 a.m. I received and acknowledged from the British Consulate your official letter on the same day at Cairo, about noon. No steamer leaves Alexandria before the 20th inst.; it is therefore evident that I could not possibly obey the order within the limits specified.

" No mention was made about my returning to England by the next steamer, probably because the Court-Martial pending upon Colonel A. Shirley will before that time have come to a close. I need scarcely say, that should I, on arrival at Bombay, find an order to that effect, it shall be instantly and implicitly obeyed.

" Considering, however, that I have already stated all that I know upon the subject of the Court-Martial in question—that I was not subpœnaed in England—that I am under directions of the Royal Geographical Society, and employed with an Expedition under the patronage of the Foreign Office—that without my proceeding to Bombay, valuable Government property would most probably have been lost, and the preparations for the Expedition have suffered from serious delay—and lastly, that by the loss of a few weeks a whole year's exploration must be allowed to pass by—I venture respectfully to hope that I have taken the proper course, and that should I, on my arrival in India, find no express and positive order for an immediate return to Europe, I may be permitted to proceed forthwith to Africa.

" As a servant of the East India Company, in whose interests I have conscientiously and energetically exerted myself for the space of 14 years, I cannot but request the Court of Directors to use their powerful influence in my behalf. Private interests cannot be weighed against public duty. At the same time, I have already embarked a considerable sum in the materiel of the Expedition, paid passage money, and devoted time, which might otherwise have been profitably employed, to the subject of Equatorial Africa. I remained long enough in London to enable the War Office to call for my presence as a witness, and I ascertained personally from Major-General Beatson that he had not placed me upon his list. And finally, I venture to observe, that by returning to Europe now, I should be compromising the interests of the Royal Geographical Society, under which I am in fact virtually serving."

4.

" *To the Secretary of the Royal Geographical Society, London.*

" Sir,—I have the honour to forward, for the information of the President and members of the Expeditionary Committee, a copy of a communication to my address from the Military Secretary to the Court of Directors, together with my reply thereto. On perusal of these documents, you will perceive that my presence is urgently demanded in England to give evidence on a Court-Martial, and that the letter desiring me to proceed forthwith to England arrived too late in Egypt to admit of my obeying that order. Were I now to proceed directly from Bombay to England, it is evident that the Expedition which I am undertaking under your direction, must be deferred to a future and uncertain date. With a view to obviate this uncalled-for delay, I have the honour to request that you will use your interest to the effect that, as an officer virtually in your service, I may be permitted to carry out the views of your Society ; and that my evidence, which can be of no importance to either prosecutor or defendant in the Court-Martial in question, may be dispensed with. I start this evening for Bombay, and will report departure from that place.

" I have, &c.,

" R. F. BURTON.

"Camp, Aden, 14th November, 1856."

5.

" *To the Secretary of the Royal Geographical Society, London.*

" Sir,—I have the honour to inform you that on the 1st Dec. 1856, I addressed to you a letter which I hope has been duly received. On the 2nd instant, in company with Lt. Speke, I left Bombay Harbour, on board the H.E.I.C's. ship of war ' *Elphinstone* ' (Capt. Frushard, I.N., commanding), *en route* to East Africa. I have little to report that may be interesting to geographers ; but perhaps some account of political affairs in the Red Sea may be deemed worthy to be transmitted by you to the Court of Directors or to the Foreign Office.

" As regards the Expedition, copies of directions and a memorandum on instruments and observations for our guidance have come to hand. For observations, Lt. Speke and I must depend upon our own exertions, neither serjeants nor native students being procurable at the Bombay Observatory. The case of instruments and the mountain barometer have not been forwarded, but may still find us at Zanzibar. Meanwhile I have obtained from the Commanding Engineer, Bombay, one six-inch sextant, one five and a-half ditto, two prismatic compasses, five thermometers (of which two are B.P.), a patent log, taper, protractors, stands, &c.; also two pocket chronometers from the Observatory, duly rated; and Dr. Buist, Secretary, Bombay Geographical Society, has obliged me with a mountain barometer and various instructions about points of interest. Lt. Speke has been recommended by the local government to the Government of India for duty in East Africa, and the services of Dr. Steinhaeuser, who is most desirous to join us, have been applied for from the Medical Board, Bombay. I have strong hopes that both these officers will be allowed to accompany me, and that the Royal Geographical Society will use their efforts to that effect.

" By the subjoined detailed account of preliminary expenses at Bombay, it will be seen that I have expended £70 out of £250, for which I was permitted to draw.

" Although, as I before mentioned, the survey of Eastern Intertropical Africa has for the moment been deferred, the necessity still exists. Even in the latest editions of *Horsburgh*, the mass of matter relative to Zanzibar is borrowed from the observations of Capt. Bissel, who navigated the coast in H.M's. ships '*Leopard*' and '*Orestes*' about A.D. 1799. Little is known of the great current which, setting periodically from and to the Red Sea and the Persian Gulf, sweeps round the Eastern Horn of Africa. The reefs are still formidable to navigators; and before these seas can be safely traversed by steamers from the Cape, as is now proposed, considerable additions must be made to Capt. Owen's survey in A.D. 1823-24. Finally, operations on the coast will form the best introduction to the geographical treasures of the interior.

" The H.E.I. Company's surveying brig '*Tigris*' will shortly be out of dock, where she has been undergoing a thorough repair, and if fitted up with a round house on the quarter-deck would answer the purpose well. She might be equipped in a couple of months, and dispatched to her ground before the South-west Monsoon sets in, or be usefully employed in observing at Zanzibar instead of lying idle in Bombay Harbour. On former surveys of the Arabian and African Coasts, a small tender of from thirty to forty tons has always been granted, as otherwise operations are much crippled in boisterous weather and exposed on inhospitable shores.   Should no other vessel be available, one of the smallest of the new Pilot Schooners now unemployed at Bombay might be directed to wait upon the 'Tigris.' Lt. H. G. Fraser, I.N., has volunteered for duty upon the African Coast, and I have the honour to transmit his letter.   Nothing more would be required were some junior officer of the Indian Navy stationed at Zanzibar for the purpose of registering tidal, barometric, and thermometric observations, in order that something of the meteorology of this unknown region may be accurately investigated.

"When passing through Aden I was informed that the blockade of the Somali Coast had been raised without compensation for the losses sustained on my last journey.   This step appears, politically speaking, a mistake.   In the case of the 'Mary Ann' brig, plundered near Berberah in A.D. 1825, due compensation was demanded and obtained.   Even in India, an officer travelling through the states not under British rule, can, if he be plundered, require an equivalent for his property.   This is indeed our chief protection,—semi-barbarians and savages part with money less willingly than with life.   If it be determined for social reasons at Aden that the blockade should cease and mutton become cheap, a certain per-centage could be laid upon the exports of Berberah till such time as our losses, which, including those of government, amount to 1380l., are made good.

"From Harar news has reached Aden that the Amir Abubakr, dying during the last year of chronic consumption, has been succeeded by a cousin, one Abd el Rahman, a bigoted Moslem, and a violent hater of the Gallas.   His success in feud and foray, however, have not prevented the wild tribes from hemming him in, and unless fortune interfere, the city must fall into their hands.   The rumour prevalent at Cairo, namely, that Harar had been besieged and taken by Mr. Bell, now serving under 'Theodorus, Emperor of Ethiopia' (the chief Cássái), appears premature.   At Aden I met in exile Sharmarkay bin Ali Salih, formerly governor of Zayla.   He has been ejected in favour of a Dankali chief by the Ottoman authorities of Yemen, a circumstance the more to be regretted as he has ever been a firm friend to our interests.

"The present defenceless state of Berberah still invites our presence.   The eastern coast of the Red Sea is almost entirely under the Porte.   On the western shore, Cosseir is Egyptian, Masawwah, Sawakin, and Zayla, Turkish, and Berberah, the best port of all, unoccupied.   I have frequently advocated the establishment of a British agency at this place, and venture to do so once more. This step would tend to increase trade, to obviate accidents in case of shipwreck, and materially assist in civilizing the Somal of the interior. The Government of Bombay has doubtless preserved copies of my reports, plans, and estimates concerning the proposed agency, and I would request the Royal Geographical Society to inquire into a project peculiarly fitted to promote their views of exploration in the Eastern Horn of Africa. Finally, this move would checkmate any ambitious projects in the Red Sea. The Suez Canal may be said to have commenced. It appears impossible that the work should pay in a commercial sense. Politically it may, if, at least, its object be, as announced by the Count d'Escayrac de Lauture, at the Société de Geographie, to 'throw open the road of India to the Mediterranean coasting trade, to democratise commerce and navigation.' The first effect of the highway would be, as that learned traveller justly remarks, to open a passage through Egypt to the speronari and feluccas of the Levant, the light infantry of a more regular force.

"The next step should be to provide ourselves with a more efficient naval force at Aden, the Head-Quarters of the Red Sea Squadron. I may briefly quote as a proof of the necessity for protection, the number of British protégés in the neighbouring ports, and the present value of the Jeddah trade.

Mocha now contains about twenty-five English subjects, the principal merchants in the place. At Masawwah, besides a few French and Americans, there are from sixteen to twenty British protégés, who trade with the interior, especially for mules required at the Mauritius and our other colonies. Hodaydah has from fifty to sixty, and Jeddah, besides its dozen resident merchants, annually witnesses the transit of some hundreds of British subjects, who flock to the Haj for commerce and devotion.

"The chief emporium of the Red Sea trade has for centuries past been Jeddah, the port of Meccah. The custom-house reports of 1856 were kindly furnished to me by Capt. Frushard, I.N. (now commanding the H.E.I.C's. sloop of war, 'Elphinstone,') an old and experienced officer, lately employed in blockading Berberah, and who made himself instrumental in quelling certain recent attempts upon Turkish supremacy in Western Arabia. According to these documents, thirty-five ships of English build (square-rigged) arrived at and left Jeddah between the end of September and April, from and for various places in the East, China, Batavia, Singapore, Calcutta, Bombay, the Malabar Coast, the Persian Gulf, and Eastern Africa. Nearly all carried our colours, and were protected, or supposed

to be protected, by a British register : only five had on board
a European captain or sailing master, the rest being commanded and officered by Arabs and Indians.   Their cargoes
from India and the Eastern regions are rice, sugar, piece goods,
planking, pepper, and pilgrims; from Persia, dates, tobacco,
and raw silk ; and from the Mozambique, ivory, gold dust, and
similar costly articles.   These imports in 1856 are valued at
160,000*l.*   The exports for the year, consisting of a little coffee
and spice for purchase of imports, amounts, per returns, to
120,000*l.*   In addition to these square-rigged ships, the number
of country vessels, open boats, buggalows, and others, from the
Persian Gulf and the Indian Coasts, amount to 900, importing
550,000*l.*, and exporting about 400,000*l.*   I may remark, that
to all these sums at least one-third should be added, as speculation abounds, and books are kept by triple entry in the Holy
Land.

" The next port in importance to Jeddah is Hodaydah, where
vessels touch on their way northward, land piece and other goods,
and call on the return passage to fill with coffee.   As the head-
quarters of the Yemen Pashalik, it has reduced Mocha, formerly
the great coffee mart, to insignificance, and the vicinity of Aden,
a free port, has drawn off much of the stream of trade from both
these ancient emporia.   On the African Coast of the Red Sea,
Sawakin, opposite Jeddah, is a mere slave mart, and Masawwah,
opposite Hodaydah, still trades in pearls, gold dust, ivory, and
mules.

" But if the value of the Red Sea traffic calls, in the present
posture of events, for increased means of protection, the Slave-
trade has equal claims to our attention.   At Aden energetic
efforts have been made to suppress it.   It is, however, still
carried on by country boats from Sawakin, Tajurrah, Zayla,
and the Somali Coast ; — a single cargo sometimes consisting of
200 head gathered from the interior, and exported to Jeddah
and the small ports lying north and south of it.   The trade is,
I believe, principally in the hands of Arab merchants at Jeddah
and Hodaydah, and resident foreigners, principally Indian
Moslems, who claim our protection in case of disturbances, and
consequently carry on a thriving business.   Our present Squadron in the Red Sea consisting of only two sailing vessels, the
country boats in the African ports have only to wait till they
see the ship pass up or down, and then knowing the passage—
a matter of a day—to be clear, to lodge the slaves at their destination.   During the past year, this trade was much injured by
the revolt of the Arabs against the Turks, and the constant
presence of the ' *Elphinstone*,' whose reported object was to

seize all vessels carrying slaves. The effect was principally moral. Although the instructions for the guidance of the Commander enjoined him to carry out the wishes of the Home and Indian Governments for the suppression of Slavery, yet there being no published treaty between the Imperial Government and the Porte sanctioning to us the right of search in Turkish bottoms, his interference would not have been supported by the Ottoman local authorities. It may be well to state, that after a Firman had been published in the Hejaz and Gemen abolishing the trade, the Turkish Governments of Jeddah and Hodaydah declared that the English Commander might do as he pleased, but that they declined making any written request for his assistance. For its present increased duties, for the suppression of the Slave-trade, for the protection of British subjects, and for the watching over Turkish and English interests in the Red Sea, the Aden Squadron is no longer sufficient. During the last two years it has numbered two sailing vessels, the 'Elphinstone,' a sloop of war, carrying twelve 32-pounders, and two 12-pounders; and the ' Mahi,' a schooner armed with one pivot gun, 32-pounder, and two 12-pounders. Nor would it be benefited by even a considerable increase of sailing vessels. It is well known that, as the prevailing winds inside the sea are favourable for proceeding upwards from September to April, so on the return, during those months, they are strongly adverse. A fast ship, like the 'Elphinstone,' requires 30 days on the downward voyage to do the work of four. Outside the sea, during those months, the current sets inward from the Indian Ocean, and a ship, in event of very light winds falling, has been detained a whole week in sight of Aden. From April to September, on the contrary, the winds set down the Red Sea frequently with violence; the current inside the sea also turns towards the Indian Ocean, and outside the S.W. Monsoon is blowing. Finally, sailing ships draw too much water. In the last year the 'Elphinstone' kept the Arabs away from Jeddah till the meanness of the Sherif Abd el Muttalib had caused his downfall. But her great depth (about from 14·6 to 15 ft.) prevented her approaching the shore at Hodaydah near enough to have injured the insurgents, who, unaware of the fact, delayed their attack upon the town till famine and a consequent pestilence dispersed them. With little increase of present expenditure, the Red Sea might be effectually commanded. Two screw-steamers, small enough to enter every harbour, and to work steadily amongst the banks on either shore, and yet large enough to be made useful in conveying English political officers of rank and Native Princes, when necessary, would amply suffice, a vessel of the class of H.M's gun-boat, 'Flying Fish,' drawing at most 9 feet water, and carrying four 32-pounders of 25 cwt. each, as broadside, and two 32-pounders of 25 cwt. each, as pivot guns, would probably be that selected. The crews would consist of fewer men than those at present required, and means would easily be devised for increasing the accommodation of officers and men, and for securing their health and comfort during cruises that might last two months in a hot and dangerous climate.

"By means of two such steamers we shall, I believe, be prepared for any contingencies which might arise in the Red Sea; and if to this squadron be added an allowance for interpreters and a slave approver in each harbour, in fact a few of the precautions practised by the West African Squadron, the slave-trade in the Red Sea will soon have received its death-blow, and Eastern Africa its regeneration at our hands.

"I have, &c., &c.,
"R. F. BURTON,
"Commanding East African Expedition.
"H.E.I.C. Sloop of War 'Elphinstone,'
"15th December, 1856."

6.

No. 961 of 1857.

From H. L. ANDERSON, *Esquire, Secretary to Government, Bombay, to* Captain R. F. BURTON, 18th *Regiment Bombay N. I.*

Dated the 23rd July, 1857.

"Sir,—With reference to your letter, dated the 15th December, 1856, to the address of the Secretary of the Royal Geographical Society of London, communicating your views on affairs in the Red Sea, and commenting on the political measures of the Government of India, I am directed by the Right Honourable the Governor in Council to state, your want of discretion, and due respect for the authorities to whom you are subordinate, has been regarded with displeasure by Government.

"I have the honour to be, Sir,
"Your most obedient Servant,
"(Signed)   H. L. ANDERSON,
"Secretary to Government.
"Bombay Castle, 23rd July, 1857."

7.

THE MASSACRE AT JUDDAH.
(*Extract from the "Telegraph Courier," Overland Summary, Bombay, August* 4, 1858.)

"On the 30th June, a massacre of nearly all the Christians took place at Juddah on the Red Sea. Amongst the victims were Mr. Page, the British Consul, and the French Consul and his lady. Altogether the Arabs succeeded in slaughtering about twenty-five.

" H.M. steamship Cyclops was there at the time, and the captain landed with a boat's crew, and attempted to bring off some of the survivors, but he was compelled to retreat, not without having killed a number of the Arabs. The next day, however, he succeeded in rescuing the few remaining Christians, and conveyed them to Suez.

" Amongst those who were fortunate enough to escape was the daughter of the French Consul; and this she succeeded in doing through the fidelity of a native after she had killed two men with her own hands, and been severely wounded in the encounter. Telegraphic dispatches were transmitted to England and France, and the Cyclops is waiting orders at Suez. As it was apprehended that the news from Juddah might excite the Arab population of Suez to the commission of similar outrages, H.R.M's Vice-Consul at that place applied to the Pasha of Egypt for assistance, which was immediately afforded by the landing of 500 Turkish soldiers, under the orders of the Pasha of Suez."

8.

" Unyanyembe, Central Africa, 24th June, 1858.

" Sir, — I have the honour to acknowledge the receipt of your official letter, No. 961 of 1857, conveying to me the displeasure of the Government in consequence of my having communicated certain views on political affairs in the Red Sea to the R. G. S. of Great Britain.

" The paper in question was as is directly stated, and it was sent for transmission to the Board of Directors, or the Foreign Office, not for publication. I beg to express my regret that it should have contained any passages offensive to the authorities to whom I am subordinate; and to assure the Right Honourable the Governor in Council that nothing was farther from my intentions than to displease a government to whose kind consideration I have been, and am still, so much indebted.

" In conclusion, I have the honour to remind you that I have received no reply to my official letter, sent from Zanzibar, urging our claims upon the Somal for the plunder of our property.

" I have the honour to be, Sir,
" Your most obedient Servant,
" RICHARD. F. BURTON,
" Commanding East African Expedition.
" To the Secretary to Government, Bombay."

9.

No. 2845, of 1857.

"Political Department.

From H. L. ANDERSON, Esq., *Secretary to Government of Bombay,* to Capt. R. F. BURTON, *Commanding E. A. Expedition, Zanzibar.*

"Dated 13th June, 1857.

"Sir,—I am directed by the Right Honourable the Governor in Council to acknowledge the receipt of your letter dated the 26th April last, soliciting compensation on behalf of yourself and the other members of the late Somalee Expedition, for losses sustained by you and them.

"2. In reply, I am desired to inform you, that under the opinion copied in the margin, expressed by the late Governor-General of India, the Right Honourable the Governor in Council cannot accede to the application now preferred.

> Having regard to the conduct of the Expedition, His Lordship cannot think that the officers who composed it have any just claims on the Government for their personal losses.

"I have, &c.,

"(Signed)   H. L. ANDERSON,
"Secretary to Government."

END OF FIRST CORRESPONDENCE.

SECOND CORRESPONDENCE.

1.

"India Office, E. C., 8th November, 1859.

"Sir,—I am directed by the Secretary of State for India in Council to forward for your information, copy of a letter addressed by Captain Rigby, her Majesty's Consul and agent at Zanzibar, to the Government of Bombay, respecting the non-payment of certain persons hired by you to accompany the Expedition under your command into Equatorial Africa, and to request that you will furnish me with any observations which you may have to make upon the statements contained in that letter.

"Sir Charles Wood especially desires to be informed why you took no steps to bring the services of the men who accompanied you, and your obligations to them, to the notice of the Bombay Government.

"I am, Sir,

"Your obedient servant,

"(Signed)   T. Cosmo Melville.

"Captain R. Burton."

2.

"No. 70 of 1859.
"Political Department.

From Captain C. P. Rigby, *her Majesty's Consul and British agent, Zanzibar, to* H. L. Anderson, *Esquire, Secretary to Government, Bombay.*

"Zanzibar, July 15th, 1859.

"Sir, — I have the honour to report, for the information of the Right Honourable the Governor in Council, the following circumstances connected with the late East African Expedition under the command of Captain Burton.

"2. Upon the return of Captain Burton to Zanzibar in March last, from the interior of Africa, he stated that, from the funds supplied him by the Royal Geographical Society for the expenses of the Expedition, he had only a sufficient sum left to defray the passage of himself and Captain Speke to England, and in consequence the persons who accompanied the Expedition from here, viz.: the Kafila Bashi, the Belooch Sepoys, and the porters, received nothing whatever from him on their return.

"3. On quitting Zanzibar for the interior of Africa, the expedition was accompanied by a party of Belooch soldiers, consisting of a Jemadar and twelve armed men. I understand they were promised a monthly salary of five dollars each; they remained with the Expedition for twenty months, and as they received nothing from Captain Burton beyond a few dollars each before starting, his highness the Sultan has generously distributed amongst them the sum of (2300) two thousand three hundred dollars.

"4. The head clerk of the Custom House here, a Banian, by name Ramjee, procured ten men, who accompanied the Expedition as porters; they were promised five dollars each per mensem, and received pay for six months, viz.: thirty dollars each before starting for the interior. They were absent for twenty months, during three of which the Banian Ramjee states that they did not accompany the Expedition.   He now claims eleven months' pay for each of these men, as they have not been paid anything beyond the advance before starting.

" 5. The head clerk also states that after the Expedition left Zanzibar, he sent two men to Captain Burton with supplies, one of whom was absent with the Expedition seventeen months, and received nothing whatever; the other, he states, was absent fifteen months, and received six months' pay, the pay for the remaining nine months being still due to him.   Thus his claim amounts to the following sums:—

Ten men for eleven months, at five dollars per man, per month, 550 Dollars.
One man for seventeen „   „   „   „   85   „
One   „   nine   „   „   „   „   45   „
                                                      ——
                              Total dollars   -   -   680

" 6. These men were slaves, belonging to 'deewans,' or petty chiefs, on the opposite mainland. They travel far into the interior to collect and carry down ivory to the coast, and are absent frequently for the space of two or three years. When hired out, the pay they receive is equally divided between the slave and the master. Captain Speke informs me, that when these men were hired, it was agreed that one-half of their hire should be paid to the men, and the other half to Ramjee on account of their owners. When Ramjee asked Captain Burton for their pay, on his return here, he declined to give him anything, saying that they had received thirty dollars each on starting, and that he could have bought them for a less sum.

" 7. The Kafila Bashi, or chief Arab, who accompanied the Expedition, by name Said bin Salem, was twenty-two months with Captain Burton. He states, that on the first journey to Pangany and Usumbara, he received fifty (50) dollars from Captain Burton; and that before starting on the last expedition, to discover the Great Lake, the late Lieutenant-Colonel Hamerton presented him with five hundred dollars on behalf of Government for the maintenance of his family during his absence. He states that he did not stipulate for any monthly pay, as Colonel Hamerton told him, that if he escorted the gentlemen to the Great Lake in the interior, and brought them in safety back to Zanzibar, he would be handsomely rewarded; and both Captain Speke and Mr. Apothecary Frost inform me that Colonel Hamerton frequently promised Said bin Salem that he should receive a thousand dollars and a gold watch if the Expedition were successful.

" 8. As it appeared to me that Colonel Hamerton had received no authority from Government to defray any part of the expenses of this Expedition, and probably made these promises thinking that if the exploration of the unknown interior were successful a great national object would be attained, and that the chief man who conducted the Expedition would be liberally rewarded, and as Captain Burton had been furnished with funds to defray the expenses, I told him that I did not feel authorised to make any payment without the previous sanction of Government, and Said bin Salem has therefore received nothing whatever since his return.

"9. Said Bin Salem also states, that on the return of the Expedition from Lake Tanganyika, (70) seventy natives of the country were engaged as porters, and accompanied the Expedition for three months; and that on arriving at a place called 'Kootoo,' a few days' journey from the sea-coast, Captain Burton wished them to diverge from the correct route to the coast opposite Zanzibar, to accompany him south to Keelwa; but they refused to do so, saying that none of their people ever dared to venture to Keelwa; that the chief slave-trade on the east coast is carried on. No doubt their fears were well grounded. These men received nothing in payment for their three months' journey, and, as no white man had ever penetrated into their country previously, I fear that any future traveller will meet with much inconvenience in consequence of these poor people not having been paid.

"10. As I considered that my duty connected with the late Expedition was limited to affording it all the aid and support in my power, I have felt very reluctant to interfere with anything connected with the non-payment of these men; but Said bin Salem and Ramjee having appealed to me, and Captain Speke, since his departure from Zanzibar, having written me two private letters, pointing out so forcibly the claims of these men, the hardships they endured, and the fidelity and perseverance they showed, conducting them safely through unexplored countries, and stating also that the agreements with them were entered into at the British Consulate, and that they considered they were serving the British Government, that I deem it my duty to bring their claims to the notice of Government; for I feel that if these men remain unpaid, after all they have endured in the service of British officers, our name for good faith in these countries will suffer, and that any future travellers wishing to further explore the interesting countries of the interior will find no persons willing to accompany them from Zanzibar, or the opposite mainland.

"11. As there was no British agent at Zanzibar for thirteen months after the death of Colonel Hamerton, the Expedition, was entirely dependent on Luddah Damha, the Custom-master here, for money and supplies. He advanced considerable sums of money without any security, forwarded all requisite supplies, and, Captain Speke says, afforded the Expedition every assistance, in the most handsome manner. Should Government, therefore, be pleased to present him with a shawl, or some small mark of satisfaction, I am confident he is fully deserving of it, and it would gratify a very worthy man to find that his assistance to the Expedition is acknowledged.

" I have, &c.,

" (Signed) C. P. RIGBY, Captain,

" H. M.'s Consul and British Agent, Zanzibar."

3.

" East India United Service Club, St. James's Square,
11th November, 1859.

" Sir, — I have the honour to acknowledge the receipt of your official letter, dated the 8th of November, 1859, forwarding for my information copy of a letter, addressed by Captain Rigby, Her Majesty's consul and agent at Zanzibar, to the Government of Bombay, respecting the non-payment of certain persons, hired by me to accompany the Expedition under my command into Equatorial Africa, and apprising me that Sir C. Wood especially desires to be informed, why I took no steps to bring the services of the men who accompanied me, and my obligations to them, to the notice of the Bombay Government.

" In reply to Sir Charles Wood I have the honour to state that, as the men alluded to rendered me no services, and as I felt in no way obliged to them, I would not report favourably of them. The Kafilah Bashi, the Jemadar, and the Baloch were servants of H.H. Sayyid Majid, in his pay and under his command ; they were not hired by me, but by the late Lieut.-Col. Hamerton, H.M.'s Consul and H.E.I.C.'s agent at Zanzibar, and they marched under the Arab flag. On return to Zanzibar, I reported them as undeserving of reward to Lieut.-Col. Hamerton's successor, Capt. Rigby, and after return to England, when my accounts were sent in to the Royal Geographical Society, I appended a memorandum, that as those persons had deserved no reward, no reward had been applied for.

" Before proceeding to reply to Capt. Rigby's letter, paragraph by paragraph, I would briefly premise with the following remarks.

" Being ordered to report myself to Lieut.-Col. Hamerton, and having been placed under his direction, I admitted his friendly interference, and allowed him to apply to H.H. the Sultan for a guide and an escort. Lieut.-Col. Hamerton offered to defray, from public funds, which he understood to be at his disposal, certain expenses of the Expedition, and he promised, as reward to the guide and escort, sums of money, to which, had I been unfettered, I should have objected as exorbitant. But in all cases, the promises made by the late consul were purely conditional, depending entirely upon the satisfactory conduct of those employed. These facts are wholly omitted in Capt. Rigby's reports.

" 2. Capt. Rigby appears to mean that the Kafila Bashi, the Baloch sepoys, and the porters received nothing whatever on my return to Zanzibar, in March last, from the interior of Africa, because the funds supplied to me by the Royal Geographical Society for the Expenditure of the Expedition, had been exhausted. Besides the sum of (1000*l*.) one thousand pounds, granted by the Foreign Office. I had expended from private resources nearly (1400*l*.) fourteen hundred pounds, and I was ready to expend more had the expenditure been called for. But, though prepared on these occasions to reward liberally for good service, I cannot see the necessity, or rather I see the unadvisability of offering a premium to notorious misconduct. This was fully explained by me to Capt. Rigby on my return to Zanzibar.

" 3. Capt. Rigby '*understands*' that the party of Baloch sepoys, consisting of a Jemadar and twelve armed men, were promised a monthly salary of 5 dollars each. This was not the case. Lieut.-Col. Hamerton advanced to the Jemadar 25, and to each sepoy 20 dollars for an outfit; he agreed that I should provide them with daily rations, and he promised them an ample reward from the public funds in case of good behaviour. These men deserved nothing; I ignore their 'fidelity' and 'perseverance,' and I assert that if I passed safely through an unexplored country, it was in no wise by their efforts. On hearing of Lieut.-Col. Hamerton's death, they mutinied in a body. At the Tanganyika Lake they refused to escort me during the period of navigation, a month of danger and difficulty. When Capt. Speke proposed to explore the Nyanza Lake, they would not march without a present of a hundred dollars' worth of cloth. On every possible occasion they clamoured for 'Bakshish,' which, under pain of endangering the success of the Expedition, could not always be withheld. They were often warned by me that they were forfeiting all hopes of a future reward, and, indeed, they ended by thinking so themselves. They returned to Zanzibar with a number of slaves, purchased by them with money procured from the Expedition. I would not present either guide or escort to the consul; but I did not think it my duty to oppose a large reward, said to be 2,300 dollars, given to them by H.H. the Sultan, and I reported his liberality and other acts of kindness to the Bombay Government on my arrival at Aden. This fact will, I trust, exonerate me from any charge of wishing to suppress my obligations.

"4. The Banyan Ramji, head clerk of the Custom House, did not, as is stated by Capt. Rigby, procure me (10) ten men who accompanied the Expedition as porters; nor were these men, as is asserted, (in par. 6), 'Slaves belonging to deewans or petty chiefs on the opposite mainland.' It is a notorious fact that these men were private slaves, belonging to the Banyan Ramjee, who hired them to me direct, and received from me as their pay, for six months, thirty dollars each; a sum for which, as I told him, he might have bought them in the bazaar. At the end of six months I was obliged to dismiss these slaves, who, as is usually the case with the slaves of Indian subjects at Zanzibar, were mutinous in the extreme. At the same time I supplied them with cloth, to enable them to rejoin their patron. On my return from the Tanganyika Lake, they requested leave to accompany me back to Zanzibar, which I permitted, with the express warning that they were not to consider themselves re-engaged. The Banyan, their proprietor, had, in fact, sent them on a trading trip into the interior under my escort, and I found them the most troublesome of the party. When Ramji applied for additional pay, after my return to Zanzibar, I told him that I had engaged them for six months; that I had dismissed them at the end of six months, as was left optional to me; and that he had already received an unusual sum for their services. This conversation appears in a distorted form and improperly represented in the concluding sentence of Capt. Rigby's 6th paragraph.

"5 and 6. With respect to the two men sent on with supplies after the Expedition had left Zanzibar, they were not paid, on account of the prodigious disappearance of the goods intrusted to their charge, as I am prepared to prove from the original journals in my possession. They were dismissed with their comrades, and never afterwards, to the best of my remembrance, did a day's work.

"7 and 8. The Kafilah Bashi received from me for the first journey to Usumbara (50) fifty dollars. Before my departure in the second Expedition he was presented by Lieut. Colonel Hamerton with (500) five hundred dollars, almost double what he had expected. He was also promised, in case of good conduct, a gold watch, and an ample reward, which, however, was to be left to the discretion of his employers. I could not recommend him through Captain Rigby to the Government for remuneration. His only object seemed to be that of wasting our resources and of collecting slaves in return for the heavy presents made to the native chiefs by the Expedition, and the consequence of his carelessness or dishonesty was, that the expenditure on the whole march, until we had learnt sufficient to supervise him, was inordinate. When the Kafilah Bashi at last refused to accompany Captain Speke to the Nyanza Lake, he was warned that he also was forfeiting all claim to future reward, and when I mentioned this circumstance to Captain Rigby at Zanzibar, he then agreed with me that the 500 dollars originally advanced were sufficient.

"9. With regard to the statement of Said bin Salim concerning the non-payment of the seventy-three porters, I have to remark that it was mainly owing to his own fault. The men did not refuse to accompany me because I wished to diverge from the "correct route," nor was I so unreasonable as to expect them to venture into the jaws of the slave trade. Several caravans that had accompanied us on the down-march, as well as the porters attached to the Expedition, were persuaded by the slaves of Ramjee (because Zanzibar was a nearer way to their homes) not to make Kilwa. The pretext of the porters was simply that they would be obliged to march back for three days. An extra remuneration was offered to them, they refused it, and left in a body. Shortly before their departure Captain Speke proposed to pay them for their services, but being convinced that they might be prevented from desertion, I did not judge advisable by paying them to do what would be virtually dismissing them. After they had proceeded a few miles, Said bin Salim was sent to recall them, on conditions which they would have accepted; he delayed, lost time, and ended by declaring that he could not travel without his dinner. Another party was instantly sent; they also loitered on the way, and thus the porters reached the coast and dispersed. Before their departure I rewarded the Kirangozi, or chief man of the caravan, who had behaved well in exhorting his followers to remain with us. I was delayed in a most unhealthy region for the arrival of some down porters, who consented to carry our goods to the coast; and to prove to them that money was not my object, I paid the newly-engaged gang as if they had marched the whole way. Their willingness to accompany me is the best proof that I had not lost the confidence of the people. Finally, on arrival at the coast, I inquired concerning those porters who had deserted us, and was informed by the Diwan and headman of the village, that they had returned to their homes in the interior, after a stay of a few days on the seaboard. This was a regrettable occurrence, but such events are common on the slave-path in Eastern Africa, and the established custom of the Arabs and other merchants, whom I had consulted upon the subject before leaving the interior, is, not to encourage desertion by paying part of the hire, or by settling for porterage before arriving at the coasts. Of the seven gangs of porters engaged on this journey, only one, an unusually small proportion, left me without being fully satisfied.

" 10. That Said bin Salim, and Ramji, the Banyan, should have appealed to Captain Rigby, according to the fashion of Orientals, after my departure from Zanzibar, for claims which they should have advanced when I refused to admit them, I am not astonished. But I must express my extreme surprise that Captain Speke should have written two private letters, forcibly pointing out the claims of these men to Captain Rigby, without having communicated the circumstance in any way to me, the chief of the Expedition. I have been in continued correspondence with that officer since my departure from Zanzibar, and until this moment I have been impressed with the conviction that Captain Speke's opinion as to the claims of the guide and escort above alluded to was identical with my own.

" 11. With respect to the last paragraph of Captain Rigby's letter, proposing that a shawl or some small mark of satisfaction should be presented by Government to Ladha Damha, the custom-master at Zanzibar, for his assistance to the Expedition, I distinctly deny the gratuitous assertions that I was entirely dependent on him for money and supplies; that he advanced considerable sums of money without any security; that he forwarded all requisite supplies, or, as Captain Speke affirms, that he afforded the Expedition every assistance in the most handsome manner. Before quitting Zanzibar for inner Africa, I settled all accounts with him, and left a small balance in his hands, and I gave, for all subsequent supplies, an order upon Messrs. Forbes, my agents in Bombay. He, like the other Hindus at Zanzibar, utterly neglected me after the death of Lieut.-Colonel Hamerton; and Captain Rigby has probably seen some of the letters of complaint which were sent by me from the interior. In fact, my principal merit in having conducted the Expedition to a successful issue is in having contended against the utter neglect of the Hindus at Zanzibar (who had promised to Lieut.-Colonel Hamerton, in return for his many good offices, their interest and assistance), and against the carelessness and dishonesty, the mutinous spirit and the active opposition of the guide and escort.

" I admit that I was careful that these men should suffer for their misconduct. On the other hand, I was equally determined that those who did their duty should be adequately rewarded, — a fact which nowhere appears in Captain Rigby's letter. The Portuguese servants, the negro-gun carriers, the several African gangs of porters, with their leaders, and all other claimants, were fully satisfied. The bills drawn in the interior, from the Arab merchants, were duly paid at Zanzibar, and on departure I left orders that if anything had been neglected it should be forwarded to me in Europe. I regret that Captain Rigby, without thoroughly ascertaining the merits of the case (which he evidently has not done), should not have permitted me to record any remarks which I might wish to offer, before making it a matter of appeal to the Bombay Government.

" Finally, I venture to hope that Captain Rigby has forwarded the complaints of those who have appealed to him without endorsing their validity; and I trust that these observations upon the statements contained in his letter may prove that these statements were based upon no foundation of fact.

" I am, Sir,
" Your obedient Servant,
" R. F. BURTON,
" Bombay Army."

4.

" India Office, E. C., 14th January, 1860.

" Sir, — I am directed by the Secretary of State for India in council, to inform you that, having taken into consideration the explanations afforded by you in your letter of the 11th November, together with the information on the same subject furnished by Captain Speke, he is of opinion that it was your duty, knowing, as you did, that demands for wages, on the part of certain Belochs and others who accompanied you into Equatorial Africa, existed against you, not to have left Zanzibar without bringing these claims before the consul there, with a view to their being adjudicated on their own merits, the more especially as the men had been originally engaged through the intervention or the influence of the British authorities, whom, therefore, it was your duty to satisfy before leaving the country. Had this course been followed, the character of the British Government would not have suffered, and the adjustment of the dispute would, in all probability, have been effected at a comparatively small outlay.

" Your letter, and that of Captain Speke, will be forwarded to the Government of Bombay, with whom it will rest to determine whether you shall be held pecuniarily responsible for the amount which has been paid in liquidation of the claims against you.

" I am, Sir,
" Your obedient Servant,
" (Signed)   J. Cosmo Melvill."

5.

" Sir,—I have the honour to acknowledge the receipt of your official letter of the 14th January, 1860.

" In reply, I have the honour to observe that, not having been favoured with a copy of the information on the same subject furnished to you by Captain Speke, I am not in a position to understand on what grounds the Secretary of State for India in council should have arrived at so unexpected a decision as regards the alleged non-payment of certain claims made by certain persons sent with me into the African interior.

" I have the honour to observe that I did not know that demands for wages existed against me on the part of those persons, and that I believed I had satisfactorily explained the circumstances of their dismissal without payment in my official letter of the 11th November, 1859.

" Although impaired health and its consequences prevented me from proceeding in an official form to the adjudication of the supposed claims in the presence of the consular authority, I represented the whole question to Captain Rigby, who, had he then—at that time—deemed it his duty to interfere, might have insisted upon adjudicating the affair with me, or with Captain Speke, before we left Zanzibar.

" I have the honour to remark that the character of the British Government has *not*, and cannot (in my humble opinion) have suffered in any way by my withholding a purely conditional reward when forfeited by gross neglect and misconduct; and I venture to suggest that by encouraging such abuses serious obstacles will be thrown in the way of future exploration, and that the liberality of the British Government will be more esteemed by the native than its character for sound sense.

" In conclusion, I venture to express my surprise, that all my labours and long services in the cause of African Exploration should have won for me no other reward than the prospect of being mulcted in a pecuniary liability incurred by my late lamented friend, Lieut.-Colonel Hamerton, and settled without reference to me by his successor, Captain Rigby.

" I have the honour, &c. &c.,
" RICHD. F. BURTON,
" Captain, Bombay Army."
"The Under Secretary of State for India."

INDEX.

Abad bin Sulayman, rest of the party at the house of, at Kazeh, i. 323.
Abdullah, the Baloch, sketch of him, i. 136.
Abdullah bin Nasib, of Zanzibar, his kindness, i. 270.
Abdullah bin Jumah, and his flying caravan, i. 315.
Abdullah bin Salim of Kazeh, his authority there, i. 329.
Abdullah, son of Musa Mzuri, ii. 225, 226.
Ablactation, period of, in East Africa, i. 117.
Abrus precatorius used as an ornament in Karagwah, ii. 181.
Adansonia digitata, or monkey-bread of East Africa, peculiarity of, i. 47.
Africa, Central, great depression of, i. 409; ii. 8.
African proverbs, i. 131.
Africans, a weak-brained people, i. 33.
Africans, East, their character and religion, ii. 324.
Albinos, frequency of, amongst the Wazaramo tribes, i. 109. Description of them, 109.
Amayr bin Said el Shaksi, calls on Capt. Burton, ii. 228. His adventures, 228.
Ammunition, danger of, in African travelling, i. 264.
Androgyne, the, ii. 159.
Animals, wild, of Uzaramo, i. 63. Of Dut'humi, 87. Of Zungomero, 95. Of the Mrima, 103, 104. Of K'hutu, 160. Of the Usagara mountains, 162. Of the plains beyond the Rufuta, 181, 183. Of Ugogi, 242. Of the road to Ugogo, 247. In Ugogo, 300. Of Unyamwezi, ii. 15. Of Ujiji, 60.
Antelopes in the Doab of the Mgeta river, i. 81. In the Rufuta plains, 183. Of East Africa, 268, 269. On the Mgunda Mk'hali, 289. Of Ugogo, i. 300.

Ant-hills of East Africa, i. 202, 203. In Unyamwezi, ii. 19. Clay of, chewed in Unyamwezi, 28.
Anthropophagi of Murivumba, ii. 114.
Ants in the Doab of the Mgeta river, i. 82. Red, of the banks of rivers in East Africa, 186. Maji m'oto, or "hot water" ants, 187. Near the Marenga Mk'hali river, 201. Account of them, 202. Annoyance of, at K'hok'ho, 276. Of Rubuga, 317. Of East Africa, 371. Of Unyanwezi, ii. 19. Of Ujiji, 64.
Apples' wood, at Mb'hali, i. 401.
Arab caravans, description of, in East Africa, i. 342.
Arab proverbs, i. 50, 86, 133, 135.
Arabs of the East coast of Africa, i. 30. The half-castes described, 32. Those settled in Unyanyembe, 323. History and description of their settlements, 327. Tents of, on their march, 353.
Arachis Hypogæa, as an article of food, i. 198.
Arak tree in Ugogo, i. 300.
Archery in East Africa, ii. 301.
Armanika, Sultan of Karagwah, account of, ii. 183. His government, 183, 184. Besieged by his brother, ii. 224.
Arms of the Wazaramo, i. 110. Of the Wadoe, 124. Of the Baloch mercenaries, 133. Of the "Sons of Ramji," 140. Required for the expedition, 152. Of the Wasagara tribe, 199, 237. Of the Wahehe, 240. Of the Wagogo, 304. Of the Wahamba, 312. Of the porters of caravans, 350. Of the Wakimbu, ii. 20. Of the Wanzamwezi, 30. Of the Wajiji, 66. Of the Wavinza, 75. Of the Watuta, 77. Of the people of Karagwah, 182.
Army of Uganda, ii. 189.
Artémise frigate, i. 1.
Atmosphere, brilliancy of the, in Ugogo, i. 297.

Asclepias in the Usagara mountains, i. 165.

Ashmed bin Nuuman, the Wajhayn or "two faces," i. 3.

Assegais of the Wasagara tribe, i. 237. Of the Wanyamwezi, ii. 22. Of East Africa generally, 301.

Ass, the African, described, i. 85. Those of the expedition, 151. Loss of, 180. Fresh asses purchased from a down caravan, 209.

Asthma, or zik el nafas, remedy in East Africa for, i. 96.

Atheism, aboriginal, ii. 342.

Bakera, village of, i. 92.

Bakshshish, in the East, ii. 84, 85. The propriety of rewarding bad conduct, 85. Influence of, ii. 172.

Balochs, the, of Zanzibar, described, i. 14. Their knavery, 85. Their behaviour on the march, 127. Sketch of their character, 132. Their quarrels with the "Sons of Ramji," 163. Their desertion and return, 173. Their penitence, 177. Their character, 177, 178. Their discontent and complaints about food, 212, 221. And proposed desertion, 273, 278. Their bile cooled, 274. Their injury to the expedition, 319. Their breakfast on the march, 345. Their manœuvres at Kazeh, 376. Their desertion, ii. 111. Influenced by bakhshish, 217. Their quarrel with the porters, 253. Doing "Zam," ii. 276. Sent home, 277.

Bana Dirungá, village of, i. 71.

Banadir, Barr el, or harbour-land, geography of, i. 30.

Bangwe, islet of, in Lake Tanganyika, ii. 53. Described 99.

Banyans, the, of the East Coast of Africa, i. 19.

Baobab Tree of East Africa, i. 47.

Barghash, Sayyid, of Zanzibar, a state prisoner at Bombay, i. 3.

Barghumi, the, of East Africa, ii. 294.

Bark-cloth, price of, at Uvira, ii. 121.

Basket making in East Africa, ii. 316.

Basts of East Africa, ii. 317.

Battle-axes of the Wanyamwezi, ii. 23. Of the East Africans, 307.

Bazar-gup, or tittle-tattle in the East, i. 12.

Bdellium Tree, or Mukl, of Ugogo, i. 299. Uses of, among the Wagogo, 300.

Beads, mode of carrying, in the expedition, i. 145. Account of African beads of commerce, 146. Currency at Msene, 398. Those most highly valued in Ujiji, ii. 72. Bead trade of Zanzibar, 390.

Bedding required for the expedition, i. 154.

Beds and bedding of the East Africans, i. 370.

Beef, roast, and plum-pudding at Msene, i. 400.

Bee-hives, seen for the first time at Marenga Mk'hali, i. 200. Their shape, 200. Of Rubuga, 317.

Beer in East Africa, ii. 285. Mode of making it, 286.

Bees in K'hutu, i. 120. But no bee-hives, 120. Wild, attack the caravan, i. 176, 248, 249. Annoyance of, at K'hok'ho, 276. Of East Africa, ii. 287.

Beetles in houses at Ujiji, ii. 91, note. One in the ear of Captain Speke, 91, note.

Belok, the Baloch, sketch of him, i. 135.

Bérard, M., his kindness, i. 22.

Berberah, disaster at, referred to, i. 68.

Bhang plant, the, in Zungomero, i. 95. Smoked throughout East Africa, 96. Effects produced by, 96. Used in Ujiji, ii. 70.

Billhooks carried by the Wasagara tribe, i. 238.

Birds, mode of catching them, i. 160. Scarcity of, in East Africa, 270. Of Ugogo, 300. Period of nidification and incubation of, ii. 13. Of Unyamwezi, 16. Of Ujiji, 60.

Births and deaths amongst the Wazaramo, customs at, i. 115, 116, 118, 119.

Bivouac, a pleasant, i. 245.

Black Magic. See Uchawi.

Blackmail of the Wazaramo, i. 70, 113. Of the Wak'hutu, 121. Of the Wazegura, 125. At Ugogo, 252. Account of the blackmail of East Africa, 253. At Kirufuru, 264. At Kanyenye, 265. In K'hok'ho, 274. At Mdaburu, 279. At Wanyika, 407. At Ubwari island, ii. 114.

Blood of cattle, drunk in East Africa, ii. 282.

Boats of the Tanganyika Lake, described, ii. 94.

Boatmen of the Tanganyika Lake, ii. 101.

Bomani, "the stockade," village of, i. 47. Halt at, 47. Vegetation of, 47, 48. Departure from, 51.

Bombax, or silk cotton tree, of Uzaramo, i. 60.

Bonye fiumara, accident to a caravan in the, ii. 270.

Books required for the expedition, i. 155.

Borassus flabelliformis, or Palmyra tree, in the plains, i. 180. Toddy drawn from, 181.

Bos Caffer, or Mbogo, in the plains of East

Africa, i. 181. Described, 181. In Ugogo, 300.

Botanical collection stolen, i. 319. Difficulty of taking care of the collection on the upward march, 320. Destroyed by damp at Ujiji, ii. 81.

Boulders of granite on the Mgunda Mk'-hali, i. 284. Picturesque effects of the, 285, 286.

Bows and arrows of the Wagogo, i. 504. Of the Wanyamwezi, ii. 22. Of the East Africans, 301. Poisoned arrows, 305.

Brab tree, or Ukhindu, of the Mrima, i. 48.

Breakfast in the caravan described, i. 345. An Arab's, at Kazeh, ii. 167.

Buffaloes on the road to Ugogo, i. 247. In Unyamwezi, ii. 15. On the Rusugi river, ii. 40.

Bumbumu, Sultan, of the Wahehe, i. 239.

Burial ceremonies of the Wanyamwezi, ii. 25.

Burkene, route to, ii. 179.

Burton, Captain, quits Zanzibar Island, i. 1.
The personnel and materiel of the expedition, i. 3, 10, 11.
Smallness of the grant allowed by government, i. 4, note.
The author's proposal to the Royal Geographical Society, i. 5.
Anchors off Wale Point, i. 8.
His difficulties, i. 19.
His MS. lost, i. 21.
Melancholy parting with Col. Hamerton, i. 22.
Lands at Kaole, i. 22.
Melancholy reflections, i. 24.
Transit of the valley of the Kingani and the Mgeta rivers, i. 41.
The first departure, i. 43, 46.
Tents pitched at Bomani, i. 51.
Delay the second, i. 49.
Departure from Bomani, i. 51.
Arrives at the village of Mkwaju la Mvuani, i. 52.
The third departure, i. 53.
Halt at Nzasa, in Uzaramo, i. 54.
Start again, i. 57.
First dangerous station, i. 59.
Second one, i. 63.
Adventure at Makutaniro, i. 70.
Author attacked by fever, i. 71.
Third dangerous station, i. 73.
Encamps at Madege Madogo, i. 79.
And at Kidunda, i. 79.
Loses his elephant-gun, i. 80.
Arrives at a place of safety, i. 81.
Enters K'hutu, i. 82.
Has a hammam, i. 82.
Thoroughly prostrated, i. 84.
His troubles, i. 86.

Burton, Captain — continued.
Prepares a report for the Royal Geographical Society, i. 89.
Advances from Dut'humi, i. 91.
Halts at Zungomero, i. 127.
Leaves Zungomero, i. 158.
Arrives at Mzizi Mdogo, i. 161.
Recovery of health at, i. 161.
Leaves Mzizi Mdogo, i. 165.
Halts at Cha K'henge, i. 167.
Desertion of the Baloch, i. 173.
Their return, i. 174.
Halts at Muhama, i. 178.
Again attacked by fever, i. 179.
Resumes the march, i. 180.
Contrasts in the scenery, i. 184.
Fords the Mukondokwa river, i. 188.
Reaches Kadetamare, i. 189.
Loss of instruments, i. 189.
Halts at Muinyi, i. 193.
Resumes the journey, i. 194.
Halts at Ndábi, i. 196.
Resumes the march and rests at Rumuma, i. 198.
Abundance of its supplies, i. 198.
Reaches Marenga Mk'hali, i. 203.
Approaches the bandit Wahumba, i. 203.
Leaves Marenga Mk'hali, i. 204.
Halts at the basin of Inenge, i. 208.
Wholesome food obtained there, i. 208.
Exchange of civilities with a down caravan, i. 208.
Painful ascent of the Rubeho, or Windy Pass, i. 213.
Halt at the Great Rubeho, i. 215.
Ascent of the Little Rubeho, i. 215
Descent of the counterslope of the Usagara mountains, i. 219.
First view of the Ugogo mountains, i. 220.
Halts at the third Rubeho, i. 221.
Marches on the banks of the Dungomaro, i. 222.
Reaches the plains of Ugogo, i. 223.
Losses during the descent, i. 224.
Halts at Ugogi, i. 241.
Engages the services of fifteen Wanyamwezi porters, i. 244.
Leaves Ugogi, i. 244.
The caravan dislodged by wild bees, i. 248.
Loses a valuable portmanteau, i. 249.
Halts on the road for the night, i. 250.
Leaves the jungle-kraal, i. 250.
Sights the Ziwa, or Pond, i. 251.
Provisions obtained there, i. 255.
Recovery of the lost portmanteau, i. 257.
Joins another up-caravan, i. 257, 258.

Burton, Captain — *continued.*
Enters Ugogo, i. 259.
Astonishment of the Wagogo, i. 263.
Delayed at Kifukuru for blackmail, i. 264.
Leaves Kifukuru, i. 265.
Accident in the jungle, i. 265.
Interview with Magomba, sultan of Kanyenye, i. 266.
Hurried march from Kanyenye, i. 271.
Arrives at Usek'he and K'hok'ho, i. 272.
Difficulties of blackmail at K'hok'ho, i. 274.
Departs from K'hok'ho, i. 275.
Desertion of fifteen porters, i. 275.
Trying march in the Mdáburu jungle, i. 277.
Reaches Uyanzi, i. 279.
Traverses the Fiery Field, i. 283.
Arrives at the Mabunguru fiumara, i. 285.
Losses on the march, i. 285.
Reaches Jiwe la Mkoa, i. 286. 288.
And Kirurumo and Jiweni, i. 289.
Marches to Mgono T'hembo, i. 290.
Arrives at the Tura Nullah, i. 291.
And at the village of Tura, the frontier of Unyamwezi, i. 292. 313.
Proceeds into Unyamwezi, i. 314.
Halts at the Kwale nullah, i. 315.
Visited by Abdullah bin Jumah and his flying caravan, i. 315.
And by Sultan Maura, i. 316.
Reaches Ukona, i. 318.
Leaves Ukona and halts at Kigwa or Mkigwa, i. 319.
Enters the dangerous Kigwa forest, i. 319.
Loss of papers there, i. 319.
Reaches the rice-lands of the Unyamyembe district, i. 321.
Enters Kazeh in grand style, i. 322.
Hospitality of the Arabs there, i. 323.
Difficulties of the preparations for re-commencing the journey, i. 377.
Sickness of the servants, i. 379.
Author attacked by fever, i. 380.
Leaves Kazeh and proceeds to Zimbili, i. 386.
Proceeds and halts at Yombo, i. 386, 387.
Leaves Yombo and reaches Pano and Mfuto, i. 389.
Halts at Irora, i. 389.
Marches to Wilyankuru, i. 390.
Hospitality of Salim bin Said, i. 391.
And of Masid ibn Musallam el Wardi, at Kirira, i. 392.
Leaves Kirira, and marches to Msene, i. 395.

Burton, Captain — *continued.*
Delayed there, i. 399.
Marches to the village of Mb'hali, i. 401.
And to Sengati and the deadly Sorora, i. 401.
Desertions and dismissals at Sorora, i. 402.
Marches to Kajjanjeri, i. 403.
Detained there by dangerous illness, i. 403.
Proceeds and halts at Usagozi, i. 406.
Some of the party afflicted by ophthalmia, i. 406.
Quits Usagozi, and marches to Masenza, i. 406, 407.
Reaches the Mukozimo district, i. 407.
Spends a night at Rukunda, i. 407.
Sights the plain of the Malagarazi river, i. 407.
Halts at Wanyika, i. 407.
Settlement of blackmail at, i. 408.
Resumes the march, i. 408.
Arrives at the bank of the Malagarazi river, i. 408.
Crosses over to Mpete, i. 410.
Marches to Kinawani, ii. 35.
And to Jambeho, ii. 36.
Fords the Rusugi river, ii. 37.
Fresh desertions, ii. 38.
Halts on the Ungwwe river, ii. 40.
First view of the Tanganyika Lake, ii. 42.
Arrives at Ukaranga, ii. 44.
And at Ujiji, ii. 46.
Visits the headman Kannena, ii. 81.
Incurs his animosity, ii. 82, 84.
Ill effects of the climate and food of Ujiji, ii. 85.
Captain Speke sent up the Lake, ii. 87.
Mode of spending the day at Ujiji, ii. 87.
Failure of Capt. Speke's expedition, ii. 90.
The author prepares for a cruise, ii. 93.
The voyage, ii. 99.
Halts and encamps at Kigari, ii. 101.
Enters the region of Urundi, ii. 101.
Reaches and halts at Wafanya, ii. 106.
Sails for the island of Ubwari, ii. 112.
Anchors there, ii. 113.
Leaves there and arrives at Murivumba, ii. 114.
Reaches the southern frontier of Uvira, ii. 115.
Further progress stopped, ii. 117, 119.
Returns, ii. 121.
Storm on the Lake, ii. 123.
Passes the night at Wafanya, ii. 123.

Burton, Captain — *continued.*
A slave accidentally shot there, ii. 124.
Returns to Kawele, ii. 124.
Improvement in health, ii. 129.
The outfit reduced to a minimum, ii. 130.
Arrival of supplies, but inadequate, ii. 132.
Preparations for the return to Unyanyembe, ii. 155.
The departure, ii. 157.
The return-march, ii. 160.
Pitches tents at Uyonwa, ii. 161.
Desertions, ii. 161.
Returns to the ferry of the Malagarazi, ii. 164.
Marches back to Unyanyembe, ii. 165.
Halts at Yombo, ii. 166.
Re-enters Kazeh, ii. 167.
Sends his companion on an expedition to the north, ii. 173.
His mode of passing time at Kazeh, ii. 173, 198.
Preparations for journeying, ii. 200.
Shortness of funds, ii. 221.
Outfit for the return, ii. 229.
Departs from Kazeh, ii. 231.
Halts at Hanga, ii. 232.
Leaves Hanga, ii. 240.
Returns through Ugogo, ii. 244.
The letters with the official " wigging," ii. 247.
Takes the Kiringawana route, ii. 249.
Halts at a den of thieves, ii. 252.
And at Maroro, ii. 255.
Marches to Kiperepeta, ii. 256.
Fords the Yovu, ii. 258.
Halts at Ruhembe rivulet, ii. 261.
And on the Makata plain, ii. 262.
Halts at Uziraha, ii. 263.
Returns to Zungomero, ii. 264.
Proposes a march to Kilwa, ii. 265.
Desertion of the porters, ii. 266.
Engages fresh ones, ii. 267.
Leaves Zungomero, and resumes the march, ii. 276.
Re-enters Uzaramo, ii. 277.
And Konduchi, ii. 278.
Sights the sea, ii. 278.
Sets out for Kilwa, ii. 372.
Returns to Zanzibar, ii. 379.
Leaves Zanzibar for Aden, ii. 384.
Returns to Europe, ii. 384.
Butter in East Africa, ii. 284.

Cacti in the Usagara Mountains, i. 165. Of Mgunda M'Khali, 286.
Calabash-tree of East Africa, described, i. 147. In the Usagara mountains, i. 164,
229. Magnificence of, at Ugogo, 260. The only large tree in Ugogo, 299.
Camp furniture required for the expedition, i. 152.
Cannibalism of the Wadoe tribe, i. 123. Of the people of Murivumba, ii. 114.
Cannabis Indica in Unyamwezi, i. 318.
Canoes built of mvule trees, ii. 147. Mode of making them, 147.
Canoes on the Malagarazi river, i. 409. On the " Ghaut," 411.
Capparis sodata, verdure of the, in Ugogo, i. 300.
Carriage, cost of, in East Africa, ii. 414.
Caravans of ivory, i. 17. Slave caravans, 17, 62. Mode of collecting a caravan in East Africa, 143. Attacked by wild bees, 4, 176. And by small-pox, 179. In East Africa, description of, 337. Porters, 337–339. Seasons for travelling, 339. The three kinds of caravan, 341. That of the Wanyamwezi, 341. Those made up by the Arab merchants, 342. Those of the Wasawahili, &c., 344. Sketch of a day's march of an East African caravan, 344. Mode of forming a caravan, 348. Dress of the caravan, 349. Ornaments and arms worn by the porters, 349. Recreations of the march, 350. Meeting of two caravans, 351. Halt of a caravan, 351. Lodgings on the march, 353. Cooking, 355, 356. Greediness of the porters, 356, 357. Water, 359. Night, 359. Dances of the porters, 360. Their caravan, 361, 362. Rate of caravan travelling, 362. Custom respecting caravans in Central Africa, ii. 54. Those on the Uruwwa route, 148. Accident to a, 270.
Carissa Carandas, the Corinda bush in Uzaramo, i. 60.
Carpentering in East Africa, ii. 309.
Carvings, rude, of the Wanyamwezi, ii. 26.
Castor plants of East Africa, i. 48. Mode of extracting the oil, 48.
Cats, wild, in Unyamwezi, ii. 15.
Cattle, horned, of Ujiji, ii. 59. Of Karagwah, 181.
Cattle trade of East Africa, ii. 413.
Cereals of East Africa, ii. 414.
Ceremoniousness of the Wajiji, ii. 69.
Ceremony and politeness, miseries of, in the East, i. 392.
Cha K'henge, halt of the party at, i. 167.
Chamærops humilis, or Nyara tree, of the Mrima, f. 48.
Chawambi, Sultan of Unyoro, ii. 198.
Chhaga, ii. 179.
Chiefs of the Wazaramo, i. 113.

Chikichi, or palm oil, trade in, at Wafanya, ii. 107.
Childbirth, ceremonies of, in Unyamwezi ii. 23. Twins, 23.
Children, mode of carrying, in Uzaramo, i. 110.
Children, Wasagara mode of carrying, i. 237.
Children, mode of carrying amongst the Wanyamwezi, ii. 22.
Children, education of, in Unyamwezi, ii. 23, 24.
Chomwi, or headman, of the Wamrima, i. 16. His privileges, 16, 17.
Chumbi, isle of, i. 1.
Chunga Mchwa, or ant, of the sweet red clay of East Africa, described, i. 201, 202.
Chungo-fundo or siyafu, or pismires of the river banks of East Africa, described, i. 186.
Chyámbo, the locale of the coast Arabs, i. 397.
Circumcision, not practised by the Wazaramo, i. 108. Nor in the Unyamwezi, ii. 23.
Clay chewed, when tobacco fails, in Unyamwezi, ii. 28.
Climate of —
    Bomani, i. 49.
    Dut'humi, i. 89, 92.
    East Africa, during the wet season, i. 379.
    Inenge, i. 208.
    Kajjanjeri, ii. 403.
    Karagwah, ii. 180.
    Kawele, ii. 130.
    Kirira, i. 394.
    Kuingani, i. 44.
    Marenga Mk'hali, i. 203.
    Mrima, i. 102, 104.
    Msene, i. 400.
    Muhama, i. 179.
    Mzizi Mdogo, i. 161.
    Rumuma, i. 199.
    Sorora, i. 401.
    Tanganyika Lake, i. 142.
    Ugogo, i. 243, 259, 297.
    Ujiji, ii. 81.
    Unyamwezi, ii. 8—14.
    Usagara, i. 221, 222, 231.
    Wafanya, ii. 107.
    Zungomero, i. 94, 127, 156, 161, 163.
Cloth, mode of carrying, in the expedition, i. 145. As an article of commerce, 148.
Clothing required for the expedition, i. 154. Of travellers in East Africa, ii. 201.
Clouds in Unyamwezi, ii. 12.
Cockroaches in houses in East Africa, i. 370.
Cocoa-nut, use of the, in East Africa, i. 36.
Cocoa-tree, its limits inland, i. 160.

Coffee, wild, or mwami, of Karagwah, ii. 180, 181, 187.
Commando, pitiable scene presented after one, i. 185.
Commerce of the Mrima, i. 39. Of Zungomero, 95. Of Uzaramo, 119. Of Ugogo, 308. Of the Wanyamwezi, ii. 29. Of the Nyanza Lake, 215. African, 224. Of Ubena, 270. Of Uvira, ii. 120. Of East Africa, 387.
Conversation, specimen of, in East Africa, ii. 243, 244.
Copal tree, or Msandarusi, of Uzaramo, i. 63.
Copal trade of East Africa, ii. 403.
Copper in Katata, ii. 148. In East Africa, 312.
Cotton in Unyamwezi, i. 318. In Ujiji, i. 57. In East Africa, 417.
Cowhage on the banks of the Mgeta river, i. 166.
Cowries of Karagwah, ii. 185. Of East Africa, 416.
Crickets of the Usagara mountains, i. 162. House, in East Africa, i. 370.
Crocodiles of the Kingani river, i. 56. In Unyamwezi, ii. 15. In the Sea of Ujiji, 60. Of the Ruche River, 158.
Crops of the Mrima, i. 102, et seq.
Cucumbers at Marenga Mk'hali, i. 201. Wild, of Unyanyembe, ii. 285
Cultivation in the Mukondokwa hills, i.196, 197. In the Usagara mountains, 229.
Currency of East Africa, stock may be recruited at Kazeh, i. 334. Of Msene, i. 398. Of Ujiji, ii. 73. Of Karagwah, 185. Of Ubena, 270. Cynhyænas of Ugogo, i. 302. In Unyamwezi, ii. 15.
Cynocephalus, the, in Unyamwezi, ii. 15. The terror of the country, 15.

Dancing of the Wazaramo women, i. 55. African, described, 360; ii. 291, 298.
Darwayash, the Baloch, sketch of him, i. 137.
"Dash," i. 58. See Blackmail.
Datura plant of Zungomero, i. 95. Smoked in East Africa, 96. In Unyamwezi, 318.
Day, an African's mode of passing the, ii. 289, 290.
Death, African fear of, ii. 331.
Defences of the Wazaramo, i. 111, 117.
Dege la Mhora, "the large jungle bird," village of, i. 72. Fate of M. Maizan at, 73.
Det'he, or Kidete of East Africa, ii. 293.
Devil's trees of East Africa, ii. 353.
Dialects of the Wazaramo, i. 107. The Wagogo, 306. The Wahumba, 311. The Wanyamwezi, ii. 5. The Wakimbu, 20. The Wanyamwezi, 30.

Diseases of the maritime region of East Africa, i. 105. Of the people of Usagara, 233. Of Ugogo, 299. Of caravans in East Africa, 342. Of Unyamwezi, ii. 11, 13, 14. Of East Africa, 318. Remedies, 321. Mystical remedies, 352, 353.

Dishdasheh, El, or turban of the coast Arabs, i. 32.

Divorce amongst the Wazaramo, i. 118. Amongst the East Africans generally, ii. 333.

Drawing materials required for the expedition, i. 155.

Dress, articles of, of the East Africans, i. 148. Of the Wamrima, 33, 34. Of the Wazaramo, 109. Of the Wak'hutu, 120. Of the Wasagara, 253. Of the Wahete, Of the Wagogo, 305. Of the Wahumba, 312. Of the Wakalaganza, 406. Of the Wakimbu, ii. 20. Of the Wanyamwezi, 21. Of the Wajiji, 64. Of the Warundi, 146. Of the Wavinza, 75. Of the Watuta, 77. Of the Wabuta, 78. Of the people of Karagwah, 182. Of the Wahinda, 220. Of the Warori, 271.

Dodges of the ferrymen, 164, 165.

Dragon-flies in Unyamwezi, ii. 18.

Drinking-bouts in East Africa, ii. 295, 335.

Drinking-cups in East Africa, ii. 295.

Drums and drumming of East Africa, ii. 295.

Drunkenness of the Wazaramo, i. 118. Of the Wak'hutu, 120. And debauchery of the people of Msene, 398. Prevalence of, near the Lake Tanganyika, ii. 59. Of the Wajiji, 69.

Dogs, wild, in Unyamwezi, ii. 16. Pariah, in the villages of Ujiji, 60. Rarely heard to bark, 60.

Dolicos pruriens on the banks of the Mgeta. river, i. 166.

Donkey-men of the expedition, i. 143.

Dub-grass in the Usagara mountains, i. 171.

Dunda, or "the Hill," district of, i. 54.

Dunda Nguru, or "Seer- fish-hill." i. 69.

Dungomaro, or Mandama, river, arrival of the caravan at the, i. 222. Description of the bed of the, 223.

Dut'humi, mountain crags of, i. 65, 83, 86. Illness of the chiefs of the expedition at, 84. Description of the plains of, 86.

Eagles, fish, of Ujiji, ii. 60.

Ear-lobes distended by the Wasagara, i. 235. And by the Wahehe, 239. By the Wagogo, 304. And by the Wahumba, 312. Enlarged by the Wanyamwezi, ii. 21.

Earth-fruit of India, i. 198.

Earthquakes in Unyamwezi, ii. 13.

Earwigs in East African houses, i. 370.

Ebb and flow of the Tanganyika Lake, ii. 143. Causes of, 143, 144.

Education of children in Unyamwezi, ii. 23, 24.

Eels of the Tanganyika Lake, ii. 68.

Eggs not eaten by the Wanyamwezi, ii. 29 Nor by the people of Ujiji, 59.

Elæis Guiniensis, or Mchikichi tree, in Ujiji, ii 58.

Elephants at Dut'humi, i. 87. In Ugogi, 242. At Ziwa, or the Pond, 251. On the road to Ugogo, 247. On the Mgunda Mk'hali, 287, 289. In Ugogo, 300. On the banks of the Malagarazi river, 408. In Unyamwezi, ii. 15. Near the sea of Ujiji, 60. In East Africa, 297.

Elephant hunting in East Africa, ii. 298.

English, the, how regarded in Africa, i. 31.

Erhardt, M., his proposed expedition to East Africa, i. 3.

Ethnology of East Africa, i. 106. Of the second region, 225, et seq.

Euphorbiæ at Mb'hali, i. 401. In Ugogo, 300. In the Usagara mountains, i. 165.

Evil eye unknown to the Wazaramo, i. 116.

Exorcism in East Africa, ii. 352.

Falsehood of the coast clans of East Africa, i. 37. General in East Africa, ii. 328.

Faraj, sketch of him and his wife, the lady Halimah, i. 129.

Fauna of Ujiji, ii. 60.

Fetiss-huts of the Wazaramo described, i. 57. Of East Africa, 369 ; ii. 346.

Fetissism of East Africa, ii. 341, et seq.

Fever, marsh, cure in Central Asia for, i. 82. The author prostrated by, 84. Delirium of, 84. Of East Africa generally described, 105. The author and his companion again attacked by, at Muhama, 179. Common in the Usagara mountains, 233. Seasoning fever of East Africa, generally, 379. Miasmatic, described, 403. Low type, 406. Seasoning fever at Unyamwezi described, ii. 14.

Fire-arms and Gunpowder in East Africa, ii. 308.

Fires in Africa, ii. 259.

Fish of the Kingani river, i. 56. Of the Tanganyika Lake, ii. 59. Varieties of, 67. Narcotised in Uzaramo, 67. At Wafanya, 108. Considered as an article of diet in East Africa, 280.

Fishing in the Tanganyika Lake, ii. 66.

Fisi, or cynhyæna, of Uzaramo, i. 63. The scavenger of the country, i. 64.

Flies in Unyamwezi, ii. 18. Fatal bite of one in, 19.

Flowers of Usagara, i. 328. At Msene, 397.

Fly, a stinging, the tzetze, i. 187.

Fog-rainbow in the Usagara mountains, i. 222.

Food of the Wamrima, i. 35. Of the Wazaramo, 56. Of the people of Zungomero, 95, 96, 97. Of the Wak'hutu, 120. Of the expedition, 151, 198. Of the people of Marenga Mk'hali, 201. Of the Wagogo, 310, 311. Of Rubuga, 317. Of Kazeh, 329. Of Arabs of, 331—334. Of Wilyanhuru, 392—394. Of Unyamwezi, ii. 28, 29. Of Ujiji, 70, 88. Of Karagwah, 180, 181. Of Uganda, 196, 197. Of the Warori tribe, 273. East Africa generally, 280.

Fords in East Africa, i. 336.

Fowls not eaten by the Wanyamwezi, ii. 29. Nor by the people of Ujiji, 59.

Frankincense of Ugogo, i. 299.

Frogs in Unyamwezi, ii. 17. Night concerts of, 17. Of the sea of Ujiji, 61.

Frost, Mr., of the Zanzibar consulate, i. 3, 21.

Fruits of East Africa, i. 48, 201. Of Usagara, 228. Of Yombo, 387. Of Mb'hali, 401. Of Ujiji, ii. 58.

Fundi, or itinerant slave-artizans of Unyanyembe, i. 328. Caravans of the, 344.

Fundikira, Sultan of Unyamwezi, notice of him, ii. 31.

Fundikira, Sultan of Ititenza, i. 326.

Funerals of the Wazaramo, i. 119. Of the Wadoe, 124.

Funza, brother of Sultan Matanza of Msene, i. 396.

Furniture of East African houses, i. 371. Kitanda, or bedstead, 371. Bedding, 371. Of the houses of the Wanyamwezi, ii. 26.

Gadflies, annoyance of, at K'hok'ho, i. 276.

Gaetano, the Goanese servant, sketch of his character, i. 131. Taken ill, 380. His epileptic fits at Msene, 395, 399.

Gama river, i. 123.

Gambling in East Africa, ii. 279.

Game in Uzaramo, i. 59, 71. In the Doab of the Mgeta river, 81. In K'huta, 120. In the plains between the Rufuta and the Mukondokwa mountains, 181. In Ugogi, 242. At Ziwa, or the Pond, 251. At Kanyenye, 268. Scarcity of, in East Africa generally, 268.

Ganza Mikono, sultan of Usek'he, i. 272.

Geography of the second region, i. 225, et seq. Of Ugogo, 295. Arab oral, ii. 144—154.

Geology of the maritime region of East Africa, i. 102. Of the Usagara mountains, 227. Of the road to Ugogo, 247.

Of Mgunda Mk'hali, i. 282—284. Of Ugogo, i. 295. Of Unyamwezi, ii. 6.

Ghost-faith of the Africans, ii. 344.

Gingerbread tree, described, i. 47.

Ginyindo, march to, ii. 253. Quarrel of the Baloch and porters at, 253.

Giraffes in Ugogi, i. 242. Native names of the, 242, 243. Use made of them, 243. At Ziwa, or the Pond, 251. On the Mgunda Mk'hali, 289. In Unyamwezi, ii. 15.

Girls of the Wanyamwezi, strange custom of the, ii. 24.

Gnus in the Doab of the Mgeta river, i. 81. At Dut'humi, 87.

Goats of Ujiji, ii. 59.

Goma pass, the, i. 168, 170.

Gombe, mud-fish in the nullah of, i. 334.

Gombe Nullah, i. 395, 397, 401, 403, ii. 8.

Goose, ruddy, Egyptian, i. 317.

Gourd, the, a musical instrument in East Africa, ii. 294.

Gourds of the Myombo tree in Usagara, i. 229.

Government of the Wazaramo, i. 113. Of the Wak'hutu, 120, 121. Of the Wanyamwezi, ii. 31. Of the Wajiji, 71. Of the northern kingdoms of Africa, 174. Mode of, in Uganda, 192. Forms of, in East Africa, 360.

Grain, mode of grinding, in East Africa, i. 111, 372. That of Msene, 397, 398. Of Ujiji, ii. 57.

Grapes, wild, seen for the first time, ii. 41.

Grasses of the swamps and marshes of the Mrima, i. 103, 104. The dub of the Usagara mountains, 171.

Graveyards, absence of, in East Africa, ii. 25.

Ground-fish of the Tanganyika Lake, ii. 68.

Ground-nut oil in East Africa, ii. 285.

Grouse, sand, at Ziwa, i. 251.

Guest welcome, or hishmat l'il gharib, of the Arabs of Kazeh, i. 329.

Gugu-mbua, or wild sugar-cane, i. 71.

Guinea-fowls in the Doab of the Mgeta river, i. 81. Of the Rufuta plains, 183. Of Ugogi, 242.

Guinea-palm of Ujiji, ii. 58.

Gul Mohammed, a Baloch of the party, sketch of him, i. 139. His conversation with Muzungu Mbaya, ii. 244.

Gulls, sea, of the sea of Ujiji, ii. 60.

Gungu, district of, in Ujiji, ii. 53. Its former and present chiefs, 53. Plundered by the Watuta tribe, 76.

Hail-storms in Unyamwezi, ii. 10.

Hair, mode of dressing the, amongst the

Wazaramo, i. 108. And the Wak'hutu, 120. Wasagara fashions of dressing the, 234. Wagogo mode, 304. Amongst the Wanyamwezi, ii. 26. Wabuha mode of dressing the, 78. And in Uganda, 189.

Halimah, the lady, sketch of, i. 129. Taken ill, 200. Returns home, ii. 277.

Hamdan, Sayyid, of Zanzibar, his death, i. 2.

Hamerton, Lieut.-Col., his friendship with the late Sultan of Zanzibar, i. 2. Interest taken by him in the expedition, 3. His objections to an expedition into the interior viâ Kilwa, 5. His death, 66. His character, 69.

Hamid bin Salim, his journey to the Wahumba tribe, i. 311.

Hammals of the Wanyamwezi, character of the, ii. 162.

Hammam, or primitive form of the lampbath, i. 82.

Hanga, journey to, ii. 232. Difficulties with the porters there, 232.

Hartebeest in the Doab of the Mgeta river, i. 81.

Hawks of the Usagara mountains, i. 162.

Hembe, or "the wild buffalo's horn," his village, i. 72.

Hides, African mode of dressing, i. 236.

Hilal bin Nasur, his information respecting the southern provinces, ii. 228.

Hippopotami on the east coast of Africa, i. 9, 12, 24, 56. In Unyamwezi, ii. 15. In the Ruche river, 52, 158. In the sea of Ujiji, 60.

Hishmat l'il gharib, or guest welcome of the Arabs of Kazeh, i. 323, 329.

Hogs of Ugogo, i. 300.

Home, African attachment for, ii. 333.

Honey in Ujiji, ii. 59. Abundance of, in East Africa, 287. Two kinds of, 288.

Houses of Kuingani, i. 43. The wayside, or kraals, 53, 181, 230. Of the Wak'hutu, 97, 121. Of the Wazaramo, 110. Of the Wagogo, 306. Of the Arabs in Unyanyembe, 328, 329. Of stone, ignored by Inner Africa, 93. Of the country beyond Marenga Mk'hali, called "Tembe," 207. The Tembe of the Wahete, 240. The Khambi or, Kraal, 354. The Tembe of the Usagara, 366. Houses of East Africa generally described, 364, ii. 334. Pests of the houses, i. 370. Furniture, 371. Of the Wanyamwezi, ii. 26. Of Karagwah, 182, 183.

Hullak, the buffoon, i. 46.

Hunting season in East Africa, ii. 296.

Hyænas in Ugogo, i. 276. In Ujiji, ii. 60.

Hyderabad, story of the police officer of, i. 217.

Ibanda, second sultan of Ukerewe, ii. 214.

Id, son of Muallim Salim, his civility at Msene, i. 399.

Iguanas of the Usagara mountains, i. 162.

Ihara or Kwihara, physical features of the plain of, i. 326.

Ikuka of Uhehe, march to, ii. 252.

Illness of the whole party at Ujiji, ii. 85, 86.

Immigration in Central Africa, ii. 19.

Imports and exports in East Africa, ii. 387.

Indian Ocean, evening on the, i. 1. View of the Mrima from the, 8.

Industry, commercial, of the Wanyamwezi, ii. 29.

Inenge, basin of, i. 208. Halt at the, 208.

Influenza, the, in Unyamwezi, ii. 13.

Influenza, remedy in East Africa for, i. 96.

Inhospitality of Africans, ii. 131, 327.

Inhumanity of the Africans, ii. 329.

Insects in East Africa, i. 186, 187, 201, 202. In houses in East Africa, 370. In Ujiji, ii. 61.

Instruments required for the expedition, i. 153. Breakage of, on the road, 169. Accidents to which they are liable in East African travels, 189, 191.

Intellect of the East African, ii. 337.

Iron in Karagwah, ii. 185. In Urori, 27. And in Ubena, 27. Of East Africa generally, 311.

Ironga, sultan of U'ungu, defeats the Warori, ii. 75.

Ironware of Uvira, ii. 121.

Irora, village of, i. 389. Halt at, 389. Sultan of, 389. Return to, ii. 166.

Irrigation, artificial, in K'hutu, i. 86.

Isa bin Hijji, the Arab merchant, exchange of civilities with, i. 208, 211. Places a tembe at Kazeh at the disposal of the party, 323.

Isa bin Hosayn, the favourite of the Sultan of Uganda, ii. 193.

Ismail, the Baloch, illness of, i. 381.

Ititenya, settlement of, i. 326.

Ivory, caravan of, i. 17. Frauds perpetrated on the owners of tusks, 17. Mode of buying and selling in East Africa, 39. Touters of Zungomero, 97. Mode of carrying large tusks of, 341, 348. Price of, at Uvira, ii. 120, 121. Ivory of Ubena, 270. Trade in Ivory, 408.

Iwanza, or public-houses, in Unyamwezi, ii. 1, 27. Described, 27, 279, 285.

Iwemba, province of, ii. 153.

Jackal, silver, of Ugogi, i. 242.

Jambeho, arrival of the party at the settlements of, ii. 36. Cultivation of, 36. Scarcity of food in, 36. Revisited, 163.

Jami of Harar, Shaykh, of the Somal, i. 33.

Jamshid, Sayyid, of Zanzibar, his death, i. 2.

Jasmine, the, in Usagara, i. 228.

Jealousy of the Wazaramo, i. 61.

Jelai, Seedy, the Baloch, sketch of him, i. 137.

Jezirah, island of, ii. 212.

Jiwe la Mkoa, or the round rock, arrival of the party at, i. 286. Description of it, 287 ; ii. 242. Halt at, 242.

Jiweni, arrival of the expedition at, i. 289. Water at, 289.

Jongo, or millepedes, in Unyamwezi, ii. 18.

Jua, Dar el, or home of hunger, i. 69.

Juma Mfumbi, Diwan of Saadani, his exaction of tribute from the Wadoe, i. 123.

Jungle, insect pests of the, i. 186. Fire in the jungle in summer, ii. 163.

Jungle-thorn, on the road to Ugogo, i. 246. Near Kanyenye, 271.

Kadetamare, arrival of the party at, i. 189. Loss of instruments at, 189, 190.

Kaffirs of the Cape, date of their migration to the banks of the Kei, ii. 5.

Kafuro, district of, in Karagwah, ii. 177.

Kajjanjeri, village of, arrival of the party at, i. 403. Deadly climate of, 403.

Kannena, headman of Kawele, visit to, ii. 81. Description of him, 81. His mode of opening trade, 82. His ill-will, 83, 84. Agrees to take the party to the northern extremity of the lake, 93. His surly and drunken conduct, 97. Starts on the voyage, 98. His covetousness, 109. His extravagance, 120. His drunkenness and fate, 156.

Kanoni, sultan of the Wahha tribe, ii. 79.

Kanoni, minor chief of Wafanya, visit from, ii. 107. His blackmail, 107. Outrage committed by his people, 124.

Kanyenye, country of, described, i. 265. Blackmail at, 265. Sultan Magomba of, 265.

Kaole, settlement of, described, i. 12, 13. The landing place of the expedition, 22.

Karagwah, kingdom of, ii. 177. Extent of, 177. Boundaries of, 178. Climate of, 180. People of, 181. Dress of, 182. Weapons of, 182. Houses of, 182. Sultan of, 183. Government of, 183.

Karagwah, mountains of, ii. 48, 144, 177.

Kariba, river, ii. 146.

Karindira, river, ii. 146.

Karungu, province of, ii. 149.

Kasangare, a Mvinza sultan, his subjects, i. 328.

Kaskazi, or N. E. monsoon, i. 83.

Kata, or sand-grouse, at Ziwa, i. 251.

Katata, or Katanga, copper in, ii. 148.

Katonga, river, ii. 187.

Kawele, principal village of Ujiji, ii. 53. Attacked by the Watuta tribe, ii. 76. Return of the expedition to, 126.

Kaya, or fenced hamlets, i. 407.

Kazeh, arrival at, i. 321, 322. Abdullah bin Salih's caravan plundered at, 321. Hospitality of the Arabs there, 323. Revisited, ii. 167.

Kazembe, sultan of Usenda, ii. 148. Account of him, 148.

Khalfan bin Muallim Salim, commands an up caravan, i. 179. His caravan attacked by small-pox, 179, 201. His falsehoods, 179. Spreads malevolent reports at Ugogo, 262.

Khalfan bin Khamis, his penny wise economy, i. 288. Bids adieu to the caravan, 291. Overtaken half-way to Unyanyembe, 221. His civility at Msene, 399.

Khambi, or substantial kraals, of the wayside described, i. 53, 134.

Khamisi, Muinyi, and the lost furniture, ii. 168.

K'hok'ho, in Ugogo, dangers of, i. 272, 274. Its tyrant sultan, 274. Insect annoyances at, 276.

Khudabakhsh, the Baloch, sketch of him, i. 138. His threats to murder the author, 174. His illness in the Windy Pass, 214. His conduct at Wafanya, ii. 110. Reaches Kawele by land, 111.

K'hutu, expedition enters the country of, i. 86. Irrigation in, 86. Hideous and grotesque vegetation of, 91. Climate of, 92. Salt-pits of, 92. Country of, described, 119. Roads in, 335. Return to, ii. 264. Desolation of, 264.

K'hutu, river i. 86.

Kibaiba river, ii. 146.

Kibuga, in Uganda, distance from the Kitangure river to, ii. 186. Road to, 186, 187. Described, 188.

Kibuya, sultan of Mdabura, blackmail of, i. 279. Description of him, 279.

Kichyoma-chyoma, " the little irons," Captain Speke afflicted with, ii. 234. The disease described, 320.

Kidogo, Muinyi, sketch of him, i. 140. His hatred of Said bin Salim, 164. His advice to the party at Marenga Mk'hali, 203. His words of wisdom on the road to Ugogo, 250. His management, 254. His quarrel with Said bin Salim, 255. Makes oath at Kanyenye, that the white man would not smite the land, 267. Loses his heart to a slave girl, 314. His demands at Kazeh, 377. Dismissed at Sorora, 402. Flogs Sangora, 403. Sent home, ii. 277.

Kidunda, or the "little hill," camping ground of, i. 79. Scenery of, 79.

Kifukuru, delay of the caravan at, i. 264. Question of blackmail at, 264. Sultan of, 264.

Kigari, on the Tanganyika Lake, halt of the party at, ii. 101.

Kigwa, or Mkigwa, halt of the caravan at, i. 319. The ill-omened forest of, 319. Sultan Manwa, 319.

Kikoboga, basin of, traversed, ii. 262.

Kikoboga river, ii. 263.

Kilwa, dangers of, as an ingress point, i. 4, 5.

Kimanu, the sultan of Ubena, ii. 270.

Kinanda, or harp, of East Africa, ii. 298.

Kinawani, village of, arrival of the caravan at, ii. 35.

Kindunda, "the hillock," i. 64.

Kinganguku, march to, ii. 251.

Kingani river described, i. 56. Valley of the, 56. Hippopotami and crocodiles of the, 56. Fish of the, 56. Its malarious plain, 69. Rise of the, 87.

Kingfishers on the lake of Tanganyika, ii. 61.

Kipango, or tzetze fly, of East Africa, i. 187.

Kiperepeta, march to, ii. 256.

Kiranga-Ranga, the first dangerous station in Uzaramo, i. 59.

Kirangozi, guide or guardian, carried by mothers in Uzaramo, i. 116.

Kirangozi, or guide of the caravan, his wrath, i. 221. Description of one, 346. Meeting of two, 351. His treatment of his slave-girl, ii. 161. His fear of travelling northward, 172.

Kiringawana mountains, i. 233.

Kiringawana route in the Usagara mountains described, ii. 249.

Kiringawana, sultan, ii. 258.

Kirira, halt of the party at, i. 392. Hospitality of an Arab merchant at, 392—394. Climate of, 394.

Kiruru, or "palm leaves," village of, i. 82.

Kirurumo, on the Mgunda Mk'hali, i. 289. Water obtained at, 289.

Kisanga, basin of, described, ii. 257.

Kisabengo, the chief headman of Inland Magogoni, i. 88. Account of his depredations, 88.

Kisawhili language, remarks on the, i. 15, note; ii. 198.

Kisesa, sultan, his blackmail, ii. 114.

Kitambi, sultan of Uyuwwi, recovers part of the stolen papers, i. 320.

Kitangure, or river of Karagwah, i. 409; ii. 144, 177, 186.

Kiti, or stool, of East Africa, i. 373.

Kittara, in Kingoro, road to, ii. 187. Wild coffee of, 187.

Kivira river, ii. 197.

Kiyombo, sultan of Urawwa, ii. 147.

Kizaya, the P'hazi, i. 54. Accompanies the expedition a part of their way, 55.

Knobkerries of Africa, ii. 306.

Kombe la Simba, the P'hazi, i. 54.

Konduchi, march to, ii. 274. Revisited, 276.

Koodoo, the, at Dut'humi, i. 87.

Koodoo horn, the bugle of East Africa, i. 203.

Kraals of thorn, in the Usagara mountains, i. 230. Of East Africa, 354.

Krapf, Dr., result of his mission, i. 6. His information, 7. His etymological errors, 36, note.

Kuhonga, or blackmail, at Ugogo, i. 252. Account of the blackmail of East Africa, 253.

Kuingani, "the cocoa-nut plantation near the sea," i. 42. Described, 43. Houses of, 43. Climate of, 44.

Kumbeni, isles of, i. 1.

Kuryamavenge river, ii. 146.

Kwale, halt at the nullah of, i. 315.

Kwihanga, village of, described, i. 396.

Ladha Damha, pushes the expedition forward, i. 11. His conversation with Ramji, 23.

Lakes,—Nyanza, or Ukerewe, i. 311, 409, ii. 175, 176, 179, 195. Tanganyika, ii. 42, et seq.; 134, et seq. Mukiziwa, ii. 147.

Lakit, Arab law of, i. 258.

Lamp-bath of Central Asia, i. 82.

Land-crabs in the Doab of the Mgeta river, i. 81.

Language of the Wagogo, i. 306. Of the Wahumba, 311. Of the Wanyamwezi, ii. 5. Of the Wakimbu, 20. Of the Wanyamwezi, 30. Specimens of the various dialects collected, 198. Of the East Africans, 336.

Leeches in Unyamwezi, ii. 18.

Leopards in Ugogo, i. 302. In Unyamwezi, ii. 15.

Leucæthiops amongst the Wazaramo, i. 109.

Libellulæ in Unyamwezi, ii. 18.

Lions in Uzaramo, i. 63. Signs of, on the road, 172. In Ugogo, 300, 301. In Unyamwezi, ii. 15.

Lizards in the houses in East Africa, i. 371.

Locusts, or nzige, flights of, in Unyamwezi, ii. 18. Varieties of, 18. Some considered edible, 18.

Lodgings on the march in East Africa, i. 353. In Ugogo, 354. In Unyamwezi, 354. In Uvinza, 354. At Ujiji, 354.

Looms in Unyamwezi, i. 318; ii. 1.

Lues in East Africa, ii. 321.

Lunar Mountains, ii. 48, 144.

Lurinda, chief of Gungu, ii. 53. Supplies a boat on the Tanganyika lake, 87. Enters into brotherhood with Said bin Salim, ii. 125.

Lying, habit of, of the African, ii. 328.

Mabruki, Muinyi, henchman in the expedition, sketch of the character of, i. 130. His slave boy, ii. 162. His bad behaviour, 173.

Mabruki Pass, descent of the, ii. 263.

Mabunguru fiumara, i. 283. Shell-fish and Silurus of the, 284. Arrival of the party at the, 285.

Macaulay, Lord, quoted, i. 393.

Machunda, chief sultan of Ukerewe, ii. 214.

Madege Madogo, the "little birds," district of, i. 79.

Madege Mkuba, "the great birds," district of, 179.

Magic, black, or Uchâwi, how punished by the Wazaramo, i. 113, 265. Mode of proceeding for ascertaining the existence of, ii. 32. See Mganga.

Magogoni, inland, country of, i. 87.

Magomba, sultan of Kanyenye, i. 265. Blackmail levied by, 265. Interview with him and his court, 266. Description of him, 266.

Magugi, in Karagwah, ii. 177.

Maizan, M., his death, i. 6. Sketch of his career, 73.

Maji m'ote, or "hot water" ant, of East Africa, i. 187.

Maji ya W'heta, or jetting water, the thermal spring of, i. 159. Return to, ii. 264.

Majid, Sayyid, sultan of Zanzibar, i. 2. Gives letters of introduction to the author, 3.

Makata tank, i. 181. Forded by the expedition, 181. Return to, ii. 262.

Makata plain, march over the, ii. 261.

Makimoni, on the Tanganyika lake, ii. 126.

Makutaniro, adventures at, i. 69.

Malagarazi river, i. 334, 337. ii. 36, 39, 47, 49. First sighted by the party, 407. Described, 408, 409. Courses of the 409. Crossed, 410. Return of the party to the, 164.

Mallok, the Jemadar, sketch of his character and personal appearance, i. 133. His desertion, and return, 173. Becomes troublesome, 381, 382. His refusal to go northwards, ii. 172. Influence of bakhshish, 172. Sent home, ii. 277.

Mamaletua, on the Tanganyika lake, halt of the party at, ii. 115. Civility of the people of, 115.

M'ana Miaha, sultan of K'hok'ho, i. 272. Description of him, 274. His extortionate blackmail, 274.

Mananzi, or pine-apple, of East Africa, i. 66.

Manda, the petty chief at Dut'humi, i. 89. Expedition sent against him, 89.

Mandama, or Dungomaro, river, arrival of the caravan at the, i. 222. Description of the bed of the, 223.

Mangrove forest on the east coast of Africa, i. 9. Of the Uzaramo, 62.

Manners and customs of the Wamrima, i. 35, 37. Of the Wasawahili, 37. Of the Wazaramo, 108 et seq. Of the Wak'hutu, 120. Of the Wadoe, 124. Of the Wasagara, 235. Of the Wagogo, 309, 310. Of the Wahumba, 312. Of the Wanyamwesi, ii. 23. Of the Wambozwa, 152.

Mansanza, sultan of Msene, i. 396. His hospital, 396. His firm rule, 396. His wives, 396, 399. His visits to the author, 399.

Manufactures of Msene, i. 398.

Manyora, fiumara of, i. 80.

Manwa, Sultan of Kigwa, his murders and robberies, i. 319. His adviser, Mansur, 319.

Maraim, Ahl, or Washhenzi, the, i. 30.

Mariki, sultan of Uyonwa, ii. 78.

Marema, sultan, at the Ziwa, i. 254.

Marenga Mk'hali, or "brackish water," river, i. 200, 201, 259. Climate of, 203. Upper, water of the, 247, 271.

Maroro, basin of, its fertility, ii. 254. The place described, 255.

Maroro river, i. 231.

Marriage amongst the Wazaramo, i. 118. In Unyamwezi, ii. 24. In East Africa generally, 332.

Marsh fever, i. 82, 84. Delirium of, 84.

Martins in the Rufuta plains, i. 183. In Unyamwezi, ii. 17.

"Marts," custom of, in South Africa, ii. 54.

Marungu, land of, ii. 149. Provinces of, 149. Roads in, 149. Description of the country, 150. History of an Arab caravan in, 151. People of, 152.

Maruta, sultan of Uvira, ii. 116. Visit from his sons, 117. Description of them, 117. His blackmail, 120.

Masenza, arrival of the party at the village of, i. 406, 407.

Masika, or rainy season, in the second region, i. 231, 232. Of East Africa, 378.

Mason-wasps of the houses in East Africa, i. 370.

Masud ibn Musallam el Wardi, sent to Msimbira to recover the stolen papers, i. 325. His hospitality, 392.

Masui, village of, ii. 229, 231.

Masury, M. Sam., his kindness to the author, i. 22.

Mat-weaving in East Africa, ii. 316.

Maunga Tafuna, province of, ii. 153.

Maura, or Maula, a sultan of the Wanyamwezi, i. 316. Visits the caravan, 316. His hospitality, 316. Description of him, 316.

Mauta, Wady el, or Valley of Death, i. 69.

Mawa, or plantain wine, ii. 180, 197. Mode of making, 287.

Mawiti, colony of Arabs at, i. 326.

Mazinga, or cannons, bee-hives so called in the interior, i. 200. Described, 200.

Mazita, account of, ii. 212.

Mazungera, P'hazi of Dege la Mhora, i. 75. Murders his guest, M. Maizan, 75, 76. Haunted by the P'hepo, or spirit of his guest, 76.

Mbarika tree, or Palma Christi, of East Africa, i. 48.

Mbega, or tippet-monkey, in Unyamwezi, ii. 15.

Mb'hali, village of, described, i. 401.

Mbembu, a kind of medlar, in Ugogo, i. 300.

Mbogo, or Bos Caffer, in the plains of East Africa, i. 181. Described, 181. In Ugogo, 300. On the Rusugi river, ii. 40.

Mboni, son of Ramji, carries off a slave girl, i. 290.

Mbono tree of East Africa, i. 48.

Mbugani, "in the wild," settlement of, described, i. 397.

Mbugu, or tree-bark, used for clothing in Ujiji, ii. 64. Mode of preparing it, 64.

Mbumi, the deserted village, i. 185.

Mbungo-bungo tree, a kind of nux vomica, i. 48.

Mbuyu, or calabash tree, of East Africa, described, i. 47.

Mchikichi tree of Ujiji, ii. 58.

Mdaburu, trying march in the jungle of, i. 277, 278. Description of, 279.

Mdimu nullah, i. 88.

Meals at Ujiji, ii. 89. In East Africa, 280, 334.

Measures of length in East Africa, ii. 388.

Medicine chest required for the expedition, i. 155.

Melancholy, inexplicable, of travellers in tropical countries, ii. 130.

Metrongoma, a wild fruit of Yombo, i. 387.

Mfu'uni, hill of, i. 170. Its former importance, 171.

Mfuto mountains, i. 326.

Mfuto, clearing of, i. 389.

Mganga, or medicine-man of East Africa, described, i. 38. His modus operandi, 44; ii. 358. His office as a priest, 350. As a physician, 352. As a detector of sorcery, 356. As a rain-maker, 357. As a prophet, 358. His minor duties, 359.

Mganga, or witch of East Africa, i. 380.

Mgazi river, i. 86.

Mgege fish of the Tanganyika Lake, ii. 67.

Mgeta river, the, i. 80, 159, 160, 166; ii. 268. Head of the, 80. Mode of crossing the swollen river, 80. Pestilence of the banks of the, i. 127. Fords of the, i. 336; ii. 268.

Mgongo T'hembo, the Elephant's Back, arrival of the caravan at, i. 290. Description of, 290. Inhabitants of, 290.

Mgude, or Mparamusi, tree, described, i. 47, 60, 83.

Mgute fish of the Tanganyika Lake, ii. 67.

Mgunda Mk'hali, or "the Fiery Field," i. 281. Description of, 281, 282. Stunted vegetation of, 282. Geology of, 282. Scarcity of water in, 283. Traversed by the caravan, 283. Features of the, 283, 292.

Miasma of Sorora and Kajjanjeri, i. 403.

Mikiziwa Lake, in Uguhha, ii. 147.

Milk of cows in Ujiji, ii. 60. As food in East Africa, 283. Preparations of, 283.

Millepedes, or jongo, in Unyamwezi, ii. 18.

Mimosa trees, i. 83. Flowers of the, in Usagara, 228. Trees in Usagara, 229. In Unyamwezi, 318. Of the Usagara mountains, 165.

Miyandozi, sultan of Kifukaru, i. 264. Levies blackmail on the caravan, 264.

Mji Mpia, "new town," settlement of, described, i. 397. Bazar of, 397.

Mkora tree, uses of the wood of the, i. 374.

Mkorongo tree, uses of the, in East Africa, i. 374.

Mkuba, or wild edible plum of Yombo, i. 387.

Mkuyu, or sycamore tree, its magnificence in East Africa, i. 195. Its two varieties, 195, 196.

Mkwaju la Mouani, the "Tamarind in the rains," the village of, described, i. 52.

Mninga tree, wood of the, i. 373. Use of the wood, 373.

Mnya Mtaza, headman of Ukaranga, ii. 45.

Mohammed bin Khamis, sailing-master of the Artemise, i. 8.

Mohammed, the Baloch, the Rish Safid, or greybeard, sketch of him, i. 134. At Kazeh, 381.

Molongwe river, ii. 146.

Money in East Africa, ii. 388.

Mombas Mission, the, i. 6, 7.

Mongo Nullah, the, i. 289. Water obtained at the, 289.

Mongoose, the, at Dut'humi, i. 87.

Monkeys of Muhinyera, i. 64. Of Usagara mountains, 162. In Unyamwezi, ii. 15.

Monkey-bread, ii. 221.

Monsoon, the N.E., or Kaskazi, of East Africa, i. 83, 102. In Unyamwezi, ii. 9. Origin of the S.W. monsoon, 50. Failure of the opportunity for comparing the hygrometry of the African and Indian monsoons, 93.

Moon, Land of the. See Unyamwezi.

Moon, her splendour at the equator, i. 162. Halo or corona round the, in Unyamwezi, ii. 11, 12.

Morality, deficiency of, of the East Africans, ii. 335.

Morus alba, the, in Uzaramo, i. 60.

Mosquitoes of East Africa described, i. 182. On the Ruche river, ii. 52, 158.

Mouma islands, ii. 153.

Moumo tree (Borassus flabelliformis), of East Africa, i. 47, 180. Toddy drawn from, 181.

Mountains :—

    Dut'humi, i. 65, 83, 86, 119.

    Jiwe la Mkoa, i. 286, 287, 295.

    Karagwah, ii. 48, 144, 177.

    Kilima Ngao, ii. 179.

    Kiringawana, i. 233.

    Lunar, ii. 144, 178.

    Mfuto, i. 326.

    Mukondokwa, i. 180, 185, 194, 203, 233.

    Ngu, or Nguru, i. 87, 125, 225.

    Njesa, i. 226.

    Rubeho, i. 203, 211, 214, 218, 245.

    Rufuta, i. 167, 170, 180.

    Uhha, ii. 160.

    Urundi, i. 409; ii. 48.

    Usagara, i. 101, 119, 159, 160, 215, 219, 225, 297.

    Wahumba, i. 295.

    Wigo, i. 159.

Mountains, none in Unyamwezi, ii. 6.

Mpagamo of Kigandu, defeated by Msimbira, i. 327.

Mparamusi, or Mgude, tree, i. 47, 60, 83.

Mpete, on the Malagarazi river, i. 410.

Mpingu tree, i. 373. Uses of the wood of the, 373.

Mporota, a den of thieves, halt at, ii. 252.

Mrima, or "hill-land," of the East African coast, described, i. 8, 30. Inhabitants of, 30. Their mode of life, 35. Mode of doing business in, 39. Vegetation of the, 47. Geography of the, 100. Climate of the, 102, 104. Diseases of the, 105. Roads of the, 105, 106. Ethnology of the, 106.

Mororwa, sultan of Wilyankuru, i. 391.

Msandarusi, or copal-tree, of Uzaramo, i. 63.

Msene, settlement of, arrival of the party at, i. 395. Description of, 395, 396. Sultan Masawza of, 396. Prices at, 397. Productions of, 397, 398. Currency of, 398. Industry of, 398. Habits of the people of, 398. Climate of, 399.

Msimbira, sultan of the Wasukuma, i. 319. Papers of the party stolen and carried to him, 320. Refuses to restore them, 320. Send a party to cut off the road, 321. Defeats Sultan Mpagamo, 327.

Msopora, Sultan, restores the stolen goods, ii. 166.

Msufi, a silk-cotton tree, in Uzaramo, i. 60.

Msukulio tree of Uzaramo, i. 61, 83.

Mtanda, date of the establishment of the kingdom of, ii. 5.

Mtego, or elephant traps, i. 287. Disappearance of the Jemadar in one, 288.

Mt'hipit'hipi, or Abras precatorius, seeds of, used as an ornament, ii. 181.

Mtogwe tree, a variety of Nux vomica, i. 48. In Unyamwezi, 318, 401.

Mtumbara, Sultan, and his quarrel, ii. 157.

Mtunguja tree of the Mrima, i. 48.

Mtungulu apples in Ugogo, i. 300.

Mtuwwa, in Ubwari island, halt of the party at, ii. 114. Blackmail at, 112.

Mud-fish, African mode of catching, i. 315.

Mud-fish in the Gombe nullah, i. 334.

Mud, Yegea, i. 83.

Muhama, halt at the nullah of, i. 176, 178.

Muhinna bin Sulayman of Kazeh, his arrival at Kawele, ii. 133. His extortion, 133.

Muhinna bin Sulayman, the Arab merchant of Kazeh, i. 323.

Muhiyy-el-Din, Shafehi Hazi of Zanzibar, i. 7.

Muhiyy-el-Din, Kazi, of the Wasawahili, i. 33.

Muhonge, settlement of, described, i. 63.

Muhonyera, district of, described, i. 63. Wild animals, 63.

Mui' Gumbi, Sultan of the Warori, ii. 271. Defeated by Sultan Ironga, 75. Description of him, 271.

Muikamba, on the Tanganyika Lake, night spent at, ii. 115.

Muingwira river, ii. 211.

Muinyi Wazira, engaged to travel with the

expedition, i. 52. Sketch of his character, 129. Requests to be allowed to depart, 314. His debauch and dismissal, 399. Reappears at Kazeh, ii. 168. Ejected, 168.

Muinyi, halt of the party at, i. 193. Determined attitude of the people of, 194.

Muinyi Chandi, passed through, i. 390.

Mukondokwa mountains, i. 180, 185, 196, 197, 203, 233. Bleak raw air of the, 197.

Mukondokwa river, i. 88, 181, 188, 192, 311. Ford of, 188. Valley of the, 192.

Mukozimo district, arrival of the party at the, i. 407. Inhospitality of the chiefs of, 407.

Mukunguru, or seasoning fever, of Unyamwezi, ii. 14.

Mulberry, the whitish-green, of Uzaramo, i. 60.

Murchison, Sir R., his triumphant geological hypothesis, i. 409. His notice respecting the interior of Africa, 409, note.

Murunguru river, ii. 154.

Murivumba, tents of the party pitched at, ii. 114. Cannibal inhabitants of, 114.

Murundusi, march to, ii. 250.

Musa, the assistant Rish Safid of the party, sketch of him, i. 138.

Musa Mzuri, handsome Moses, of Kazeh, i. 323. His return to Kazeh, ii. 223. His history, 223. His hospitality, 226. Visits the expedition at Masui, 231. His kindness, 231.

Music and musical instruments in East Africa, described, ii. 291, 338. Of the Wajiji, 98.

Mutware, or Mutwale, the Lord of the Ferry of the Malagarazi river, i. 409.

Muzungu, or white man, dangers of accompanying a, in Africa, i. 10, 11.

Muzunga Mbaya, the wicked white man, the plague of the party, ii. 239. His civility near home, 240. Sketch of his personal appearance, and specimen of his conversation, 244.

Mvirama, a Mzaramo chief, demands rice, i. 80.

Mviraru, a Wazaramo chief, bars the road, i. 58.

Mvoro fish in the Tanganyika Lake, ii. 67.

Mvule trees used for making canoes, ii. 147.

Mwami, or wild coffee of Karagwah, ii. 180, 181, 187.

Mwimbe, or mangrove trees, of the coast of East Africa, i. 9. Those of Uzaramo, 62.

Mwimbi, bad camping ground of, ii. 262.

Mwongo fruit tree, in Mb'hali, i. 401.

Mgombi river, i. 183.

Myombo tree of East Africa described, i. 184. Of Usagara, 229.

Mzimu, or Fetiss hut, of the Wazaramo, described, i. 57. In Ubwari Island, halt at, ii. 113. Re-visited, 121.

Mziga Mdogo, or " The Little Tamarind," arrival of the party at, i. 161.

Mziga-ziga, a mode of carrying goods, i. 341.

Mzogera, Sultan of Uvinza, i. 408. His power, 408. Settlement of blackmail with envoys of, 408.

Names given to children by the Wazaramo, i. 116.

Nakl, or first stage of departure, i. 43.

Nur, Beni, "sons of fire," the English so called in Africa, i. 31.

Nautch at Kuingani described, i. 45.

Ndabi tree, i. 196. Fruit of the, 196.

Ndabi, halt of the caravan at, i. 196.

Navigation of the Tanganyika Lake, antiquity of the mode of, ii. 96.

Necklaces of shells worn in Ujiji, ii. 65.

Nge, or scorpions, of East Africa, i. 370.

Ngole, or Dendraspis, at Dut'humi, i. 87.

Night in the Usagara mountains, i. 162. In the caravan, described, 359.

Nile, White, Ptolemy's notion of the origin of the, ii. 178. Captain Speke's supposed discovery of the sources of the, 204.

Njasa, Sultan of the Wasagara, his visit to the expedition, i. 199. Description of him, 199. Makes "sare" or brotherhood with Said bin Salim, 199.

Njesa mountains, i. 226.

Njugu ya Nyassa, the Arachis Hypogæa, as an article of food, i. 198.

Northern kingdoms of Africa. See Karagwah, Uganda, and Ungoro.

Nose pincers of the Wajiji tribe, ii. 65.

Nullahs, or watercourses of East Africa, i. 102.

Nutmeg, wild, of Usui, ii. 176.

Nyakahanga, in Karagwah, ii. 177.

Nyanza, or Ukerewe, Lake, i. 311, 439; ii. 175, 176, 179. Chances of exploration of the, 195. Geography of the, 206, 210, et seq. Size of the, 212. Position of the, 211. Commerce of the, 215. Savage races of the, 215. Reasons why it is not the head stream of the White Nile, 218. Tribes dwelling near the, 219.

Nyara, or Chamærops humilis, of the Mrima, i. 48.

Nyasanga, fishing village on the Tanganyika lake, ii. 101.

Nzasa, halt at the, i. 54.

Nzige, or locusts, flights of, in Unyamwezi, ii. 18. Varieties of, 18.

Oars not used on the Tanganyika Lake, ii. 96.

Ocelot, the, of Ugogi, 1. 242.

Oil, common kind of, in East Africa, ii. 285. Various kinds of, 285.

Olive-tree unknown in East Africa, ii. 285.

Olympus, the Æthiopian, ii. 179.

Onions cultivated in Unyamwezi, i. 330.

Ophthalmia, several of the party suffer from, in Unyamwezi, i. 406.

Ophidia in Unyamwezi, ii. 17.

Ordeal for witchcraft, ii. 357. Amongst the Wazaramo, i. 114.

Ornaments worn by the Wazaramo, i. 110. By the Wak'hutu, 120. Fondness of the Africans for, 147, 148, 150. Of the Wasagara tribe, 199, 237. Of the Wagogo, 305. Of the Wahumba, 312. Of the porters of caravans, 349. Of sultans in East Africa, 396. Of the Wakimba, ii. 20. Of the Wanyamwezi, 22. Of the Wabuha, 78. Of the Wabwari islanders, 113. Of the people of Karagwah, 181.

Ostriches in Ugogo, i, 301. Value of feathers in East Africa, i. 301.

Outfit of the expedition, articles required for the, i. 151.

Oxen of Ujiji, ii. 59.

Paddles used on the Tanganyika lake, ii. 96. Described, 96.

Palm, Syphæna, i. 82, 83.

Palma Christi, or Mbarika, of East Africa, i. 48.

Palm-oil, or mawezi, of the shores of the lake Tanganyika, ii. 58. Mode of extracting it, 58, 59. Price at the lake, 59. Uses to which it is applied, 59. Trade in, at Wafanya, 107.

Palmyra tree (Borassus flabelliformis), in the plains, i. 180. Toddy drawn from, 181. At Yambo, 387. And at Mb'hali, 401. Tapped for toddy at Msene, 398.

Pangani river, ii. 179.

Papazi, pest of, in East Africa, i. 371.

Papilionaceæ in Unyamwezi, ii. 18.

Panda, village of, i. 403.

Pano, village of, i. 389.

Parugerero, district of, in Unyamwezi, ii. 37. Salt manufacture of, 37.

Partridges in the Doab of the Mgeta river i. 81.

Pazi bug, the, of East Africa, i. 371.

Peewit, the, in the Rufuta plains, i. 183.

Phantasmata in East Africa, ii. 352.

P'hazi, or headmen of the Wazaramo, i. 54. 113. Of the Wak'hutu, 121.

P'hepo, ghost or devil, African belief in, i. 88 ; ii. 352. Exorcism, 352.

Phlebotomy in East Africa, ii. 322.

Pig-nuts of East Africa, i. 198.

Pillaw in Africa, i. 393. How to boil rice, 393.

Pine-apple, or Mananzi, of East Africa, i. 66.

Pipes in East Africa, ii. 315.

Pismires, chungo-fundo or siyafu, of the banks of the rivers in East Africa, described, i. 186. Its enemy, the maji m'oto, 187.

Pismires black, annoyance of, at K'hok'ho, i. 276.

Plantain wine of Karagwah, ii. 180. And of Uganda, 197. Mode of making it, 287.

Plantains near the Unguwwe river, ii. 41. Of Ujiji, 58. The staff of life in many places, 58. Luxuriance of it, 58. Varieties, 58. Of Uganda, 196.

Playfair, Captain R. L., his " History of Arabia Felix" quoted, i. 68, note.

Plum, wild, of Yombo, i. 387.

Plundering expeditions of the Wazaramo, i. 112.

Poisons used for arrows in Africa, ii. 301.

Polygamy amongst the Wanyamwezi, ii. 24.

Pombe beer, of East Africa, i. 95, 116, 333 ; ii. 180, 285. Universal use of, i. 309 ; ii. 29. Mode of making it, 286.

Porcupines in K'hutu, i. 160.

Porridge of the East Africans, i. 35.

Porridge flour, of the Wanyamwezi, ii. 29.

Porters, or Pagazi, the Wanyamwezi, of the expedition, i. 143. Character of East African, 144. In East Africa, 337. Variations of porterage, 339. Great weight carried sometimes by, 341. Their discontent, 343. Desertion of in Wilyankuru, 391. Description of those hired in Ujiji, ii. 157. Of the Warori, 271.

Pottery, art of, in East Africa, ii. 313.

Prices at Msene, i. 397. In the market at Unyanyembe, 333. In Ujiji, ii. 72. At Wafanya, 107. At Uvira, 120, 121.

Proverbs, Arab, i. 50, 86, 130, 133, 135, 382.
—— African, i. 31.
—— Moslem, ii. 131.
—— Persian, ii, 237.
—— Sanscrit, i. 133.
—— Wanyamwezi, i. 338.

Pumpkins, junsal or boga, grown at Marenga Mk'hali, i. 201.

Punishments in Uganda, ii. 192.

Punishments in East Africa, ii, 364.

Punneeria coagulans of the Mrima, i. 48.

Quaggas in Unyamwezi, ii. 15.

Races of the Northern Kingdoms of Africa, ii. 174, 175.
Rahmat, the Baloch, i. 46.
Rain at Zungomero, i. 156. Autumnal, at Muhama, 179. In the Usagara mountains, 218, 231, 232. In Ugogo, 298. The Masika or wet season, 378. In Unyamwezi, ii. 8—10. In the valley of the Malagarazi river, 49. In Karagwah, 180.
Ranibow, fog, in the Usagara mountains, i. 222.
Ramji, the Banyan of Cutch, engaged to accompany the expedition, i. 10. His commercial speculation, 20. His conversation with Ladha Damha, 23. Visits the author at Kuingani, 43. Account of him, 43, 44. His advice, 45.
Ramji, "sons" of, sketch of them, i. 140. Their ever-increasing baggage, 182. Their quarrels with the Baloch soldiers, 163. Their insolence, 164. Reappear at Kazeh, ii. 168. Allowed to take the places of porters, 227. Return home, ii. 277.
Ranæ of Unyamwezi, ii. 17. Of the Tanganyika Lake, ii. 61.
Rats, field, i. 160. On the banks of the Mukondokwa river, 193. House rats of Ujiji, ii. 60.
Ravens of the Usagara mountains, i. 162.
Religion of the Wazaramo, i. 115. Of the East Africans, ib.; ii. 341. An African's notion of God, 348 note.
Reptiles in Unyamwezi, ii. 17.
Respect, tokens of, amongst the Wajiji, ii. 69.
Revenge of the African, ii. 329.
Revenue, sources of, in East Africa, ii. 365.
Rhinoceroses at Dut'humi, i. 87. On the road to Ugogo, 247. On the Mgunda Mk'hali, 289. In Ugogo, 300. In Unyamwezi, ii. 15. The Rhinoceros horn trade of East Africa, 413.
Rice, how to cook, i. 393. Red, density and rapidity of growth of, at Msene, 397. Luxuriance of, in Ujiji, ii. 57. Allowed to degenerate, 57. Unknown in Karagwah, 180.
Ricinæ of East Africa, i. 371.
Rigby, Captain, at Zanzibar, ii. 382.
Rivers:—
    Dungomaro, or Mandama, i. 222.
    Gama, i. 123.
    Kariba, ii. 146.
    Karindire, ii. 146.
    Katonga, ii. 187.
    K'hutu, i. 86.
    Kibaiba, ii. 146.
    Kingani, i. 56, 69, 87, 101, 123, 231.
    Kikoboga, ii. 263.
    Kitangure, or Karagwah, i. 409; ii. 144, 177, 186.
    Kuryamavenge, ii. 146.
    Malagarazi, i. 334, 337, 407, 408; ii. 36, 39, 47, 49, 164.
    Mandama, or Dungomero, 222.
    Marenga Mk'hali, i. 200, 201.
    Marenga Mk'hali, upper, i. 247.
    Maroro, i. 231.
    Molongwe, ii. 146.
    Mgazi, i. 86.
    Mgeta, i. 80, 86, 87, 88, 101, 119, 127, 159, 160, 336; ii. 264, 268, 274.
    Muingwira, ii. 187.
    Mukondokwa, i. 88, 181, 188, 192, 216, 311.
    Myombo, i, 181.
    Mwega, ii. 256.
    Pangani, i. 125; ii. 179,
    Ruche, ii. 46, 52, 157, 158.
    Rufiji, or Rwaha, i. 30, 101, 119, 216, 220, 225, 231.; ii. 257, 270, 379.
    Rufuta, i. 167.
    Ruguvu, or Luguvu, ii. 40, 52.
    Rumangwa, ii. 149, 153.
    Rumuma, i. 197.
    Rusizi, or Lusizi, ii. 117, 146.
    Rusugi, ii. 37, 161.
    Rwaha, or Rufiti, i. 216, 220, 225, 231, 295; ii. 8.
    Tumbiri of Dr. Krapf, ii. 217.
    Unguwwe, or Uvungwe, ii, 40, 52.
    Yovu, ii. 257, 258.
    Zohnwe, i. 127.
Riza, the Baloch, sketch of him, i. 139.
Roads in the maritime region of East Africa described, i. 105, 106. In the Usagara Mountains, 230. From Ugogo to Unyamwezi, 281. In Ugogo, 302. In Unyanyembe, 325. Description of the roads in East Africa, 335. In Unyamwezi, ii. 19. From the Malagarazi Ferry, 51.
Rubeho Mountains, i. 233, 211, 245, 233.
Rubeho, or "Windy Pass," painful ascent of the, i. 213. Scenery from the summit, 214. Village of Wasagara at the summit, 218.
Rubeho, the Great, halt at the, i. 215. Dangerous illness of Capt. Speke at, 215. His restoration, 215.
Rubeho, the Little, ascent of the, i. 215. Fight between the porters and the four Wak'hutu, 216.
Rubeho, the Third, halt of the caravan at, i. 221.
Rubuga, arrival of the caravan at, i. 315. Visit from Abdullah bin Jumah and his flying caravan, 315. Flood at, 317.

Ruche river, ii. 52. Mouth of the, 46, 157.

Rudi, march to, ii. 251.

Rufiji river, the, i. 30, 216, 220, 225, 231 ; ii. 257, 379. Races on the, i. 30.

Rufita Pass in Umgara, ii. 259.

Rufuta fiumara, the, i. 167.

Ruguvu, or Luguvu, river, ii. 40, 52. Fords of the, i. 336.

Ruhembe rivulet, the, ii. 261. Halt in the basin of the, 261.

Ruhembe, Sultan, slain by the Watuta, ii. 76.

Rukunda, or Lukunda, night spent at, i. 407.

Rumanika of Karagwah, his rebellion and defeat, ii. 183. Besieges his brother, 224.

Rumuma river, described, i. 197.

Rumuma, halt of the caravan at, i. 198. Abundance of its supplies, 198. Visit from the Sultan Njasa at, 199. Climate of, 199.

Rusimba, Sultan of Ujiji, ii. 70.

Rusizi river, ii. 117, 146.

Rusugi river, described, ii. 37. Forded, 37,

Ruwere, chief of Jambeho, levies " dash " on the party, ii. 36.

Rwaha river, i. 295, 216, 220, 225, 231, ii. 257.

Sage, in Usagara, i. 228.

Sangale fish in the Tanganyika Lake, ii. 67.

Said, Sayyid, Sultan of Zanzibar, the " Imaum of Muscat," i. 2. His sons, 2.

Salim bin Rashid, the Arab merchant, calls on Captain Burton, ii. 228.

Said bin Salim, appointed Ras Kafilah, or caravan guide, to the expedition, i. 9, 10. Attacked by fever, 71. His terror of the Wazaramo, 73. His generosity through fear, 90. His character, 129. His hatred of the Baloch, 163. His covetousness, 163, 164. Insolence of his slaves, 164. His dispute with Kidogo, 255. His fears, and neglect at Ugogo, 280. His inhospitality, 287. His change of behaviour, 382. His punishment, 384. His selfishness, 391. His fears, ii. 125. Enters into brotherhood with Lurinda, 125. And afterwards with Kannena, 126. His carelessness of the supplies, 127. His impertinence, 159, 160. His attempts to thwart the expedition, 172. Pitches tents outside Kazeh, 227. Moves to the village of Masui, 229. Dismissed from his stewardship, 237. His news from Zanzibar, 261. His terror in Uzaramo, 275. Leaves for home, 277. Visits the author at Zanzibar, 382.

Said bin Ali el Hinawi, the Arab merchant of Kazeh, i. 323.

Said bin Majid, the Arab merchant of Kazeh, i. 323. Return of the expedition with his caravan, ii. 157. Separation from him, 165. Treatment of his people at Ujiji, 84.

Said bin Mohammed of Mbuamaji, and his caravan i. 257. Account of him and his family, 258.

Said bin Mohammed, Sultan of Irora, i. 389. His surliness, 389. Brought to his senses, 389, 390.

Salim bin Said, the Arab merchant in Wilyankuru, i. 391. His hospitality, 391.

Salim bin Masud, the Arab merchant, murdered, i. 328, 391.

Sanscrit proverb, i. 133.

Salt, demand for, in Ujiji, ii. 82. Scarcity of, at Wafanya, 108. Stock laid in, ii. 161.

Salt-pits of K'hutu, i. 92.

Salt-trade of Parugerero, ii. 37. Quality of the salt, 37.

Salsaparilla vine of Uzaramo, i. 60.

Sare, or brother oath, of the Wazaramo, i. 114. Mode of performing the ceremony, 114. Ceremony of, performed between Sultan Njasa and Said bin Salim, i. 199.

Sawahil, or " the shores," geographical position of the, i. 29, 30. People of, described, 30.

Sayf bin Salim, the Arab merchant, account of, i. 83. Returns to Dut'humi, 128. His covetousness, 128. Crushes a servile rebellion, 125.

Scorpions of East Africa, i. 370. In the houses in Ujiji, ii. 61.

Seasons, aspect of the, in Ugogo, i. 298. Eight in Zanzibar, ii. 8. Two in Unyamwezi, 8.

Seedy Mubarak Bombay, gun-carrier in the expedition, character of, i. 130, 279. His demand of bakhshish, ii. 173. His peculiarities, 236. Appointed steward, 237.

Σελήνης ὅρος of the Greeks, locality of the, ii. 4.

Servile war in East Africa, i. 125.

Shahdad, the Baloch, sketch of him, i. 135. Left behind at Kazeh, 381.

Sharm, or shame, Oriental, i. 23.

Sheep of Ujiji, ii. 59.

Shehe, son of Ramji, appointed Kirangozi, ii. 232. Dismissed, 238.

Shields of the Wasagara tribe, i. 238. Unknown to the Wagogo, 304. Carried by the Wahumba, 312. In Unyamwezi, ii. 23.

Shoes required for the expedition, i. 154.

Shoka, or battle-axes of the East Africans, ii. 307.

Shukkah, or loin cloth, of East Africa, i. 149. Of the Wasagara, 235. Materials of which it is made, 236.

Siki, or vinegar of East Africa, ii. 288.

Sikujui, the lady, added to the caravan, i. 210. Description of her, 210, 221.

Silurus, the, of the Mabunguru fiumara, i. 284.

Sime, or double-edged knives, of the Wasagara, i. 240. Of the Wagogo, 306. Of the Wanyamwezi, ii. 22. Of East Africa generally, 307.

Singa fish of the Tanganyika Lake, ii. 68.

Siroccos at Ugogo, i. 260.

Siyafu, or black pismires, annoyances of, at K'hok'ho, i. 276.

Skeletons on the road side, i. 165, 168.

Skin, colour of the, of the Wazaramo, i. 108. Of the Wak'hutu, 120. Of the Wadoe, 124. Of the Wagogo, 304. Sebaceous odour of the, of the Wazaramo, 309. Of the Wanyamwezi, ii. 20. Warundi, 145. Karagwah people, 181. Skin diseases of East Africa, 320.

Slave caravans of East Africa, i. 17. At Tumba Ihere, 62. At Zanzibar, 50.

Slaves and slavery: kidnapping in Inland Magogoni, i. 88. In Dut'humi, 89. Slavery in K'hutu, 97, 98, 121. Kidnappings of the Wazegura, 125. Pitiable scene presented by a village after a commando, 185. In Ugogo, 309. In Unyamwezi, ii. 23. Of Ujiji, 61, 71. Prices of slaves in, 62, 71. Prices of Wahha slaves at Msene, 79. Not trustworthy in Africa, 111. Their modes of murdering their patrons, 111. Prices of, in Uvira, 121. In Karagwah, 184. In Ubena, 270. Degrading effects of the slave trade, 340, 366. Origin of the slave trade of East Africa, 366. Treatment of slaves, 367, 369. Two kinds of slave trade, 368. Kidnapping, 369. Character of slaves, 371. Revenge of slaves, 374, 375. Female slaves, 375. Prices of slaves, 375. Number of slaves imported yearly into Zanzibar, 377. Ease with which the slave-trade at Zanzibar could be abolished, 377.

Smallpox in the Usagara mountains, i. 166. And in the up caravans, 179. The porters of the party attacked by, 180, 184, 190. In Khalfan's caravan, 201. In the caravans in East Africa, 342. In East Africa generally, ii. 318.

Smoking parties of women at Yombo, i. 388.

Snay bin Amir, the Arab merchant of Kazeh, i. 323. Performs the guest rites there, 323, 324. Sketch of his career, 324. His visit to the Sultan of Ugunda, ii. 193. His kindness, i. 384; ii. 231.

Snakes at Unyamwezi, ii. 17. In the houses in Ujiji, 61.

Snuff, Wajiji mode of taking, ii. 65.

Soil, fertility of the, at Msene, i. 397. Character of the, in Unyamwezi, ii. 6. Wondrous fertility of the, in the valley of the Malagarazi river, 49. And of that of Ujiji, 57.

Soma Giri, of the Hindus, locality of the, ii. 4.

Songs of the porters of the caravan, ii. 361, 362. Of East Africa, ii. 291.

Sorghum cultivated in Ujiji, ii. 57.

Sorora, or Solola, in Unyamwezi, arrival of the party at, i. 401. Its deadly climate, 401.

Speke, Capt., his illness in Uzaramo, i. 62, 65, 69. Shakes off his preliminary symptoms, 71. Lays the foundation of a fever, 82. Thoroughly prostrated, 84. Recovers his health at Mzizi Mdogo, 161. Again attacked at Muhama, 179. And by "liver" at Rumuma, 200. Dangerous illness at the Windy Pass, 214. Restored, 215. Unable to walk, 286. Awaits reserve supplies at Kazeh, 386. Rejoins the caravan, 390. Tormented by ophthalmia, 406, ii. 86. Starts on an expedition to explore the northern extremity of the Tanganyika Lake, 87. Returns moist and mildewed, and nothing done, 90. His "Journal" in "Blackwood" referred to, 90. Quoted, 91 note. A beetle in his ear, 91 note. Joins the second expedition, 99. Improvement in his health, 129. Return journey, 157. His deafness and dimness of vision, 169. Leaves Kazeh for the north, 173. Returns, 204. His supposed discovery of the sources of the White Nile, 204. Taken ill at Hanga, 233. Convalescent, 240. Sights the sea at Konduchi, 279. Returns home, 384.

Spears and assegais of the Wasagara tribe, i. 237. Of the Wagogo, 306. Of the Wahumba, 311. Of the Wanyamwezi, ii. 22. Of East Africa generally, 301.

Spiders of East Africa, i. 371. In the houses of Ujiji, ii. 61.

Sport in East Africa, remarks on, i. 268.

Spring, hot, of Maji ya W'heta, i. 159.

Squirrels, red, in K'hutu, i. 160.

Stars, their splendour at the equator, i. 163.

Stares, category of in Africa, ii. 129.

Stationery required for the expedition, i. 153.

Steinhæuser, Dr., i. 25.

Storm in Uzaramo, i. 69. Those of the rainy monsoon in Unyamwezi, ii. 9. On the Tanganyika Lake, description of a, 122.

Succession and inheritance, in Unyamwezi, ii. 23.

Sugar-cane, wild, or Gugu-mbua, i. 71. In Ujiji, ii. 58. Chewed, 288.

Sugar made of granulated honey, i. 397.

Suiya, antelope, i. 269.

Sulphur in Karagwah, ii. 185.

Sultans, burial-places of, in Unyamwezi, ii. 26. Power of the Sultan in this country, 31 And in East Africa generally, ii. 362.

Sun, his splendour at the equator, i. 162. Ring-cloud tempering the rays of the, in Unyamwezi, ii. 11, 12.

Suna, Sultan of Uganda, ii. 188. The Arabs' description of him, 189. His hundred sons, 192. His chief officers, and mode of government, 192. Account of a visit to him, 193.

Sunset-hour on the Indian Ocean, i. 1. In the Land of the Moon, 387. In Unyamwezi, ii. 7. In Ujiji, 89. In East Africa generally, 289.

Sunrise on the Tanganyika Lake, ii. 156.

Superstitions of the Wamrima, i. 38. Of the Wagogoni, inland, 88. Of the Wazaramo, 112, 114, 115.

Supplies, shortness of, ii. 130. Arrival of some, but inadequate for the purpose, 130.

Surgery in East Africa, ii. 322.

Suwarora, Sultan, his exorbitant black-mail, ii. 176.

Swallows in Unyamwezi, ii. 17.

Swords in East Africa, ii. 308.

Sycomore tree of East Africa, the Mkuyu, its magnificence, i. 195. Its two varieties, 195, 196. Its magnificence in Usagara, 229.

Tailoring in Africa, ii. 201.

Tamarind trees of the Usagara Mountains, i. 165, 229. Modes of preparing the fruit, 165. At Mfuto, 389.

Tanganyika Lake, first view of the, described, ii. 42, 43. A boat engaged on the, 45. Seen from Ujiji, 47. Hippopotami and crocodiles in, 60. People of the shores of, 62, et seq. Fishing in, 66. Varieties of fish in, 67. Failure of Captain Speke's expedition for exploring the northern shores of, 90. Preparations for another cruise, 93. Description of the boats of the lake, 94. Navigation of the, 94. Voyage up the, 99. Eastern shores of the, described, 100. Fishing villages, 100. Remarks on boating and voyaging on the lake, 101. Account of the island of Ubwari, 108. Visit to the island, 113. Further progress stopped, 117, 119. Storm on the lake, 122. History of the lake, ii. 134 et seq. Meaning of the name, 137. Extent and general direction of, 137. Altitude of, 139. Sweetness of its water, 139. Its colour, 140. Its depth, 140. Its affluents, 140. Its coasts, 141. No effluents, 141. Its temperature, 142. Its ebb and flow, 143. Physical and ethnological features of its periplus, 144. Sunrise scenery on the lake, 156.

Targes of the East Africans described, ii. 307.

Tattoo, not general amongst the Wazaramo, i. 108. Nor amongst the Wak'hutu, 120. Practised by the Wadoe, 124. Of the Wanyamwezi, ii. 21. Amongst the Wajiji, 63. Of the Warundi, 145.

Teeth, chipped to points by the Wasagara tribe, i. 235.

Tembe, the houses beyond Marenga Mk'-hali so called, i. 207. Description of the Tembe of East Africa, 366.

Tembo, or palm-toddy, a favourite inebrient in Ujiji, ii. 70.

Tenga, in Karagwah, ii. 177.

Tent-making in Africa, ii. 201.

Termites of East Africa, i. 201, 202. In the houses of Ujiji, ii. 61.

Tetemeka, or earthquakes in Unyamwezi, ii. 13.

Thermometers in Africa, i. 169.

Thiri, or Ut'hiri, district of, ii. 215.

Thirst, impatience and selfishness of, of the Baloch guard, i. 205. African impatience of, 359 ; ii. 334.

Thorns, nuisance of, on the road to Ugogo, i. 246.

Thunder and lightning in Unyamwezi, ii. 9. In the Malagarazi valley, 50. In Karagwah, 180.

Timber of East Africa, ii. 415.

Time, difficulty of keeping, by chronometers in East African travel, i. 189, 190. Second-hand watches to be preferred, 190.

Tirikeza, or afternoon march of a caravan, i. 203, 221. Incidents of one, 204, 205.

Tobacco, trade of, in East Africa, ii. 418.

Tobacco, use of, in East Africa, i. 36. Smoked by women in Unyamwezi, 388. Chewed by Unyamwezi, ii. 28. Tobacco of Uganda, 196. Tobacco trade of East Africa, ii, 418.

Tobacco-pipes of Eastern Africa, i. 388 ; ii. 315.

Toddy obtained from the palmyra of Msene only, i. 398. Extracted from the Guinea-palm in Ujiji, ii. 59. Prevalence of the use of, in Ujiji, 59, 70. Of Zanzibar, 287.

Togwa, a drink in Unyamwezi, i. 333. And in East Africa generally, ii. 286.

Tombs of the Wamrima and Wazaramo, i. 57.

Tools required for the expedition, i. 153.

Tramontana of the Rubeho, or Windy Pass, i. 214.

Travellers in Africa, advice to, ii. 82. Melancholy of which travellers in tropical countries complain, 130.

Travelling, characteristics of Arab, in Eastern Africa, ii. 157. Expense of travelling in East Africa, 229.

Trees in East Africa. See Vegetation.

Tree-bark used for clothing in Ujiji, ii. 64. Mode of preparing it, 64.

Trove, treasure, Arab care of, i. 258.

Tumba Ihere, the P'hazi, i. 54. His station, 62. Slave caravans at, 62. Accompanies the expedition, 62, 65.

Tumbiri river of Dr. Krapf, ii. 217.

Tunda, " the fruit," malaria of the place, i. 71.

Tura, arrival of the caravan at the nullah of, i. 291. And at the village of, 292. Astonishment of the inhabitants, 292. Description of, 313. Return to, ii. 241.

Turmeric at Muinyi Chandi, i. 390.

Twanigana, elected Kirangozi, ii. 239. His conversation, 243.

Twins amongst the Wazaramo, i. 116. Treatment of, in Unyamwezi, ii. 23.

Tzetze, a stinging jungle fly, i. 187. At K'hok'ho, 276. On the Mgunda Mk'hali, 289.

Ubena, land of, described, ii. 269. People of, 270. Commerce and currency of 270.

Ubeyya, province of, ii. 153.

Ubwari, island of, ii. 108. De Barros' account of, quoted, 108. Size and position of, 108. The expedition sails for, 112. Inhabitants of, 113. Halt at, 114. Portuguese accounts of, 135.

Uchawi, or black magic, how punished by the Wazaramo, i. 113. Described, 265. Not generally believed in Ugogo, 307. Mode of proceeding in cases of, ii. 32. Belief of the East Africans generally in, 347. Office of the mganga, 356.

Ufipa, district of, on the Tanganyika Lake, i. 153. Its fertility, 135. People of, 153.

Ufyoma, a province of Unyamwezi, ii. 6.

Ugaga, delay at the village of, i. 408, 410.

Ugali, or flour porridge, the common food

of East Africa, i. 35. Of the Wanyamwezi, ii. 29.

Uganda, road to, ii. 187. Sultan of, and his government, 188.

Uganza, arrival of the caravan at, i. 407.

Ugogi, halt of the party at, i. 241. Abundance of provisions at, 241. Geography of, 242. People of, 242. Animals of, 242. Pleasant position of, 243. Its healthiness, 243.

Ugogo, first view of, from the Usagara mountains, i. 220. The plains of, reached by the caravan, 223. Scenery on the road near, 245. Blackmail at, 252. Entrance into, 259. Description of the surrounding country, 259. The calabash tree at, 260. Siroccos at, 260. Reception of the caravan at, 261. Incidents of the march through, 261-280. Roads from Ugogo to Unyamwezi, 281. Geography of Ugogo, 294. Boundaries of, 294. No rivers in, 295. Igneous formation of, 295. Houses of, 296. Subsoil of, 296. Climate of, 297. Diseases of, 299. Vegetation of, 299, 300. Animals of, 300. Roads of, 302. Description of the tribes of, 303. Lodging for caravans in, 354. Return through, ii. 246.

Ugoyye, district of, in Ujiji, ii. 53.

Uhha, land of, now a desert, ii. 53. Laid waste by the Watuta tribe, 76, 78.

Uhehe, march through, ii. 250. People of, 251.

Ujiji, Sea of. See Tanganyika, Lake of.

Ujiji, town of, lodgings for caravans in, i. 354. Arrival of the party at the, ii. 46. Scene there, 47. Climate of, 50, 51. Boundaries of, 53. Villages and districts of, 53. Camping ground of caravans near, 54. Distance of Ujiji from the coast, and number of stages, 55. History of the country, 56. Trade of, 57. Fertility of the soil of, 57. Bazar of, 59. Fauna of, 60. Slave trade of, 61. Principal tribes in, 62. Inconveniences of a halt at, and of a return journey from, 74. Mode of spending the day at, 87.

Ukami, depopulation of, i. 88.

Ukaranga, or "land of ground-nuts," on the Tanganyika Lake, arrival at, ii. 44. Boundaries of, 52. Wretched villages of, 52. Apathy of the people, 52. Etymology of the name, 52.

Ukerewe, ii. 212. Account of, 212, 213. People of, 212. Commerce of, 213.

Ukhindu, or brab-tree, i. 48.

Ukona, reached by the caravan, i. 318.

Ukungwe, village of, i. 403.

Ukungwe, islands of, ii. 151.

Umbilical region, protrusion of the, in the children of the Wazaramo, ii. 117.
Unguwwe, or Uvungwe, river, ii. 40, 52. Forded, 40.
Unyanguruwwe, settlement of, i. 408.
Unyangwira, a province of Unyamwezi, ii. 6.
Unyanyembe district, rice lands of the, i. 321. Aspect of the land, 321. Description of it, 325; ii. 5. Roads in, i. 325. Its physical features, 326. Its villages, 326. History of the Arab settlements in, 327. Food in, 329, 331—334. Prices in, 333.
Unyamwezi, or the Land of the Moon, i. 313. Arrival of the caravan in the, 314. Lodgings for caravans in, 354. Geography of, ii. 1. Boundaries and extent of, 2. Altitude of, 2. The country as known to the Portuguese, 2. Corruptions of the name, 2, 3. Etymology of the word, 3, 4. Barbarous traditions of its having been a great empire, 4. Portuguese accounts of its former greatness, 5. Its present political condition, 5. Its dialects, 5. Provinces into which it is divided, 5. General appearance of the country, 6. Its geology, 6. Peaceful rural beauty of the country, 7. Water and rice fields 7. Versant of Unyamwezi, 8. Its two seasons, 8. Its rainy monsoon, 8—10. The hot season, 11. Diseases of the country, 11, 13, 14. Whirlwinds and earthquakes, 11, 13. Curious effects of the climate, 14. Fauna of Unyamwezi, 15. Roads in, 19. Notice of the races of, 19.
Unyoro, dependent, ii. 187.
Unyoro, independent, land of, ii. 197. People of, 197.
Urundi, mountains of, i. 409; ii. 48. Arrival of the expedition in the region of, 101. People of, 107, 117. Description of the kingdom of, 144. Governments of, 145. People of, 145. Route to, 169.
Uruwwa, the present terminus of trade, ii. 147. People of, 147. Prices at, 147.
Usagara mountains, i. 87, 159, 215, 297, 335. Ascent of the, 160. Halt in the, 161. Healthiness of the, 161. Vegetation of the, 162, 165. Water in the, 218. Descent of the counterslope of the, 219. View from the, 220. Geography of the, 225, et seq. Geology of the, 227. Fruits and flowers of the, 228. Magnificent trees of the, 129. Water-channels and cultivation of the ground in the, 229. Village of the, 229. Supplies of food in the, 229. Roads of the, 230. Water

for drinking in the, 230. Climate of the, 231. Diseases of the, 233. The tribes inhabiting the, 233.
Usagozi, a province of Unyamwezi, ii. 6. March to, i. 405. Insolence of the men of, 405. Description of the town of, and country around, 405. Sultan and people of, 406.
Usek'he, in Ugogo, i. 272.
Usenda, capital of the Sultan Kazembe, ii. 148. Trade of Usenda, 148.
Usenge, arrival of the party at the clearing of, i. 407.
Usoga, Land of, ii. 197. People of, 197.
Usui, road and route from Unyanyembe to, ii. 175. Description of, 176. People of, 176.
Usukama, a province of Unyamwezi, ii. 5.
Usumbwa, a province of Unyamwezi, ii. 6.
Utakama, a province of Unyamwezi, ii. 5.
Utambara, near Marungu, district of, ii. 151.
Ut'hongwe, country of, ii. 52.
Utumbara, a province of Unyamwezi, ii. 6, 176. People of 176.
Uvinza, lodgings for caravans in, i. 354. Geography of, ii. 1, 48. The two seasons of, 8.
Uvira, southern frontier of, reached by the expedition, ii. 115, 116. Sultan of, 116. Blackmail at, 120. Commerce of, 120.
Uyanzi, land of, description of the, i. 279.
Uyonwa, principal village of Uvinza, ii. 78. Sultan Mariki of, 78. Tents pitched at, 161.
Uyuwwi, Kitambi, sultan of, i. 320.
Uzaramo, the first district of, i. 54. Fertility of, 60. Wild animals of, 63. Storm in, 60. Boundaries of the territory of, 107. Roads in, 335. Art of narcotising fish in, ii. 67. Re-entered, 275.
Uzige, land of, described, ii. 146. People of, 146. Rivers of, 146.
Uziraha, plain of, ii. 263.
Uzungu, or White Land, African curiosity respecting, i. 261.

Valentine, the Goanese servant, sketch of his character, i. 131. Taken ill, i. 200, 379; ii. 169. Cured by the tinctura Warburgii, 169. His reception by the Wagogo, 263. Sent to learn cooking, 384. Suffers from ophthalmia, 406. Mortally wounds a Wayfanya, ii. 124.
Vegetables in East Africa, i. 201; ii. 283.
Vegetation of—
    Bomani, road to, i. 47.
    Dut'humi, i. 87.
    Eastern Africa generally, i. 228.
    Karagwah, ii. 180.

Katonga river, ii. 187.
K'hutu, i. 91.
Kingani river, valley of the, i. 56, 69.
Kiranga-Ranga, i. 60.
Kirira, i. 395.
Kiruru, i. 83.
Kuingani, i. 43.
Makata tank, i. 181.
Mgeta river, i. 166.
Mgunda Mk'hali, i. 282.
Mrima, the, i. 101, 103, 104.
Msene, i. 397, note.
Muhogwe, i. 63.
Mukondokwa mountains, i. 195.
Murundusi, ii. 250.
Rufuta fiumara, i. 168.
—— plains, i. 180.
Tanganyika Lake shores, ii. 141.
The road beyond Marenga Mk'hali, i. 205.
The road to Ugogo, i. 246.
Tumba Ihere, i. 62.
Ugogo, i. 275, 299, 300.
Ugoma, ii. 147.
Ujiji, ii. 57.
Unguwwe river, ii. 40.
Unyamwezi, ii. 6.
Usagara mountains, i. 162, 165, 220.
Uvinza in June, ii. 163.
Yombo, i. 387.
Zungomero, i. 95.
Veneration, African want of, ii. 336.
Village life in East Africa, described, ii. 278.
Villages of the Mrima, i. 102. Of the Wak'hutu, 121. A deserted village described, 185. Villages of the Usagara mountains, 229. Of the Wahehe, 240. Of East Africa generally, 364, et seq. In Unyamwezi, ii. 7. Of Ukaranga, 52.
Vinegar of East Africa, ii. 288.
Voandzeia subterranea, a kind of vetch, i. 196, 198.

Wabembe tribe, their cannibal practices, ii. 114, 146.
Wabena tribes, i. 304. Described by the Arab merchants, ii. 270.
Wabha tribe, their habitat, ii. 78. Their chief village, 78. Their personal appearance and dress, 78. Their arms, 78. Their women, 78.
Wabisa tribe, habitat of the, ii. 150. Their dress, 150. Their manners and customs, 150.
Wabwari, or people of Ubwari island, described, ii. 113. Women of the, 113.
Wadoe tribe, their habitat, i. 123. Their history, 123. Their cannibalism, 123. Their distinctive marks, 124. Their

arms, 124. Their customs, 124. Subdivisions of the tribe, 124.
Wafanya, halt at the village of, ii. 106. Visit from the chief of, 107. Blackmail, at, 107. Climate of, 107. Prices at, 107.
Wafipa tribe, habitat of the, ii. 153. Their personal appearance, 153.
Wafyoma race, described, ii. 176.
Waganda races, described, ii. 196. Their language, 196. Their dress, 196.
Waganga, or priests, of Urundi, their savage appearance, ii. 145. See Mganga.
Wagara, or Wagala, tribe, i. 407.
Wagogo, their astonishment at the white man, i. 263. Habitat of the, 303, 304. Extent of the country of the, 304. Complexion of the, 304. The ear-ornaments of the, 304. Distinctive mark of the, 304. Modes of wearing the hair, 304. Women of the, 305. Dress of the, 305. Ornaments of the, 305. Arms of the, 306. Villages of the, 306. Language of the, 306. Their dislike of the Wanyamwezi, 307. Their strength of numbers, 307. Not much addicted to black magic, 307. Their commerce, 308. Their greediness, 308. Their thievish propensities, 309. Their idleness and debauchery, 309. Their ill manners, 309. Their rude hospitality, 310. Authority of the Sultan of Ugogo, 310. Food in, 310, 311.
Wagoma tribe, their habitat, ii. 147.
Waguhha tribe, habitat of the, ii. 147. Lake in their country, 147. Roads, 147.
Wahayya tribe, the, ii. 187.
Wahehe tribe, their habitat, i. 239. Their thievish propensities, 239. Their distension of their ear-lobes, 239. Distinctive marks of the tribe, 239. Their dress, 239. Their arms, 240. Their villages, flocks, and herds, 240.
Wahha tribe, their country laid waste, ii. 76, 78. Their present habitat, 79. Wahha slaves, 79.
Wahinda tribe, account of the, ii. 219. Their habitat, 219. Their dress, 220. Their manners and customs, 220.
Wahuma class of Karagwah, described, ii. 181, 182.
Wahumba tribe, the bandit, i. 203. Haunts of the, seen in the distance, 205.
Wahumba, or Wamasai, tribe, ii. 215. Attack the villages of Inenge, i. 213. Haunts of, 259. Slavery among the, 309. Dialect of the, 311. Habitat of the, 311. Seldom visited by travellers, 311. Complexion of the, 311. Dress, manners, and customs of the, 312. Dwellings of the, 312. Arms of the, 312.

Wahumba Hills, i. 295, 297.
Wajiji tribe, the, described, ii. 62. Rudeness and violence of, 62, 68. Diseases of, 63. Practice of tattooing amongst, 63. Ornaments and dress of, 63, 64. Cosmetics of, 63. Mode of taking snuff of, 65. Fishermen of the lake of Tanganyika, 66. Ceremoniousness of the Wajiji, 69. Absence of family affection amongst them, 69. Their habits of intoxication, 69. Power and rights of their sultan, 70. Their government, 71. Their commerce, 71. Prices in Ujiji, 72. Currency in, 73. Musical instruments of the Wajiji, 98. Inquisitive wonder of the people, 128. Category of stares, 128.

Wakaguru tribe, villages of the, i. 168.

Wakalaganza tribe, the i. 406. Dress of the, 406.

Wakamba, the, a sub-tribe of the Wazaramo, i. 108.

Wakarenga tribe, wretched villages of the, ii. 52. Their want of energy and civilisation, 52, 74, 75.

Wakatete tribe, habitat of the, ii. 149.

Wakimbu race, account of the, ii. 19. villages of the, 19. Dress and characteristic marks of the, 20. Arms of the, 20. Ornaments of the, 20. Language of the, 20.

Wakumbaku tribe, country of the, i. 88.

Wak'hutu race, the, described, i. 97. The ivory touters of, 97. Their territory, 119. Their physical and mental qualities, 120. Their dress, 120. Their drunkenness, 120. Their food, 120. Their government, 121. Their dwellings, 121.

Wakwafi tribe, slavery among the, i. 309. Their untaineable character, 309.

Wall point, i. 8.

Wamasai tribe, slavery among the, i. 309.

Wambele, Chomwi la Mtu Mku, or Headman Great Man of Precedence, i. 156.

Wambozwa tribe, habitat of the, ii. 149. Their government, 152. Their personal appearance, 152. Their manners and customs, 152.

Wamrima, or "people of the Mrima," described, i. 16, 30, 32. Their chomwi, or headmen, 16. Their dress, 33. Their women, 34. Their mode of life, 35. Their national characteristics, 36. Their habits and customs, 37. Their tombs, 57. Wamrima caravans, description of, 344. Hospitality of the people, 353.

Wanguru porters, desertion of the, i. 52.

Wanyambo, the poor class of Karagwah, described, ii. 182.

Wanyamwezi porters of the expedition, i. 143. Account of the Wanyamwezi tribe, ii. 20. Colour of the skin of the, 20. Effluvium from their skins, 20. Mode of dressing the hair, 20. Elongation of the mammæ of the women, 21. Mark of the tribe, 21. Dress of the, 21. Ornaments of the, 22. Arms of the, 22. Manners and customs of the, 23. Ceremonies of childbirth, 23. Of marriage, 24. Funerals, 25. Houses of the Wanyamwezi, 24. Iwanza, or public-house of the, 27. Food of the people, 28. Their commercial industry, 29. Their language, 30. Cultivation of the ground, 30, 31. Slavery amongst them, 31, 33. Government of the people, 31. Notice of Sultan Fundikira, 31, 32. Desertion of the porters, in Ugogo, 277. Their fear of the Wagogo, 307. Greeting of porters of the, on the road, 291.

Wanyika, halt of the party at the settlement of, i. 407. Blackmail at, 407.

Wanyora race described, ii. 197.

Wap'hangara, the, a subtribe of the Wazaramo, i. 108.

Wapoka, country of the, ii. 153.

Warburg's tincture, an invaluable medicine, ii. 169.

Warori, their meeting with the caravan, ii. 251. The tribe described, 272. Their raids, 272, 273. Their personal appearance, 273. Dress and weapons, 273. Their food and habitations, 273.

Warufiji, or people of the Rufiji river, i. 30.

Warudi tribe, ii. 215, 219.

Warugaru tribe, country of the, i. 88. Their language, 89.

Warundi tribe, noise and insolence of the, ii. 107. Their inhospitality, 108, 117. Their habitat, 144. Their mode of government, 145. Their complexion, 145. Their personal appearance, 145. Their dress, arms, and ornaments, 145. Their women, 146.

Wasagara tribe, thievish propensities of the, i. 229. Villages of the, 168. Those of Rumuma described, 198. Their ornaments and arms, 199. Village of, on the summit of Rubeho, 218. Villages of, on the slopes, 221. Their habitat, 234. Colour of their skins, 234. Modes of wearing the hair, 234. Distension of the ear-lobe, 235. Distinctive marks of the tribe, 235. Dress of the, 235. Arms of the, 237. Government of the, 238. Houses of the, 366.

Wasawahili, or people of the Sawahil, described, i. 30. National characteristics of the, 36. Their habits and customs, 37. Caravans of, 344.

Wasenze tribe, their habitat, ii. 147.

Washaki tribe, the, ii. 215, 219.

Washenzi, or barbarians from the interior, i. 18. Curiosity of, 394.

Washenzi, "the conquered," or Ahl Maraim, the, i. 30.

Wasps, mason, of the houses in East Africa, i. 370.

Wasui tribe, described, ii. 176.

Wasukuma tribe, their thievery, i. 319. Punishment of some of them, 320, 321. Their sultan, Msimbira, 319-321.

Wasumbwa tribe, in Msene, i. 395.

Wasuop'hángá tribe, country of the, i. 88.

Watatura tribes, i. 304; ii. 215, 220. Their habitat, 220. Recent history of them, 220, 221.

Watches, a few second-hand, the best things for keeping time in East African travel, i. 190.

Water-courses, or nullahs, of East Africa, i. 102. In the Usagara mountains, 229, 230.

Water in the Mrima, i. 102. In the Usagara mountains, 218. Scarcity of, near Marenga Mk'hali, 203. Impatience and selfishness of thirst of the Baloch guard, 205. In the Usagara mountains, 230. On the road to Ugogo, 247. Permission required for drawing, 252. Scarcity of, at Kanyenye, 265. Inhospitality of the people there, respecting, 267. Scarcity of, in Mgunda Mk'hali, 282. At the Jiwe la Mkoa, 287: At Kirurumo, 289. At Jiweni, 289. On the march of the caravan, 359. In Unyamwezi, ii. 7. Of the Tanganyika Lake, its sweetness, 139. Want of, on the return journey, 239.

Water-melons at Marenga Mk'hali, i. 201. Cultivation of, 201.

Wat'hembe tribe, the, ii. 154.

Wat'hembwe tribe, habitat of the, ii. 149.

Wat'hongwe tribe, country of the, ii. 154.

Wat'hongwe Kapana, Sultan, ii. 154.

Watosi tribe in Msene, i. 396. Their present habitat, ii. 185. Account of them and their manners and customs, 185.

Watuta tribe, hills of the, i. 408. History of, ii. 75. Their present habitat, 76. Their wanderings and forays, 76, 77. Their women, 77. Their arms, 77. Their tactics, 77. Their fear of fire-arms, 77. Their hospitality and strange traits, 77. Their attack on the territory of Kannena, ii. 156.

Wavinza tribe, i. 407. Personal appearance and character of the, ii. 75. Arms of the, 75. Inhospitality of the, 75. Drunkenness of the, 75.

Wavira tribe, civility of the, ii. 115.

Wayfanya, return to, ii. 123.   A slave mortally wounded at, 124.

Wazaramo tribe, the, i. 19.

Wazaramo, or Wazalamo, territory of the, i. 54. Visit from the P'hazi, or headmen, i. 54. Women's dance of ceremony, 55. Tombs of the tribe, 57. Stoppage of the guard of the expedition by the Wazaramo, 70. Ethnology of the race, 107. Their dialect, 107. Subtribes of, 108. Distinctive marks of the tribe, 108. Albinos of the, 109. Dress of the, 109. Ornaments and arms of the, 110. Houses of the, 110. Character of the, 112. Their government, 113. The Sare, or brother oath, of the, 114. Births and deaths, 118. Funeral ceremonies, 118, 119. "Industry" of the tribe, 119.

Wazegura tribe, i. 124. Their habitat, 125. Their arms, 125. Their kidnapping practices, 125. Their government, 125. Their character, 126.

Wazige tribe described, ii. 146.

Waziraha, a subtribe of the Wak'hutu, i. 122. Described, 123.

Weights and measures in Zanzibar, ii. 389, 391.

Weapons in East Africa, ii. 300.

Weaving in East Africa, ii. 309.

White land, African curiosity respecting, i. 261.

Whirlwinds in Unyamwezi, ii. 11, 13.

Wife of Sultan Magomba, i. 266.

Wigo hill, i. 93, 159.

Wilyankuru, Eastern, passed through, i. 390.

Winds in Unyamwezi, ii. 9, 10. In Central Africa, 50. Periodical of Lake Tanganyika, 143. In Karagwah, ii. 180.

Windy Pass, or Pass of Rubeho, painful ascent of, i. 213. Village of Wasagara at, 218.

Wine, plantain, of Karagwah, ii. 180. And of Uganda, 197.

Wire, mode of carrying, in the expedition, i. 145. As an article of commerce, 146, 150

Witch, or mganga, of East Africa, i. 380.

Witchcraft, belief in, in East Africa, ii. 347. Office of the mganga, 356.

Women in East Africa, ii. 298, 330, 332, 334.

———— of Karagwah, ii. 182.

———— of the Wabu ha, ii. 78.

————————— Wagogo, i. 304, 305, 310.

————————— Wahehe, i. 239.

————————— Wajiji, ii. 62—64.

————————— Wak'hutu, i. 120.

————————— Wamrima, i. 16, 34.

————————— Wanyamwezi, i. 388, 396, 398; ii. 21, 23, 24.

————————— Warundi, ii. 146.

Women of the Wasagara, i. 234, 236.
———— —— Wataturu, ii. 221.
———— —— Watuta, ii. 77.
———— —— Wazaramo, i. *55*, 61, 63,
110, 116, 118. ·
—— " Lulliloo " of the Wanyamwezi,
i. 291.
—— physicians in East Africa, ii. 323.
—— Dance by themselves in East
Africa, i. 361.
—— Handsome, at Yombo, i. 388.
—— Slave-girls of the coast Arabs on
the march up country, i. 314.
—— The Iwanza, or publichouses of the
women of Unyamwezi, ii. 27.
—— Of the Wabwari islanders, ii. 113.
Wood-apples in Unyamwezi, i. 318.
Woodward, Mr. S. P., his description of
shells brought from Tanganyika Lake, ii.
102, *note*.

Xylophagus, the, in East African houses, i.
370.

Yegea mud, i. 83.
Yombo, halt of the party at, i. 387.   De-
scription of, 387.   The sunset hour at,
387.   Return to, ii. 166.
Yovu, river, ii. 257, 258.   Forded, 258.
Yovu, village of, described, i. 396.

Zanzibar, view of, from the sea, i. 1.   What
the island is not, 2.   Family, 2, 3.   History of the word " Zanzibar," 28.   Its
geographical position, 29.   Weakness of
the government of, in the interior of the
continent, 98.   The eight seasons of, ii.
8.   Slave-trade of, 377.   Troubles in,
380.   General trade of, Appendix to
vol. ii.
Zawada, the lady, added to the caravan, i.
210.   Her services to Capt. Speke, ii.
277.
Zebras, in the Rufuta plains, i. 183.   At
Ziwa, 251.   In Unyamwezi, ii. 15.
Zemzemiyah of East Africa, ii. 239.
Zeze, or guitar, of East Africa, ii. 291.
Zik el nafas, or asthma, remedy in East
Africa for, i. 96.
Zimbili, halt of the caravan at, i. 386.   De-
scription of, 386.
Ziwa, or the Pond, i. 244.   Water obtained
from the, 250.   Description of the, 251.
Troubles of the expedition at, 254.
Zohnwe river, i. 172.
Zohnwe settlement, i. 173.   Adventures of
the expedition at, 173.
Zungomero, district of, described, i. 93.
Commerce of, 95.   Attractions of, 95.
Food of, 95—97.   Cause of the ivory
touters of, 97.   Halt of the expedition at,
i. 127.   Pestilence of, 127, 163.   Fresh
porters engaged at, 128.   Life at, 156.
Return to, ii. 264.   Departure from,
276.

THE END.